FEDERAL RULES OF CIVIL PROCEDURE 2025-2026

With Study Resources

FEDERAL RULES OF CIVIL PROCEDURE 2025-2026

With Study Resources

Including Selected Provisions of the U.S. Code, U.S. Constitution, Federal Rules of Appellate Procedure, Administrative Office of U.S. Courts Forms and Statistics, State Long-Arm Statutes, Venue Provisions, Service Rules, and Relation-Back of Amendments Materials, Recent Case Law, and FRCP Essentials: Your Exam Checklist

Thomas O. Main

WILLIAM S. BOYD PROFESSOR OF LAW
WILLIAM S. BOYD SCHOOL OF LAW
UNIVERSITY OF NEVADA, LAS VEGAS

ASPEN PUBLISHING

To contact Customer Service, e-mail customer.service@aspenpublishing.com, call 1-800-950-5259, or mail correspondence to:

Aspen Publishing
Attn: Order Department
1 Wall Street
Burlington, MA 01803

1 2 3 4 5 6 7 8 9 0

ISBN 979-8-8941-0374-7

Library of Congress Cataloging-in-Publication Data

ABOUT ASPEN PUBLISHING

Aspen Publishing is a leading provider of legal education content and digital learning solutions in the United States and globally. Our innovative products and platforms—designed based on best practices in learning science—engage students and enhance outcomes. From textbooks and audiobooks authored by renowned experts to digital platforms and products like LEAF, Connected eBooks, Connected Quizzing, PracticePerfect, and JD-Next, we empower the next generation of legal professionals with innovative, trusted, and accessible resources.

The Aspen Casebook Series, affectionately known as the "red and black" casebooks among law faculty and students, includes hundreds of highly regarded textbooks across more than 80 disciplines. These range from foundational courses like Torts and Contracts to emerging electives such as Sustainability and the Law of Policing. Our study aids, including the popular *Examples & Explanations* series, help law students master complex topics with clarity and confidence.

Aspen's expertise extends to undergraduate education with our Paralegal, Criminal Justice, and Business Law series, offering the same hallmark quality to a broader audience. JD-Next, our groundbreaking online law school prep course and admissions test, provides a realistic preview of law school, equips students with essential skills for academic success, and evaluates their readiness for legal studies.

Aspen Publishing Is Proud to Be a UWorld Company

Since 2003, UWorld has been a global leader in developing high-quality learning tools for students preparing for high-stakes exams. With a commitment to excellence, UWorld has helped millions of students in undergraduate, graduate, and professional programs in fields such as medicine, nursing, finance, and law achieve their academic and career goals.

Founded by Chandra S. Pemmasani, M.D., during his medical residency, UWorld began focusing on medical education and has since expanded into various academic fields, including law. In 2020, UWorld launched its Legal vertical, starting with its comprehensive Multistate Bar Exam (MBE®) Question Bank, followed by the acquisition of Themis Bar Review, which integrated resources to provide a complete bar exam preparation experience. In 2024, UWorld expanded its offerings by acquiring Aspen Publishing, enhancing its suite of legal education products.

Today, UWorld offers an unparalleled range of study materials that blend active learning methods with expert content, ensuring students and educators can access the most effective resources. From bar preparation to law school success, UWorld is committed to supporting the next generation of legal professionals. Learn more at uworld.com.

CONTENTS

PREFACE

This book was prepared as a resource to supplement any Civil Procedure course. It includes amendments to the Federal Rules that may take effect on December 1, 2025.

The federal judiciary's website is an additional resource for national and local rules, for proposed and pending amendments, and for other information about the courts, including statistical data. Consult www.uscourts.gov.

FEDERAL RULES OF CIVIL PROCEDURE

I. Scope of Rules; Form of Action

Rule 1. Scope and Purpose

These rules govern the procedure in all civil actions and proceedings in the United States district courts, except as stated in Rule 81. They should be construed, administered, and employed by the court and the parties to secure the just, speedy, and inexpensive determination of every action and proceeding.

Rule 2. One Form of Action

There is one form of action — the civil action.

II. Commencing an Action; Service of Process, Pleadings, Motions, and Orders

Rule 3. Commencing an Action

A civil action is commenced by filing a complaint with the court.

Rule 4. Summons

(a) Contents; Amendments

(1) Contents. A summons must:

(A) name the court and the parties;

(B) be directed to the defendant;

(C) state the name and address of the plaintiff's attorney or — if unrepresented — of the plaintiff;

(D) state the time within which the defendant must appear and defend;

(E) notify the defendant that a failure to appear and defend will result in a default judgment against the defendant for the relief demanded in the complaint;

(F) be signed by the clerk; and

(G) bear the court's seal.

(2) Amendments. The court may permit a summons to be amended.

(b) Issuance. On or after filing the complaint, the plaintiff may present a summons to the clerk for signature and seal. If the summons is properly completed, the clerk must sign, seal, and issue it to the plaintiff for service on the defendant. A summons — or a copy of a summons that is addressed to multiple defendants — must be issued for each defendant to be served.

(c) Service

(1) In General. A summons must be served with a copy of the complaint. The plaintiff is responsible for having the summons and complaint served within the time allowed by Rule 4(m) and must furnish the necessary copies to the person who makes service.

(2) By Whom. Any person who is at least 18 years old and not a party may serve a summons and complaint.

(3) By a Marshall or Someone Specially Appointed. At the plaintiff's request, the court may order that service be made by a United States marshal or deputy marshal or by a person specially appointed by the court. The court must so order if the plaintiff is authorized to proceed in forma pauperis under 28 U.S.C. § 1915 or as a seaman under 28 U.S.C. § 1916.

(d) Waiving Service

(1) Requesting a Waiver. An individual, corporation, or association that is subject to service under Rule 4(e), (f), or (h) has a duty to avoid unnecessary expenses of serving the summons. The plaintiff may notify such a defendant that an action has been commenced and request that the defendant waive service of a summons. The notice and request must:

(A) be in writing and be addressed:

(i) to the individual defendant; or

(ii) for a defendant subject to service under Rule 4(h), to an officer, a managing or general agent, or any other agent authorized by appointment or by law to receive service of process;

(B) name the court where the complaint was filed;

(C) be accompanied by a copy of the complaint, 2 copies of the waiver form appended to this Rule 4, and a prepaid means for returning the form;

(D) inform the defendant, using the form appended to this Rule 4, of the consequences of waiving and not waiving service;

(E) state the date when the request is sent;

(F) give the defendant a reasonable time of at least 30 days after the request was sent — or at least 60 days if sent to the defendant outside any judicial district of the United States — to return the waiver; and

(G) be sent by first-class mail or other reliable means.

(2) Failure to Waive. If a defendant located within the United States fails, without good cause, to sign and return a waiver requested by a plaintiff located within the United States, the court must impose on the defendant:

(A) the expenses later incurred in making service; and

(B) the reasonable expenses, including attorney's fees, of any motion required to collect those service expenses.

(3) Time to Answer After a Waiver. A defendant who, before being served with process, timely returns a waiver need not serve an answer to the complaint until 60 days after the request was sent — or until 90 days after it was sent to the defendant outside any judicial district of the United States.

(4) Results of Filing a Waiver. When the plaintiff files a waiver, proof of service is not required and these rules apply as if a summons and complaint had been served at the time of filing the waiver.

(5) Jurisdiction and Venue Not Waived. Waiving service of a summons does not waive any objection to personal jurisdiction or to venue.

(e) Serving an Individual Within a Judicial District of the United States. Unless federal law provides otherwise, an individual — other than a minor, an incompetent person, or a person whose waiver has been filed — may be sued in a judicial district of the United States by:

(1) following state law for serving a summons in an action brought in courts of general jurisdiction in the state where the district court is located or where service is made; or

(2) doing any of the following:

(A) delivering a copy of the summons and of the complaint to the individual personally;

(B) leaving a copy of each at the individual's dwelling or usual place of abode with someone of suitable age and discretion who resides there; or

(C) delivering a copy of each to an agent authorized by appointment or by law to receive service of process.

(f) Serving an Individual in a Foreign Country. Unless federal law provides otherwise, an individual — other than a minor, an incompetent person, or a person whose waiver has been filed — may be served at a place not within any judicial district of the United States:

(1) by any internationally agreed means of service that is reasonably calculated to give notice, such as those authorized by the Hague Convention on the Service Abroad of Judicial and Extrajudicial Documents;

(2) if there is no internationally agreed means, or if an international agreement allows but does not specify other means, by a method that is reasonably calculated to give notice:

(A) as prescribed by the foreign country's law for service in that country in an action in its courts of general jurisdiction;

(B) as the foreign authority directs in response to a letter rogatory or letter of request; or

(C) unless prohibited by the foreign country's law, by:

(i) delivering a copy of the summons and of the complaint to the individual personally; or

(ii) using any form of mail that the clerk addresses and sends to the individual and that requires a signed receipt; or

(3) by other means not prohibited by international agreement, as the court orders.

(g) **Serving a Minor or an Incompetent Person.** A minor or an incompetent person in a judicial district of the United States must be served by following state law for serving a summons or like process on such a defendant in an action brought in the courts of general jurisdiction of the state where service is made. A minor or an incompetent person who is not within any judicial district of the United States must be served in the manner prescribed by Rule 4(f)(2)(A), (f)(2)(B), or (f)(3).

(h) **Serving a Corporation, Partnership, or Association.** Unless federal law provides otherwise or the defendant's waiver has been filed, a domestic or foreign corporation, or a partnership or other unincorporated association that is subject to suit under a common name, must be served:

(1) in a judicial district of the United States:

(A) in the manner prescribed by Rule 4(e)(1) for serving an individual; or

(B) by delivering a copy of the summons and of the complaint to an officer, a managing or general agent, or any other agent authorized by appointment or by law to receive service of process and — if the agent is one authorized by statute and the statute so requires — by also mailing a copy of each to the defendant; or

(2) at a place not within any judicial district of the United States, in any manner prescribed by Rule 4(f) for serving an individual, except personal delivery under (f)(2)(C)(i).

(i) **Serving the United States and Its Agencies, Corporations, Officers, or Employees**

(1) United States. To serve the United States, a party must:

(A) (i) deliver a copy of the summons and of the complaint to the United States attorney for the district where the action is brought — or to an assistant United States attorney or clerical employee whom the United States attorney designates in a writing filed with the court clerk — or

(ii) send a copy of each by registered or certified mail to the civil-process clerk at the United States attorney's office;

(B) send a copy of each by registered or certified mail to the Attorney General of the United States at Washington, D.C.; and

(C) if the action challenges an order of a nonparty agency or officer of the United States, send a copy of each by registered or certified mail to the agency or officer.

(2) Agency; Corporation; Officer or Employee Sued in an Official Capacity. To serve a United States agency or corporation, or a United States officer or employee sued only in an official capacity, a party must serve the United States and also send a copy of the summons and of the complaint by registered or certified mail to the agency, corporation, officer, or employee.

(3) Officer or Employee Sued Individually. To serve a United States officer or employee sued in an individual capacity for an act or omission occurring in connection with duties performed on the United States' behalf (whether or not the officer or employee is also sued in an official capacity), a party must serve the United States and also serve the officer or employee under Rule 4(e), (f), or (g).

(4) Extending Time. The court must allow a party a reasonable time to cure its failure to:

(A) serve a person required to be served under Rule 4(i)(2), if the party has served either the United States attorney or the Attorney General of the United States; or

(B) serve the United States under Rule 4(i)(3), if the party has served the United States officer or employee.

(j) Serving a Foreign, State, or Local Government

(1) Foreign State. A foreign state or its political subdivision, agency, or instrumentality must be served in accordance with 28 U.S.C. § 1608.

(2) State or Local Government. A state, a municipal corporation, or any other state-created governmental organization that is subject to suit must be served by:

(A) delivering a copy of the summons and of the complaint to its chief executive officer; or

(B) serving a copy of each in the manner prescribed by that state's law for serving a summons or like process on such a defendant.

(k) Territorial Limits of Effective Service

(1) In General. Serving a summons or filing a waiver of service establishes personal jurisdiction over a defendant:

(A) who is subject to the jurisdiction of a court of general jurisdiction in the state where the district court is located;

(B) who is a party joined under Rule 14 or 19 and is served within a judicial district of the United States and not more than 100 miles from where the summons was issued; or

(C) when authorized by a federal statute.

(2) Federal Claim Outside State-Court Jurisdiction. For a claim that arises under federal law, serving a summons or filing a waiver of service establishes personal jurisdiction over a defendant if:

(A) the defendant is not subject to jurisdiction in any state's courts of general jurisdiction; and

(B) exercising jurisdiction is consistent with the United States Constitution and laws.

(l) Proving Service

(1) Affidavit Required. Unless service is waived, proof of service must be made to the court. Except for service by a United States marshal or deputy marshal, proof must be made by the server's affidavit.

(2) Service Outside the United States. Service not within any judicial district of the United States must be proved as follows:

(A) if made under Rule 4(f)(1), as provided in the applicable treaty or convention; or

(B) if made under Rule 4(f)(2) or (f)(3), by a receipt signed by the addressee, or by other evidence satisfying the court that the summons and complaint were delivered to the addressee.

(3) Validity of Service; Amending Proof. Failure to prove service does not affect the validity of service. The court may permit proof of service to be amended.

(m) Time Limit for Service. If a defendant is not served within 90 days after the complaint is filed, the court — on motion or on its own after notice to the plaintiff — must dismiss the action without prejudice against that defendant or order that service be made within a specified time. But if the plaintiff shows good cause for the failure, the court must extend the time for service for an appropriate period. This subdivision (m) does not apply to service in a foreign country under Rule 4(f), 4(h)(2), or 4(j)(1), or to service of a notice under Rule 71.1(d)(3)(A).

(n) Asserting Jurisdiction over Property or Assets

(1) Federal Law. The court may assert jurisdiction over property if authorized by a federal statute. Notice to claimants of the property must be given as provided in the statute or by serving a summons under this rule.

(2) State Law. On a showing that personal jurisdiction over a defendant cannot be obtained in the district where the action is brought by reasonable efforts to serve a summons under this rule, the court may assert jurisdiction over the defendant's assets found in the district. Jurisdiction is acquired by seizing the assets under the circumstances and in the manner provided by state law in that district.

Rule 4 Notice of a Lawsuit and Request to Waive Service of Summons.

(Caption)

To (*name the defendant or — if the defendant is a corporation, partnership, or association — name an officer or agent authorized to receive service*):

Why are you getting this?

A lawsuit has been filed against you, or the entity you represent, in this court under the number shown above. A copy of the complaint is attached.

This is not a summons, or an official notice from the court. It is a request that, to avoid expenses, you waive formal service of a summons by signing and returning the enclosed waiver. To avoid these expenses, you must return the signed waiver within (*give at least 30 days or at least 60 days if the defendant is outside any judicial district of the United States*) from the date shown below, which is the date this notice was sent. Two copies of the waiver form are enclosed, along with a stamped, self-addressed envelope or other prepaid means for returning one copy. You may keep the other copy.

What happens next?

If you return the signed waiver, I will file it with the court. The action will then proceed as if you had been served on the date the waiver is filed, but no summons will be served on you and you will have 60 days from the date this notice is sent (see the date below) to answer the complaint (or 90 days if this notice is sent to you outside any judicial district of the United States).

If you do not return the signed waiver within the time indicated, I will arrange to have the summons and complaint served on you. And I will ask the court to require you, or the entity you represent, to pay the expenses of making service.

Please read the enclosed statement about the duty to avoid unnecessary expenses.

I certify that this request is being sent to you on the date below.

Date: ______

____

(Signature of the attorney or unrepresented party)

____

(Printed name)

____

(Address)

____

(E-mail address)

____

(Telephone number)

Rule 4 Waiver of the Service of Summons

(Caption)

To (*name the plaintiff's attorney or the unrepresented plaintiff*):

I have received your request to waive service of a summons in this action along with a copy of the complaint, two copies of this waiver form, and a prepaid means of returning one signed copy of the form to you.

I, or the entity I represent, agree to save the expense of serving a summons and complaint in this case.

I understand that I, or the entity I represent, will keep all defenses or objections to the lawsuit, the court's jurisdiction, and the venue of the action, but that I waive any objections to the absence of a summons or of service.

I also understand that I, or the entity I represent, must file and serve an answer or a motion under Rule 12 within 60 days from_, the date when this request was sent (or 90 days if it was sent outside the United States). If I fail to do so, a default judgment will be entered against me or the entity I represent.

Date: ______

____

(Signature of the attorney or unrepresented party)

____

(Printed name)

____

(Address)

____

(E-mail address)

____

(Telephone number)

____

[Attach the following]

____

Duty to Avoid Unnecessary Expenses of Serving a Summons

Rule 4 of the Federal Rules of Civil Procedure requires certain defendants to cooperate in saving unnecessary expenses of serving a summons and complaint. A defendant who is located in the United Sates and who fails to return a signed waiver of service requested by a plaintiff located in the United States will be required to pay the expenses of service, unless the defendant shows good cause for the failure.

"Good cause" does not include a belief that the lawsuit is groundless, or that it has been brought in an improper venue, or that the court has no jurisdiction over this matter or over the defendant or the defendant's property.

If the waiver is signed and returned, you can still make these and all other defenses and objections, but you cannot object to the absence of a summons or of service.

If you waive service, then you must, within the time specified on the waiver form, serve an answer or a motion under Rule 12 on the plaintiff and file a copy with the court. By signing and returning the waiver form, you are allowed more time to respond than if a summons had been served.

Rule 4.1. Serving Other Process

(a) **In General.** Process — other than a summons under Rule 4 or a subpoena under Rule 45 — must be served by a United States marshal or deputy marshal or by a person specially appointed for that purpose. It may be served anywhere within the territorial limits of the state where the district court is located and, if authorized by a federal statute, beyond those limits. Proof of service must be made under Rule 4(l).

(b) **Enforcing Orders: Committing for Civil Contempt.** An order committing a person for civil contempt of a decree or injunction issued to enforce federal law may be served and enforced in any district. Any other order in a civil-contempt proceeding may be served only in the state where the issuing court is located or elsewhere in the United States within 100 miles from where the order was issued.

Rule 5. Serving and Filing Pleadings and Other Papers

(a) **Service: When Required**

(1) In General. Unless these rules provide otherwise, each of the following papers must be served on every party:

(A) an order stating that service is required;

(B) a pleading filed after the original complaint, unless the court orders otherwise under Rule 5(c) because there are numerous defendants;

(C) a discovery paper required to be served on a party, unless the court orders otherwise;

(D) a written motion, except one that may be heard ex parte; and

(E) a written notice, appearance, demand, or offer of judgment, or any similar paper.

(2) If a Party Fails to Appear. No service is required on a party who is in default for failing to appear. But a pleading that asserts a new claim for relief against such a party must be served on that party under Rule 4.

(3) Seizing Property. If an action is begun by seizing property and no person is or need be named as a defendant, any service required before the filing of an appearance, answer, or claim must be made on the person who has custody or possession of the property when it was seized.

(b) Service: How Made

(1) Serving an Attorney. If a party is represented by an attorney, service under this rule must be made on the attorney unless the court orders service on the party.

(2) Service in General. A paper is served under this rule by:

(A) handing it to the person;

(B) leaving it:

(i) at the person's office with a clerk or other person in charge or, if no one is in charge, in a conspicuous place in the office; or

(ii) if the person has no office or the office is closed, at the person's dwelling or usual place of abode with someone of suitable age and discretion who resides there;

(C) mailing it to the person's last known address — in which event service is complete upon mailing;

(D) leaving it with the court clerk if the person has no known address;

(E) sending it to a registered user by filing it with the court's electronic-filing system or sending it by other electronic means that the person consented to in writing — in either of which events service is complete upon filing or sending, but is not effective if the filer or sender learns that it did not reach the person to be served; or

(F) delivering it by any other means that the person consented to in writing — in which event service is complete when the person making service delivers it to the agency designated to make delivery.

(3) Using Court Facilities. [Abrogated (Apr., 2018, eff. Dec. 1, 2018.)]

(c) Serving Numerous Defendants

(1) In General. If an action involves an unusually large number of defendants, the court may, on motion or on its own, order that:

(A) defendants' pleadings and replies to them need not be served on other defendants;

(B) any crossclaim, counterclaim, avoidance, or affirmative defense in those pleadings and replies to them will be treated as denied or avoided by all other parties; and

(C) filing any such pleading and serving it on the plaintiff constitutes notice of the pleading to all parties.

(2) Notifying Parties. A copy of every such order must be served on the parties as the court directs.

(d) Filing

(1) Required Filings; Certificate of Service

(A) Papers after the Complaint. Any paper after the complaint that is required to be served must be filed no later than a reasonable time after service. But disclosures under Rule 26(a)(1) or (2) and the following discovery requests and responses must not be filed until they are used in the proceeding or the court orders filing; depositions: interrogatories, requests for documents or tangible things or to permit entry onto land, and requests for admission.

(B) Certificate of Service. No certificate of service is required when a paper is served by filing it with the court's electronic-filing system. When a paper that is required to be served is served by other means:

(i) if the paper is filed, a certificate of service must be filed with it or within a reasonable time after service; and

(ii) if the paper is not filed, a certificate of service need not be filed unless filing is required by court order or by local rule.

(2) Nonelectronic Filing. A paper not filed electronically is filed by delivering it:

(A) to the clerk; or

(B) to a judge who agrees to accept it for filing, and who must then note the filing date on the paper and promptly send it to the clerk.

(3) Electronic Filing and Signing

(A) By a Represented Person — Generally Required; Exceptions. A person represented by an attorney must file electronically, unless nonelectronic filing is allowed by the court for good cause or is allowed or required by local rule.

(B) By an Unrepresented Person — When Allowed or Required. A person not represented by an attorney:

(i) may file electronically only if allowed by court order or by local rule; and

(ii) may be required to file electronically only by court order, or by a local rule that includes reasonable exceptions.

(C) Signing. A filing made through a person's electronic-filing account and authorized by that person, together with that person's name on a signature block, constitutes the person's signature.

(D) Same as a Written Paper. A paper filed electronically is a written paper for purposes of these rules.

(4) Acceptance by the Clerk. The clerk must not refuse to file a paper solely because it is not in the form prescribed by these rules or by a local rule or practice.

Rule 5.1. Constitutional Challenge to a Statute — Notice, Certification, and Intervention

(a) Notice By A Party. A party that files a pleading, written motion, or other paper drawing into question the constitutionality of a federal or state statute must promptly:

(1) file a notice of constitutional question stating the question and identifying the paper that raises it, if:

(A) a federal statute is questioned and the parties do not include the United States, one of its agencies, or one of its officers or employees in an official capacity; or

(B) a state statute is questioned and the parties do not include the state, one of its agencies, or one of its officers or employees in an official capacity; and

(2) serve the notice and paper on the Attorney General of the United States if a federal statute is questioned — or on the state attorney general if a state statute is questioned — either by certified or registered mail or by sending it to an electronic address designated by the attorney general for this purpose.

(b) Certification by the Court. The court must, under 28 U.S.C. § 2403, certify to the appropriate attorney general that a statute has been questioned.

(c) Intervention; Final Decision on the Merits. Unless the court sets a later time, the attorney general may intervene within 60 days after the notice is filed or after the court certifies the challenge, whichever is earlier. Before the time to intervene expires, the court may reject the constitutional challenge, but may not enter a final judgment holding the statute unconstitutional.

(d) No Forfeiture. A party's failure to file and serve the notice, or the court's failure to certify, does not forfeit a constitutional claim or defense that is otherwise timely asserted.

Rule 5.2. Privacy Protection for Filings Made with the Court

(a) Redacted Filings. Unless the court orders otherwise, in an electronic or paper filing with the court that contains an individual's social-security number, taxpayer-identification number, or birth date, the name of an individual known to be a minor, or a financial-account number, a party or nonparty making the filing may include only:

(1) the last four digits of the social-security number and taxpayer-identification number;

(2) the year of the individual's birth;

(3) the minor's initials; and

(4) the last four digits of the financial-account number.

(b) Exemptions from the Redaction Requirement. The redaction requirement does not apply to the following:

(1) a financial-account number that identifies the property allegedly subject to forfeiture in a forfeiture proceeding;

(2) the record of an administrative or agency proceeding;

(3) the official record of a state-court proceeding;

(4) the record of a court or tribunal, if that record was not subject to the redaction requirement when originally filed;

(5) a filing covered by Rule 5.2(c) or (d); and

(6) a pro se filing in an action brought under 28 U.S.C. §§ 2241, 2254, or 2255.

(c) Limitations on Remote Access to Electronic Files; Social-Security Appeals and Immigration Cases. Unless the court orders otherwise, in an action for benefits under the Social Security Act, and in an action or proceeding relating to an order of removal, to relief from removal, or to immigration benefits or detention, access to an electronic file is authorized as follows:

(1) the parties and their attorneys may have remote electronic access to any part of the case file, including the administrative record;

(2) any other person may have electronic access to the full record at the courthouse, but may have remote electronic access only to:

(A) the docket maintained by the court; and

(B) an opinion, order, judgment, or other disposition of the court, but not any part of the case file or the administrative record.

(d) Filings Made Under Seal. The court may order that a filing be made under seal without redaction. The court may later unseal the filing or order the person who made the filing to file a redacted version for the public record.

(e) Protective Orders. For good cause, the court may by order in a case:

(1) require redaction of additional information; or

(2) limit or prohibit a nonparty's remote electronic access to a document filed with the court.

(f) Option for Additional Unredacted Filing Under Seal. A person making a redacted filing may also file an unredacted copy under seal. The court must retain the unredacted copy as part of the record.

(g) Option for Filing a Reference List. A filing that contains redacted information may be filed together with a reference list that identifies each item of redacted information and specifies an appropriate identifier that uniquely corresponds to each item listed. The list must be filed under seal and may be amended as of right. Any reference in the case to a listed identifier will be construed to refer to the corresponding item of information.

(h) Waiver of Protection of Identifiers. A person waives the protection of Rule 5.2(a) as to the person's own information by filing it without redaction and not under seal.

Rule 6. Computing and Extending Time; Time for Motion Papers

(a) Computing Time. The following rules apply in computing any time period specified in these rules, in any local rule or court order, or in any statute that does not specify a method of computing time.

(1) Period Stated in Days or a Longer Unit. When the period is stated in days or a longer unit of time:

(A) exclude the day of the event that triggers the period;

(B) count every day, including intermediate Saturdays, Sundays, and legal holidays;

and

(C) include the last day of the period, but if the last day is a Saturday, Sunday, or legal holiday, the period continues to run until the end of the next day that is not a Saturday, Sunday, or legal holiday.

(2) Period Stated in Hours. When the period is stated in hours:

(A) begin counting immediately on the occurrence of the event that triggers the period;

(B) count every hour, including hours during intermediate Saturdays, Sundays, and legal holidays; and

(C) if the period would end on a Saturday, Sunday, or legal holiday, the period continues to run until the same time on the next day that is not a Saturday, Sunday, or legal holiday.

(3) Inaccessibility of the Clerk's Office. Unless the court orders otherwise, if the clerk's office is inaccessible:

(A) on the last day for filing under Rule 6(a)(1), then the time for filing is extended to the first accessible day that is not a Saturday, Sunday, or legal holiday; or

(B) during the last hour for filing under Rule 6(a)(2), then the time for filing is extended to the same time on the first accessible day that is not a Saturday, Sunday, or legal holiday.

(4) "Last Day" Defined. Unless a different time is set by a statute, local rule, or court order, the last day ends:

(A) for electronic filing, at midnight in the court's time zone; and

(B) for filing by other means, when the clerk's office is scheduled to close.

(5) "Next Day" Defined. The "next day" is determined by continuing to count forward when the period is measured after an event and backward when measured before an event.

(6) "Legal Holiday" Defined. "Legal holiday" means:

(A) the day set aside by statute for observing New Year's Day, Martin Luther King Jr.'s Birthday, Washington's Birthday, Memorial Day, Juneteenth National Independence Day, Independence Day, Labor Day, Columbus Day, Veterans' Day, Thanksgiving Day, or Christmas Day;

(B) any day declared a holiday by the President or Congress; and

(C) for periods that are measured after an event, any other day declared a holiday by the state where the district court is located.

(b) Extending Time

(1) In General. When an act may or must be done within a specified time, the court may, for good cause, extend the time:

(A) with or without motion or notice if the court acts, or if a request is made, before the original time or its extension expires; or

(B) on motion made after the time has expired if the party failed to act because of excusable neglect.

(2) Exceptions. A court must not extend the time to act under Rules 50(b) and (d), 52(b), 59(b), (d), and (e), and 60(b).

(c) Motions, Notices of Hearing, and Affidavits

(1) In General. A written motion and notice of the hearing must be served at least 14 days before the time specified for the hearing, with the following exceptions:

(A) when the motion may be heard ex parte;

(B) when these rules set a different time; or

(C) when a court order — which a party may, for good cause, apply for ex parte — sets a different time.

(2) Supporting Affidavit. Any affidavit supporting a motion must be served with the motion. Except as Rule 59(c) provides otherwise, any opposing affidavit must be served at least 7 days before the hearing, unless the court permits service at another time.

(d) Additional Time after Certain Kinds of Service. When a party may or must act within a specified time after being served and service is made under Rule 5(b)(2)1(C) (mail), (D) (leaving with the clerk), or (F) (other means consented to), 3 days are added after the period would otherwise expire under Rule 6(a).

III. Pleadings and Motions

Rule 7. Pleadings Allowed; Form of Motions and Other Papers

(a) Pleadings. Only these pleadings are allowed:

(1) a complaint;

(2) an answer to a complaint;

(3) an answer to a counterclaim designated as a counterclaim;

(4) an answer to a crossclaim;

(5) a third-party complaint;

(6) an answer to a third-party complaint; and
(7) if the court orders one, a reply to an answer.

(b) Motions and Other Papers

(1) In General. A request for a court order must be made by motion. The motion must:

(A) be in writing unless made during a hearing or trial;
(B) state with particularity the grounds for seeking the order; and
(C) state the relief sought.

(2) Form. The rules governing captions and other matters of form in pleadings apply to motions and other papers.

Rule 7.1. Disclosure Statement

(a) Who Must File; Contents

(1) Nongovernmental Corporations. A nongovernmental corporate party or a nongovernmental corporation that seeks to intervene must file a statement that:

(A) identifies any parent corporation and any publicly held corporation owning 10% or more of its stock; or
(B) states that there is no such corporation.

(2) Parties or Intervenors in a Diversity Case. In an action in which jurisdiction is based on diversity under 28 U.S.C. § 1332(a), a party or intervenor must, unless the court orders otherwise, file a disclosure statement. The statement must name — and identify the citizenship of — every individual or entity whose citizenship is attributed to that party or intervenor:

(A) when the action is filed in or removed to federal court, and
(B) when any later event occurs that could affect the court's jurisdiction under § 1332(a).

(b) Time to File; Supplemental Filing. A party, intervenor, or proposed intervenor must:

(1) file the disclosure statement with its first appearance, pleading, petition, motion, response, or other request addressed to the court; and
(2) promptly file a supplemental statement if any required information changes.

Rule 8. General Rules of Pleading

(a) Claim for Relief. A pleading that states a claim for relief must contain:

(1) a short and plain statement of the grounds for the court's jurisdiction, unless the court already has jurisdiction and the claim needs no new jurisdictional support;

(2) a short and plain statement of the claim showing that the pleader is entitled to relief; and

(3) a demand for the relief sought, which may include relief in the alternative or different types of relief.

(b) Defenses; Admissions and Denials

(1) In General. In responding to a pleading, a party must:

(A) state in short and plain terms its defenses to each claim asserted against it; and

(B) admit or deny the allegations asserted against it by an opposing party.

(2) Denials — Responding to the Substance. A denial must fairly respond to the substance of the allegation.

(3) General and Specific Denials. A party that intends in good faith to deny all the allegations of a pleading — including the jurisdictional grounds — may do so by a general denial. A party that does not intend to deny all the allegations must either specifically deny designated allegations or generally deny all except those specifically admitted.

(4) Denying Part of an Allegation. A party that intends in good faith to deny only part of an allegation must admit the part that is true and deny the rest.

(5) Lacking Knowledge or Information. A party that lacks knowledge or information sufficient to form a belief about the truth of an allegation must so state, and the statement has the effect of a denial.

(6) Effect of Failing to Deny. An allegation — other than one relating to the amount of damages — is admitted if a responsive pleading is required and the allegation is not denied. If a responsive pleading is not required, an allegation is considered denied or avoided.

(c) Affirmative Defenses

(1) In General. In responding to a pleading, a party must affirmatively state any avoidance or affirmative defense, including:

- accord and satisfaction;
- arbitration and award;
- assumption of risk;
- contributory negligence;
- duress;
- estoppel;
- failure of consideration;
- fraud;
- illegality;
- injury by fellow servant;
- laches;
- license;
- payment;

- release;
- res judicata;
- statute of frauds;
- statute of limitations; and
- waiver.

(2) Mistaken Designation. If a party mistakenly designates a defense as a counterclaim, or a counterclaim as a defense, the court must, if justice requires, treat the pleading as though it were correctly designated, and may impose terms for doing so.

(d) Pleading to Be Concise and Direct; Alternative Statements; Inconsistency

(1) In General. Each allegation must be simple, concise, and direct. No technical form is required.

(2) Alternative Statements of a Claim or Defense. A party may set out two or more statements of a claim or defense alternatively or hypothetically, either in a single count or defense or in separate ones. If a party makes alternative statements, the pleading is sufficient if any one of them is sufficient.

(3) Inconsistent Claims or Defenses. A party may state as many separate claims or defenses as it has, regardless of consistency.

(e) Construing Pleadings. Pleadings must be construed so as to do justice.

Rule 9. Pleading Special Matters

(a) Capacity or Authority to Sue; Legal Existence

(1) In General. Except when required to show that the court has jurisdiction, a pleading need not allege:

(A) a party's capacity to sue or be sued;

(B) a party's authority to sue or be sued in a representative capacity;

(C) the legal existence of an organized association of persons that is made a party.

(2) Raising Those Issues. To raise any of those issues, a party must do so by a specific denial, which must state any supporting facts that are peculiarly within the party's knowledge.

(b) Fraud or Mistake; Condition of Mind. In alleging fraud or mistake, a party must state with particularity the circumstances constituting fraud or mistake. Malice, intent, knowledge, and other conditions of a person's mind may be alleged generally.

(c) Conditions Precedent. In pleading conditions precedent, it suffices to allege generally that all conditions precedent have occurred or been performed. But when denying that a condition precedent has occurred or been performed, a party must do so with particularity.

(d) Official Document or Act. In pleading an official document or official act, it suffices to allege that the document was legally issued or the act legally done.

(e) Judgment. In pleading a judgment or decision of a domestic or foreign court, a judicial or quasi-judicial tribunal, or a board or officer, it suffices to plead the judgment or decision without showing jurisdiction to render it.

(f) Time and Place. An allegation of time or place is material when testing the sufficiency of a pleading.

(g) Special Damages. If an item of special damage is claimed, it must be specifically stated.

(h) Admiralty or Maritime Claim

(1) How Designated. If a claim for relief is within the admiralty or maritime jurisdiction and also within the court's subject-matter jurisdiction on some other ground, the pleading may designate the claim as an admiralty or maritime claim for purposes of Rules 14(c), 38(e), and 82 and the Supplemental Rules for Admiralty or Maritime Claims and Asset Forfeiture Actions. A claim cognizable only in the admiralty or maritime jurisdiction is an admiralty or maritime claim for those purposes, whether or not so designated.

(2) Designation for Appeal. A case that includes an admiralty or maritime claim within this subdivision (h) is an admiralty case within 28 U.S.C. § 1292(a)(3).

Rule 10. Form of Pleadings

(a) Caption; Names of Parties. Every pleading must have a caption with the court's name, a title, a file number, and a Rule 7(a) designation. The title of the complaint must name all the parties; the title of other pleadings, after naming the first party on each side, may refer generally to other parties.

(b) Paragraphs; Separate Statements. A party must state its claims or defenses in numbered paragraphs, each limited as far as practicable to a single set of circumstances. A later pleading may refer by number to a paragraph in an earlier pleading. If doing so would promote clarity, each claim founded on a separate transaction or occurrence — and each defense other than a denial — must be stated in a separate count or defense.

(c) Adoption by Reference; Exhibits. A statement in a pleading may be adopted by reference elsewhere in the same pleading or in any other pleading or motion. A copy of a written instrument that is an exhibit to a pleading is a part of the pleading for all purposes.

Rule 11. Signing Pleadings, Motions, and Other Papers; Representations to the Court; Sanctions

(a) Signature. Every pleading, written motion, and other paper must be signed by at least one attorney of record in the attorney's name — or by a party personally if the party is unrepresented. The paper must state the signer's address, e-mail address, and telephone number. Unless a rule or statute specifically states otherwise, a pleading need not be verified or accompanied by an affidavit. The court must strike an unsigned paper unless the omission is promptly corrected after being called to the attorney's or party's attention.

(b) Representations to the Court. By presenting to the court a pleading, written motion, or other paper — whether by signing, filing, submitting, or later advocating it — an attorney or unrepresented party certifies that to the best of the person's knowledge, information, and belief, formed after an inquiry rea- sonable under the circumstances:

(1) it is not being presented for any improper purpose, such as to harass, cause unnecessary delay, or needlessly increase the cost of litigation;

(2) the claims, defenses, and other legal contentions are warranted by existing law or by a nonfrivolous argument for extending, modifying, or reversing existing law or for establishing new law;

(3) the factual contentions have evidentiary support or, if specifically so identified, will likely have evidentiary support after a reasonable opportunity for further investigation or discovery; and

(4) the denials of factual contentions are warranted on the evidence or, if specifically so identified, are reasonably based on belief or a lack of information.

(c) Sanctions

(1) In General. If, after notice and a reasonable opportunity to respond, the court determines that Rule 11(b) has been violated, the court may impose an appropriate sanction on any attorney, law firm, or party that violated the rule or is responsible for the violation. Absent exceptional circumstances, a law firm must be held jointly responsible for a violation committed by its partner, associate, or employee.

(2) Motion for Sanctions. A motion for sanctions must be made separately from any other motion and must describe the specific conduct that allegedly violates Rule 11(b). The motion must be served under Rule 5, but it must not be filed or be presented to the court if the challenged paper, claim, defense, contention, or denial is withdrawn or appropriately corrected within 21 days after service or within another time the court sets. If warranted, the court may award to the prevailing party the reasonable expenses, including attorney's fees, incurred for the motion.

(3) On the Court's Initiative. On its own, the court may order an attorney, law firm, or party to show cause why conduct specifically described in the order has not violated Rule 11(b).

(4) Nature of a Sanction. A sanction imposed under this rule must be limited to what suffices to deter repetition of the conduct or comparable conduct by others similarly situated. The sanction may include nonmonetary directives; an order to pay a penalty into court; or, if imposed on motion and warranted for effective deterrence, an order directing payment to the movant of part or all of the reasonable attorney's fees and other expenses directly resulting from the violation.

(5) Limitations on Monetary Sanctions. The court must not impose a monetary sanction:

(A) against a represented party for violating Rule 11(b)(2); or

(B) on its own, unless it issued the show-cause order under Rule 11(c)(3) before voluntary dismissal or settlement of the claims made by or against the party that is, or whose attorneys are, to be sanctioned.

(6) Requirements for an Order. An order imposing a sanction must describe the sanctioned conduct and explain the basis for the sanction.

(d) Inapplicability to Discovery. This rule does not apply to disclosures and discovery requests, responses, objections, and motions under Rules 26 through 37.

Rule 12. Defenses and Objections: When and How Presented; Motion for Judgment on the Pleadings; Consolidating Motions; Waiving Defenses; Pretrial Hearing

(a) Time to Serve a Responsive Pleading

(1) In General. Unless another time is specified by a federal statute, the time for serving a responsive pleading is as follows:

(A) A defendant must serve an answer:

(i) within 21 days after being served with the summons and complaint; or

(ii) if it has timely waived service under Rule 4(d), within 60 days after the request for a waiver was sent, or within 90 days after it was sent to the defendant outside any judicial district of the United States.

(B) A party must serve an answer to a counterclaim or crossclaim within 21 days after being served with the pleading that states the counterclaim or crossclaim.

(C) A party must serve a reply to an answer within 21 days after being served with an order to reply, unless the order specifies a different time.

(2) United States and Its Agencies, Officers, or Employees Sued in an Official Capacity. The United States, a United States agency, or a United States officer or employee sued only in an official capacity must serve an answer to a complaint, counterclaim, or crossclaim within 60 days after service on the United States attorney.

(3) United States Officers or Employees Sued in an Individual Capacity. A United States officer or employee sued in an individual capacity for an act or omission occurring in connection with duties performed on the United States' behalf must serve an answer to a complaint, counterclaim, or crossclaim within 60 days after service on the officer or employee or service on the United States attorney, whichever is later.

(4) Effect of a Motion. Unless the court sets a different time, serving a motion under this rule alters these periods as follows:

(A) if the court denies the motion or postpones its disposition until trial, the responsive pleading must be served within 14 days after notice of the court's action; or

(B) if the court grants a motion for a more definite statement, the responsive pleading must be served within 14 days after the more definite statement is served.

(b) How to Present Defenses. Every defense to a claim for relief in any pleading must be asserted in the responsive pleading if one is required. But a party may assert the following defenses by motion:

(1) lack of subject-matter jurisdiction;
(2) lack of personal jurisdiction;
(3) improper venue;
(4) insufficient process;
(5) insufficient service of process;
(6) failure to state a claim upon which relief can be granted; and
(7) failure to join a party under Rule 19.

A motion asserting any of these defenses must be made before pleading if a responsive pleading is allowed. If a pleading sets out a claim for relief that does not require a responsive pleading, an opposing party may assert at trial any defense to that claim. No defense or objection is waived by joining it with one or more other defenses or objections in a responsive pleading or in a motion.

(c) Motion for Judgment on the Pleadings. After the pleadings are closed — but early enough not to delay trial — a party may move for judgment on the pleadings.

(d) Result of Presenting Matters Outside the Pleadings. If, on a motion under Rule 12(b)(6) or 12(c), matters outside the pleadings are presented to and not excluded by the court, the motion must be treated as one for summary judgment under Rule 56. All parties must be given a reasonable opportunity to present all the material that is pertinent to the motion.

(e) Motion for a More Definite Statement. A party may move for a more definite statement of a pleading to which a responsive pleading is allowed but which is so vague or ambiguous that the party cannot reasonably prepare a response. The motion must be made before filing a responsive pleading and must point out the defects complained of and the details desired. If the court orders a more definite statement and the order is not obeyed within 14 days after notice of the order or within the time the court sets, the court may strike the pleading or issue any other appropriate order.

(f) Motion to Strike. The court may strike from a pleading an insufficient defense or any redundant, immaterial, impertinent, or scandalous matter. The court may act:

(1) on its own; or

(2) on motion made by a party either before responding to the pleading or, if a response is not allowed, within 21 days after being served with the pleading.

(g) Joining Motions

(1) Right to Join. A motion under this rule may be joined with any other motion allowed by this rule.

(2) Limitation on Further Motions. Except as provided in Rule 12(h)(2) or (3), a party that makes a motion under this rule must not make another motion under this rule raising a defense or objection that was available to the party but omitted from its earlier motion.

(h) Waiving and Preserving Certain Defenses

(1) When Some Are Waived. A party waives any defense listed in Rule 12(b)(2)-(5) by:

(A) omitting it from a motion in the circumstances described in Rule 12(g)(2); or

(B) failing to either

(i) make it by motion under this rule; or

(ii) include it in a responsive pleading or in an amendment allowed by Rule 15(a)(1) as a matter of course.

(2) When to Raise Others. Failure to state a claim upon which relief can be granted, to join a person required by Rule 19(b), or to state a legal defense to a claim may be raised:

(A) in any pleading allowed or ordered under Rule 7(a);

(B) by a motion under Rule 12(c); or
(C) at trial.

(3) Lack of Subject-Matter Jurisdiction. If the court determines at any time that it lacks subject matter jurisdiction, the court must dismiss the action.

(i) Hearing Before Trial. If a party so moves, any defense listed in Rule 12(b)(1)-(7) — whether made in a pleading or by motion — and a motion under Rule 12(c) must be heard and decided before trial unless the court orders a deferral until trial.

Rule 13. Counterclaim and Crossclaim

(a) Compulsory Counterclaim

(1) In General. A pleading must state as a counterclaim any claim that — at the time of its service — the pleader has against an opposing party if the claim:

(A) arises out of the transaction or occurrence that is the subject matter of the opposing party's claim; and

(B) does not require adding another party over whom the court cannot acquire jurisdiction.

(2) Exceptions. The pleader need not state the claim if:

(A) when the action was commenced, the claim was the subject of another pending action; or

(B) the opposing party sued on its claim by attachment or other process that did not establish personal jurisdiction over the pleader on that claim, and the pleader does not assert any counterclaim under this rule.

(b) Permissive Counterclaim. A pleading may state as a counterclaim against an opposing party any claim that is not compulsory.

(c) Relief Sought in a Counterclaim. A counterclaim need not diminish or defeat the recovery sought by the opposing party. It may request relief that exceeds in amount or differs in kind from the relief sought by the opposing party.

(d) Counterclaim Against the United States. These rules do not expand the right to assert a counterclaim — or to claim a credit — against the United States or a United States officer or agency.

(e) Counterclaim Maturing or Acquired After Pleading. The court may permit a party to file a supplemental pleading asserting a counterclaim that matured or was acquired by the party after serving an earlier pleading.

(f) [Abrogated]

(g) **Crossclaim Against a Coparty.** A pleading may state as a crossclaim any claim by one party against a coparty if the claim arises out of the transaction or occurrence that is the subject matter of the original action or of a counterclaim, or if the claim relates to any property that is the subject matter of the original action. The crossclaim may include a claim that the coparty is or may be liable to the crossclaimant for all or part of a claim asserted in the action against the crossclaimant.

(h) **Joining Additional Parties.** Rules 19 and 20 govern the addition of a person as a party to a counterclaim or crossclaim.

(i) **Separate Trials; Separate Judgments.** If the court orders separate trials under Rule 42(b), it may enter judgment on a counterclaim or crossclaim under Rule 54(b) when it has jurisdiction to do so, even if the opposing party's claims have been dismissed or otherwise resolved.

Rule 14. Third-Party Practice

(a) When a Defending Party May Bring in a Third Party

(1) Timing of the Summons and Complaint. A defending party may, as third-party plaintiff, serve a summons and complaint on a nonparty who is or may be liable to it for all or part of the claim against it. But the third-party plaintiff must, by motion, obtain the court's leave if it files the third-party complaint more than 14 days after serving its original answer.

(2) Third-Party Defendant's Claims and Defenses. The person served with the summons and third-party complaint — the "third-party defendant":

(A) must assert any defense against the third-party plaintiff 's claim under Rule 12;

(B) must assert any counterclaim against the third-party plaintiff under Rule 13(a), and may assert any counterclaim against the third-party plaintiff under Rule 13(b) or any crossclaim against another third-party defendant under Rule 13(g);

(C) may assert against the plaintiff any defense that the third-party plaintiff has to the plaintiff 's claim; and

(D) may also assert against the plaintiff any claim arising out of the transaction or occurrence that is the subject matter of the plaintiff 's claim against the third-party plaintiff.

(3) Plaintiff 's Claims Against a Third-Party Defendant. The plaintiff may assert against the third-party defendant any claim arising out of the transaction or

occurrence that is the subject matter of the plaintiff 's claim against the third-party plaintiff. The third-party defendant must then assert any defense under Rule 12 and any counterclaim under Rule 13(a), and may assert any counterclaim under Rule 13(b) or any crossclaim under Rule 13(g).

(4) Motion to Strike, Sever or Try Separately. Any party may move to strike the third-party claim, to sever it, or to try it separately.

(5) Third-Party Defendant's Claim Against a Nonparty. A third-party defendant may proceed under this rule against a non-party who is or may be liable to the third-party defendant for all or part of any claim against it.

(6) Third-Party Complaint In Rem. If it is within the admiralty or maritime jurisdiction, a third-party complaint may be in rem. In that event, a reference in this rule to the "summons" includes the warrant of arrest, and a reference to the defendant or third-party plaintiff includes, when appropriate, a person who asserts a right under Supplemental Rule C(6)(a)(i) in the property arrested.

(b) When a Plaintiff May Bring in a Third Party. When a claim is asserted against a plaintiff, the plaintiff may bring in a third party if this rule would allow a defendant to do so.

(c) Admiralty or Maritime Claim

(1) Scope of Impleader. If a plaintiff asserts an admiralty or maritime claim under Rule 9(h), the defendant or a person who asserts a right under Supplemental Rule C(6)(a)(i) may, as a third-party plaintiff, bring in a third-party defendant who may be wholly or partly liable — either to the plaintiff or to the third-party plaintiff — for remedy over, contribution, or otherwise on account of the same transaction, occurrence, or series of transactions or occurrences.

(2) Defending Against a Demand for Judgment for the Plaintiff. The third-party plaintiff may demand judgment in the plaintiff 's favor against the third-party defendant. In that event, the third-party defendant must defend under Rule 12 against the plaintiff 's claim as well as the third-party plaintiff 's claim; and the action proceeds as if the plaintiff had sued both the third-party defendant and the third-party plaintiff.

Rule 15. Amended and Supplemental Pleadings

(a) Amendments Before Trial

(1) Amending as a Matter of Course. A party may amend its pleadings once as a matter of course within:

(A) 21 days after serving it, or

(B) if the pleading is one to which a responsive pleading is required, 21 days after service of a responsive pleading or 21 days after service of a motion under Rule 12(b), (e), or (f), whichever is earlier.

(2) Other Amendments. In all other cases, a party may amend its pleading only with the opposing party's written consent or the court's leave. The court should freely give leave when justice so requires.

(3) Time to Respond. Unless the court orders otherwise, any required response to an amended pleading must be made within the time remaining to respond to the original pleading or within 14 days after service of the amended pleading, whichever is later.

(b) Amendments During and After Trial

(1) Based on an Objection at Trial. If, at trial, a party objects that evidence is not within the issues raised in the pleadings, the court may permit the pleadings to be amended. The court should freely permit an amendment when doing so will aid in presenting the merits and the objecting party fails to satisfy the court that the evidence would prejudice that party's action or defense on the merits. The court may grant a continuance to enable the objecting party to meet the evidence.

(2) For Issues Tried by Consent. When an issue not raised by the pleadings is tried by the parties' express or implied consent, it must be treated in all respects as if raised in the pleadings. A party may move — at any time, even after judgment — to amend the pleadings to conform them to the evidence and to raise an unpleaded issue. But failure to amend does not affect the result of the trial of that issue.

(c) Relation Back of Amendments

(1) When an Amendment Relates Back. An amendment to a pleading relates back to the date of the original pleading when:

(A) the law that provides the applicable statute of limitations allows relation back;

(B) the amendment asserts a claim or defense that arose out of the conduct, transaction, or occurrence set out — or attempted to be set out — in the original pleading; or

(C) the amendment changes the party or the naming of the party against whom a claim is asserted, if Rule 15(c)(1)(B) is satisfied and if, within the period provided by Rule 4(m) for serving the summons and complaint, the party to be brought in by amendment:

(i) received such notice of the action that it will not be prejudiced in defending on the merits; and

(ii) knew or should have known that the action would have been brought against it, but for a mistake concerning the proper party's identity.

(2) Notice to the United States. When the United States or a United States officer or agency is added as a defendant by amendment, the notice requirements of Rule 15(c)(1)(C)(i) and (ii) are satisfied if, during the stated period, process was delivered or mailed to the United States attorney or the United States attorney's designee, to the Attorney General of the United States, or to the officer or agency.

(d) Supplemental Pleadings. On motion and reasonable notice, the court may, on just terms, permit a party to serve a supplemental pleading setting out any transaction, occurrence, or event that happened after the date of the pleading to be supplemented. The court may permit supplementation even though the original pleading is defective in stating a claim or defense. The court may order that the opposing party plead to the supplemental pleading within a specified time.

Rule 16. Pretrial Conferences; Scheduling; Management[1]

(a) Purposes of a Pretrial Conference. In any action, the court may order the attorneys and any unrepresented parties to appear for one or more pretrial conferences for such purposes as:

(1) expediting disposition of the action;

(2) establishing early and continuing control so that the case will not be protracted because of lack of management;

(3) discouraging wasteful pretrial activities;

(4) improving the quality of the trial through more thorough preparation; and

(5) facilitating settlement.

(b) Scheduling

(1) Scheduling Order. Except in categories of actions exempted by local rule, the district judge — or a magistrate judge when authorized by local rule — must issue a scheduling order:

(A) after receiving the parties' report under Rule 26(f); or

(B) after consulting with the parties' attorneys and any unrepresented parties at a scheduling conference.

(2) Time to Issue. The judge must issue the scheduling order as soon as practicable, but unless the judge finds good cause for delay, the judge must issue it within the earlier of 90 days after any defendant has been served with the complaint or 60 days after any defendant has appeared.

(3) Contents of the Order

(A) Required Contents. The scheduling order must limit the time to join other parties, amend the pleadings, complete discovery, and file motions.

(B) Permitted Contents. The scheduling order may:

(i) modify the timing of disclosures under Rules 26(a)and 26(e)(1);

(ii) modify the extent of discovery;

(iii) provide for disclosure, discovery, or preservation of electronically stored information;

1. There is a pending amendment to Rule 16(b) that may take effect December 1, 2025. See details, *infra*.

(iv) include any agreements the parties reach for asserting claims of privilege or of protection as trial-preparation material after information is produced, including agreements reached under Federal Rule of Evidence 502;

(v) direct that before moving for an order relating to discovery, the movant must request a conference with the court;

(vi) set dates for pretrial conferences and for trial; and

(vii) include other appropriate matters.

(4) Modifying a Schedule. A schedule may be modified only for good cause and with the judge's consent.

(c) Attendance and Matters for Consideration at a Pretrial Conference

(1) Attendance. A represented party must authorize at least one of its attorneys to make stipulations and admissions about all matters that can reasonably be anticipated for discussion at a pretrial conference. If appropriate, the court may require that a party or its representative be present or reasonably available by other means to consider possible settlement.

(2) Matters for Consideration. At any pretrial conference, the court may consider and take appropriate action on the following matters:

(A) formulating and simplifying the issues, and eliminating frivolous claims or defenses;

(B) amending the pleadings if necessary or desirable;

(C) obtaining admissions and stipulations about facts and documents to avoid unnecessary proof, and ruling in advance on the admissibility of evidence;

(D) avoiding unnecessary proof and cumulative evidence, and limiting the use of testimony under Federal Rule of Evidence 702;

(E) determining the appropriateness and timing of summary adjudication under Rule 56;

(F) controlling and scheduling discovery, including orders affecting disclosures and discovery under Rule 26 and Rules 29 through 37;

(G) identifying witnesses and documents; scheduling the filing and exchange of any pretrial briefs, and setting dates for further conferences and for trial;

(H) referring matters to a magistrate judge or a master;

(I) settling the case and using special procedures to assist in resolving the dispute when authorized by statute or local rule;

(J) determining the form and content of the pretrial order;

(K) disposing of pending motions;

(L) adopting special procedures for managing potentially difficult or protracted actions that may involve complex issues, multiple parties, difficult legal questions, or unusual proof problems;

(M) ordering a separate trial under Rule 42(b) of a claim, counterclaim, crossclaim, third-party claim, or particular issue;

(N) ordering the presentation of evidence early in the trial on a manageable issue that might, on the evidence, be the basis for a judgment as a matter of law under Rule 50(a) or a judgment on partial findings under Rule 52(c);

(O) establishing a reasonable limit on the time allowed to present evidence; and

(P) facilitating in other ways the just, speedy, and inexpensive disposition of the action.

(d) Pretrial Orders. After any conference under this rule, the court should issue an order reciting the action taken. This order controls the course of the action unless the court modifies it.

(e) Final Pretrial Conferences and Orders. The court may hold a final pretrial conference to formulate a trial plan, including a plan to facilitate the admission of evidence. The conference must be held as close to the start of trial as is reasonable, and must be attended by at least one attorney who will conduct the trial for each party and by any unrepresented party. The court may modify the order issued after a final pretrial conference only to prevent manifest injustice.

(f) Sanctions

(1) In General. On motion or on its own, the court may issue any just orders, including those authorized by Rule 37(b)(2)(A)(ii)-(vii), if a party or by its attorney:

(A) fails to appear at a scheduling or other pretrial conference;

(B) is substantially unprepared to participate — or does not participate in good faith — in the conference; or

(C) fails to obey a scheduling or other pretrial order.

(2) Imposing Fees and Costs. Instead of or in addition to any other sanction, the court must order the party, its attorney, or both to pay the reasonable expenses — including attorney's fees — incurred because of any noncompliance with this rule, unless the noncompliance was substantially justified or other circumstances make an award of expenses unjust.

Pending Amendment to Rule 16(b) that may take effect December 1, 2025

(b) Scheduling and Management

. . .

(3) Contents of the Order

. . .

(B) Permitted Contents

. . .

(iv) include the timing and method for complying with Rule 26(b)(5)(A) and any agreements the parties reach for asserting claims of privilege or of protection as trial-preparation material after information is produced, including agreements reached under Federal Rule of Evidence 502;

. . .

Pending Amendment to add new Rule 16.1 that may take effect December 1, 2025

Rule 16.1. Multidistrict Litigation

(a) Initial Management Conference. After the Judicial Panel on Multidistrict Litigation transfers actions, the transferee court should schedule an initial management conference to develop an initial plan for orderly pretrial activity in the MDL proceedings.

(b) Report for the Conference

(1) Submitting a Report. The transferee court should order the parties to meet and to submit a report to the court before the conference.

(2) Required Content: the Parties' Views on Leadership Control and Other Matters. The report must address any matter the court designates — which may include any matter in Rule 16 — and, unless the court orders otherwise, the parties' views on:

(A) whether leadership counsel should be appointed and, if so:

(i) the timing of the appointments;

(ii) the structure of leadership counsel;

(iii) the procedure for selecting leadership and whether the appointments should be reviewed periodically;

(iv) their responsibilities and authority in conducting pretrial activities and any role in facilitating resolution of the MDL proceedings;

(v) the proposed methods for regularly communicating with and reporting to the court and nonleadership counsel;

(vi) any limits on activity by nonleadership counsel; and

(vii) whether and when to establish a means for compensating leadership counsel;

(B) any previously entered scheduling or other orders that should be vacated or modified;

(C) a schedule for additional management conferences with the court;

(D) how to manage the direct filing of new actions in the MDL proceedings; and

(E) whether related actions have been — or are expected to be — filed in other courts, and whether to adopt methods for coordinating them.

(3) Additional Required Content: the Parties' Initial Views on Various Matters. Unless the court orders otherwise, the report also must address the parties' initial views on:

(A) whether consolidated pleadings should be prepared;

(B) how and when the parties will exchange information about the factual bases for their claims and defenses;

(C) discovery; including any difficult issues that may arise;

(D) any likely pretrial motions;

(E) whether the court should consider any measures to facilitate resolving some or all actions before the court;

(F) whether any matters should be referred to a magistrate judge or a master; and

(G) the principal factual and legal issues likely to be presented.

(4) Permitted Content. The report may include any other matter that the parties wish to bring to the court's attention.

(c) Initial Management Order. After the conference, the court should enter an initial management order addressing the matters in Rule 16.1(b) and, in the court's discretion, any other matters. This order controls the course of the proceedings unless the court modifies it.

IV. Parties

Rule 17. Plaintiff and Defendant; Capacity; Public Officers

(a) Real Party In Interest

(1) Designation in General. An action must be prosecuted in the name of the real party in interest. The following may sue in their own names without joining the person for whose benefit the action is brought:

(A) an executor;

(B) an administrator;

(C) a guardian;

(D) a bailee;

(E) a trustee of an express trust;

(F) a party with whom or in whose name a contract has been made for another's benefit; and

(G) a party authorized by statute.

(2) Action in the Name of the United States for Another's Use or Benefit. When a federal statute so provides, an action for another's use or benefit must be brought in the name of the United States.

(3) Joinder of the Real Party in Interest. The court may not dismiss an action for failure to prosecute in the name of the real party in interest until, after an objection, a reasonable time has been allowed for the real party in interest to ratify, join, or be substituted into the action. After ratification, joinder, or substitution, the action proceeds as if it had been originally commenced by the real party in interest.

(b) Capacity to Sue or Be Sued. Capacity to sue or be sued is determined as follows:

(1) for an individual who is not acting in a representative capacity, by the law of the individual's domicile;

(2) for a corporation, by the law under which it was organized; and

(3) for all other parties, by the law of the state where the court is located, except that:

(A) a partnership or other unincorporated association with no such capacity under that state's law may sue or be sued in its common name to enforce a substantive right existing under the United States Constitution or laws; and

(B) 28 U.S.C. §§ 754 and 959(a) govern the capacity of a receiver appointed by a United States court to sue or be sued in a United States court.

(c) Minor or Incompetent Person

(1) With a Representative. The following representatives may sue or defend on behalf of a minor or an incompetent person:

(A) a general guardian;

(B) a committee;

(C) a conservator; or

(D) a like fiduciary.

(2) Without a Representative. A minor or an incompetent person who does not have a duly appointed representative may sue by a next friend or by a guardian ad litem. The court must appoint a guardian ad litem — or issue another appropriate order — to protect a minor or incompetent person who is unrepresented in an action.

(d) Public Officer's Title and Name. A public officer who sues or is sued in an official capacity may be designated by official title rather than by name, but the court may order that the officer's name be added.

Rule 18. Joinder of Claims

(a) In General. A party asserting a claim, counterclaim, crossclaim, or third-party claim may join, as independent or alternative claims, as many claims as it has against an opposing party.

(b) Joinder of Contingent Claims. A party may join two claims even though one of them is contingent on the disposition of the other; but the court may grant relief only in accordance with the parties' relative substantive rights. In particular, a plaintiff may state a claim for money and a claim to set aside a conveyance that is fraudulent as to that plaintiff, without first obtaining a judgment for the money.

Rule 19. Required Joinder of Parties

(a) Persons Required to Be Joined if Feasible

(1) Required Party. A party who is subject to service of process and whose joinder will not deprive the court of subject-matter jurisdiction must be joined as a party if:

(A) in that person's absence, the court cannot accord complete relief among existing parties; or

(B) that person claims an interest to the subject of the action and is so situated that disposing of the action in the person's absence may:

(i) as a practical matter impair or impede the person's ability to protect the interest; or

(ii) leave an existing party subject to a substantial risk of incurring double, multiple, or otherwise inconsistent obligations because of the interest.

(2) Joinder by Court Order. If a person has not been joined as required, the court must order that the person be made a party. A person who refuses to join as a plaintiff may be made either a defendant or, in a proper case, an involuntary plaintiff.

(3) Venue. If a party objects to venue and the joinder would make venue improper, the court must dismiss that party.

(b) When Joinder Is Not Feasible. If a person who is required to be joined if feasible cannot be joined, the court must determine whether in equity and good conscience the action should proceed among the existing parties or should be dismissed. The factors for the court to consider include:

(1) the extent to which a judgment rendered in the person's absence might prejudice that person or the existing parties;

(2) the extent to which any prejudice could be lessened or avoided by:

(A) protective provisions in the judgment;

(B) shaping the relief; or

(C) other measures;

(3) whether a judgment rendered in the person's absence would be adequate; and

(4) whether the plaintiff would have an adequate remedy if the action were dismissed for nonjoinder.

(c) Pleading the Reasons for Nonjoinder. When asserting a claim for relief, a party must state:

(1) the name, if known, of any person who is required to be joined if feasible but is not joined; and

(2) the reasons for not joining that person.

(d) Exception for Class Actions. This rule is subject to Rule 23.

Rule 20. Permissive Joinder of Parties

(a) Persons Who May Join or Be Joined

(1) Plaintiffs. Persons may join in one action as plaintiffs if:

(A) they assert any right to relief jointly, severally, or in the alternative with respect to or arising out of the same transaction, occurrence, or series of transactions or occurrences; and

(B) any question of law or fact common to all plaintiffs will arise in the action.

(2) Defendants. Persons — as well as a vessel, cargo, or other property subject to admiralty process in rem — may be joined in one action as defendants if:

(A) any right to relief is asserted against them jointly, severally, or in the alternative with respect to or arising out of the same transaction, occurrence, or series of transactions or occurrences; and

(B) any question of law or fact common to all defendants will arise in the action.

(3) Extent of Relief. Neither a plaintiff nor a defendant need be interested in obtaining or defending against all the relief demanded. The court may grant judgment to one or more plaintiffs according to their rights, and against one or more defendants according to their liabilities.

(b) Protective Measures. The court may issue orders — including an order for separate trials — to protect a party against embarrassment, delay, expense, or other prejudice that arises from including a person against whom the party asserts no claim and who asserts no claim against the party.

Rule 21. Misjoinder and Nonjoinder of Parties

Misjoinder of parties is not a ground for dismissing an action. On motion or on its own, the court may at any time, on just terms, add or drop a party. The court may also sever any claim against a party.

Rule 22. Interpleader

(a) Grounds

(1) By a Plaintiff. Persons with claims that may expose a plaintiff to double or multiple liability may be joined as defendants and required to interplead. Joinder for interpleader is proper even though:

(A) the claims of the several claimants, or the titles on which their claims depend, lack a common origin or are adverse and independent rather than identical; or

(B) the plaintiff denies liability in whole or in part to any or all of the claimants.

(2) By a Defendant. A defendant exposed to similar liability may seek interpleader through a crossclaim or counterclaim.

(b) Relation to Other Rules and Statutes. This rule supplements — and does not limit — the joinder of parties allowed by Rule 20. The remedy this rule provides is in addition to — and does not supersede or limit — the remedy provided by 28 U.S.C. §§ 1335, 1397, and 2361. An action under those statutes must be conducted under these rules.

Rule 23. Class Actions

(a) Prerequisites. One or more members of a class may sue or be sued as representative parties on behalf of all members only if:

(1) the class is so numerous that joinder of all members is impracticable;

(2) there are questions of law or fact common to the class;

(3) the claims or defenses of the representative parties are typical of the claims or defenses of the class; and

(4) the representative parties will fairly and adequately protect the interests of the class.

(b) Types of Class Actions. A class action may be maintained if Rule 23(a) is satisfied and if:

(1) prosecuting separate actions by or against individual class members would create a risk of:

(A) inconsistent or varying adjudications with respect to individual class members that would establish incompatible standards of conduct for the party opposing the class; or

(B) adjudications with respect to individual class members that, as a practical matter, would be dispositive of the interests of the other members not parties to the individual adjudications or would substantially impair or impede their ability to protect their interests;

(2) the party opposing the class has acted or refused to act on grounds that apply generally to the class, so that final injunctive relief or corresponding declaratory relief is appropriate respecting the class as a whole; or

(3) the court finds that the questions of law or fact common to class members predominate over any questions affecting only individual members, and that a class action is superior to other available methods for fairly and efficiently adjudicating the controversy. The matters pertinent to these findings include:

(A) the class members' interests in individually controlling the prosecution or defense of separate actions;

(B) the extent and nature of any litigation concerning the controversy already begun by or against class members;

(C) the desirability or undesirability of concentrating the litigation of the claims in the particular forum; and

(D) the likely difficulties in managing a class action.

(c) Certification Order; Notice to Class Members; Judgment; Issues Classes; Subclasses

(1) Certification Order

(A) Time to Issue. At an early practicable time after a person sues or is sued as a class representative, the court must determine by order whether to certify the action as a class action.

(B) Defining the Class; Appointing Class Counsel. An order that certifies a class action must define the class and the class claims, issues, or defenses, and must appoint class counsel under Rule 23(g).

(C) Altering or Amending the Order. An order that grants or denies class certification may be altered or amended before final judgment.

(2) Notice

(A) For (b)(1) or (b)(2) Classes. For any class certified under Rule 23(b)(1) or (b)(2), the court may direct appropriate notice to the class.

(B) For (b)(3) Classes. For any class certified under Rule 23(b)(3) — or upon ordering notice under Rule 23(e)(1) to a class proposed to be certified for purposes of settlement under Rule 23(b)(3) — the court must direct to class members the best notice that is practicable under the circumstances, including individual notice to all members who can be identified through reasonable effort. The notice may be by one or more of the following: United States mail, electronic means, or other appropriate means. The notice must clearly and concisely state in plain, easily understood language:

(i) the nature of the action;

(ii) the definition of the class certified;

(iii) the class claims, issues, or defenses;

(iv) that a class member may enter an appearance through an attorney if the member so desires;

(v) that the court will exclude from the class any member who requests exclusion;

(vi) the time and manner for requesting exclusion; and

(vii) the binding effect of a class judgment on members under Rule 23(c)(3).

(3) Judgment. Whether or not favorable to the class, the judgment in a class action must:

(A) for any class certified under Rule 23(b)(1) or (b)(2), include and describe those whom the court finds to be class members; and

(B) for any class certified under Rule 23(b)(3), include and specify or describe those to whom the Rule 23(c)(2) notice was directed, who have not requested exclusion, and whom the court finds to be class members.

(4) Particular Issues. When appropriate, an action may be brought or maintained as a class action with respect to particular issues.

(5) Subclasses. When appropriate, a class may be divided into subclasses that are each treated as a class under this rule.

(d) Conducting the Action

(1) In General. In conducting an action under this rule, the court may issue orders that:

(A) determine the course of proceedings or prescribe measures to prevent undue repetition or complication in presenting evidence or argument;

(B) require — to protect class members and fairly conduct the action — giving appropriate notice to some or all class members of:

(i) any step in the action;

(ii) the proposed extent of the judgment; or

(iii) the members' opportunity to signify whether they consider the representation fair and adequate, to intervene and present claims or defenses, or to otherwise come into the action;

(C) impose conditions on the representative parties or on intervenors;

(D) require that the pleadings be amended to eliminate allegations about representation of absent persons and that the action proceed accordingly; or

(E) deal with similar procedural matters.

(2) Combining and Amending Orders. An order under Rule 23(d)(1) may be altered or amended from time to time and may be combined with an order under Rule 16.

(e) Settlement, Voluntary Dismissal, or Compromise. The claims, issues, or defenses of a certified class — or a class proposed to be certified for purposes of settlement — may be settled, voluntarily dismissed, or compromised only with the court's approval. The following procedures apply to a proposed settlement, voluntary dismissal, or compromise:

(1) Notice to the Class

(A) Information That Parties Must Provide to the Court. The parties must provide the court with information sufficient to enable it to determine whether to give notice of the proposal to the class.

(B) Grounds for a Decision to Give Notice. The court must direct notice in a reasonable manner to all class members who would be bound by the proposal if giving notice is justified by the parties' showing that the court will likely be able to:

(i) approve the proposal under Rule 23(e)(2); and

(ii) certify the class for purposes of judgment on the proposal.

(2) Approval of the Proposal. If the proposal would bind class members, the court may approve it only after a hearing and only on finding that it is fair, reasonable, and adequate after considering whether:

(A) the class representatives and class counsel have adequately represented the class;

(B) the proposal was negotiated at arm's length;

(C) the relief provided for the class is adequate, taking into account:

(i) the costs, risks, and delay of trial and appeal;

(ii) the effectiveness of any proposed method of distributing relief to the class, including the method of processing class-member claims;

(iii) the terms of any proposed award of attorney's fees, including timing of payment; and

(iv) any agreement required to be identified under Rule 23(e)(3); and

(D) the proposal treats class members equitably relative to each other.

(3) Identifying Agreements. The parties seeking approval must file a statement identifying any agreement made in connection with the proposal.

(4) New Opportunity to Be Excluded. If the class was previously certified under Rule 23(b)(3), the court may refuse to approve a settlement unless it affords a new opportunity to request exclusion to individual class members who had an earlier opportunity to request exclusion but did not do so.

(5) Class-Member Objections

(A) In General. Any class member may object to the proposal if it requires court approval under this subdivision (e). The objection must state whether it applies only to the objector, to a specific subset of the class, or to the entire class, and also state with specificity the grounds for the objection.

(B) Court Approval Required for Payment in Connection with an Objection. Unless approved by the court after a hearing, no payment or other consideration may be provided in connection with:

(i) forgoing or withdrawing an objection, or

(ii) forgoing, dismissing, or abandoning an appeal from a judgment approving the proposal.

(C) Procedure for Approval After an Appeal. If approval under Rule 23(e)(5)(B) has not been obtained before an appeal is docketed in the court of appeals, the procedure of Rule 62.1 applies while the appeal remains pending.

(f) Appeals. A court of appeals may permit an appeal from an order granting or denying class-action certification under this rule, but not from an order under Rule 23(e)(1). A party must file a petition for permission to appeal with the circuit clerk within 14 days after the order is entered, or within 45 days after the order is entered if any party is the United States, a United States agency, or a United States officer or employee sued for an act or omission occurring in connection with duties performed on the United States' behalf. An appeal does not stay proceedings in the district court unless the district judge or the court of appeals so orders.

(g) Class Counsel

(1) Appointing Class Counsel. Unless a statute provides otherwise, a court that certifies a class must appoint class counsel. In appointing class counsel, the court:

(A) must consider:

(i) the work counsel has done in identifying or investigating potential claims in this action;

(ii) counsel's experience in handling class actions, other complex litigation, and the type of claims asserted in the action;

(iii) counsel's knowledge of the applicable law; and

(iv) the resources that counsel will commit to representing the class;

(B) may consider any other matter pertinent to counsel's ability to fairly and adequately represent the interests of the class;

(C) may order potential class counsel to provide information on any subject pertinent to the appointment and to propose terms for attorney's fees and nontaxable costs;

(D) may include in the appointing order provisions about the award of attorney's fees or nontaxable costs under Rule 23(h); and

(E) may make further orders in connection with the appointment.

(2) Standard for Appointing Class Counsel. When one applicant seeks appointment as class counsel, the court may appoint that applicant only if the applicant is adequate under Rule 23(g)(1) and (4). If more than one adequate applicant seeks appointment, the court must appoint the applicant best able to represent the interests of the class.

(3) Interim Counsel. The court may designate interim counsel to act on behalf of a putative class before determining whether to certify the action as a class action.

(4) Duty of Class Counsel. Class counsel must fairly and adequately represent the interests of the class.

(h) Attorney's Fees and Nontaxable Costs. In a certified class action, the court may award reasonable attorney's fees and nontaxable costs that are authorized by law or by the parties' agreement. The following procedures apply:

(1) A claim for an award must be made by motion under Rule 54(d)(2), subject to the provisions of this subdivision (h), at a time the court sets. Notice of the

motion must be served on all parties and, for motions by class counsel, directed to class members in a reasonable manner.

(2) A class member, or a party from whom payment is sought, may object to the motion.

(3) The court may hold a hearing and must find the facts and state its legal conclusions under Rule 52(a).

(4) The court may refer issues related to the amount of the award to a special master or a magistrate judge, as provided in Rule 54(d)(2)(D).

Rule 23.1. Derivative Actions

(a) Prerequisites. This rule applies only when one or more shareholders or members of a corporation or an unincorporated association bring a derivative action to enforce a right that the corporation or association may properly assert but has failed to enforce. The derivative action may not be maintained if it appears that the plaintiff does not fairly and adequately represent the interests of shareholders or members who are similarly situated in enforcing the right of the corporation or association.

(b) Pleading Requirements. The complaint must be verified and must:

(1) allege that the plaintiff was a shareholder or member at the time of the transaction complained of, or that the plaintiff 's share or membership later devolved on it by operation of law;

(2) allege that the action is not a collusive one to confer jurisdiction that the court would otherwise lack; and

(3) state with particularity:

(A) any effort by the plaintiff to obtain the desired action from the directors or comparable authority and, if necessary, from the shareholders or members; and

(B) the reasons for not obtaining the action or not making the effort.

(c) Settlement, Dismissal, and Compromise. A derivative action may be settled, voluntarily dismissed, or compromised only with the court's approval. Notice of a proposed settlement, voluntary dismissal, or compromise must be given to shareholders or members in the manner that the court orders.

Rule 23.2. Actions Relating to Unincorporated Associations

This rule applies to an action brought by or against the members of an unincorporated association as a class by naming certain members as representative parties. The action may be maintained only if it appears that those parties will fairly and adequately protect the interests of the association and its members.

In conducting the action, the court may issue any appropriate orders corresponding with those in Rule 23(d), and the procedure for settlement, voluntary dismissal, or compromise must correspond with the procedure in Rule 23(e).

Rule 24. Intervention

(a) **Intervention of Right.** On timely motion, the court must permit anyone to intervene who:

(1) is given an unconditional right to intervene by a federal statute; or

(2) claims an interest relating to the property or transaction that is the subject of the action, and is so situated that disposing of the action may as a practical matter impair or impede the movant's ability to protect its interest, unless existing parties adequately represent that interest.

(b) **Permissive Intervention**

(1) In General. On timely motion, the court may permit anyone to intervene who:

(A) is given a conditional right to intervene by a federal statute; or

(B) has a claim or defense that shares with the main action a common question of law or fact.

(2) By a Government Officer or Agency. On timely motion, the court may permit a federal or state governmental officer or agency to intervene if a party's claim or defense is based on:

(A) a statute or executive order administered by the officer or agency; or

(B) any regulation, order, requirement, or agreement issued or made under the statute or executive order.

(3) Delay or Prejudice. In exercising its discretion, the court must consider whether the intervention will unduly delay or prejudice the adjudication of the original parties' rights.

(c) **Notice and Pleading Required.** A motion to intervene must be served on the parties as provided in Rule 5. The motion must state the grounds for intervention and be accompanied by a pleading that sets out the claim or defense for which intervention is sought.

Rule 25. Substitution of Parties

(a) **Death**

(1) Substitution if the Claim is Not Extinguished. If a party dies and the claim is not extinguished, the court may order substitution of the proper party. A motion for substitution may be made by any party or by the decedent's successor

or representative. If the motion is not made within 90 days after service of a statement noting the death, the action by or against the decedent must be dismissed.

(2) Continuation Among the Remaining Parties. After a party's death, if the right sought to be enforced survives only to or against the remaining parties, the action does not abate, but proceeds in favor of or against the remaining parties. The death should be noted on the record.

(3) Service. A motion to substitute, together with a notice of hearing, must be served on the parties as provided in Rule 5 and on nonparties as provided in Rule 4. A statement noting death must be served in the same manner. Service may be made in any judicial district.

(b) Incompetency. If a party becomes incompetent, the court may, on motion, permit the action to be continued by or against the party's representative. The motion must be served as provided in Rule 25(a)(3).

(c) Transfer of Interest. If an interest is transferred, the action may be continued by or against the original party unless the court, on motion, orders the transferee to be substituted in the action or joined with the original party. The motion must be served as provided in Rule 25(a)(3).

(d) Public Officers; Death or Separation from Office. An action does not abate when a public officer who is a party in an official capacity dies, resigns, or otherwise ceases to hold office while the action is pending. The officer's successor is automatically substituted as a party. Later proceedings should be in the substituted party's name, but any misnomer not affecting the parties' substantial rights must be disregarded. The court may order substitution at any time, but the absence of such an order does not affect the substitution.

V. Disclosures and Discovery

Rule 26. Duty to Disclose; General Provisions Governing Discovery[2]

(a) Required Disclosures

(1) Initial Disclosure

(A) In General. Except as exempted by Rule 26(a)(1)(B) or as otherwise stipulated or ordered by the court, a party must, without awaiting a discovery request, provide to the other parties:

2. There is a pending amendment to Rule 26(f) that may take effect December 1, 2025. See details, *infra*.

(i) the name and, if known, the address and telephone number of each individual likely to have discoverable information — along with the subjects of that information — that the disclosing party may use to support its claims or defenses, unless the use would be solely for impeachment;

(ii) a copy — or a description by category and location — of all documents, electronically stored information, and tangible things that the disclosing party has in its possession, custody, or control and may use to support its claims or defenses, unless the use would be solely for impeachment;

(iii) a computation of each category of damages claimed by the disclosing party — who must also make available for inspection and copying as under Rule 34 the documents or other evidentiary material, unless privileged or protected from disclosure, on which each computation is based, including materials bearing on the nature and extent of injuries suffered; and

(iv) for inspection and copying as under Rule 34, any insurance agreement under which an insurance business may be liable to satisfy all or part of a possible judgment in the action or to indemnify or reimburse for payments made to satisfy the judgment.

(B) Proceedings Exempt from Initial Disclosure. The following proceedings are exempt from initial disclosure:

(i) an action for review on an administrative record;

(ii) a forfeiture action in rem arising from a federal statute;

(iii) a petition for habeas corpus or any other proceeding to challenge a criminal conviction or sentence;

(iv) an action brought without an attorney by a person in the custody of the United States, a state, or a state subdivision;

(v) an action to enforce or quash an administrative summons or subpoena;

(vi) an action by the United States to recover benefit payments;

(vii) an action by the United States to collect on a student loan guaranteed by the United States;

(viii) a proceeding ancillary to a proceeding in another court; and

(ix) an action to enforce an arbitration award.

(C) Time for Initial Disclosures — In General. A party must make the initial disclosures at or within 14 days after the parties' Rule 26(f) conference unless a different time is set by stipulation or court order, or unless a party objects during the conference that initial disclosures are not appropriate in this action and states the objection in the proposed discovery plan. In ruling on the objection, the court must determine what disclosures, if any, are to be made and must set the time for disclosure.

(D) Time for Initial Disclosures — For Parties Served or Joined Later. A party that is first served or otherwise joined after the Rule 26(f) conference must make the initial disclosures within 30 days after being served or joined, unless a different time is set by stipulation or court order.

(E) Basis for Initial Disclosure; Unacceptable Excuses. A party must make its initial disclosures based on the information then reasonably available to it. A party is not excused from making its disclosures because it has not fully investigated the case or because it challenges the sufficiency of another party's disclosures or because another party has not made its disclosures.

(2) Disclosure of Expert Testimony

(A) In General. In addition to the disclosures required by Rule 26(a)(1), a party must disclose to the other parties the identity of any witness it may use at trial to present evidence under Federal Rule of Evidence 702, 703, or 705.

(B) Witnesses Who Must Provide a Written Report. Unless otherwise stipulated or ordered by the court, this disclosure must be accompanied by a written report — prepared and signed by the witness — if the witness is one retained or specially employed to provide expert testimony in the case or one whose duties as the party's employee regularly involve giving expert testimony. The report must contain:

(i) a complete statement of all opinions the witness will express and the basis and reasons for them;

(ii) the facts or data considered by the witness in forming them;

(iii) any exhibits that will be used to summarize or support them;

(iv) the witness's qualifications, including a list of all publications authored in the previous 10 years;

(v) a list of all other cases in which, during the previous 4 years, the witness testified as an expert at trial or by deposition; and

(vi) a statement of the compensation to be paid for the study and testimony in the case.

(C) Witnesses Who Do Not Provide a Written Report. Unless otherwise stipulated or ordered by the court, if the witness is not required to provide a written report, this disclosure must state:

(i) the subject matter on which the witness is expected to present evidence under Federal Rule of Evidence 702, 703, or 705; and

(ii) a summary of the facts and opinions to which the witness is expected to testify.

(D) Time to Disclose Expert Testimony. A party must make these disclosures at the times and in the sequence that the court orders. Absent a stipulation or a court order, the disclosures must be made:

(i) at least 90 days before the date set for trial or for the case to be ready for trial;

or

(ii) if the evidence is intended solely to contradict or rebut evidence on the same subject matter identified by another party under Rule 26(a)(2)(B) or (C), within 30 days after the other party's disclosure.

(E) Supplementing the Disclosure. The parties must supplement these disclosures when required under Rule 26(e).

(3) Pretrial Disclosures

(A) In General. In addition to the disclosures required by Rule 26(a)(1) and (2), a party must provide to the other parties and promptly file the following information about the evidence that it may present at trial other than solely for impeachment:

(i) the name and, if not previously provided, the address and telephone number of each witness — separately identifying those the party expects to present and those it may call if the need arises;

(ii) the designation of those witnesses whose testimony the party expects to present by deposition and, if not taken stenographically, a transcript of the pertinent parts of the deposition; and

(iii) an identification of each document or other exhibit, including summaries of other evidence — separately identifying those items the party expects to offer and those it may offer if the need arises.

(B) Time for Pretrial Disclosures; Objections. Unless the court orders otherwise, these disclosures must be made at least 30 days before trial. Within 14 days after they are made, unless the court sets a different time, a party may serve and promptly file a list of the following objections: any objections to the use under Rule 32(a) of a deposition designated by another party under Rule 26(a)(3)(A)(ii); and any objection, together with the grounds for it, that may be made to the admissibility of materials identified under Rule 26(a)(3)(A)(iii). An objection not so made — except for one under Federal Rule of Evidence 402 or 403 — is waived unless excused by the court for good cause.

(4) Form of Disclosures. Unless the court orders otherwise, all disclosures under Rule 26(a) must be in writing, signed, and served.

(b) Discovery Scope and Limits

(1) Scope in General. Unless otherwise limited by court order, the scope of discovery is as follows: Parties may obtain discovery regarding any nonprivileged matter that is relevant to any party's claim or defense and proportional to the needs of the case, considering the importance of the issues at stake in the action, the amount in controversy, the parties' relative access to relevant information, the parties' resources, the importance of the discovery in resolving the issues, and whether the burden or expense of the proposed discovery outweighs its likely benefit. Information within this scope of discovery need not be admissible in evidence to be discoverable.

(2) Limitations on Frequency and Extent

(A) When Permitted. By order, the court may alter the limits in these rules on the number of depositions and interrogatories or on the length of depositions under Rule 30. By order or local rule, the court may also limit the number of requests under Rule 36.

(B) Specific Limitations on Electronically Stored Information. A party need not provide discovery of electronically stored information from sources that the party identifies as not reasonably accessible because of undue burden or cost. On motion to compel discovery or for a protective order, the party from whom discovery is sought must show that the information is not reasonably accessible because of undue burden or cost. If that showing is made, the court may nonetheless order discovery from such sources if the requesting party shows good cause, considering the limitations of Rule 26(b)(2)(C). The court may specify conditions for the discovery.

(C) When Required. On motion or on its own, the court must limit the frequency or extent of discovery otherwise allowed by these rules or by local rule if it determines that:

(i) the discovery sought is unreasonably cumulative or duplicative, or can be obtained from some other source that is more convenient, less burdensome, or less expensive;

(ii) the party seeking discovery has had ample opportunity to obtain the information by discovery in the action; or

(iii) the proposed discovery is outside the scope permitted by Rule 26(b)(1).

(3) Trial Preparation; Materials

(A) Documents and Tangible Things. Ordinarily, a party may not discover documents and tangible things that are prepared in anticipation of litigation or for trial by or for another party or its representative (including the other party's attorney, consultant, surety, indemnitor, insurer, or agent). But, subject to Rule 26(b)(4), those materials may be discovered if:

(i) they are otherwise discoverable under Rule 26(b)(1); and

(ii) the party shows that it has substantial need for the materials to prepare its case and cannot, without undue hardship, obtain their substantial equivalent by other means.

(B) Protection Against Disclosure. If the court orders discovery of those materials, it must protect against disclosure of the mental impressions, conclusions, opinions, or legal theories of a party's attorney or other representative concerning the litigation.

(C) Previous Statement. Any party or other person may, on request and without the required showing, obtain the person's own previous statement about the action or its subject matter. If the request is refused, the person may move for a court order, and Rule 37(a)(5) applies to the award of expenses. A previous statement is either:

(i) a written statement that the person has signed or otherwise adopted or approved; or

(ii) a contemporaneous stenographic, mechanical, electrical, or other recording — or a transcription of it — that recites substantially verbatim the persons' oral statement.

(4) Trial Preparation: Experts

(A) Deposition of an Expert Who May Testify. A party may depose any person who has been identified as an expert whose opinions may be presented at trial. If Rule 26(a)(2)(B) requires a report from the expert, the deposition may be conducted only after the report is provided.

(B) Trial-Preparation Protection for Draft Reports or Disclosures. Rules 26(b)(3)(A) and (B) protect drafts of any report or disclosure required under Rule 26(a)(2), regardless of the form in which the draft is recorded.

(C) Trial-Preparation Protection for Communications Between a Party's Attorney and Expert Witness. Rules 26(B)(3)(A) and (B) protect communications between the party's attorney and any witness required to provide a report under Rule 26(a)(2)(B), regardless of the form of the communications, except to the extent that the communications:

(i) relate to compensation for the expert's study or testimony;

(ii) identify facts or data that the party's attorney provided and that the expert considered in forming the opinions to be expressed; or

(iii) identify assumptions that the party's attorney provided and that the expert relied on in forming the opinions to be expressed.

(D) Expert Employed Only for Trial Preparation. Ordinarily, a party may not, by interrogatories or deposition, discover facts known or opinions held by an expert who has been retained or specially employed by another party in anticipation of litigation or to prepare for trial and who is not expected to be called as a witness at trial. But a party may do so only:

(i) as provided in Rule 35(b); or

(ii) on showing exceptional circumstances under which it is impracticable for the party to obtain facts or opinions on the same subject by other means.

(E) Payment. Unless manifest injustice would result, the court must require that the party seeking discovery:

(i) pay the expert a reasonable fee for time spent in responding to discovery under Rule 26(b)(4)(A) or (D); and

(ii) for discovery under (D), also pay the other party a fair portion of the fees and expenses it reasonably incurred in obtaining the expert's facts and opinions.

(5) Claiming Privilege or Protecting Trial-Preparation Materials

(A) Information Withheld. When a party withholds information otherwise discoverable by claiming that the information is privileged or subject to protection as trial-preparation material, the party must:

(i) expressly make the claim; and

(ii) describe the nature of the documents, communications, or things not produced or disclosed — and do so in a manner that, without revealing information itself privileged or protected, will enable other parties to assess the claim.

(B) Information Produced. If information produced in discovery is subject to a claim of privilege or of protection as trial-preparation material, the party making the claim may notify any party that received the information of the claim and the basis for it. After being notified, a party must promptly return, sequester, or destroy the specified information and any copies it has; must not use or disclose the information until the claim is resolved; must take reasonable steps to retrieve the information if the party disclosed it before being notified; and may promptly present the information to the court under seal for a determination of the claim. The producing party must preserve the information until the claim is resolved.

(c) Protective Orders

(1) In General. A party or any person from whom discovery is sought may move for a protective order in the court where the action is pending — or as an alternative on matters relating to a deposition, in the court for the district where the deposition will be taken. The motion must include a certification that the movant has in good faith conferred or attempted to confer with other affected parties in an effort to resolve the dispute without court action. The court may, for good cause, issue an order to protect a party or person from annoyance, embarrassment, oppression, or undue burden or expense, including one or more of the following:

(A) forbidding the disclosure or discovery;

(B) specifying terms, including time and place or the allocation of expenses, for the disclosure or discovery;

(C) prescribing a discovery method other than the one selected by the party seeking discovery;

(D) forbidding inquiry into certain matters, or limiting the scope of disclosure or discovery to certain matters;

(E) designating the persons who may be present while the discovery is conducted;

(F) requiring that a deposition be sealed and opened only on court order;

(G) requiring that a trade secret or other confidential research, development, or commercial information not be revealed or be revealed only in a specified way; and

(H) requiring that the parties simultaneously file specified documents or information in sealed envelopes, to be opened as the court directs.

(2) Ordering Discovery. If a motion for a protective order is wholly or partly denied, the court may, on just terms, order that any party or person provide or permit discovery.

(3) Awarding Expenses. Rule 37(a)(5) applies to the award of expenses.

(d) Timing and Sequence of Discovery

(1) Timing. A party may not seek discovery from any source before the parties have conferred as required by Rule 26(f), except in a proceeding exempted from initial disclosure under Rule 26(a)(1)(B), or when authorized by these rules, by stipulation, or by court order.

(2) Early Rule 34 Requests

(A) Time to Deliver. More than 21 days after the summons and complaint are served on a party, a request under Rule 34 may be delivered:

(i) to that party by any other party, and

(ii) by that party to any plaintiff or to any other party that has been served.

(B) When Considered Served. The request is considered to have been served at the first Rule 26(f) conference.

(3) Sequence. Unless the parties stipulate or the court orders otherwise for the parties' and witnesses' convenience and in the interests of justice:

(A) methods of discovery may be used in any sequence; and

(B) discovery by one party does not require any other party to delay its discovery.

(e) Supplementing Disclosures and Responses

(1) In General. A party who has made a disclosure under Rule 26(a) — or who has responded to an interrogatory, request for production, or request for admission — must supplement or correct its disclosure or response:

(A) in a timely manner if the party learns that in some material respect the disclosure or response is incomplete or incorrect, and if the additional or corrective information has not otherwise been made known to the other parties during the discovery process or in writing; or

(B) as ordered by the court.

(2) Expert Witness. For an expert whose report must be disclosed under Rule 26(a)(2(B), the party's duty to supplement extends both to information included in the report and to information given during the expert's deposition. Any additions or changes to this information must be disclosed by the time the party's pretrial disclosures under Rule 26(a)(3) are due.

(f) Conference of the Parties; Planning for Discovery

(1) Conference Timing. Except in a proceeding exempted from initial disclosure under Rule 26(a)(1)(B) or when the court orders otherwise, the parties must confer as soon as practicable — and in any event at least 21 days before a scheduling conference is to be held or a scheduling order is due under Rule 16(b).

(2) Conference Content; Parties' Responsibilities. In conferring, the parties must consider the nature and basis of their claims and defenses and the possibilities for promptly settling or resolving the case; make or arrange for the disclosures required by Rule 26(a)(1); discuss any issues about preserving discoverable information; and develop a proposed discovery plan. The attorneys of record and all unrepresented parties that have appeared in the case are jointly responsible for arranging the conference, for attempting in good faith to agree on the proposed discovery plan, and for submitting to the court within 14 days after the conference a written report outlining the plan. The court may order the parties or attorneys to attend the conference in person.

(3) Discovery Plan. A discovery plan must state the parties' views and proposals on:

(A) what changes should be made in the timing, form, or requirement for disclosures under Rule 26(a), including a statement of when initial disclosures were made or will be made;

(B) the subjects on which discovery may be needed, when discovery should be completed, and whether discovery should be conducted in phases or be limited to or focused on particular issues;

(C) any issues about disclosure, discovery, or preservation of electronically stored information, including the form or forms in which it should be produced;

(D) any issues about claims of privilege or of protection as trial-preparation materials, including — if the parties agree on a procedure to assert these claims after production — whether to ask the court to include their agreement in an order under Federal Rule of Evidence 502;

(E) what changes should be made in the limitations on discovery imposed under these rules or by local rule, and what other limitations should be imposed; and

(F) any other orders that the court should issue under Rule 26(c) or under Rule 16(b) and (c).

(4) Expedited Schedule. If necessary to comply with its expedited schedule for Rule 16(b) conferences, a court may by local rule:

(A) require the parties' conference to occur less than 21 days before the scheduling conference is held or a scheduling order is due under Rule 16(b); and

(B) require the written report outlining the discovery plan to be filed less than 14 days after the parties' conference, or excuse the parties from submitting a written report and permit them to report orally on their discovery plan at the Rule 16(b) conference.

(g) Signing Disclosures and Discovery Requests, Responses, and Objections

(1) Signature Required; Effect of Signature. Every disclosure under Rule 26(a)(1) or (a)(3) and every discovery request, response, or objection must be signed by at least one attorney of record in the attorney's own name — or by the party personally, if unrepresented — and must state the signer's address, e-mail address, and telephone number. By signing, an attorney or party certifies that to the best of the person's knowledge, information, and belief formed after a reasonable inquiry:

(A) with respect to a disclosure, it is complete and correct as of the time it is made; and

(B) with respect to a discovery request, response, or objection, it is:

(i) consistent with these rules and warranted by existing law or by a nonfrivolous argument for extending, modifying, or reversing existing law, or for establishing new law;

(ii) not interposed for any improper purpose, such as to harass, cause unnecessary delay, or needlessly increase the cost of litigation; and

(iii) neither unreasonable nor unduly burdensome or expensive, considering the needs of the case, prior discovery in the case, the amount in controversy, and the importance of the issues at stake in the action.

(2) Failure to Sign. Other parties have no duty to act on an unsigned disclosure, request, response, or objection until it is signed, and the court must strike it unless a signature is promptly supplied after the omission is called to the attorney's or party's attention.

(3) Sanction for Improper Certification. If a certification violates this rule without substantial justification, the court, on motion or on its own, must impose an appropriate sanction on the signer, the party on whose behalf the signer was acting, or both. The sanction may include an order to pay the reasonable expenses, including attorney's fees, caused by the violation.

Pending Amendment to Rule 26(f) that may take effect December 1, 2025

(f) Conference of the Parties; Planning for Discovery

. . .

(3) Discovery Plan. A discovery plan must state the parties' views and proposals on:

. . .

(D) any issues about claims of privilege or of protection as trial-preparation materials, including the timing and method for complying with Rule 26(b)(5)(A) and — if the parties agree on a procedure to assert these claims after production — whether to ask the court to include their agreement in an order under Federal Rule of Evidence 502;

. . .

Rule 27. Depositions to Perpetuate Testimony

(a) Before an Action Is Filed

(1) Petition. A person who wants to perpetuate testimony about any matter cognizable in a United States court may file a verified petition in the district court for the district where any expected adverse party resides. The petition must ask for an order authorizing the petitioner to depose the named persons in order to perpetuate their testimony. The petition must be titled in the petitioner's name and must show:

(A) that the petitioner expects to be a party to an action cognizable in a United States court but cannot presently bring it or cause it to be brought;

(B) the subject matter of the expected action and the petitioner's interest;

(C) the facts that the petitioner wants to establish by the proposed testimony and the reasons to perpetuate it;

(D) the names or a description of the persons whom the petitioner expects to be adverse parties and their addresses, so far as known; and

(E) the name, address, and expected substance of the testimony of each deponent.

(2) Notice and Service. At least 21 days before the hearing date, the petitioner must serve each expected adverse party with a copy of the petition and a notice stating the time and place of the hearing. The notice may be served either inside or outside the district or state in the manner provided in Rule 4. If that service cannot be made with reasonable diligence on an expected adverse party, the court may order service by publication or otherwise. The court must appoint an attorney to represent persons not served in the manner provided in Rule 4 and to cross-examine the deponent if an unserved person is not otherwise represented. If any expected adverse party is a minor or is incompetent, Rule 17(c) applies.

(3) Order and Examination. If satisfied that perpetuating the testimony may prevent a failure or delay of justice, the court must issue an order that designates or describes the persons whose depositions may be taken, specifies the subject matter of the examinations, and states whether the depositions will be taken orally or by written interrogatories. The depositions may then be taken under these rules, and the court may issue orders like those authorized by Rules 34 and 35. A reference in these rules to the court where an action is pending means, for purposes of this rule, the court where the petition for the deposition was filed.

(4) Using the Deposition. A deposition to perpetuate testimony may be used under Rule 32(a) in any later-filed district-court action involving the same subject matter if the deposition either was taken under these rules or, although not so taken, would be admissible in evidence in the courts of the state where it was taken.

(b) Pending Appeal

(1) In General. The court where a judgment has been rendered may, if an appeal has been taken or may still be taken, permit a party to depose witnesses to perpetuate their testimony for use in the event of further proceedings in that court.

(2) Motion. The party who wants to perpetuate testimony may move for leave to take the depositions, on the same notice and service as if the action were pending in the district court. The motion must show:

(A) the name, address, and expected substance of the testimony of each deponent; and

(B) the reasons for perpetuating the testimony.

(3) Court Order. If the court finds that perpetuating the testimony may prevent a failure or delay of justice, the court may permit the depositions to be taken and may issue orders like those authorized by Rules 34 and 35. The depositions

may be taken and used as any other deposition taken in a pending district-court action.

(c) Perpetuation by an Action. This rule does not limit a court's power to entertain an action to perpetuate testimony.

Rule 28. Persons Before Whom Depositions May Be Taken

(a) Within the United States

(1) In General. Within the United States or a territory or insular possession subject to United States jurisdiction, a deposition must be taken before:

(A) an officer authorized to administer oaths either by federal law or by the law in the place of examination; or

(B) a person appointed by the court where the action is pending to administer oaths and take testimony.

(2) Definition of "Officer." The term "officer" in Rules 30, 31, and 32 includes a person appointed by the court under this rule or designated by the parties under Rule 29(a).

(b) In a Foreign Country

(1) In General. A deposition may be taken in a foreign country:

(A) under an applicable treaty or convention;

(B) under a letter of request, whether or not captioned a "letter rogatory";

(C) on notice, before a person authorized to administer oaths either by federal law or by the law in the place of examination; or

(D) before a person commissioned by the court to administer any necessary oath and take testimony.

(2) Issuing a Letter of Request or a Commission. A letter of request, a commission, or both may be issued:

(A) on appropriate terms after an application and notice of it; and

(B) without a showing that taking the deposition in another manner is impracticable or inconvenient.

(3) Form of a Request, Notice, or Commission. When a letter of request or any other device is used according to a treaty or convention, it must be captioned in the form prescribed by that treaty or convention. A letter of request may be addressed "To the Appropriate Authority in [name of country]." A deposition notice or a commission must designate by name or descriptive title the person before whom the deposition is to be taken.

(4) Letter of Request — Admitting Evidence. Evidence obtained in response to a letter of request need not be excluded merely because it is not a verbatim transcript, because the testimony was not taken under oath, or because of any similar departure from the requirements for depositions taken within the United States.

(c) Disqualification. A deposition must not be taken before a person who is any party's relative, employee, or attorney; who is related to or employed by any party's attorney; or who is financially interested in the action.

Rule 29. Stipulations About Discovery Procedure

Unless the court orders otherwise, the parties may stipulate that:

(a) a deposition may be taken before any person, at any time or place, on any notice, and in the manner specified — in which event it may be used in the same way as any other deposition; and

(b) other procedures governing or limiting discovery be modified — but a stipulation extending the time for any form of discovery must have court approval if it would interfere with the time set for completing discovery, for hearing a motion, or for a trial.

Rule 30. Depositions by Oral Examination

(a) When a Deposition May Be Taken

(1) Without Leave. A party may, by oral questions, depose any person, including a party, without leave of court except as provided in Rule 30(a)(2). The deponent's attendance may be compelled by subpoena under Rule 45.

(2) With Leave. A party must obtain leave of court, and the court must grant leave to the extent consistent with Rule 26(b)(1) and (2):

(A) if the parties have not stipulated to the deposition and:

(i) the deposition would result in more than 10 depositions being taken under this rule or Rule 31 by the plaintiffs, or by the defendants, or by the third-party defendants;

(ii) the deponent has already been deposed in the case; or

(iii) the party seeks to take the deposition before the time specified in Rule 26(d), unless the party certifies in the notice, with supporting facts, that the deponent is expected to leave the United States and be unavailable for examination in this country after that time; or

(B) if the deponent is confined in prison.

(b) Notice of the Deposition; Other Formal Requirements

(1) Notice in General. A party who wants to depose a person by oral questions must give reasonable written notice to every other party. The notice must state the time and place of the deposition and, if known, the deponent's name and address. If the name is unknown, the notice must provide a general description

sufficient to identify the person or the particular class or group to which the person belongs.

(2) Producing Documents. If a subpoena duces tecum is to be served on the deponent, the materials designated for production, as set out in the subpoena, must be listed in the notice or in an attachment. The notice to a party deponent may be accompanied by a request under Rule 34 to produce documents and tangible things at the deposition.

(3) Method of Recording

(A) Method Stated in the Notice. The party who notices the deposition must state in the notice the method for recording the testimony. Unless the court orders otherwise, testimony may be recorded by audio, audiovisual, or stenographic means. The noticing party bears the recording costs. Any party may arrange to transcribe a deposition.

(B) Additional Method. With prior notice to the deponent and other parties, any party may designate another method for recording the testimony in addition to that specified in the original notice. That party bears the expense of the additional record or transcript unless the court orders otherwise.

(4) By Remote Means. The parties may stipulate — or the court may on motion order — that a deposition be taken by telephone or other remote means. For the purpose of this rule and Rules 28(a), 37(a)(2), and 37(b)(1), the deposition takes place where the deponent answers the questions.

(5) Officer's Duties

(A) Before the Deposition. Unless the parties stipulate otherwise, a deposition must be conducted before an officer appointed or designated under Rule 28. The officer must begin the deposition with an on-the-record statement that includes:

(i) the officer's name and business address;

(ii) the date, time, and place of the deposition;

(iii) the deponent's name;

(iv) the officer's administration of the oath or affirmation to the deponent; and

(v) the identity of all persons present.

(B) Conducting the Deposition: Avoiding Distortion. If the deposition is recorded nonstenographically, the officer must repeat the items in Rule 30(b)(5)(A)(i)(iii) at the beginning of each unit of the recording medium. The deponent's and attorneys' appearance or demeanor must not be distorted through recording techniques.

(C) After the Deposition. At the end of each deposition, the officer must state on the record that the deposition is complete and must set out any stipulations made by the attorneys about custody of the transcript or recording and of the exhibits, or about any other pertinent matters.

(6) Notice or Subpoena Directed to an Organization. In its notice or subpoena, a party may name as the deponent a public or private corporation,

a partnership, an association, a governmental agency, or other entity and must describe with reasonable particularity the matters for examination. The named organization must designate one or more officers, directors, or managing agents, or designate other persons who consent to testify on its behalf; and it may set out the matters on which each person designated will testify. Before or promptly after the notice or subpoena is served, the serving party and the organization must confer in good faith about the matters for examination. A subpoena must advise a nonparty organization of its duty to confer with the serving party and to designate each person who will testify. The persons designated must testify about information known or reasonably available to the organization. This paragraph (6) does not preclude a deposition by any other procedure allowed by these rules.

(c) Examination and Cross-Examination; Record of the Examination; Objections; Written Questions

(1) Examination and Cross-Examination. The examination and cross-examination of a deponent proceed as they would at trial under the Federal Rules of Evidence, expect Rules 103 and 615. After putting the deponent under oath or affirmation, the officer must record the testimony by the method designated under Rule 30(b)(3)(A). The testimony must be recorded by the officer personally or by a person acting in gthe presence and under the direction of the officer.

(2) Objections. An objection at the time of the examination — whether to evidence, to a party's conduct, to the officer's qualifications, to the manner of taking the deposition, or to any other aspect of the deposition — must be noted on the record, but the examination still proceeds; the testimony is taken subject to any objection. An objection must be stated concisely in a nonargumentative and nonsuggestive manner. A person may instruct a deponent not to answer only when necessary to preserve a privilege, to enforce a limitation ordered by the court, or to present a motion under 30(d)(3).

(3) Participating Through Written Questions. Instead of participating in the oral examination, a party may serve written questions in a sealed envelope on the party noticing the deposition, who must deliver them to the officer. The officer must ask the deponent these questions and record the answers verbatim.

(d) Duration; Sanction; Motion to Terminate or Limit

(1) Duration. Unless otherwise stipulated or ordered by the court, a deposition is limited to one day of 7 hours. The court must allow additional time consistent with Rule 26(b)(1) and (2) if needed to fairly examine the deponent or if the deponent, another person, or any other circumstance impedes or delays the examination.

(2) Sanction. The court may impose an appropriate sanction — including the reasonable expenses and attorney's fees incurred by any party — on a person who impedes, delays, or frustrates the fair examination of the deponent.

(3) Motion to Terminate or Limit

(A) Grounds. At any time during a deposition, the deponent or a party may move to terminate or limit it on the ground that it is being conducted in bad faith or in a manner that unreasonably annoys, embarrasses, or oppresses the deponent or party. The motion may be filed in the court where the action is pending or the deposition is being taken. If the objecting deponent or party so demands, the deposition must be suspended for the time necessary to obtain an order.

(B) Order. The court may order that the deposition be terminated or may limit its scope and manner as provided in Rule 26(c). If terminated, the deposition may be resumed only by order of the court where the action is pending.

(C) Award of Expenses. Rule 37(a)(5) applies to the award of expenses.

(e) Review by the Witness; Changes

(1) Review; Statement of Changes. On request by the deponent or a party before the deposition is completed, the deponent must be allowed 30 days after being notified by the officer that the transcript or recording is available in which:

(A) to review the transcript or recording; and

(B) if there are changes in form or substance, to sign a statement listing the changes and the reasons for making them.

(2) Changes Indicated in the Officer's Certificate. The officer must note in the certificate prescribed by Rule 30(f)(1) whether a review was requested and, if so, must attach any changes the deponent makes during the 30-day period.

(f) Certification and Delivery; Exhibits; Copies of the Transcript or Recording; Filing

(1) Certification and Delivery. The officer must certify in writing that the witness was duly sworn and that the deposition accurately records the witness's testimony. The certificate must accompany the record of the deposition. Unless the court orders otherwise, the of- ficer must seal the deposition in an envelope or package bearing the title of the action and marked "Deposition of [witness's name]" and must promptly send it to the attorney who arranged for the transcript or recording. The attorney must store it under conditions that will protect it against loss, destruction, tampering, or deterioration.

(2) Documents and Tangible Things

(A) Originals and Copies. Documents and tangible things produced for inspection during a deposition must, on a party's request, be marked for identification and attached to the deposition. Any party may inspect and copy them. But if the person who produced them wants to keep the originals, the person may:

(i) offer copies to be marked, attached to the deposition, and then used as originals — after giving all parties a fair opportunity to verify the copies by comparing them with the originals; or

(ii) give all parties a fair opportunity to inspect and copy the originals after they are marked — in which event the originals may be used as if attached to the deposition.

(B) Order Regarding the Originals. Any party may move for an order that the originals be attached to the deposition pending final disposition of the case.

(3) Copies of the Transcript or Recording. Unless otherwise stipulated or ordered by the court, the officer must retain the stenographic notes of a deposition taken stenographically or a copy of the recording of a deposition taken by another method. When paid reasonable charges, the officer must furnish a copy of the transcript or recording to any party or the deponent.

(4) Notice of Filing. A party who files the deposition must promptly notify all other parties of the filing.

(g) Failure to Attend a Deposition or Serve a Subpoena; Expenses. A party who, expecting a deposition to be taken, attends in person or by an attorney may recover reasonable expenses for attending, including attorney's fees, if the noticing party failed to:

(1) attend and proceed with the deposition; or

(2) serve a subpoena on a nonparty deponent, who consequently did not attend.

Rule 31. Depositions by Written Questions

(a) When a Deposition May Be Taken

(1) Without Leave. A party may, by written questions, depose any person, including a party, without leave of court except as provided in Rule 31(a)(2). The deponent's attendance may be compelled by subpoena under Rule 45.

(2) With Leave. A party must obtain leave of court, and the court must grant leave to the extent consistent with Rule 26(b)(1) and (2):

(A) if the parties have not stipulated to the deposition and:

(i) the deposition would result in more than 10 depositions being taken under this rule or Rule 30 by the plaintiffs, or by the defendants, or by the third-party defendants;

(ii) the deponent has already been deposed in the case; or

(iii) the party seeks to take a deposition before the time specified in Rule 26(d);

or

(B) if the deponent is confined to prison.

(3) Service; Required Notice. A party who wants to depose a person by written questions must serve them on every other party, with a notice stating, if known, the deponent's name and address. If the name is unknown, the notice must provide

a general description sufficient to identify the person or the particular class or group to which the person belongs. The notice must also state the name or descriptive title and the address of the officer before whom the deposition will be taken.

(4) Questions Directed to an Organization. A public or private corporation, a partnership, an association, or a governmental agency may be deposed by written questions in accordance with Rule 30(b)(6).

(5) Questions from Other Parties. Any questions to the deponent from other parties must be served on all parties as follows: cross-questions, within 14 days after being served with the notice and direct questions; redirect questions, within 7 days after being served with cross-questions; and recross-questions, within 7 days after being served with redirect questions. The court may, for good cause, extend or shorten these times.

(b) Delivery to the Officer; Officer's Duties. The party who noticed the deposition must deliver to the officer a copy of all the questions served and of the notice. The officer must promptly proceed in the manner provided in Rule 30(c), (e), and (f) to:

(1) take the deponent's testimony in response to the questions;

(2) prepare and certify the deposition; and

(3) send it to the party, attaching a copy of the questions and of the notice.

(c) Notice of Completion or Filing

(1) Completion. The party who noticed the deposition must notify all other parties when it is completed.

(2) Filing. A party who files the deposition must promptly notify all other parties of the filing.

Rule 32. Using Depositions in Court Proceedings

(a) Using Depositions

(1) In General. At a hearing or trial, all or part of a deposition may be used against a party on these conditions:

(A) the party was present or represented at the taking of the deposition or had reasonable notice of it;

(B) it is used to the extent it would be admissible under the Federal Rules of Evidence if the deponent were present and testifying; and

(C) the use is allowed by Rule 32(a)(2) through (8).

(2) Impeachment and Other Uses. Any party may use a deposition to contradict or impeach the testimony given by the deponent as a witness, or for any other purpose allowed by the Federal Rules of Evidence.

(3) Deposition of Party, Agent, or Designee. An adverse party may use for any purpose the deposition of a party or anyone who, when deposed, was the party's officer, director, managing agent, or designee under Rule 30(b)(6) or 31(a)(4).

(4) Unavailable Witness. A party may use for any purpose the deposition of a witness, whether or not a party, if the court finds:

(A) that the witness is dead;

(B) that the witness is more than 100 miles from the place of hearing or trial or is outside the United States, unless it appears that the witness's absence was procured by the party offering the deposition;

(C) that the witness cannot attend or testify because of age, illness, infirmity, or imprisonment;

(D) that the party offering the deposition could not procure the witness's attendance by subpoena; or

(E) on motion and notice, that exceptional circumstances make it desirable — in the interest of justice and with due regard to the importance of live testimony in open court — to permit the deposition to be used.

(5) Limitations on Use

(A) Deposition Taken on Short Notice. A deposition must not be used against a party who, having received less than 14 days' notice of the deposition, promptly moved for a protective order under Rule 26(c)(1)(B) requesting that it not be taken or be taken at a different time or place — and this motion was still pending when the deposition was taken.

(B) Unavailable Deponent; Party Could Not Obtain an Attorney. A deposition taken without leave of court under the unavailability provision of Rule 30(a)(2)(A)(iii) must not be used against a party who shows that, when served with the notice, it could not, despite diligent efforts, obtain an attorney to represent it at the deposition.

(6) Using Part of a Deposition. If a party offers in evidence only part of a deposition, an adverse party may require the offeror to introduce other parts that in fairness should be considered with the part introduced, and any party may itself introduce any other parts.

(7) Substituting a Party. Substituting a party under Rule 25 does not affect the right to use a deposition previously taken.

(8) Deposition Taken in an Earlier Action. A deposition lawfully taken and, if required, filed in any federal- or state-court action may be used in a later action involving the same subject matter between the same parties, or their representatives or successors in interest, to the same extent as if taken in the later action. A deposition previously taken may also be used as allowed by the Federal Rules of Evidence.

(b) Objections to Admissibility. Subject to Rules 28(b) and 32(d)(3), an objection may be made at a hearing or trial to the admission of any deposition testimony that would be inadmissible if the witness were present and testifying.

(c) Form of Presentation. Unless the court orders otherwise, a party must provide a transcript of any deposition testimony the party offers, but may provide the court with the testimony in nontranscript form as well. On any party's request, deposition testimony offered in a jury trial for any purpose other than impeachment must be presented in nontranscript form, if available, unless the court for good cause orders otherwise.

(d) Waiver of Objections

(1) To the Notice. An objection to an error or irregularity in a deposition notice is waived unless promptly served in writing on the party giving the notice.

(2) To the Officer's Qualification. An objection based on disqualification of the officer before whom a deposition is to be taken is waived if not made:

(A) before the deposition begins; or

(B) promptly after the basis for disqualification becomes known or, with reasonable diligence, could have been known.

(3) To the Taking of the Deposition

(A) Objection to Competence, Relevance, or Materiality. An objection to a deponent's competence — or to the competence, relevance, or materiality of testimony — is not waived by a failure to make the objection before or during the deposition, unless the ground for it might have been corrected at that time.

(B) Objection to an Error or Irregularity. An objection to an error or irregularity at an oral examination is waived if:

(i) it relates to the manner of taking the deposition, the form of a question or answer, the oath or affirmation, a party's conduct, or other matters that might have been corrected at that time; and

(ii) it is not timely made during the deposition.

(C) Objection to a Written Question. An objection to the form of a written question under Rule 31 is waived if not served in writing on the party submitting the question within the time for serving responsive questions or, if the question is a recross-question, within 7 days after being served with it.

(4) To Completing and Returning the Deposition. An objection to how the officer transcribed the testimony — or prepared, signed, certified, sealed, endorsed, sent, or otherwise dealt with the deposition — is waived unless a motion to suppress is made promptly after the error or irregularity becomes known or, with reasonable diligence, could have been known.

Rule 33. Interrogatories to Parties

(a) In General

(1) Number. Unless otherwise stipulated or ordered by the court, a party may serve on any other party no more than 25 written interrogatories, including all discrete subparts. Leave to serve additional interrogatories may be granted to the extent consistent with Rule 26(b)(1) and (2).

(2) Scope. An interrogatory may relate to any matter that may be inquired into under Rule 26(b). An interrogatory is not objectionable merely because it

asks for an opinion or contention that relates to fact or the application of law to fact, but the court may order that the interrogatory need not be answered until designated discovery is complete, or until a pretrial conference or some other time.

(b) Answers and Objections

(1) Responding Party. The interrogatories must be answered:

(A) by the party to whom they are directed; or

(B) if that party is a public or private corporation, a partnership, an association, or a governmental agency, by any officer or agent, who must furnish the information available to the party.

(2) Time to Respond. The responding party must serve its answers and any objections within 30 days after being served with the interrogatories. A shorter or longer time may be stipulated to under Rule 29 or be ordered by the court.

(3) Answering Each Interrogatory. Each interrogatory must, to the extent it is not objected to, be answered separately and fully in writing under oath.

(4) Objections. The grounds for objecting to an interrogatory must be stated with specificity. Any ground not stated in a timely objection is waived unless the court, for good cause, excuses the failure.

(5) Signature. The person who makes the answers must sign them, and the attorney who objects must sign any objections.

(c) Use. An answer to an interrogatory may be used to the extent allowed by the Federal Rules of Evidence.

(d) Option to Produce Business Records. If the answer to an interrogatory may be determined by examining, auditing, compiling, abstracting, or summarizing a party's business records (including electronically stored information), and if the burden of deriving or ascertaining the answer will be substantially the same for either party, the responding party may answer by

(1) specifying the records that must be reviewed, in sufficient detail to enable the interrogating party to locate and identify them as readily as the responding party could; and

(2) giving the interrogating party a reasonable opportunity to examine and audit the records and to make copies, compilations, abstracts, or summaries.

Rule 34. Producing Documents, Electronically Stored Information, and Tangible Things, or Entering onto Land, for Inspection and Other Purposes

(a) In General. A party may serve on any other party a request within the scope of Rule 26(b):

(1) to produce and permit the requesting party or its representative to inspect, copy, test, or sample the following items in the responding party's possession, custody, or control:

(A) any designated documents or electronically stored information — including writings, drawings, graphs, charts, photographs, sound recordings, images, and other data or data compilations — stored in any medium from which information can be obtained either directly or, if necessary, after translation by the responding party into a reasonably usable form; or

(B) any designated tangible things; or

(2) to permit entry onto designated land or other property possessed or controlled by the responding party, so that the requesting party may inspect, measure, survey, photograph, test, or sample the property or any designated object or operation on it.

(b) Procedure

(1) Contents of the Request. The request:

(A) must describe with reasonable particularity each item or category of items to be inspected;

(B) must specify a reasonable time, place, and manner for the inspection and for performing the related acts; and

(C) may specify the form or forms in which electronically stored information is to be produced.

(2) Responses and Objections

(A) Time to Respond. The party to whom the request is directed must respond in writing within 30 days after being served or — if the request was delivered under Rule 26(d)(2) — within 30 days after the parties' first Rule 26(f) conference. A shorter or longer time may be stipulated to under Rule 29 or be ordered by the court.

(B) Responding to Each Item. For each item or category, the response must either state that inspection and related activities will be permitted as requested or state with specificity the grounds for objecting to the request, including the reasons. The responding party may state that it will produce copies of documents or of electronically stored information instead of permitting inspection. The production must then be completed no later than the time for inspection specified in the request or another reasonable time specified in the response.

(C) Objections. An objection must state whether any responsive materials are being withheld on the basis of that objection. An objection to part of a request must specify the part and permit inspection of the rest.

(D) Responding to a Request for Production of Electronically Stored Information. The response may state an objection to a requested form for producing electronically stored information. If the responding party objects to a requested form — or if no form was specified in the request — the party must state the form or forms it intends to use.

(E) Producing the Documents or Electronically Stored Information. Unless otherwise stipulated or ordered by the court, these procedures apply to producing documents or electronically stored information:

(i) A party must produce documents as they are kept in the usual course of business or must organize and label them to correspond to the categories in the request;

(ii) If a request does not specify a form for producing electronically stored information, a party must produce it in a form or forms in which it is ordinarily maintained or in a reasonably usable form or forms; and

(iii) A party need not produce the same electronically stored information in more than one form.

(c) Nonparties. As provided in Rule 45, a nonparty may be compelled to produce documents and tangible things or to permit an inspection.

Rule 35. Physical and Mental Examinations

(a) Order for an Examination

(1) In General. The court where the action is pending may order a party whose mental or physical condition — including blood group — is in controversy to submit to a physical or mental examination by a suitably licensed or certified examiner. The court has the same authority to order a party to produce for examination a person who is in its custody or under its legal control.

(2) Motion and Notice; Contents of the Order. The order:

(A) may be made only on motion for good cause and on notice to all parties and the person to be examined; and

(B) must specify the time, place, manner, conditions, and scope of the examination, as well as the person or persons who will perform it.

(b) Examiner's Report

(1) Request by the Party or Person Examined. The party who moved for the examination must, on request, deliver to the requester a copy of the examiner's report, together with like reports of all earlier examinations of the same condition. The request may be made by the party against whom the examination order was issued or by the person examined.

(2) Contents. The examiner's report must be in writing and must set out in detail the examiner's findings, including diagnoses, conclusions, and the results of any tests.

(3) Request by the Moving Party. After delivering the reports, the party who moved for the examination may request — and is entitled to receive — from the party against whom the examination order was issued like reports of all earlier or later examinations of the same condition. But those reports need not be delivered

by the party with custody or control of the person examined if the party shows that it could not obtain them.

(4) Waiver of Privilege. By requesting and obtaining the examiner's report, or by deposing the examiner, the party examined waives any privilege it may have — in that action or any other action involving the same controversy — concerning testimony about all examinations of the same condition.

(5) Failure to Deliver a Report. The court on motion may order — on just terms — that a party deliver the report of an examination. If the report is not provided, the court may exclude the examiner's testimony at trial.

(6) Scope. The subdivision (b) applies also to an examination made by the parties' agreement, unless the agreement states otherwise. This subdivision does not preclude obtaining an examiner's report or deposing an examiner under other rules.

Rule 36. Requests for Admission

(a) Scope and Procedure

(1) Scope. A party may serve on any other party a written request to admit, for purposes of the pending action only, the truth of any matters within the scope of Rule 26(b)(1) relating to:

(A) facts, the application of law to fact, or opinions about either; and

(B) the genuineness of any described documents.

(2) Form; Copy of a Document. Each matter must be separately stated. A request to admit the genuineness of a document must be accompanied by a copy of the document unless it is, or has been, otherwise furnished or made available for inspection and copying.

(3) Time to Respond; Effect of Not Responding. A matter is admitted unless, within 30 days after being served, the party to whom the request is directed serves on the requesting party a written answer or objection addressed to the matter and signed by the party or its attorney. A shorter or longer time for responding may be stipulated to under Rule 29 or be ordered by the court.

(4) Answer. If a matter is not admitted, the answer must specifically deny it or state in detail why the answering party cannot truthfully admit or deny it. A denial must fairly respond to the substance of the matter; and when good faith requires that a party qualify an answer or deny only a part of a matter, the answer must specify the part admitted and qualify or deny the rest. The answering party may assert lack of knowledge or information as a reason for failing to admit or deny only if the party states that it has made reasonable inquiry and that the information it knows or can readily obtain is insufficient to enable it to admit or deny.

(5) Objections. The grounds for objecting to a request must be stated. A party must not object solely on the ground that the request presents a genuine issue for trial.

(6) Motion Regarding the Sufficiency of an Answer or Objection. The requesting party may move to determine the sufficiency of an answer or objection. Unless the court finds an objection justified, it must order that an answer be served. On finding that an answer does not comply with this rule, the court may order either that the matter is admitted or that an amended answer be served. The court may defer its final decision until a pretrial conference or a specified time before trial. Rule 37(a)(5) applies to an award of expenses.

(b) Effect of an Admission; Withdrawing or Amending it. A matter admitted under this rule is conclusively established unless the court, on motion, permits the admission to be withdrawn or amended. Subject to Rule 16(e), the court may permit withdrawal or amendment if it would promote the presentation of the merits of the action and if the court is not persuaded that it would prejudice the requesting party in maintaining or defending the action on the merits. An admission under this rule is not an admission for any other purpose and cannot be used against the party in any other proceeding.

Rule 37. Failure to Make Disclosures or to Cooperate in Discovery; Sanctions

(a) Motion for an Order Compelling Disclosure or Discovery

(1) In General. On notice to other parties and all affected persons, a party may move for an order compelling disclosure or discovery. The motion must include a certification that the movant has in good faith conferred or attempted to confer with the person or party failing to make disclosure or discovery in an effort to obtain it without court action.

(2) Appropriate Court. A motion for an order to a party must be made in the court where the action is pending. A motion for an order to a nonparty must be made in the court where the discovery is or will be taken.

(3) Specific Motions

(A) To Compel Disclosure. If a party fails to make a disclosure required by Rule 26(a), any other party may move to compel disclosure and for appropriate sanctions.

(B) To Compel a Discovery Response. A party seeking discovery may move for an order compelling an answer, designation, production, or inspection. This motion may be made if:

(i) a deponent fails to answer a question asked under Rule 30 or 31;

(ii) a corporation or other entity fails to make a designation under Rule 30(b)(6) or 31(a)(4);

(iii) a party fails to answer an interrogatory submitted under Rule 33; or

(iv) a party fails to produce documents or fails to respond that inspection will be permitted — or fails to permit inspection — as requested under Rule 34.

(C) Related to a Deposition. When taking an oral deposition, the party asking a question may complete or adjourn the examination before moving for an order.

(4) Evasive or Incomplete Disclosure, Answer, or Response. For purposes of this subdivision (a), an evasive or incomplete disclosure, answer, or response must be treated as a failure to disclose, answer, or respond.

(5) Payment of Expenses; Protective Orders

(A) If the Motion Is Granted (or Disclosure or Discovery Is Provided After Filing). If the motion is granted — or if the disclosure or requested discovery is provided after the motion was filed — the court must, after giving an opportunity to be heard, require the party or deponent whose conduct necessitated the motion, the party or attorney advising that conduct, or both to pay the movant's reasonable expenses incurred in making the motion, including attorney's fees. But the court must not order this payment if:

(i) the movant filed the motion before attempting in good faith to obtain the disclosure or discovery without court action;

(ii) the opposing party's nondisclosure, response, or objection was substantially justified; or

(iii) other circumstances make an award of expenses unjust.

(B) If the Motion is Denied. If the motion is denied, the court may issue any protective order authorized under Rule 26(c) and must, after giving an opportunity to be heard, require the movant, the attorney filing the motion, or both to pay the party or deponent who opposed the motion its reasonable expenses incurred in opposing the motion, including attorney's fees. But the court must not order this payment if the motion was substantially justified or other circumstances make an award of expenses unjust.

(C) If the Motion is Granted in Part and Denied in Part. If the motion is granted in part and denied in part, the court may issue any protective order authorized under Rule 26(c) and may, after giving an opportunity to be heard, apportion the reasonable expenses for the motion.

(b) Failure to Comply with a Court Order

(1) Sanctions Sought in the District Where the Deposition Is Taken. If the court where the discovery is taken orders a deponent to be sworn or to answer a question and the deponent fails to obey, the failure may be treated as contempt of court. If a deposition- related motion is transferred to the court where the action is pending, and that court orders a deponent to be sworn or to answer a question and the deponent fails to obey, the failure may be treated as contempt of either the court where the discovery is taken or the court where the action is pending.

(2) Sanctions Sought in the District Where the Action Is Pending

(A) For Not Obeying a Discovery Order. If a party or a party's officer, director, or managing agent — or a witness designated under Rule 30(b)(6) or 31(a)(4) — fails to obey an order to provide or permit discovery, including an order under

Rule 26(f), 35, or 37(a), the court where the action is pending may issue further just orders. They may include the following:

(i) directing that the matters embraced in the order or other designated facts be taken as established for purposes of the action, as the prevailing party claims;

(ii) prohibiting the disobedient party from supporting or opposing designated claims or defenses, or from introducing designated matters in evidence;

(iii) striking pleadings in whole or in part;

(iv) staying further proceedings until the order is obeyed;

(v) dismissing the action or proceeding in whole or in part;

(vi) rendering a default judgment against the disobedient party; or

(vii) treating as contempt of court the failure to obey any order except an order to submit to a physical or mental examination.

(B) For Not Producing a Person for Examination. If a party fails to comply with an order under Rule 35(a) requiring it to produce another person for examination, the court may issue any of the orders listed in Rule 37(b)(2)(A)(i)-(vi), unless the disobedient party shows that it cannot produce the other person.

(C) Payment of Expenses. Instead of or in addition to the orders above, the court may order the disobedient party, the attorney advising that party, or both to pay the reasonable expenses, including attorney's fees, caused by the failure, unless the failure was substantially justified or other circumstances make an award of expenses unjust.

(c) Failure to Disclose, to Supplement an Earlier Response, or to Admit

(1) Failure to Disclose or Supplement. If a party fails to provide information or identify a witness as required by Rule 26(a) or (e), the party is not allowed to use that information or witness to supply evidence on a motion, at a hearing, or at a trial, unless the failure was substantially justified or is harmless. In addition to or instead of this sanction, the court, on motion and after giving an opportunity to be heard:

(A) may order payment of the reasonable expenses, including attorney's fees, caused by the failure;

(B) may inform the jury of the party's failure; and

(C) may impose other appropriate sanctions, including any of the orders listed in Rule 37(b)(2)(A)(i)-(vi).

(2) Failure to Admit. If a party fails to admit what is requested under Rule 36 and if the requesting party later proves a document to be genuine or the matter true, the requesting party may move that the party who failed to admit pay the reasonable expenses, including attorney's fees, incurred in making that proof. The court must so order unless:

(A) the request was held objectionable under Rule 36(a);

(B) the admission sought was of no substantial importance;

(C) the party failing to admit had a reasonable ground to believe that it might prevail on the matter; or

(D) there was other good reason for the failure to admit.

(d) Party's Failure to Attend Its Own Deposition, Serve Answers to Interrogatories, or Respond to a Request for Inspection

(1) In General

(A) Motion; Ground for Sanctions. The court where the action is pending may, on motion, order sanctions if:

(i) a party or a party's officer, director, or managing agent — or a person designated under Rule 30(b)(6) or 31(a)(4) — fails, after being served with proper notice, to appear for that person's deposition; or

(ii) a party, after being properly served with interrogatories under Rule 33 or a request for inspection under Rule 34, fails to serve its answers, objections, or written response.

(B) Certification. A motion for sanctions for failing to answer or respond must include a certification that the movant has in good faith conferred or attempted to confer with the party failing to act in an effort to obtain the answer or response without court action.

(2) Unacceptable Excuse for Failing to Act. A failure described in Rule 37(d)(1)(A) is not excused on the ground that the discovery sought was objectionable, unless the party failing to act has a pending motion for a protective order under Rule 26(c).

(3) Types of Sanctions. Sanctions may include any of the orders listed in Rule 37(b)(2) (A) (i)-(vi). Instead of or in addition to these sanctions, the court must require the party failing to act, the attorney advising that party, or both to pay the reasonable expenses, including attorney's fees, caused by the failure, unless the failure was substantially justified or other circumstances make an award of expenses unjust.

(e) Failure to Provide Electronically Stored Information. If electronically stored information that should have been preserved in the anticipation or conduct of litigation is lost because a party failed to take reasonable steps to preserve it, and it cannot be restored or replaced through additional discovery, the court:

(1) upon finding prejudice to another party from loss of the information, may order measures no greater than necessary to cure the prejudice; or

(2) only upon finding that the party acted with the intent to deprive another party of the information's use in the litigation may:

(A) presume that the lost information was unfavorable to the party;

(B) instruct the jury that it may or must presume the information was unfavorable to the party; or

(C) dismiss the action or enter a default judgment.

(f) Failure to Participate in Framing a Discovery Plan. If a party or its attorney fails to participate in good faith in developing and submitting a proposed discovery plan as required by Rule 26(f), the court may, after giving an opportunity to be heard, require that party or attorney to pay to any other party the reasonable expenses, including attorney's fees, caused by the failure.

VI. Trials

Rule 38. Right to a Jury Trial; Demand

(a) Right Preserved. The right of trial by jury as declared by the Seventh Amendment to the Constitution — or as provided by a federal statute — is preserved to the parties inviolate.

(b) Demand. On any issue triable of right by a jury, a party may demand a jury trial by:

(1) serving the other parties with a written demand — which may be included in a pleading — no later than 14 days after the last pleading directed to the issue is served; and

(2) filing the demand in accordance with Rule 5(d).

(c) Specifying Issues. In its demand, a party may specify the issues that it wishes to have tried by a jury; otherwise, it is considered to have demanded a jury trial on all the issues so triable. If the party has demanded a jury trial on only some issues, any other party may — within 14 days after being served with the demand or within a shorter time ordered by the court — serve a demand for a jury trial on any other or all factual issues triable by jury.

(d) Waiver; Withdrawal. A party waives a jury trial unless its demand is properly served and filed. A proper demand may be withdrawn only if the parties consent.

(e) Admiralty and Maritime Claims. These rules do not create a right to a jury trial on issues in a claim that is an admiralty or maritime claim under Rule 9(h).

Rule 39. Trial by Jury or by the Court

(a) When a Demand Is Made. When a jury trial has been demanded under Rule 38, the action must be designated on the docket as a jury action. The trial on all issues so demanded must be by jury unless:

(1) the parties or their attorneys file a stipulation to a nonjury trial or so stipulate on the record; or

(2) the court, on motion or on its own, finds that on some or all of those issues there is no federal right to a jury trial.

(b) When No Demand Is Made. Issues on which a jury trial is not properly demanded are to be tried by the court. But the court may, on motion, order a jury trial on any issue for which a jury might have been demanded.

(c) Advisory Jury; Jury Trial by Consent. In an action not triable of right by a jury, the court, on motion or on its own:

(1) may try any issue with an advisory jury; or

(2) may, with the parties' consent, try any issue by a jury whose verdict has the same effect as if a jury trial had been a matter of right, unless the action is against the United States and a federal statute provides for a nonjury trial.

Rule 40. Scheduling Cases for Trial

Each court must provide by rule for scheduling trials. The court must give priority to actions entitled to priority by a federal statute.

Rule 41. Dismissal of Actions

(a) Voluntary Dismissal

(1) By the Plaintiff

(A) Without a Court Order. Subject to Rules 23(e), 23.1(c), 23.2, and 66 and any applicable federal statute, the plaintiff may dismiss an action without a court order by filing:

(i) a notice of dismissal before the opposing party serves either an answer or a motion for summary judgment; or

(ii) a stipulation of dismissal signed by all parties who have appeared.

(B) Effect. Unless the notice or stipulation states otherwise, the dismissal is without prejudice. But if the plaintiff previously dismissed any federal- or state-court action based on or including the same claim, a notice of dismissal operates as an adjudication on the merits.

(2) By Court Order; Effect. Except as provided in Rule 41(a)(1), an action may be dismissed at the plaintiff 's request only by court order, on terms that the court considers proper. If a defendant has pleaded a counterclaim before being served with the plaintiff 's motion to dismiss, the action may be dismissed over the defendant's objection only if the counterclaim can remain pending for independent adjudication. Unless the order states otherwise, a dismissal under this paragraph (2) is without prejudice.

(b) Involuntary Dismissal; Effect. If the plaintiff fails to prosecute or to comply with these rules or a court order, a defendant may move to dismiss the action or any claim against it. Unless the dismissal order states otherwise, a dismissal under this subdivision (b) and any dismissal not under this rule — except one for lack of jurisdiction, improper venue, or failure to join a party under Rule 19 — operates as an adjudication on the merits.

(c) Dismissing a Counterclaim, Crossclaim, or Third-Party Claim. This rule applies to a dismissal of any counterclaim, crossclaim, or third-party claim. A claimant's voluntary dismissal under Rule 41(a)(1)(A)(i) must be made:

(1) before a responsive pleading is served; or

(2) if there is no responsive pleading, before evidence is introduced at a hearing or trial.

(d) Costs of a Previously Dismissed Action. If a plaintiff who previously dismissed an action in any court files an action based on or including the same claim against the same defendant, the court:

(1) may order the plaintiff to pay all or part of the costs of that previous action; and

(2) may stay the proceedings until the plaintiff has complied.

Rule 42. Consolidation; Separate Trials

(a) Consolidation. If actions before the court involve a common question of law or fact, the court may:

(1) join for hearing or trial any or all matters at issue in the actions;

(2) consolidate the actions; or

(3) issue any other orders to avoid unnecessary cost or delay.

(b) Separate Trials. For convenience, to avoid prejudice, or to expedite and economize, the court may order a separate trial of one or more separate issues, claims, crossclaims, counterclaims, or third-party claims. When ordering a separate trial, the court must preserve any federal right to a jury trial.

Rule 43. Taking Testimony

(a) In Open Court. At trial, the witnesses' testimony must be taken in open court unless a federal statute, the Federal Rules of Evidence, these rules, or other rules adopted by the Supreme Court provide otherwise. For good cause in compelling circumstances and with appropriate safeguards, the court may permit testimony in open court by contemporaneous transmission from a different location.

(b) Affirmation Instead of an Oath. When these rules require an oath, a solemn affirmation suffices.

(c) Evidence on a Motion. When a motion relies on facts outside the record, the court may hear the matter on affidavits or may hear it wholly or partly on oral testimony or on depositions.

(d) Interpreter. The court may appoint an interpreter of its choosing; fix reasonable compensation to be paid from funds provided by law or by one or more parties; and tax the compensation as costs.

Rule 44. Proving an Official Record

(a) Means of Proving

(1) Domestic Record. Each of the following evidences an official record — or an entry in it — that is otherwise admissible and is kept within the United States, any state, district, or commonwealth, or any territory subject to the administrative or judicial jurisdiction of the United States:

(A) an official publication of the record; or

(B) a copy attested by the officer with legal custody of the record — or by the officer's deputy — and accompanied by a certificate that the officer has custody. The certificate must be made under seal:

(i) by a judge of a court of record in the district or political subdivision where the record is kept; or

(ii) by any public officer with a seal of office and with official duties in the district or political subdivision where the record is kept.

(2) Foreign Record

(A) In General. Each of the following evidences a foreign official record — or an entry in it — that is otherwise admissible:

(i) an official publication of the record; or

(ii) the record — or a copy — that is attested by an authorized person and is accompanied either by a final certification of genuineness or by a certification under a treaty or convention to which the United States and the country where the record is located are parties.

(B) Final Certification of Genuineness. A final certification must certify the genuineness of the signature and official position of the attester or of any foreign official whose certificate of genuineness relates to the attestation or is in a chain of certificates of genuineness relating to the attestation. A final certification may be made by a secretary of a United States embassy or legation; by a consul general, vice consul, or consular agent of the United States; or by a diplomatic or consular official of the foreign country assigned or accredited to the United States.

(C) Other Means of Proof. If all parties have had a reasonable opportunity to investigate a foreign record's authenticity and accuracy, the court may, for good cause, either:

(i) admit an attested copy without final certification; or

(ii) permit the record to be evidenced by an attested summary with or without a final certification.

(b) Lack of Record. A written statement that a diligent search of designated records revealed no record or entry of a specified tenor is admissible as evidence that the records contain no such record or entry. For domestic records, the statement must be authenticated under Rule 44(a)(1). For foreign records, the statement must comply with (a)(2)(C)(ii).

(c) Other Proof. A party may prove an official record — or an entry or lack of an entry in it — by any other method authorized by law.

Rule 44.1. Determining Foreign Law

A party who intends to raise an issue about a foreign country's law must give notice by a pleading or other writing. In determining foreign law, the court may consider any relevant material or source, including testimony, whether or not submitted by a party or admissible under the Federal Rules of Evidence. The court's determination must be treated as a ruling on a question of law.

Rule 45. Subpoena

(a) In General

(1) Form and Contents

(A) Requirements — In General. Every subpoena must:

(i) state the court from which it issued;

(ii) state the title of the action and its civil-action number;

(iii) command each person to whom it is directed to do the following at a specified time and place: attend and testify; produce designated documents, electronically stored information, or tangible things in that person's possession, custody, or control; or permit the inspection of the premises; and

(iv) set out the text of Rule 45(d) and (e).

(B) Command to Attend a Deposition — Notice of the Recording Method. A subpoena commanding attendance at a deposition must state the method for recording the testimony.

(C) Combining or Separating a Command to Produce or to Permit Inspection; Specifying the Form for Electronically Stored Information.

A command to produce documents, electronically stored information, or tangible things or to permit the inspection of premises may be included in a subpoena commanding attendance at a deposition, hearing, or trial, or may be set out in a separate subpoena. A subpoena may specify the form or forms in which electronically stored information is to be produced.

(D) Command to Produce; Included Obligations. A command in a subpoena to produce documents, electronically stored information, or tangible things requires the responding person to permit inspection, copying, testing, or sampling of the materials.

(2) Issuing Court. A subpoena must issue from the court where the action is pending.

(3) Issued by Whom. The clerk must issue a subpoena, signed but otherwise in blank, to a party who requests it. That party must complete it before service. An attorney also may issue and sign a subpoena if the attorney is authorized to practice in the issuing court.

(4) Notice to Other Parties Before Service. If the subpoena commands the production of documents, electronically stored information, or tangible things or the inspection of premises before trial, then before it is served on the person to whom it is directed, a notice and a copy of the subpoena must be served on each party.

(b) Service

(1) By Whom and How; Tendering Fees. Any person who is at least 18 years old and not a party may serve a subpoena. Serving a subpoena requires delivering a copy to the named person and, if the subpoena requires that person's attendance, tendering the fees for 1 day's attendance and the mileage allowed by law. Fees and mileage need not be tendered when the subpoena issues on behalf of the United States or any of its officers or agencies.

(2) Service in the United States. A subpoena may be served at any place within the United States.

(3) Service in a Foreign Country. 28 U.S.C. § 1783 governs issuing and serving a subpoena directed to a United States national or resident who is in a foreign country.

(4) Proof of Service. Proving service, when necessary, requires filing with the issuing court a statement showing the date and manner of service and the names of the persons served. The statement must be certified by the server.

(c) Place of compliance

(1) For a Trial, Hearing, or Deposition. A subpoena may command a person to attend a trial, hearing, or deposition only as follows:

(A) within 100 miles of where the person resides, is employed, or regularly transacts business in person; or

(B) within the state where the person resides, is employed, or regularly transacts business in person, if the person

(i) is a party or a party's officer; or

(ii) is commanded to attend a trial and would not incur substantial expense.

(2) For Other Discovery. A subpoena may command:

(A) production of documents, electronically stored information, or tangible things at a place within 100 miles of where the person resides, is employed, or regularly transacts business in person; and

(B) inspection of premises at the premises to be inspected.

(d) Protecting a Person Subject to a Subpoena: Enforcement

(1) Avoiding Undue Burden or Expense; Sanctions. A party or attorney responsible for issuing and serving a subpoena must take reasonable steps to avoid imposing undue burden or expense on a person subject to the subpoena. The court for the district where compliance is required must enforce this duty and impose an appropriate sanction — which may include lost earnings and reasonable attorney's fees — on a party or attorney who fails to comply.

(2) Command to Produce Materials or Permit Inspection

(A) Appearance Not Required. A person commanded to produce designated documents, electronically stored information, or tangible things, or to permit the inspection of premises, need not appear in person at the place of production or inspection unless also commanded to appear for a deposition, hearing, or trial.

(B) Objections. A person commanded to produce documents or tangible things or to permit inspection may serve on the party or attorney designated in the subpoena a written objection to inspecting, copying, testing, or sampling any or all of the designated materials or to inspecting the premises — or to producing electronically stored information in the form or forms requested. The objection must be served before the earlier of the time specified for compliance or 14 days after the subpoena is served. If an objection is made, the following rules apply:

(i) At any time, on notice to the commanded person, the serving party may move the court for the district where compliance is required for an order compelling production or inspection.

(ii) These acts may be required only as directed in the order, and the order must protect a person who is neither a party nor a party's officer from significant expense resulting from compliance.

(3) Quashing or Modifying a Subpoena

(A) When Required. On timely motion, the court for the district where compliance is required must quash or modify a subpoena that:

(i) fails to allow a reasonable time to comply;

(ii) requires a person to comply beyond the geographical limits specified in Rule 45(c);

(iii) requires disclosure of privileged or other protected matter, if no exception or waiver applies; or

(iv) subjects a person to undue burden.

(B) When Permitted. To protect a person subject to or affected by a subpoena, the court for the district where compliance is required may, on motion, quash or modify the subpoena if it requires:

(i) disclosing a trade secret or other confidential research, development, or commercial information;

(ii) disclosing an unretained expert's opinion or information that does not describe specific occurrences in dispute and results from the expert's study that was not requested by a party.

(C) Specifying Conditions as an Alternative. In the circumstances described in Rule 45(d)(3)(B), the court may, instead of quashing or modifying a subpoena, order appearance or production under specified conditions if the serving party:

(i) shows a substantial need for the testimony or material that cannot be otherwise met without undue hardship; and

(ii) ensures that the subpoenaed person will be reasonably compensated.

(e) Duties in Responding to a Subpoena

(1) Producing Documents or Electronically Stored Information. These procedures apply to producing documents or electronically stored information:

(A) Documents. A person responding to a subpoena to produce documents must produce them as they are kept in the ordinary course of business or must organize and label them to correspond to the categories in the demand.

(B) Form for Producing Electronically Stored Information Not Specified. If a subpoena does not specify a form for producing electronically stored information, the person responding must produce it in a form or forms in which it is ordinarily maintained or in a reasonably usable form or forms.

(C) Electronically Stored Information Produced in Only One Form. The person responding need not produce the same electronically stored information in more than one form.

(D) Inaccessible Electronically Stored Information. The person responding need not provide discovery of electronically stored information from sources that the person identifies as not reasonably accessible because of undue burden or cost. On motion to compel discovery or for a protective order, the person responding must show that the information is not reasonably accessible because of undue burden or cost. If that showing is made, the court may nonetheless order discovery from such sources if the requesting party shows good cause, considering the limitations of Rule 26(b)(2)(C). The court may specify conditions for the discovery.

(2) Claiming Privilege or Protection

(A) Information Withheld. A person withholding subpoenaed information under a claim that it is privileged or subject to protection as trial-preparation material must:

(i) expressly make the claim; and

(ii) describe the nature of the withheld documents, communications, or tangible things in a manner that, without revealing information itself privileged or protected, will enable the parties to assess the claim.

(B) Information Produced. If information produced in response to a subpoena is subject to a claim of privilege or of protection as trial-preparation material, the person making the claim may notify any party that received the information of the claim and the basis for it. After being notified, a party must promptly return, sequester, or destroy the specified information and any copies it has; must not use or disclose the information until the claim is resolved; must take reasonable steps to retrieve the information if the party disclosed it before being notified; and may promptly present the information under seal to the court for the district where compliance is required for a determination of the claim. The person who produced the information must preserve the information until the claim is resolved.

(f) Transferring a Subpoena-Related Motion. When the court where compliance is required did not issue the subpoena, it may transfer a motion under this rule to the issuing court if the person subject to the subpoena consents or if the court finds exceptional circumstances. Then, if the attorney for a person subject to a subpoena is authorized to practice in the court where the motion was made, the attorney may file papers and appear on the motion as an officer of the issuing court. To enforce its order, the issuing court may transfer the order to the court where the motion was made.

(g) Contempt. The court for the district where compliance is required — and also, after a motion is transferred, the issuing court — may hold in contempt a person who, having been served, fails without adequate excuse to obey the subpoena or an order related to it.

Rule 46. Objecting to a Ruling or Order

A formal exception to a ruling or order is unnecessary. When the ruling or order is requested or made, a party need only state the action that it wants the court to take or objects to, along with the grounds for the request or objection. Failing to object does not prejudice a party who had no opportunity to do so when the ruling or order was made.

Rule 47. Selecting Jurors

(a) **Examining Jurors.** The court may permit the parties or their attorneys to examine prospective jurors or may itself do so. If the court examines the jurors, it must permit the parties or their attorneys to make any further inquiry it considers proper, or must itself ask any of the additional questions it considers proper.

(b) **Peremptory Challenges.** The court must allow the number of peremptory challenges provided by 28 U.S.C. § 1870.

(c) **Excusing a Juror.** During trial or deliberation, the court may excuse a juror for good cause.

Rule 48. Number of Jurors; Verdict; Polling

(a) **Number of Jurors.** A jury must begin with at least 6 and no more than 12 members, and each juror must participate in the verdict unless excused under Rule 47(c).

(b) **Verdict.** Unless the parties stipulate otherwise, the verdict must be unanimous and must be returned by a jury of at least 6 members.

(c) **Polling.** After a verdict is returned but before the jury is discharged, the court must on a party's request, or may on its own, poll the jurors individually. If the poll reveals a lack of unanimity or lack of assent by the number of jurors that the parties stipulated to, the court may direct the jury to deliberate further or may order a new trial.

Rule 49. Special Verdict; General Verdict and Questions

(a) **Special Verdict**

(1) In General. The court may require a jury to return only a special verdict in the form of a special written finding on each issue of fact. The court may do so by:

(A) submitting written questions susceptible of a categorical or other brief answer;

(B) submitting written forms of the special findings that might properly be made under the pleadings and evidence; or

(C) using any other method that the court considers appropriate.

(2) Instructions. The court must give the instructions and explanations necessary to enable the jury to make its findings on each submitted issue.

(3) Issues Not Submitted. A party waives the right to a jury trial on any issue of fact raised by the pleadings or evidence but not submitted to the jury unless, before the jury retires, the party demands its submission to the jury. If the party does not demand submission, the court may make a finding on the issue. If the court makes no finding, it is considered to have made a finding consistent with its judgment on the special verdict.

(b) General Verdict with Answers to Written Questions

(1) In General. The court may submit to the jury forms for a general verdict, together with written questions on one or more issues of fact that the jury must decide. The court must give the instructions and explanations necessary to enable the jury to render a general verdict and answer the questions in writing, and must direct the jury to do both.

(2) Verdict and Answers Consistent. When the general verdict and the answers are consistent, the court must approve, for entry upon Rule 58, an appropriate judgment on the verdict and answers.

(3) Answers Inconsistent with the Verdict. When the answers are consistent with each other but one or more is inconsistent with the general verdict, the court may:

(A) approve, for entry under Rule 58, an appropriate judgment according to the answers, notwithstanding the general verdict;

(B) direct the jury to further consider its answers and verdict; or

(C) order a new trial.

(4) Answers Inconsistent with Each Other and the Verdict. When the answers are inconsistent with each other and one or more is also inconsistent with the general verdict, judgment must not be entered; instead, the court must direct the jury to further consider its answers and verdict, or must order a new trial.

Rule 50. Judgment as a Matter of Law in a Jury Trial; Related Motion for a New Trial; Conditional Ruling

(a) Judgment as a Matter of Law

(1) In General. If a party has been fully heard on an issue during a jury trial and the court finds that a reasonable jury would not have a legally sufficient evidentiary basis to find for the party on that issue, the court may:

(A) resolve the issue against the party; and

(B) grant a motion for judgment as a matter of law against the party on a claim or defense that, under the controlling law, can be maintained or defeated only with a favorable finding on that issue.

(2) Motion. A motion for judgment as a matter of law may be made at any time before the case is submitted to the jury. The motion must specify the judgment sought and the law and facts that entitle the movant to the judgment.

(b) Renewing the Motion After Trial; Alternative Motion for a New Trial. If the court does not grant a motion for judgment as a matter of law made under Rule 50(a), the court is considered to have submitted the action to the jury subject to the court's later deciding the legal questions raised by the motion. No later than 28 days after the entry of judgment — or if the motion addresses a jury issue not decided by a verdict, no later than 28 days after the jury was discharged — the movant may file a renewed motion for judgment as a matter of law and may include an alternative or joint request for a new trial under Rule 59. In ruling on the renewed motion, the court may:

(1) allow judgment on the verdict, if the jury returned a verdict;

(2) order a new trial; or

(3) direct the entry of judgment as a matter of law.

(c) Granting the Renewed Motion; Conditional Ruling on a Motion for New Trial

(1) In General. If the court grants a renewed motion for judgment as a matter of law, it must also conditionally rule on any motion for a new trial by determining whether a new trial should be granted if the judgment is later vacated or reversed. The court must state the grounds for conditionally granting or denying the motion for a new trial.

(2) Effect of a Conditional Ruling. Conditionally granting the motion for a new trial does not affect the judgment's finality; if the judgment is reversed, the new trial must proceed unless the appellate court orders otherwise. If the motion for a new trial is conditionally denied, the appellee may assert error in that denial; if the judgment is reversed, the case must proceed as the appellate court orders.

(d) Time for a Losing Party's New-Trial Motion. Any motion for a new trial under Rule 59 by a party against whom judgment as a matter of law is rendered must be filed no later than 28 days after the entry of the judgment.

(e) Denying the Motion for Judgment as a Matter of Law; Reversal on Appeal. If the court denies the motion for judgment as a matter of law, the prevailing party may, as appellee, assert grounds entitling it to a new trial should the appellate court conclude that the trial court erred in denying the motion. If the appellate court reverses the judgment, it may order a new trial, direct the trial court to determine whether a new trial should be granted, or direct the entry of judgment.

Rule 51. Instructions to the Jury; Objections; Preserving a Claim of Error

(a) Requests

(1) Before or at the Close of the Evidence. At the close of the evidence or at any earlier reasonable time that the court orders, a party may file and furnish

to every other party written requests for the jury instructions it wants the court to give.

(2) After the Close of the Evidence. After the close of the evidence a party may:

(A) file requests for instructions on issues that could not reasonably have been anticipated by an earlier time that the court set for requests; and

(B) with the court's permission, file untimely requests for instructions on any issue.

(b) Instructions. The court:

(1) must inform the parties of its proposed instructions and proposed action on the requests before instructing the jury and before final jury arguments;

(2) must give the parties an opportunity to object on the record and out of the jury's hearing before the instructions and arguments are delivered; and

(3) may instruct the jury at any time before the jury is discharged.

(c) Objections

(1) How to Make. A party who objects to an instruction or the failure to given an instruction must do so on the record, stating distinctly the matter objected to and the grounds for the objection.

(2) When to Make. An objection is timely if:

(A) a party objects at the opportunity provided under Rule 51(b)(2); or

(B) a party was not informed of an instruction or action on a request before that opportunity to object, and the party objects promptly after learning that the instruction or request will be, or has been, given or refused.

(d) Assigning Error; Plain Error

(1) Assigning Error. A party may assign as error:

(A) an error in an instruction actually given, if that party properly objected; or

(B) a failure to give an instruction, if that party properly requested it and — unless the court rejected the request in a definitive ruling on the record — also properly objected.

(2) Plain Error. A court may consider a plain error in the instructions that has not been preserved as required by Rule 51(d)(1) if the error affects substantial rights.

Rule 52. Findings and Conclusions by the Court; Judgment on Partial Findings

(a) Findings and Conclusions

(1) In General. In an action tried on the facts without a jury or with an advisory jury, the court must find the facts specially and state its conclusions of law separately. The findings and conclusions may be stated on the record after the

close of the evidence or may appear in an opinion or a memorandum of decision filed by the court. Judgment must be entered under Rule 58.

(2) For an Interlocutory Injunction. In granting or refusing an interlocutory injunction, the court must similarly state the findings and conclusions that support its action.

(3) For a Motion. The court is not required to state findings or conclusions when ruling on a motion under Rule 12 or 56 or, unless these rules provide otherwise, on any other motion.

(4) Effect of a Master's Findings. A master's findings, to the extent adopted by the court, must be considered the court's findings.

(5) Questioning the Evidentiary Support. A party may later question the sufficiency of the evidence supporting the findings, whether or not the party requested findings, objected to them, moved to amend them, or moved for partial findings.

(6) Setting Aside the Findings. Findings of fact, whether based on oral or other evidence must not be set aside unless clearly erroneous, and the reviewing court must give due regard to the trial court's opportunity to judge the witnesses' credibility.

(b) Amended or Additional Findings. On a party's motion filed no later than 28 days after the entry of judgment, the court may amend its findings — or make additional findings — and may amend the judgment accordingly. The motion may accompany a motion for a new trial under Rule 59.

(c) Judgment on Partial Findings. If a party has been fully heard on an issue during a nonjury trial and the court finds against the party on that issue, the court may enter judgment against the party on a claim or defense that, under the controlling law, can be maintained or defeated only with a favorable finding on that issue. The court may, however, decline to render any judgment until the close of the evidence. A judgment on partial findings must be supported by findings of fact and conclusions of law as required by Rule 52(a).

Rule 53. Masters

(a) Appointment

(1) Scope. Unless a statute provides otherwise, a court may appoint a master only to:

(A) perform duties consented to by the parties;

(B) hold trial proceedings and make or recommend findings of fact on issues to be decided without a jury if appointment is warranted by:

(i) some exceptional condition; or

(ii) the need to perform an accounting or resolve a difficult computation of damages; or

(C) address pretrial and posttrial matters that cannot be effectively and timely addressed by an available district judge or magistrate judge of the district.

(2) Disqualification. A master must not have a relationship to the parties, attorneys, action, or court that would require disqualification of a judge under 28 U.S.C. § 455, unless the parties, with the court's approval, consent to the appointment after the master discloses any potential grounds for disqualification.

(3) Possible Expense or Delay. In appointing a master, the court must consider the fairness of imposing the likely expenses on the parties and must protect against unreasonable expense or delay.

(b) Order Appointing a Master

(1) Notice. Before appointing a master, the court must give the parties notice and an opportunity to be heard. Any party may suggest candidates for appointment.

(2) Contents. The appointing order must direct the master to proceed with all reasonable diligence and must state:

(A) the master's duties, including any investigation or enforcement duties, and any limits on the master's authority under Rule 53(c);

(B) the circumstances, if any, in which the master may communicate ex parte with the court or a party;

(C) the nature of the materials to be preserved and filed as the record of the master's activities;

(D) the time limits, method of filing the record, other procedures, and standards for reviewing the master's orders, findings, and recommendations; and

(E) the basis, terms, and procedure for fixing the master's compensation under Rule 53(g).

(3) Issuing. The court may issue the order only after:

(A) the master files an affidavit disclosing whether there is any ground for disqualification under 28 U.S.C. § 455; and

(B) if a ground is disclosed, the parties, with the court's approval, waive the disqualification.

(4) Amending. The order may be amended at any time after notice to the parties and an opportunity to be heard.

(c) Master's Authority

(1) In General. Unless the appointing order directs otherwise, a master may:

(A) regulate all proceedings;

(B) take all appropriate measures to perform the assigned duties fairly and efficiently; and

(C) if conducting an evidentiary hearing, exercise the appointing court's power to compel, take, and record evidence.

(2) Sanctions. The master may by order impose on a party any noncontempt sanction provided by Rule 37 or 45, and may recommend a contempt sanction against a party and sanctions against a nonparty.

(d) Master's Orders. A master who issues an order must file it and promptly serve a copy on each party. The clerk must enter the order on the docket.

(e) Master's Reports. A master must report to the court as required by the appointing order. The master must file the report and promptly serve a copy on each party, unless the court orders otherwise.

(f) Action on The Master's Order, Report, or Recommendations

(1) Opportunity for a Hearing; Action in General. In acting on a master's order, report, or recommendations, the court must give the parties notice and an opportunity to be heard; may receive evidence; and may adopt or affirm, modify, wholly or partly reject or reverse, or resubmit it to the master with instructions.

(2) Time to Object or Move to Adopt or Modify. A party may file objections to — or a motion to adopt or modify — the master's order, report, or recommendations no later than 21 days after a copy is served, unless the court sets a different time.

(3) Reviewing Factual Findings. The court must decide de novo all objections to findings of fact made or recommended by a master, unless the parties, with the court's approval, stipulate that:

(A) the findings will be reviewed for clear error; or

(B) the findings of a master appointed under Rule 53(a)(1)(A) or (C) will be final.

(4) Reviewing Legal Conclusions. The court must decide de novo all objections to conclusions of law made or recommended by a master.

(5) Reviewing Procedural Matters. Unless the appointing order establishes a different standard of review, the court may set aside a master's ruling on a procedural matter only for an abuse of discretion.

(g) Compensation

(1) Fixing Compensation. Before or after judgment, the court must fix the master's compensation on the basis and terms stated in the appointing order, but the court may set a new basis and terms after giving notice and an opportunity to be heard.

(2) Payment. The compensation must be paid either:

(A) by a party or parties; or

(B) from a fund or subject matter of the action within the court's control.

(3) Allocating Payment. The court must allocate payment among the parties after considering the nature and amount of the controversy, the parties' means, and the extent to which any party is more responsible than the other parties for the reference to a master. An interim allocation may be amended to reflect a decision on the merits.

(h) Appointing a Magistrate Judge. A magistrate judge is subject to this rule only when the order referring a matter to the magistrate judge states that the reference is made under this rule.

VII. Judgment

Rule 54. Judgment; Costs

(a) Definition; Form. "Judgment" as used in these rules includes a decree and any order from which an appeal lies. A judgment should not include recitals of pleadings, a master's report, or a record of prior proceedings.

(b) Judgment on Multiple Claims or Involving Multiple Parties. When an action presents more than one claim for relief — whether as a claim, counterclaim, crossclaim, or third-party claim — or when multiple parties are involved, the court may direct entry of a final judgment as to one or more, but fewer than all, claims or parties only if the court expressly determines that there is no just reason for delay. Otherwise, any order or other decision, however designated, that adjudicates fewer than all the claims or the rights and liabilities of fewer than all the parties does not end the action as to any of the claims or parties and may be revised at any time before the entry of a judgment adjudicating all the claims and all the parties' rights and liabilities.

(c) Demand for Judgment; Relief to Be Granted. A default judgment must not differ in kind from, or exceed in amount, what is demanded in the pleadings. Every other final judgment should grant the relief to which each party is entitled, even if the party has not demanded that relief in its pleadings.

(d) Costs; Attorney's Fees

(1) Costs Other Than Attorney's Fees. Unless a federal statute, these rules, or a court order provides otherwise, costs — other than attorney's fees — should be allowed to the prevailing party. But costs against the United States, its officers, and its agencies may be imposed only to the extent allowed by law. The clerk may tax costs on 14 days' notice. On motion served within the next 7 days, the court may review the clerk's action.

(2) Attorney's Fees

(A) Claim to Be by Motion. A claim for attorney's fees and related nontaxable expenses must be made by motion unless the substantive law requires those fees to be proved at trial as an element of damages.

(B) Timing and Content of the Motion. Unless a statute or a court order provides otherwise, the motion must:

(i) be filed no later than 14 days after the entry of judgment;

(ii) specify the judgment and the statute, rule, or other grounds entitling the movant to the award;

(iii) state the amount sought or provide a fair estimate of it; and

(iv) disclose, if the court so orders, the terms of any agreement about fees for the services for which the claim is made.

(C) Proceedings. Subject to Rule 23(h), the court must, on a party's request, give an opportunity for adversary submissions on the motion in accordance with Rule 43(c) or 78. The court may decide issues of liability for fees before receiving submissions on the value of services. The court must find the facts and state its conclusions of law as provided in Rule 52(a).

(D) Special Procedures by Local Rule; Reference to a Master or a Magistrate Judge. By local rule, the court may establish special procedures to resolve fee-related issues without extensive evidentiary hearings. Also, the court may refer issues concerning the value of services to a special master under Rule 53 without regard to the limitations of Rule 53(a) (1), and may refer a motion for attorney's fees to a magistrate judge under Rule 72(b) as if it were a dispositive pretrial matter.

(E) Exceptions. Subparagraphs (A)-(D) do not apply to claims for fees and expenses as sanctions for violating these rules or as sanctions under 28 U.S.C. § 1927.

Rule 55. Default; Default Judgment

(a) Entering a Default. When a party against whom a judgment for affirmative relief is sought has failed to plead or otherwise defend, and that failure is shown by affidavit or otherwise, the clerk must enter the party's default.

(b) Entering a Default Judgment

(1) By the Clerk. If the plaintiff 's claim is for a sum certain or a sum that can be made certain by computation, the clerk — on the plaintiff 's request, with an affidavit showing the amount due — must enter judgment for that amount and costs against a defendant who has been defaulted for not appearing and who is neither a minor nor an incompetent person.

(2) By the Court. In all other cases, the party must apply to the court for a default judgment. A default judgment may be entered against a minor or incompetent person only if represented by a general guardian, conservator, or other like fiduciary who has appeared. If the party against whom a default judgment is sought has appeared personally or by a representative, that party or its representative must be served with written notice of the application at least 7 days before the hearing. The court may conduct hearings or make referrals — preserving any

federal statutory right to a jury trial — when, to enter or effectuate judgment, it needs to:

(A) conduct an accounting;
(B) determine the amount of damages;
(C) establish the truth of any allegation by evidence; or
(D) investigate any other matter.

(c) Setting Aside a Default or a Default Judgment. The court may set aside an entry of default for good cause, and it may set aside a final default judgment under Rule 60(b).

(d) Judgment Against the United States. A default judgment may be entered against the United States, its officers, or its agencies only if the claimant establishes a claim or right to relief by evidence that satisfies the court.

Rule 56. Summary Judgment

(a) Motion for Summary Judgment or Partial Summary Judgment. A party may move for summary judgment, identifying each claim or defense — or the part of each claim or defense — on which summary judgment is sought. The court shall grant summary judgment if the movant shows that there is no genuine dispute as to any material fact and the movant is entitled to judgment as a matter of law. The court should state on the record the reasons for granting or denying the motion.

(b) Time to File a Motion. Unless a different time is set by local rule or the court orders otherwise, a party may file a motion for summary judgment at any time until 30 days after the close of all discovery.

(c) Procedures

(1) Supporting Factual Positions. A party asserting that a fact cannot be or is genuinely disputed must support the assertion by:

(A) citing to particular parts of materials in the record, including depositions, documents, electronically stored information, affidavits or declarations, stipulations (including those made for purposes of the motion only), admissions, interrogatory answers, or other materials; or

(B) showing that the materials cited do not establish the absence or presence of a genuine dispute or that an adverse party cannot produce admissible evidence to support the fact.

(2) Objection That a Fact Is Not Supported by Admissible Evidence. A party may object that the material cited to support or dispute a fact cannot be presented in a form that would be admissible in evidence.

(3) Materials Not Cited. The court need consider only the cited materials, but it may consider other materials in the record.

(4) Affidavits or Declarations. An affidavit or declaration used to support or oppose a motion must be made on personal knowledge, set out facts that would be admissible in evidence, and show that the affiant or declarant is competent to testify on the matters stated.

(d) When Facts Are Unavailable to the Nonmovant. If a nonmovant shows by affidavit or declaration that, for specified reasons, it cannot present facts essential to justify its opposition, the court may:

(1) defer considering the motion or deny it;

(2) allow time to obtain affidavits or declarations or to take discovery; or

(3) issue any other appropriate order.

(e) Failing to Properly Support or Address a Fact. If a party fails to properly support an assertion of fact or fails to properly address another party's assertion of fact as required by Rule 56(c), the court may:

(1) give an opportunity to properly support or address the fact;

(2) consider the fact undisputed for purposes of the motion;

(3) grant summary judgment if the motion and supporting materials — including the facts considered undisputed — show that the movant is entitled to it; or

(4) issue any other appropriate order.

(f) Judgment Independent of the Motion. After giving notice and a reasonable time to respond, the court may:

(1) grant summary judgment for a nonmovant;

(2) grant the motion on grounds not raised by a party; or

(3) consider summary judgment on its own after identifying for the parties material facts that may not be genuinely in dispute.

(g) Failing to Grant All the Requested Relief. If the court does not grant all the relief requested by the motion, it may enter an order stating any material fact — including an item of damages or other relief — that is not genuinely in dispute and treating the fact as established in the case.

(h) Affidavit or Declaration Submitted in Bad Faith. If satisfied that an affidavit or declaration under this rule is submitted in bad faith or solely for delay, the court — after notice and a reasonable time to respond — may order the submitting party to pay the other party the reasonable expenses, including attorney's fees, it incurred as a result. An offending party or attorney may also be held in contempt or subjected to other appropriate sanctions.

Rule 57. Declaratory Judgment

These rules govern the procedure for obtaining a declaratory judgment under 28 U.S.C. § 2201. Rules 38 and 39 govern a demand for a jury trial. The existence of another adequate remedy does not preclude a declaratory judgment that is otherwise appropriate. The court may order a speedy hearing of a declaratory-judgment action.

Rule 58. Entering Judgment

(a) Separate Document. Every judgment and amended judgment must be set out in a separate document, but a separate document is not required for an order disposing of a motion:

(1) for judgment under Rule 50(b);
(2) to amend or make additional findings under Rule 52(b);
(3) for attorney's fees under Rule 54;
(4) for a new trial, or to alter or amend the judgment, under Rule 59; or
(5) for relief under Rule 60.

(b) Entering Judgment

(1) Without the Court's Direction. Subject to Rule 54(b) and unless the court orders otherwise, the clerk must, without awaiting the court's direction, promptly prepare, sign, and enter the judgment when:

(A) the jury returns a general verdict;
(B) the court awards only costs or a sum certain; or
(C) the court denies all relief.

(2) Court's Approval Required. Subject to Rule 54(b), the court must promptly approve the form of the judgment, which the clerk must promptly enter, when:

(A) the jury returns a special verdict or a general verdict with answers to written questions; or
(B) the court grants other relief not described in this subdivision (b).

(c) Time of Entry. For purposes of these rules, judgment is entered at the following times:

(1) if a separate document is not required, when the judgment is entered in the civil docket under Rule 79(a); or

(2) if a separate document is required, when the judgment is entered in the civil docket under Rule 79(a) and the earlier of these events occurs:

(A) it is set out in a separate document; or
(B) 150 days have run from the entry in the civil docket.

(d) Request for Entry. A party may request that judgment be set out in a separate document as required by Rule 58(a).

(e) **Cost or Fee Awards.** Ordinarily, the entry of judgment may not be delayed, nor the time for appeal extended, in order to tax costs or award fees. But if a timely motion for attorney's fees is made under Rule 54(d)(2), the court may act before a notice of appeal has been filed and become effective to order that the motion have the same effect under Federal Rule of Appellate Procedure 4(a)(4) as a timely motion under Rule 59.

Rule 59. New Trial; Altering or Amending a Judgment

(a) **In General**

(1) Grounds for New Trial. The court may, on motion, grant a new trial on all or some of the issues — and to any party — as follows:

(A) after a jury trial, for any reason for which a new trial has heretofore been granted in an action at law in federal court; or

(B) after a nonjury trial, for any reason for which a rehearing has heretofore been granted in a suit in equity in federal court.

(2) Further Action After a Nonjury Trial. After a nonjury trial, the court may, on motion for a new trial, open the judgment if one has been entered, take additional testimony, amend findings of fact and conclusions of law or make new ones, and direct the entry of a new judgment.

(b) **Time to File a Motion for a New Trial.** A motion for a new trial must be filed no later than 28 days after the entry of judgment.

(c) **Time to Serve Affidavits.** When a motion for a new trial is based on affidavits, they must be filed with the motion. The opposing party has 14 days after being served to file opposing affidavits. The court may permit reply affidavits.

(d) **New Trial on the Court's Initiative or for Reasons Not in the Motion.** No later than 28 days after the entry of judgment, the court, on its own, may order a new trial for any reason that would justify granting one on a party's motion. After giving the parties notice and an opportunity to be heard, the court may grant a timely motion for a new trial for a reason not stated in the motion. In either event, the court must specify the reasons in its order.

(e) **Motion to Alter or Amend Judgment.** A motion to alter or amend a judgment must be filed no later than 28 days after the entry of the judgment.

Rule 60. Relief from a Judgment or Order

(a) **Corrections Based on Clerical Mistakes; Oversights and Omissions.** The court may correct a clerical mistake or a mistake arising from oversight or omission whenever one is found in a judgment, order, or other part of the record. The court may do so on motion or on its own, with or without notice. But after an appeal has been docketed in the appellate court and while it is pending, such a mistake may be corrected only with the appellate court's leave.

(b) **Grounds for Relief from a Final Judgment, Order, or Proceeding.** On motion and just terms, the court may relieve a party or its legal representative from a final judgment, order, or proceeding for the following reasons:

(1) mistake, inadvertence, surprise, or excusable neglect;

(2) newly discovered evidence that, with reasonable diligence, could not have been discovered in time to move for a new trial under Rule 59(b);

(3) fraud (whether previously called intrinsic or extrinsic), misrepresentation, or misconduct by an opposing party;

(4) the judgment is void;

(5) the judgment has been satisfied, released or discharged; it is based on an earlier judgment that has been reversed or vacated; or applying it prospectively is no longer equitable; or

(6) any other reason that justifies relief.

(c) **Timing and Effect of the Motion**

(1) Timing. A motion under Rule 60(b) must be made within a reasonable time — and for reasons (1), (2), and (3) no more than a year after the entry of the judgment or order or the date of the proceeding.

(2) Effect on Finality. The motion does not affect the judgment's finality or suspend its operation.

(d) **Other Powers to Grant Relief.** This rule does not limit a court's power to:

(1) entertain an independent action to relieve a party from a judgment, order, or proceeding;

(2) grant relief under 28 U.S.C. § 1655 to a defendant who was not personally notified of the action; or

(3) set aside a judgment for fraud on the court.

(e) **Bills and Writs Abolished.** The following are abolished: bills of review, bills in the nature of bills of review, and writs of coram nobis, coram vobis, and audita querela.

Rule 61. Harmless Error

Unless justice requires otherwise, no error in admitting or excluding evidence — or any other error by the court or a party — is ground for granting a new trial, for setting aside a verdict, or for vacating, modifying, or otherwise disturbing a judgment or order. At every stage of the proceeding, the court must disregard all errors and defects that do not affect any party's substantial rights.

Rule 62. Stay of Proceedings to Enforce a Judgment

(a) **Automatic Stay.** Except as provided in Rule 62(c) and (d), execution on a judgment and proceedings to enforce it are stayed for 30 days after its entry, unless the court orders otherwise.

(b) **Stay by Bond or Other Security.** At any time after judgment is entered, a party may obtain a stay by providing a bond or other security. The stay takes effect when the court approves the bond or other security and remains in effect for the time specified in the bond or other security.

(c) **Stay of an Injunction, Receivership, or Patent Accounting Order.** Unless the court orders otherwise, the following are not stayed after being entered, even if an appeal is taken:

(1) an interlocutory or final judgment in an action for an injunction or receivership; or

(2) a judgment or order that directs an accounting in an action for patent infringement.

(d) **Injunction Pending an Appeal.** While an appeal is pending from an interlocutory order or final judgment that grants, continues, modifies, refuses, dissolves, or refuses to dissolve or modify an injunction, the court may suspend, modify, restore, or grant an injunction on terms for bond or other terms that secure the opposing party's rights. If the judgment appealed from is rendered by a statutory three-judge district court, the order must be made either:

(1) by that court sitting in open session; or

(2) by the assent of all its judges, as evidenced by their signatures.

(e) **Stay Without Bond on an Appeal by the United States, Its Officers, or Its Agencies.** The court must not require a bond, obligation, or other security from the appellant when granting a stay on an appeal by the United States, its officers, or its agencies or on an appeal directed by a department of the federal government.

(f) Stay in Favor of a Judgment Debtor Under State Law. If a judgment is a lien on the judgment debtor's property under the law of the state where the court is located, the judgment debtor is entitled to the same stay of execution the state court would give.

(g) Appellate Court's Power Not Limited. This rule does not limit the power of the appellate court or one of its judges or justices:

(1) to stay proceedings — or suspend, modify, restore, or grant an injunction — while an appeal is pending; or

(2) to issue an order to preserve the status quo or the effectiveness of the judgment to be entered.

(h) Stay with Multiple Claims or Parties. A court may stay the enforcement of a final judgment entered under Rule 54(b) until it enters a later judgment or judgments, and may prescribe terms necessary to secure the benefit of the stayed judgment for the party in whose favor it was entered.

Rule 62.1. Indicative Ruling on a Motion for Relief That is Barred by a Pending Appeal

(a) Relief Pending Appeal. If a timely motion is made for relief that the court lacks authority to grant because of an appeal that has been docketed and is pending, the court may:

(1) defer considering the motion;

(2) deny the motion; or

(3) state either that it would grant the motion if the court of appeals remands for that purpose or that the motion raises a substantial issue.

(b) Notice to the Court of Appeals. The movant must promptly notify the circuit clerk under Federal Rule of Appellate Procedure 12.1 if the district court states that it would grant the motion or that the motion raises a substantial issue.

(c) Remand The district court may decide the motion if the court of appeals remands for that purpose.

Rule 63. Judge's Inability to Proceed

If a judge conducting a hearing or trial is unable to proceed, any other judge may proceed upon certifying familiarity with the record and determining that the case may be completed without prejudice to the parties. In a hearing or a nonjury trial, the successor judge must, at a party's request, recall any witness whose testimony is material and disputed and who is available to testify again without undue burden. The successor judge may also recall any other witness.

VIII. Provisional and Final Remedies

Rule 64. Seizing a Person or Property

(a) **Remedies Under State Law — In General.** At the commencement of and throughout an action, every remedy is available that, under the law of the state where the court is located, provides for seizing a person or property to secure satisfaction of the potential judgment. But a federal statute governs to the extent it applies.

(b) **Specific Kinds of Remedies.** The remedies available under this rule include the following — however designated and regardless of whether state procedure requires an independent action:

- arrest;
- attachment;
- garnishment;
- replevin;
- sequestration; and
- other corresponding or equivalent remedies.

Rule 65. Injunctions and Restraining Orders

(a) **Preliminary Injunction**

(1) Notice. The court may issue a preliminary injunction only on notice to the adverse party.

(2) Consolidating the Hearing with the Trial on the Merits. Before or after beginning the hearing on a motion for a preliminary injunction, the court may advance the trial on the merits and consolidate it with the hearing. Even when consolidation is not ordered, evidence that is received on the motion and that would be admissible at trial becomes part of the trial record and need not be repeated at trial. But the court must preserve any party's right to a jury trial.

(b) **Temporary Restraining Order**

(1) Issuing Without Notice. The court may issue a temporary restraining order without written or oral notice to the adverse party or its attorney only if:

(A) specific facts in an affidavit or a verified complaint clearly show that immediate and irreparable injury, loss, or damage will result to the movant before the adverse party can be heard in opposition; and

(B) the movant's attorney certifies in writing any efforts made to give notice and the reasons why it should not be required.

(2) Contents; Expiration. Every temporary restraining order issued without notice must state the date and hour it was issued; describe the injury and state why it is irreparable; state why the order was issued without notice; and be promptly filed in the clerk's office and entered in the record. The order expires at the time after entry — not to exceed 14 days — that the court sets, unless before that time the court, for good cause, extends it for a like period or the adverse party consents to a longer extension. The reasons for an extension must be entered in the record.

(3) Expediting the Preliminary-Injunction Hearing. If the order is issued without notice, the motion for a preliminary injunction must be set for hearing at the earliest possible time, taking precedence over all other matters except hearings on older matters of the same character. At the hearing, the party who obtained the order must proceed with the motion; if the party does not, the court must dissolve the order.

(4) Motion to Dissolve. On 2 days' notice to the party who obtained the order without notice — or on shorter notice set by the court — the adverse party may appear and move to dissolve or modify the order. The court must then hear and decide the motion as promptly as justice requires.

(c) Security. The court may issue a preliminary injunction or a temporary restraining order only if the movant gives security in an amount that the court considers proper to pay the costs and damages sustained by any party found to have been wrongfully enjoined or restrained. The United States, its officers, and its agencies are not required to give security.

(d) Contents and Scope of Every Injunction and Restraining Order

(1) Contents. Every order granting an injunction and every restraining order must:

(A) state the reasons why it issued;

(B) state its terms specifically; and

(C) describe in reasonable detail — and not by referring to the complaint or other document — the act or acts restrained or required.

(2) Persons Bound. The order binds only the following who receive actual notice of it by personal service or otherwise:

(A) the parties;

(B) the parties' officers, agents, servants, employees, and attorneys; and

(C) other persons who are in active concert or participation with anyone described in Rule 65(d)(2)(A) or (B).

(e) Other Laws Not Modified. These rules do not modify the following:

(1) any federal statute relating to temporary restraining orders or preliminary injunctions in actions affecting employer and employee;

(2) 28 U.S.C. § 2361, which relates to preliminary injunctions in actions of interpleader or in the nature of interpleader; or

(3) 28 U.S.C. § 2284, which relates to actions that must be heard and decided by a three- judge district court.

(f) **Copyright Impoundment.** This rule applies to copyright-impoundment proceedings.

Rule 65.1. Proceedings Against a Security Provider

Whenever these rules (including the Supplemental Rules for Admiralty or Maritime Claims and Asset Forfeiture Actions) require or allow a party to give security, and security is given with one or more security providers, each provider submits to the court's jurisdiction and irrevocably appoints the court clerk as its agent for receiving service of any papers that affect its liability on the security. The security provider's liability may be enforced on motion without an independent action. The motion and any notice that the court orders may be served on the court clerk, who must promptly send a copy of each to every security provider whose address is known.

Rule 66. Receivers

These rules govern an action in which the appointment of a receiver is sought or a receiver sues or is sued. But the practice in administering an estate by a receiver or a similar court-appointed officer must accord with the historical practice in federal courts or with a local rule. An action in which a receiver has been appointed may be dismissed only by court order.

Rule 67. Deposit into Court

(a) **Depositing Property.** If any part of the relief sought is a money judgment or the disposition of a sum of money or some other deliverable thing, a party — on notice to every other party and by leave of court — may deposit with the court all or part of the money or thing, whether or not that party claims any of it. The depositing party must deliver to the clerk a copy of the order permitting deposit.

(b) **Investing and Withdrawing Funds.** Money paid into court under this rule must be deposited and withdrawn in accordance with 28 U.S.C. §§ 2041 and 2042 and any like statute. The money must be deposited in an interest-bearing account or invested in a court-approved, interest-bearing instrument.

Rule 68. Offer of Judgment

(a) **Making an Offer; Judgment on an Accepted Offer.** At least 14 days before the date set for trial, a party defending against a claim may serve on an opposing party an offer to allow judgment on specified terms, with the costs then accrued. If, within 14 days after being served, the opposing party serves written notice accepting the offer, either party may then file the offer and notice of acceptance, plus proof of service. The clerk must then enter judgment.

(b) **Unaccepted Offer.** An unaccepted offer is considered withdrawn, but it does not preclude a later offer. Evidence of an unaccepted offer is not admissible except in a proceeding to determine costs.

(c) **Offer After Liability Is Determined.** When one party's liability to another has been determined but the extent of liability remains to be determined by further proceedings, the party held liable may make an offer of judgment. It must be served within a reasonable time — but at least 14 days — before the date set for a hearing to determine the extent of liability.

(d) **Paying Costs After an Unaccepted Offer.** If the judgment that the offeree finally obtains is not more favorable than the unaccepted offer, the offeree must pay the costs incurred after the offer was made.

Rule 69. Execution

(a) **In General**

(1) Money Judgment; Applicable Procedure. A money judgment is enforced by a writ of execution, unless the court directs otherwise. The procedure on execution — and in proceedings supplementary to and in aid of judgment or execution — must accord with the procedure of the state where the court is located, but a federal statute governs to the extent it applies.

(2) Obtaining Discovery. In aid of the judgment or execution, the judgment creditor or a successor in interest whose interest appears of record may obtain discovery from any person — including the judgment debtor — as provided in these rules or by the procedure of the state where the court is located.

(b) **Against Certain Public Officers.** When a judgment has been entered against a revenue officer in the circumstances stated in 28 U.S.C. § 2006, or against an officer of Congress in the circumstances stated in 2 U.S.C. § 118, the judgment must be satisfied as those statutes provide.

Rule 70. Enforcing a Judgment for a Specific Act

(a) **Party's Failure to Act; Ordering Another to Act.** If a judgment requires a party to convey land, to deliver a deed or other document, or to perform any other specific act and the party fails to comply within the time specified, the court may order the act to be done — at the disobedient party's expense — by another person appointed by the court. When done, the act has the same effect as if done by the party.

(b) **Vesting Title.** If the real or personal property is within the district, the court — instead of ordering a conveyance — may enter a judgment divesting any party's title and vesting it in others. That judgment has the effect of a legally executed conveyance.

(c) **Obtaining a Writ of Attachment or Sequestration.** On application by a party entitled to performance of an act, the clerk must issue a writ of attachment or sequestration against the disobedient party's property to compel obedience.

(d) **Obtaining a Writ of Execution or Assistance.** On application by a party who obtains a judgment or order for possession, the clerk must issue a writ of execution or assistance.

(e) **Holding in Contempt.** The court may also hold the disobedient party in contempt.

Rule 71. Enforcing Relief for or Against a Nonparty

When an order grants relief for a nonparty or may be enforced against a nonparty, the procedure for enforcing the order is the same as for a party.

IX. Special Proceedings

Rule 71.1. Condemning Real or Personal Property

(a) **Applicability of Other Rules.** These rules govern proceedings to condemn real and personal property by eminent domain, except as this rule provides otherwise.

(b) **Joinder of Properties.** The plaintiff may join separate pieces of property in a single action, no matter whether they are owned by the same persons or sought for the same use.

(c) Complaint

(1) Caption. The complaint must contain a caption as provided in Rule 10(a). The plaintiff must, however, name as defendants both the property—designated generally by kind, quantity, and location—and at least one owner of some part or interest in the property.

(2) Contents. The complaint must contain a short and plain statement of the following:

(A) the authority for the taking;

(B) the uses for which the property is to be taken;

(C) a description sufficient to identify the property;

(D) the interests to be acquired; and

(E) for each piece of property, a designation of each defendant who has been joined as an owner or owner of an interest in it.

(3) Parties. When the action commences, the plaintiff need join as defendants only those persons who have or claim an interest in the property and whose names are then known. But before any hearing on compensation, the plaintiff must add as defendants all those persons who have or claim an interest and whose names have become known or can be found by a reasonably diligent search of the records, considering both the property's character and value and the interests to be acquired. All others may be made defendants under the designation "Unknown Owners."

(4) Procedure. Notice must be served on all defendants as provided in Rule 71.1(d), whether they were named as defendants when the action commenced or were added later. A defendant may answer as provided in Rule 71.1(e). The court, meanwhile, may order any distribution of a deposit that the facts warrant.

(5) Filing; Additional Copies. In addition to filing the complaint, the plaintiff must give the clerk at least one copy for the defendants' use and additional copies at the request of the clerk or a defendant.

(d) Process

(1) Delivering Notice to the Clerk. On filing a complaint, the plaintiff must promptly deliver to the clerk joint or several notices directed to the named defendants. When adding defendants, the plaintiff must deliver to the clerk additional notices directed to the new defendants.

(2) Contents of the Notice

(A) Main Contents. Each notice must name the court, the title of the action, and the defendant to whom it is directed. It must describe the property sufficiently to identify it, but need not describe any property other than that to be taken from the named defendant. The notice must also state:

(i) that the action is to condemn property;

(ii) the interest to be taken;

(iii) the authority for the taking;

(iv) the uses for which the property is to be taken;

(v) that the defendant may serve an answer on the plaintiff's attorney within 21 days after being served with the notice;

(vi) that the failure to so serve an answer constitutes consent to the taking and to the court's authority to proceed with the action and fix the compensation; and

(vii) that a defendant who does not serve an answer may file a notice of appearance.

(B) Conclusion. The notice must conclude with the name, telephone number, and email address of the plaintiff's attorney and an address within the district in which the action is brought where the attorney may be served.

(3) Serving the Notice

(A) Personal Service. When a defendant whose address is known resides within the United States or a territory subject to the administrative or judicial jurisdiction of the United States, personal service of the notice (without a copy of the complaint) must be made in accordance with Rule 4.

(B) Service by Publication

(i) A defendant may be served by publication only when the plaintiff's attorney files a certificate stating that the attorney believes the defendant cannot be personally served, because after diligent inquiry within the state where the complaint is filed, the defendant's place of residence is still unknown or, if known, that it is beyond the territorial limits of personal service. Service is then made by publishing the notice — once a week for at least three successive weeks — in a newspaper published in the county where the property, is located or, if there is no such newspaper, in a newspaper with general circulation where the property is located. Before the last publication, a copy of the notice must also be mailed to every defendant who cannot be personally served but whose place of residence is then known. Unknown owners may be served by publication in the same manner by a notice addressed to "Unknown Owners."

(ii) Service by publication is complete on the date of the last publication. The plaintiff's attorney must prove publication and mailing by a certificate, attach a printed copy of the published notice, and mark on the copy the newspaper's name and the dates of publication.

(4) Effect of Delivery and Service. Delivering the notice to the clerk and serving it have the same effect as serving a summons under Rule 4.

(5) Amending the Notice; Proof of Service and Amending the Proof. Rule 4(a)(2) governs amending the notice. Rule 4(l) governs proof of service and amending it.

(e) Appearance or Answer

(1) Notice of Appearance. A defendant that has no objection or defense to the taking of its property may serve a notice of appearance designating the

property in which it claims an interest. The defendant must then be given notice of all later proceedings affecting the defendant.

(2) Answer. A defendant that has an objection or defense to the taking must serve an answer within 21 days after being served with the notice. The answer must:

(A) identify the property in which the defendant claims an interest;

(B) state the nature and extent of the interest; and

(C) state all the defendant's objections and defenses to the taking.

(3) Waiver of Other Objections and Defenses; Evidence on Compensation. A defendant waives all objections and defenses not stated in its answer. No other pleading or motion asserting an additional objection or defense is allowed. But at the trial on compensation, a defendant — whether or not it has previously appeared or answered — may present evidence on the amount of compensation to be paid and may share in the award.

(f) Amending Pleadings. Without leave of court, the plaintiff may — as often as it wants — amend the complaint at any time before the trial on compensation. But no amendment may be made if it would result in a dismissal inconsistent with Rule 71.1(i)(1) or (2). The plaintiff need not serve a copy of an amendment, but must serve notice of the filing, as provided in Rule 5(b), on every affected party who has appeared and, as provided in Rule 71.1(d), on every affected party who has not appeared. In addition, the plaintiff must give the clerk at least one copy of each amendment for the defendants' use, and additional copies at the request of the clerk or a defendant. A defendant may appear or answer in the time and manner and with the same effect as provided in Rule 71.1(e).

(g) Substituting Parties. If a defendant dies, becomes incompetent, or transfers an interest after being joined, the court may, on motion and notice of hearing, order that the proper party be substituted. Service of the motion and notice on a nonparty must be made as provided in Rule 71.1(d)(3).

(h) Trial of the Issues

(1) Issues Other Than Compensation; Compensation. In an action involving eminent domain under federal law, the court tries all issues, including compensation, except when compensation must be determined:

(A) by any tribunal specially constituted by a federal statute to determine compensation; or

(B) if there is no such tribunal, by a jury when a party demands one within the time to answer or within any additional time the court sets, unless the court appoints a commission.

(2) Appointing a Commission; Commission's Powers and Report

(A) Reasons for Appointing. If a party has demanded a jury, the court may instead appoint a three-person commission to determine compensation because of the character, location, or quantity of the property to be condemned or for other just reasons.

(B) Alternate Commissioners. The court may appoint up to two additional persons to serve as alternate commissioners to hear the case and replace commissioners who, before a decision is filed, the court finds unable or disqualified to perform their duties. Once the commission renders its final decision, the court must discharge any alternate who has not replaced a commissioner.

(C) Examining the Prospective Commissioners. Before making its appointments, the court must advise the parties of the identity and qualifications of each prospective commissioner and alternate, and may permit the parties to examine them. The parties may not suggest appointees, but for good cause may object to a prospective commissioner or alternate.

(D) Commission's Powers and Report. A commission has the powers of a master under Rule 53(c). Its action and report are determined by a majority. Rule 53(d), (e), and (f) apply to its action and report.

(i) Dismissal of the Action or a Defendant

(1) Dismissing the Action

(A) By the Plaintiff. If no compensation hearing on a piece of property has begun, and if the plaintiff has not acquired title or a lesser interest or taken possession, the plaintiff may, without a court order, dismiss the action as to that property by filing a notice of dismissal briefly describing the property.

(B) By Stipulation. Before a judgment is entered vesting the plaintiff with title or a lesser interest in or possession of property, the plaintiff and affected defendants may, without a court order, dismiss the action in whole or in part by filing a stipulation of dismissal. And if the parties so stipulate, the court may vacate a judgment already entered.

(C) By Court Order. At any time before compensation has been determined and paid, the court may, after a motion and hearing, dismiss the action as to a piece of property. But if the plaintiff has already taken title, a lesser interest, or possession as to any part of it, the court must award compensation for the title, lesser interest, or possession taken.

(2) Dismissing a Defendant. The court may at any time dismiss a defendant who was unnecessarily or improperly joined.

(3) Effect. A dismissal is without prejudice unless otherwise stated in the notice, stipulation, or court order.

(j) Deposit and Its Distribution

(1) Deposit. The plaintiff must deposit with the court any money required by law as a condition to the exercise of eminent domain and may make a deposit when allowed by statute.

(2) Distribution; Adjusting Distribution. After a deposit, the court and attorneys must expedite the proceedings so as to distribute the deposit and to determine and pay compensation. If the compensation finally awarded to a defendant

exceeds the amount distributed to that defendant, the court must enter judgment against the plaintiff for the deficiency. If the compensation awarded to a defendant is less than the amount distributed to that defendant, the court must enter judgment against that defendant for the overpayment.

(k) Condemnation Under a State's Power of Eminent Domain. This rule governs an action involving eminent domain under state law. But if state law provides for trying an issue by jury — or for trying the issue of compensation by jury or commission or both — that law governs.

(l) Costs. Costs are not subject to Rule 54(d).

Rule 72. Magistrate Judges; Pretrial Order

(a) Nondispositive Matters. When a pretrial matter not dispositive of a party's claim or defense is referred to a magistrate judge to hear and decide, the magistrate judge must promptly conduct the required proceedings and, when appropriate, issue a written order stating the decision. A party may serve and file objections to the order within 14 days after being served with a copy. A party may not assign as error a defect in the order not timely objected to. The district judge in the case must consider timely objections and modify or set aside any part of the order that is clearly erroneous or is contrary to law.

(b) Dispositive Motions and Prisoner Petitions

(1) Findings and Recommendations. A magistrate judge must promptly conduct the required proceedings when assigned, without the parties' consent, to hear a pretrial matter dispositive of a claim or defense or a prisoner petition challenging the conditions of confinement. A record must be made of all evidentiary proceedings and may, at the magistrate judge's discretion, be made of any other proceedings. The magistrate judge must enter a recommended disposition, including, if appropriate, proposed findings of fact. The clerk must promptly mail a copy to each party.

(2) Objections. Within 14 days after being served with a copy of the recommended disposition, a party may serve and file specific written objections to the proposed findings and recommendations. A party may respond to another party's objections within 14 days after being served with a copy. Unless the district judge orders otherwise, the objecting party must promptly arrange for transcribing the record, or whatever portions of it the parties agree to or the magistrate judge considers sufficient.

(3) Resolving Objections. The district judge must determine de novo any part of the magistrate judge's disposition that has been properly objected to. The district judge may accept, reject, or modify the recommended disposition; receive further evidence; or return the matter to the magistrate judge with instructions.

Rule 73. Magistrate Judges; Trial by Consent; Appeal

(a) Trial by Consent. When authorized under 28 U.S.C. § 636(c), a magistrate judge may, if all parties consent, conduct a civil action or proceeding, including a jury or nonjury trial. A record must be made in accordance with 28 U.S.C. § 636(c)(5).

(b) Consent Procedure

(1) In General. When a magistrate judge has been designated to conduct civil actions or proceedings, the clerk must give the parties written notice of their opportunity to consent under 28 U.S.C. § 636(c). To signify their consent, the parties must jointly or separately file a statement consenting to the referral. A district judge or magistrate judge may be informed of a party's response to the clerk's notice only if all parties have consented to the referral.

(2) Reminding the Parties About Consenting. A district judge, magistrate judge, or other court official may remind the parties of the magistrate judge's availability, but must also advise them that they are free to withhold consent without adverse substantive consequences.

(3) Vacating a Referral. On its own for good cause — or when a party shows extraordinary circumstances — the district judge may vacate a referral to a magistrate judge under this rule.

(c) Appealing a Judgment. In accordance with 28 U.S.C. § 636(c)(3), an appeal from a judgment entered at a magistrate judge's direction may be taken to the court of appeals as would any other appeal from a district-court judgment.

Rule 74. [Abrogated]

Rule 75. [Abrogated]

Rule 76. [Abrogated]

X. District Courts and Clerks Conducting Business; Issuing Orders

Rule 77. Conducting Business; Clerk's Authority; Notice of an Order or Judgment

(a) When Court Is Open. Every district court is considered always open for filing any paper, issuing and returning process, making a motion, or entering an order.

(b) Place for Trial and Other Proceedings. Every trial on the merits must be conducted in open court and, so far as convenient, in a regular courtroom. Any other act or proceeding may be done or conducted by a judge in chambers, without the attendance of the clerk or other court official, and anywhere inside or outside the district. But no hearing — other than one ex parte — may be conducted outside the district unless all the affected parties consent.

(c) Clerk's Office Hours; Clerk's Orders

(1) Hours. The clerk's office — with a clerk or deputy on duty — must be open during business hours every day except Saturdays, Sundays, and legal holidays. But a court may, by local rule or order, require that the office be open for specified hours on Saturday or a particular legal holiday other than one listed in Rule 6(a)(6)(A).

(2) Orders. Subject to the court's power to suspend, alter, or rescind the clerk's action for good cause, the clerk may:

(A) issue process;

(B) enter a default;

(C) enter a default judgment under Rule 55(b)(1); and

(D) act on any other matter that does not require the court's action.

(d) Serving Notice of an Order or Judgment

(1) Service. Immediately after entering an order or judgment, the clerk must serve notice of the entry, as provided in Rule 5(b), on each party who is not in default for failing to appear. The clerk must record that service on the docket. A party also may serve notice of the entry as provided in Rule 5(b).

(2) Time to Appeal Not Affected by Lack of Notice. Lack of notice of the entry does not affect the time for appeal or relieve — or authorize the court to relieve — a party for failing to appeal within the time allowed, except as allowed by Federal Rule of Appellate Procedure 4(a).

Rule 78. Hearing Motions; Submission on Briefs

(a) Providing a Regular Schedule for Oral Hearings. A court may establish regular times and places for oral hearings on motions.

(b) Providing for Submission on Briefs. By rule or order, the court may provide for submitting and determining motions on briefs, without oral hearings.

Rule 79. Records Kept by the Clerk

(a) Civil Docket

(1) In General. The clerk must keep a record known as the "civil docket" in the form and manner prescribed by the Director of the Administrative Office of the United States Courts with the approval of the Judicial Conference of the United States. The clerk must enter each civil action in the docket. Actions must be assigned consecutive file numbers, which must be noted in the docket where the first entry of the action is made.

(2) Items to be Entered. The following items must be marked with the file number and entered chronologically in the docket:

(A) papers filed with the clerk;

(B) process issued, and proofs of service or other returns showing execution; and

(C) appearances, orders, verdicts, and judgments.

(3) Contents of Entries; Jury Trial Demanded. Each entry must briefly show the nature of the paper filed or writ issued, the substance of each proof of service or other return, and the substance and date of entry of each order and judgment. When a jury trial has been properly demanded or ordered, the clerk must enter the word "jury" in the docket.

(b) Civil Judgments and Orders. The clerk must keep a copy of every final judgment and appealable order; of every order affecting title to or a lien on real or personal property; and of any other order that the court directs to be kept. The clerk must keep these in the form and manner prescribed by the Director of the Administrative Office of the United States courts with the approval of the Judicial Conference of the United States.

(c) Indexes; Calendars. Under the court's direction, the clerk must:

(1) keep indexes of the docket and of the judgments and orders described Rule 79(b); and

(2) prepare calendars of all actions ready for trial, distinguishing jury trials from nonjury trials.

(d) Other Records. The clerk must keep any other records required by the Director of the Administrative Office of the United States Courts with the approval of the Judicial Conference of the United States.

Rule 80. Stenographic Transcript as Evidence

If stenographically reported testimony at a hearing or trial is admissible in evidence at a later trial, the testimony may be proved by a transcript certified by the person who reported it.

XI. General Provisions

Rule 81. Applicability of the Rules in General; Removed Actions

(a) Applicability to Particular Proceedings

(1) Prize Proceedings. These rules do not apply to prize proceedings in admiralty governed by 10 U.S.C. §§ 7651-7681.

(2) Bankruptcy. These rules apply to bankruptcy proceedings to the extent provided by the Federal Rules of Bankruptcy Procedure.

(3) Citizenship. These rules apply to proceedings for admission to citizenship to the extent that the practice in those proceedings is not specified in federal statutes and has previously conformed to the practice in civil actions. The provisions of 8 U.S.C. § 1451 for service by publication and for answer apply in proceedings to cancel citizenship certificates.

(4) Special Writs. These rules apply to proceedings for habeas corpus and for quo warranto to the extent that the practice in those proceedings:

(A) is not specified in a federal statute, the Rules Governing Section 2254 Cases, or the Rules Governing Section 2255 Cases; and

(B) has previously conformed to the practice in civil actions.

(5) Proceedings Involving a Subpoena. These rules apply to proceedings to compel testimony or the production of documents through a subpoena issued by a United States officer or agency under a federal statute, except as otherwise provided by statute, by local rule, or by court order in the proceedings.

(6) Other Proceedings. These rules, to the extent applicable, govern proceedings under the following laws, except as these laws provide other procedures:

(A) 7 U.S.C. §§ 292, 499g(c), for reviewing an order of the Secretary of Agriculture;

(B) 9 U.S.C., relating to arbitration;

(C) U.S.C. § 522, for reviewing an order of the Secretary of the Interior;

(D) 15 U.S.C. § 715d(c), for reviewing an order denying a certificate of clearance;

(E) 29 U.S.C. §§ 159, 160, for enforcing an order of the National Labor Relations Board;

(F) 33 U.S.C. §§ 918, 921, for enforcing or reviewing a compensation order under the Longshore and Harbor Workers' Compensation Act; and

(G) 45 U.S.C. § 159, for reviewing an arbitration award in a railway-labor dispute.

(b) Scire Facias and Mandamus. The writs of scire facias and mandamus are abolished. Relief previously available through them may be obtained by appropriate action or motion under these rules.

(c) Removed Actions

(1) Applicability. These rules apply to a civil action after it is removed from a state court.

(2) Further Pleading. After removal, repleading is unnecessary unless the court orders it. A defendant who did not answer before removal must answer or present other defenses or objections under these rules within the longest of these periods:

(A) 21 days after receiving — through service or otherwise — a copy of the initial pleading stating the claim for relief;

(B) 21 days after being served with the summons for an initial pleading on file at the time of service; or

(C) 7 days after the notice of removal is filed.

(3) Demand for a Jury Trial

(A) As Affected by State Law. A party who, before removal, expressly demanded a jury trial in accordance with state law need not renew the demand after removal. If the state law did not require an express demand for a jury trial, a party need not make one after removal unless the court orders the parties to do so within a specified time. The court must so order at a party's request and may so order on its own. A party who fails to make a demand when so ordered waives a jury trial.

(B) Under Rule 38. If all necessary pleadings have been served at the time of removal, a party entitled to a jury trial under Rule 38 must be given one if the party serves a demand within 14 days after:

(i) it files a notice of removal; or

(ii) it is served with a notice of removal filed by another party.

(d) Law Applicable

(1) "State Law" Defined. When these rules refer to state law, the term "law" includes the state's statutes and the state's judicial decisions.

(2) "State" Defined. The term "state" includes, where appropriate, the District of Columbia and any United States commonwealth or territory.

(3) "Federal Statute" Defined in the District of Columbia. In the United States District Court for the District of Columbia, the term "federal statute" includes any Act of Congress that applies locally to the District.

Rule 82. Jurisdiction and Venue Unaffected

These rules do not extend or limit the jurisdiction of the district courts or the venue of actions in those courts. An admiralty or maritime claim under Rule 9(h) is governed by 28 U.S.C. § 1390.

Rule 83. Rules by District Courts; Judge's Directives

(a) Local Rules

(1) In General. After giving public notice and an opportunity for comment, a district court, acting by a majority of its district judges, may adopt and amend rules governing its practice. A local rule must be consistent with — but not duplicate — federal statutes and rules adopted under 28 U.S.C. §§ 2072 and 2075, and must conform to any uniform numbering system prescribed by the Judicial Conference of the United States. A local rule takes effect on the date specified by the district court and remains in effect unless amended by the court or abrogated by the judicial council of the circuit. Copies of rules and amendments must, on their adoption, be furnished to the judicial council and the Administrative Office of the United States Courts and be made available to the public.

(2) Requirement of Form. A local rule imposing a requirement of form must not be enforced in a way that causes a party to lose any right because of a nonwillful failure to comply.

(b) Procedure When There Is No Controlling Law. A judge may regulate practice in any manner consistent with federal law, rules adopted under 28 U.S.C. §§ 2072 and 2075, and the district's local rules. No sanction or other disadvantage may be imposed for noncompliance with any requirement not in federal law, federal rules, or the local rules unless the alleged violator has been furnished in the particular case with actual notice of the requirement.

Rule 84. [Abrogated]

Rule 85. Title

These rules may be cited as the Federal Rules of Civil Procedure.

Rule 86. Effective Dates

(a) In General.. These rules and any amendments take effect at the time specified by the Supreme Court, subject to 28 U.S.C. § 2074. They govern:

(1) proceedings in an action commenced after their effective date; and

(2) proceedings after that date in an action then pending unless:

(A) the Supreme Court specifies otherwise; or

(B) the court determines that applying them in a particular action would be infeasible or work an injustice.

(b) December 1, 2007 Amendments. If any provisions in Rules 1-5.1, 6-73, or 77-86 conflicts with another law, priority in time for the purpose of 28 U.S.C. § 2072(b) is not affected by the amendments taking effect on December 1, 2007.

Rule 87. Civil Rules Emergency

(a) Conditions for an Emergency. The Judicial Conference of the United States may declare a Civil Rules emergency if it determines that extraordinary circumstances relating to public health or safety, or affecting physical or electronic access to a court, substantially impair the court's ability to perform its functions in compliance with these rules.

(b) Declaring an Emergency

(1) Content. The declaration:

(A) must designate the court or courts affected;

(B) adopts all the emergency rules in Rule 87(c) unless it excepts one or more of them; and

(C) must be limited to a stated period of no more than 90 days.

(2) Early Termination. The Judicial Conference may terminate a declaration for one or more courts before the termination date.

(3) Additional Declarations. The Judicial Conference may issue additional declarations under this rule.

(c) Emergency Rules

(1) Emergency Rules 4(e), (h)(1), (j)(2), and for serving a minor or incompetent person. The court may by order authorize service on a defendant described in Rule 4(e), (h)(1), (i), or (j)(2) — or on a minor or incompetent person in a judicial district of the United States — by a method that is reasonably calculated to give notice. A method of service may be completed under the order after the declaration ends unless the court, after notice and an opportunity to be heard, modifies or rescinds the order.

(2) Emergency Rule 6(b)(2).

(A) Extension of Time to File Certain Motions. A court may, by order, apply Rule 6(b)(1)(A) to extend for a period of no more than 30 days after entry of the order the time to act under Rules 50(b) and (d), 52(b), 59(b), (d), and (e), and 60(b).

(B) Effect on Time to Appeal. Unless the time to appeal would otherwise be longer:

(i) if the court denies an extension, the time to file an appeal runs for all parties from the date of the order denying the motion to extend is entered;

(ii) if the court grants an extension, a motion authorized by the court and filed within the extended period is, for purposes of Appellate Rule 4(a)(4)(A), filed "within the time allowed by" the Federal Rules of Civil Procedure; and

(iii) if the court grants an extension and no motion authorized by the court is made within the extended period, the time to file an appeal runs for all parties from the expiration of the extended period.

(C) Declaration Ends. An act authorized by an order under this emergency rule may be completed under the order after the emergency declaration ends.

RECENT CASE LAW

Royal Canin U.S.A., Inc., v. Wullschleger

604 U.S. 22

KAGAN, J., delivered the opinion for a unanimous Court.

If a complaint filed in state court asserts federal-law claims, the defendant may remove the case to federal court. *See* 28 U. S. C. § 1441(a). And if the complaint also asserts state-law claims arising out of the same facts, the federal court may adjudicate those claims too, in the exercise of what is called supplemenftal jurisdiction. *See* § 1367.

This case presents a further question: What happens if, after removal, the plaintiff amends her complaint to delete all the federal-law claims, leaving nothing but state-law claims behind? May the federal court still adjudicate the now purely state-law suit? We hold that it may not. When an amendment excises the federal-law claims that enabled removal, the federal court loses its supplemental jurisdiction over the related state-law claims. The case must therefore return to state court.

I

A

"Federal courts," we have often explained, "are courts of limited jurisdiction." *E.g., Kokkonen v. Guardian Life Ins. Co. of America*, 511 U.S. 375, 377, 114 S. Ct. 1673, 128 L.Ed.2d 391 (1994). Limited first by the Constitution, to only the kinds of "Cases" and "Controversies" listed in Article III. And for all lower federal courts, limited as well by statute. Congress determines, through its grants of jurisdiction, which suits those courts can resolve. So, for example, Congress has always given federal courts power to decide "diversity" cases, between "citizens of different States" whose dispute involves more than a stated sum (the so-called amount-in-controversy). § 1332(a). And of special importance here, Congress has long conferred jurisdiction on federal courts to resolve cases "arising under" federal law. § 1331.

"Arising under" jurisdiction — more often known as federal-question jurisdiction — enables federal courts to decide cases founded on federal law. A suit most typically falls within that statutory grant "when federal law creates the cause of action asserted." *Gunn v. Minton*, 568 U.S. 251, 257, 133 S. Ct. 1059, 185

L.Ed.2d 72 (2013). On rare occasions, the grant also covers a suit containing state-law claims alone, because one or more of them "necessarily raise[s]" a "substantial" and "actually disputed" federal question. *Id.*, at 258, 133 S. Ct. 1059. Either way, the determination of jurisdiction is based only on the allegations in the plaintiff 's "well-pleaded complaint" — not on any issue the defendant may raise. *Franchise Tax Bd. of Cal. v. Construction Laborers Vacation Trust for Southern Cal.*, 463 U.S. 1, 9–10, 103 S. Ct. 2841, 77 L.Ed.2d 420 (1983). That longstanding rule makes the complaint — the plaintiff 's own claims and allegations — the key to "arising under" jurisdiction. If the complaint presents no federal question, a federal court may not hear the suit.

But if a complaint includes the requisite federal question, a federal court often has power to decide state-law questions too. Suppose a complaint with two claims — one based on federal, the other on state, law. This Court held in *Mine Workers v. Gibbs*, 383 U.S. 715, 725, 86 S. Ct. 1130, 16 L.Ed.2d 218 (1966), that a federal court may exercise supplemental jurisdiction over the state claim so long as it "derive[s] from" the same "nucleus of operative fact" as the federal one. The *Gibbs* Court reasoned that when the two claims are so closely related, they make up "but one constitutional 'case' "; and the Court presumed that Congress wanted in that situation to confer jurisdiction up to the Constitution's limit. *Ibid.* (quoting U. S. Const., Art. III, § 2, cl. 1); *see Exxon Mobil Corp. v. Allapattah Services, Inc.*, 545 U.S. 546, 553, 125 S. Ct. 2611, 162 L.Ed.2d 502 (2005). Congress later confirmed that view, generally codifying *Gibbs*'s supplemental-jurisdiction rule in 28 U.S.C. § 1367 (whose text we will soon consider). Under that statute, as under *Gibbs*, jurisdiction over a federal-law claim brings with it supplemental jurisdiction over a state-law claim arising from the same facts. That derivative jurisdiction, though, is to some extent discretionary; § 1367 spells out circumstances, again derived from *Gibbs*, in which a federal court may decline to hear a state claim falling within the statute's bounds. *See* § 1367(c); *Gibbs*, 383 U.S. at 726–727, 86 S. Ct. 1130.

And yet one more preparatory point: If a statute confers federal jurisdiction over a suit, not only the plaintiff but also the defendant can get it into federal court. Take the "arising under" statute: It grants federal district courts "original jurisdiction" over cases presenting a federal question. § 1331; *see* § 1332 (similarly providing "original jurisdiction" over diversity suits). The plaintiff may avail herself of that jurisdiction (and of the opportunity § 1367 affords to add supplemental state claims); but she also may file her suit in state court. If she takes the latter route, another statute then gives the defendant an option. Because the case falls within the federal courts' "original jurisdiction," the defendant may "remove[]" it from state to federal court. § 1441(a). And there the case (including supplemental state claims) usually remains. Except that "[i]f at any time before final judgment it appears that the district court lacks subject matter jurisdiction," the case must be "remanded" to state court. § 1447(c). That is because, to return to where we started, federal courts are courts of limited jurisdiction: When they do not have (or no longer have) authorization to resolve a suit, they must hand it over.

B

Before raising issues demanding a jurisdictional primer, this case was all about the marketing of dog food. Petitioner Royal Canin U. S. A., Inc., manufactures a brand of dog food available only with a veterinarian's prescription — and thus sold at a premium price. Respondent Anastasia Wullschleger purchased the food, thinking it contained medication not found in off-the-shelf products. She later learned it did not. Her suit, initially filed in a Missouri state court, contends that Royal Canin's dog food is ordinary dog food: The company sells the product with a prescription not because its ingredients make that necessary, but solely to fool consumers into paying a jacked-up price. Her original complaint asserted claims under the Missouri Merchandising Practices Act and state antitrust law. It also alleged violations of the Federal Food, Drug, and Cosmetic Act (FDCA), 21 U. S. C. § 301 et seq.

And so began the procedural back-and-forth that eventually landed Wullschleger's case in this Court. Royal Canin went first: It removed the case to federal court based on the asserted violations of the FDCA.[1] That removal properly brought to the District Court not only Wullschleger's FDCA claims, but also her factually intertwined state-law claims. The parties were thus set to litigate the entire suit in federal court. But that is not where Wullschleger wanted the case to be resolved. So she countered Royal Canin's move: She amended her complaint to delete its every mention of the FDCA, leaving her state claims to stand on their own. And with that amended, all-state-law complaint in hand, she petitioned the District Court to remand the case to state court.

Although the District Court denied Wullschleger's request, the Court of Appeals for the Eighth Circuit reversed that decision and ordered a remand. *See* 75 F.4th 918, 924 (CA8 2023). . . . In the Eighth Circuit's view, Wullschleger's amendment had eliminated any basis for federal jurisdiction. An amended complaint, the court reasoned, "[supersedes] an original complaint and renders the original complaint without legal effect." *Id.*, at 922 (alteration in original). And nothing in the amended complaint supported federal-question jurisdiction: It was, after all, now based entirely on state law. Nor could the District Court now exercise supplemental jurisdiction over Wullschleger's state-law claims. "[T]he

---

1. That first step provoked an earlier jurisdictional battle, resolved in favor of allowing removal and not at issue here. The dispute arose because Wullschleger's complaint alleged the FDCA violations not as independent federal claims, but instead in support of her state claims. Did the complaint, then, contain the needed federal question? The Court of Appeals held that it did because the meaning of the referenced FDCA provisions was thoroughly embedded in, and integral to the success of, Wullschleger's state-law claims. *See Wullschleger v. Royal Canin U. S. A., Inc.*, 953 F.3d 519, 522 (CA8 2020) (*citing Gunn v. Minton*, 568 U.S. 251, 258, 133 S. Ct. 1059, 185 L.Ed.2d 72 (2013)). We here treat that finding of federal-question jurisdiction as a given. And for ease of exposition, we take a slight liberty throughout this opinion, referring to the original complaint's FDCA allegations simply as federal claims.

possibility of supplemental jurisdiction," the court reasoned, "vanished right alongside the once-present federal questions." *Id.*, at 924. And that analysis held good even though it was Royal Canin, rather than Wullschleger, that had brought the suit to the District Court: "It makes no difference," the Eighth Circuit stated, that the case "end[ed] up in federal court through removal." *Id.*, at 922.

Other Courts of Appeals have reached the opposite conclusion, holding that a post-removal amendment cannot divest a federal court of jurisdiction. . . . On that view, "[t]he existence of subject matter jurisdiction is determined by examining the complaint as it existed at the time of removal." *Harper v. AutoAlliance Int'l, Inc.*, 392 F.3d 195, 210 (CA6 2004). So the District Court here would have retained supplemental jurisdiction over Wullschleger's state-law claims even after she amended her complaint to delete all her federal-law ones.

We granted certiorari to resolve the Circuit split, 601 U. S. ——, 144 S. Ct. 1455, 218 L.Ed.2d 688 (2024), and we now affirm the decision below.

II

When a plaintiff amends her complaint following her suit's removal, a federal court's jurisdiction depends on what the new complaint says. If (as here) the plaintiff eliminates the federal-law claims that enabled removal, leaving only state-law claims behind, the court's power to decide the dispute dissolves. With the loss of federal-question jurisdiction, the court loses as well its supplemental jurisdiction over the state claims. That conclusion fits the text of § 1367, governing supplemental jurisdiction. And it accords with a bevy of rules hinging federal jurisdiction on the allegations made in an amended complaint, because that complaint has become the operative one. Royal Canin argues that our precedent makes an exception for when an amendment follows a lawsuit's removal, but that is to read two bits of gratuitous language for a good deal more than they are worth.

A

Begin with § 1367, entitled "Supplemental jurisdiction." Subsection (a) states the basic rule:

> "Except as provided in subsections (b) and (c) or as expressly provided otherwise by Federal statute, in any civil action of which the district courts have original jurisdiction, the district courts shall have supplemental jurisdiction over all other claims that are so related to claims in the action within such original jurisdiction that they form part of the same case or controversy under Article III of the United States Constitution."

The subsection thus takes as its starting point claims within a federal district court's original jurisdiction — because, say, they turn on federal law. *See* § 1331. It then confers authority on the court to decide certain "other" claims in the same suit, involving only state law. That added authority — the court's supplemental jurisdiction — extends to claims "so related to" the claims supporting original jurisdiction as to form "part of the same [constitutional] case." And that needed relationship, *Gibbs* explains, is one of fact: The federal court has supplemental jurisdiction over state-law claims sharing a "common nucleus of operative fact" with the federal-law ones. 383 U.S. at 725, 86 S. Ct. 1130.

Skip down a bit and subsection (c) explains that the supplemental jurisdiction just conferred is in some measure discretionary. That subsection provides that a district court "may decline to exercise supplemental jurisdiction" in three specific situations: (1) if the supplemental claim "raises a novel or complex issue of State law"; (2) if the supplemental claim "substantially predominates" over the claims within the court's original jurisdiction; and (3) if the district court "has dismissed all claims over which it has original jurisdiction."[4] In all those contexts, federal law is not where the real action is. So although supplemental jurisdiction persists, the district court need not exercise it: Instead, the court may (and indeed, ordinarily should) kick the case to state court. *See Gibbs*, 383 U.S. at 726–727, 86 S. Ct. 1130.

In addressing the text of § 1367, Royal Canin argues primarily from the first subsection's grant of jurisdiction. The language there is "broad," the company says: Section 1367(a) grants "supplemental jurisdiction over 'all other claims' within the case or controversy, unless Congress 'expressly provided otherwise.'" Reply Brief 2 (emphasis in original). And Congress did not expressly provide that an amendment deleting federal claims eliminates supplemental jurisdiction. *See id.*, at 4–5. The upshot, Royal Canin says, is the rule it espouses: The amendment of a complaint following removal of a suit to federal court cannot divest that court of supplemental jurisdiction.

But that position founders on an undisputed point: Nothing in § 1367's text — including in the text Royal Canin highlights — distinguishes between cases removed to federal court and cases originally filed there. *See* Tr. of Oral Arg. 7–8. Whatever that text says about removed cases, it also says about original ones, and vice versa. That means if (as Royal Canin urges) § 1367(a)'s language prevents an amendment from ousting supplemental jurisdiction in removed cases, then so too it does in original ones. But here is the rub: In original cases, this Court has already reached the opposite conclusion. The pertinent rule comes from *Rockwell Int'l Corp. v. United States*, 549 U.S. 457, 473–474, 127 S. Ct. 1397, 167 L.Ed.2d 190 (2007): "[W]hen a plaintiff files a complaint in federal court and then voluntarily amends the complaint, courts look to the amended complaint to determine jurisdiction." So when the plaintiff in an original case amends her complaint to withdraw the federal claims, leaving only state claims behind, she divests the

4. A fourth, more general provision, which neither party thinks relevant here, allows a court to decline supplemental jurisdiction "in exceptional circumstances," for "other compelling reasons." 28 U. S. C. § 1367(c)(4).

federal court of adjudicatory power. *See ibid.* Royal Canin concedes that result, as it must. *See* Tr. of Oral Arg. 6–7. The position it adopts — applying only in removed cases — is indeed designed not to collide with *Rockwell*'s ruling. But once § 1367(a) is taken as consistent with *Rockwell*, it cannot say what the company posits. Under that provision — as under *Rockwell* — an amendment excising all federal claims divests a court of supplemental jurisdiction over the remaining state claims in an original case. And if in an original case, then also in a removed case — because, again, § 1367(a) draws no distinction between the two.

The exclusion from § 1367(a) of such post-amendment state-law claims is reflected in the text of § 1367(c). Recall that § 1367(c) describes three contexts in which state-law claims, though covered by § 1367(a)'s jurisdictional grant, are often better given to state courts. If § 1367(a)'s grant included the leftover state claims in an amended complaint, they too would have appeared on § 1367(c)'s list: Even more than the claims addressed there, they are ill-suited to federal adjudication. The leftover state claims, after all, are now the entirety of the plaintiff's suit. Federal claims are not just subordinate, as in §§ 1367(c)(1) and (2), but gone. And gone for good as well. When federal claims are dismissed by the district court, as in § 1367(c)(3), an appellate court may yet revive them; but that cannot happen when the plaintiff has excised them through a proper amendment. So, again, it follows: If § 1367(a) conferred supplemental jurisdiction over the claims here, § 1367(c) would make that jurisdiction discretionary. That § 1367(c) does not do so — that even while it addresses, for example, dismissals of federal claims, it makes no mention of amendments deleting them — shows that § 1367(a) does not extend so far. Or otherwise said, there is no discretion to decline supplemental jurisdiction here because there is no supplemental jurisdiction at all. Once the plaintiff has ditched all claims involving federal questions, the leftover state claims are supplemental to nothing — and § 1367(a) does not authorize a federal court to resolve them.

That result accords with Congress's usual view of how amended pleadings can affect jurisdiction. On that view, apparent in varied federal statutes, an amendment can wipe the jurisdictional slate clean, giving rise to a new analysis with a different conclusion. Consider 28 U. S. C. § 1653: It states broadly that, in both trial and appellate courts, "[d]efective allegations of jurisdiction may be amended" to ensure that a case can go forward. So a case falling outside the federal court's jurisdiction can come within it by virtue of an amendment. Or take the statute laying out procedures for removal. It provides that even "if the case stated by the initial pleading is not removable," an amendment may make it so: The defendant can remove the case after receiving "an amended pleading" establishing that the case is newly subject to federal jurisdiction. § 1446(b)(3); *see* § 1332(d)(7) (similarly providing that an "amended complaint" in a proposed class action may create "[f]ederal jurisdiction"). In such statutes, Congress conceives of amendments as having the potential to alter jurisdiction. And just the same here. Section 1367 contemplates that when an amended complaint is filed, the jurisdictional basis for the suit is reviewed anew. If nothing in the amended complaint now falls "within [the federal court's] original jurisdiction," then neither does anything fall within the court's "supplemental jurisdiction." § 1367(a). In the superseding pleading, the state-law claims are just state-law claims, outside § 1367(a)'s purview.

B

That reading of § 1367 also parallels a slew of other, mainly judge-made procedural rules linking jurisdiction to the amended, rather than initial, complaint. In multiple contexts — involving both cases brought in federal court and cases removed there — courts conceive of amendments to pleadings as potentially jurisdiction-changing events. The amended complaint becomes the operative one; and in taking the place of what has come before, it can either create or destroy jurisdiction. Section 1367, as laid out above, fits hand in glove with — indeed, embodies — that familiar approach. A post-removal amendment can divest a federal court of its supplemental jurisdiction because — as the usual procedural principle holds — jurisdiction follows from (and only from) the operative pleading.

Begin from the beginning: The plaintiff is "the master of the complaint," and therefore controls much about her suit. *Caterpillar Inc. v. Williams*, 482 U.S. 386, 398–399, 107 S. Ct. 2425, 96 L.Ed.2d 318 (1987). She gets to determine which substantive claims to bring against which defendants. And in so doing, she can establish — or not — the basis for a federal court's subject-matter jurisdiction. She may, for example, name only defendants who come from a different State, or instead add one from her own State and thereby destroy diversity of citizenship. *See* § 1332(a). Or in cases like this one, she may decide to plead federal-law claims, or instead to allege state-law claims alone and thus ensure a state forum. *See* § 1331; *supra*, at —— (describing the well-pleaded complaint rule).

And the plaintiff 's control over those matters extends beyond the time her first complaint is filed. If a plaintiff amends her complaint, the new pleading "supersedes" the old one: The "original pleading no longer performs any function in the case." 6 C. Wright, A. Miller, & M. Kane, Federal Practice and Procedure § 1476, pp. 636–637 (3d ed. 2010). Or as we put the matter over a century ago: "When a petition is amended," the "cause proceeds on the amended petition." *Washer v. Bullitt County*, 110 U.S. 558, 562, 4 S. Ct. 249, 28 L.Ed. 249 (1884). So changes in parties, or changes in claims, effectively remake the suit. And that includes its jurisdictional basis: The reconfiguration accomplished by an amendment may bring the suit either newly within or newly outside a federal court's jurisdiction.

That idea is the one *Rockwell* invoked, as earlier noted. Recall the situation there considered: "[A] plaintiff files a complaint in federal court and later voluntarily amends the complaint" to "withdraw[]" the allegations supporting federal jurisdiction. *Rockwell*, 549 U.S. at 473–474, 127 S. Ct. 1397. Should the suit proceed? "[C]ourts," *Rockwell* replied, "look to the amended complaint to determine jurisdiction." *Id.*, at 474, 127 S. Ct. 1397. That complaint is now the operative one; the old complaint has become irrelevant. So unless the withdrawn allegations were "replaced by others" giving the court adjudicatory power, the plaintiff 's amendment "will defeat jurisdiction." *Id.*, at 473, 127 S. Ct. 1397. Or more specifically: If a plaintiff files a suit in federal court based on federal claims and later scraps those claims, the federal court cannot go forward with a now all-state-claim suit. *See id.*, at 473–474, 127 S. Ct. 1397.[5]

That rule for original federal cases has a host of variations, each tying jurisdiction to an amended pleading. If, as *Rockwell* spelled out, eliminating federal claims in such a suit can destroy federal jurisdiction, the opposite is also true: Adding federal claims can create federal jurisdiction where it once was wanting. *See, e.g., ConnectU LLC v. Zuckerberg*, 522 F.3d 82, 91 (CA1 2008) (holding that an amended complaint, which "replaced the original complaint lock, stock, and barrel," conferred jurisdiction). And so too, an amendment can either destroy or create jurisdiction in an original diversity case. The addition of a non-diverse party in such a case typically destroys diversity jurisdiction, requiring the case's dismissal. *See Owen Equipment & Erection Co. v. Kroger*, 437 U.S. 365, 374–377, 98 S. Ct. 2396, 57 L.Ed.2d 274 (1978) (stating that an amendment asserting claims against a non-diverse party "destroy[s]" complete diversity "just as surely as" joining that party in the first instance); *see also, e.g., American Fiber & Finishing, Inc. v. Tyco Healthcare Group, LP*, 362 F.3d 136, 139 (CA1 2004). . . . Conversely, the elimination of a non-diverse defendant by way of amendment ensures that a case can proceed in federal court, though it could not have done so before. *See Newman-Green, Inc. v. Alfonzo-Larrain*, 490 U.S. 826, 832–833, 109 S. Ct. 2218, 104 L.Ed.2d 893 (1989). In short, the rule in original cases that jurisdiction follows the amended (i.e., now operative) pleading applies across the board.

And still more: Similar rules have long applied in the removal context. Not across the board, of course, else this case would not have arisen: The very issue here is whether, in a removed case (as in an original one), an amended complaint dropping federal claims destroys jurisdiction. But in two of the other situations discussed above, the rule in removed cases is the same as the rule in original ones. . . . First, in removed cases too, amending a complaint to add a federal claim creates federal jurisdiction when it did not previously exist. So

---

5. The *Rockwell* Court distinguished its rule from another, operating in diversity cases, which evaluates a party's citizenship (e.g., whether the defendant is in fact from New York) at the time a suit is brought, and never again later. *See* 549 U.S. at 473, 127 S. Ct. 1397 (*citing, e.g., Anderson v. Watt*, 138 U.S. 694, 701, 11 S. Ct. 449, 34 L.Ed. 1078 (1891)). That so-called time-of-filing rule, *Rockwell* explained, concerns only the actual "state of things" relevant to jurisdiction — meaning, the facts on the ground, rather than (as addressed here) the claims and parties that the plaintiff includes in a complaint. 549 U.S. at 473, 127 S. Ct. 1397; *see* 75 F.4th 918, 922–923 (CA8 2023) (case below) (discussing that distinction).

even if removing a case was improper because the initial complaint did not contain a federal claim, the plaintiff 's later assertion of such a claim establishes jurisdiction going forward. *See Pegram v. Herdrich*, 530 U.S. 211, 215–216, and n. 2, 120 S. Ct. 2143, 147 L.Ed.2d 164 (2000); *Bernstein v. Lind-Waldock & Co.*, 738 F.2d 179, 185–186 (CA7 1984) (Posner, J.). The federal court can thus resolve both the newly added federal-law claim and the now supplemental state-law ones. *See id.*, at 186–187. And second, in removed cases too, amending a complaint to join a non-diverse party destroys diversity jurisdiction. So if such a joinder occurs after removal, the federal court must remand the case to the state court it began in. *See* § 1447(e); *Powerex Corp. v. Reliant Energy Services, Inc.*, 551 U.S. 224, 231–232, 127 S. Ct. 2411, 168 L.Ed.2d 112 (2007). Once again, federal jurisdiction — or its absence — follows from the amended complaint.[8]

The uniformity of that principle, as between original and removed cases, is not surprising. The appropriateness of federal jurisdiction — or the lack thereof — does not depend on whether the plaintiff first filed suit in federal or state court. Rather, it depends, in either event, on the substance of the suit — the legal basis of the claims (federal or state?) and the citizenship of the parties (diverse or not?). (That focus on substance is indeed why original jurisdiction and removal jurisdiction generally mirror each other in scope. *See* § 1441(a).) So in a removed no less than in an original case, the rule that jurisdiction follows the operative pleading serves a critical function. It too ensures that the case, as it will actually be litigated, merits a federal forum.

And with all that recognized, the answer to the disputed question here becomes yet more certain: On top of § 1367, a panoply of procedural rules shows that a post-removal amendment excising all federal claims destroys federal jurisdiction. Under those rules, the presence of jurisdiction, in removed as

8. Royal Canin offers up something of an exception: In both original and removed cases, an amendment reducing the alleged amount-in-controversy to below the statutory threshold — like a post-filing development that makes recovering the needed amount impossible — will usually not destroy diversity jurisdiction. *See St. Paul Mercury Indemnity Co. v. Red Cab Co.*, 303 U.S. 283, 289, 292, 58 S. Ct. 586, 82 L.Ed. 845 (1938); Brief for Petitioners 20. But that rule is inapposite here, by virtue of its subject and function alike. First, the rule more concerns a fact on the ground — that is, the value of a suit — than it does the plaintiff 's selection of claims and parties. So this Court has viewed it as analogous to the time-of-filing rule applying to citizenship, which also assesses a factual issue relevant to jurisdiction only at the suit's outset. *See St. Paul Mercury*, 303 U.S. at 294–295, 58 S. Ct. 586; *Rosado v. Wyman*, 397 U.S. 397, 405, n. 6, 90 S. Ct. 1207, 25 L.Ed.2d 442 (1970); *supra*, at ——, n. 5. Second, the rule responds to the difficulties of assessing a suit's value and the likelihood that the calculation will change over the course of litigation. Especially given that the alleged amount-in-controversy does not cap damages, "constant litigation" over the matter, having the potential to alter a court's jurisdiction, "would be wasteful." *Grupo Dataflux v. Atlas Global Group, L. P.*, 541 U.S. 567, 580–581, 124 S. Ct. 1920, 158 L.Ed.2d 866 (2004) (making the same point about changes in citizenship). But as all the examples given above show, we have never held such a concern to limit the effect of the plaintiff 's decision, as the master of her complaint, to add or subtract claims or parties.

in original cases, hinges on the amended, now operative pleading. By adding or subtracting claims or parties, and thus reframing the suit, that pleading can alter a federal court's authority. And so it is here. When a plaintiff, after removal, cuts out all her federal-law claims, federal-question jurisdiction dissolves. And with any federal anchor gone, supplemental jurisdiction over the residual state claims disappears as well. The operative pleading no longer supports federal jurisdiction, and the federal court must remand the case to the state court where it started.

C

Royal Canin contends that this Court has twice before reached the opposite conclusion — first, in *Carnegie-Mellon Univ. v. Cohill*, 484 U.S. 343, 108 S. Ct. 614, 98 L.Ed.2d 720 (1988), and next in *Rockwell*, in a footnote to the analysis we have related above. But in each case, the relied-on passage is extraneous to the Court's holding and reasoning, and so cannot bear the weight of Royal Canin's argument.

Begin with *Cohill*, which shares the procedural posture of this case but asked and answered a different question. There, as here, the plaintiff filed a suit in state court, asserting both federal and state claims; the defendant removed the suit to federal court; and the plaintiff then dropped her federal claim and sought a remand. The District Court granted that request over the defendant's objection. But in opposing that ruling, the defendant did not argue (à la Royal Canin) that the court should have held on to the case. Rather, the defendant urged that the court should have dismissed the case outright instead of remanding it. (The difference mattered because the statute of limitations had by then expired, and a dismissal would have ended the suit.) The disputed issue was thus not about keeping the case in federal court, but about two different ways of expelling it. Or as *Cohill* put it: The question "present[ed] is whether the District Court could relinquish jurisdiction over the case only by dismissing it without prejudice or whether the District Court could relinquish jurisdiction over the case by remanding it to state court as well." 484 U.S. at 351, 108 S. Ct. 614. We held that the federal court could remand as well as dismiss, even though no statute then authorized the former action. *Id.*, at 357, 108 S. Ct. 614; *see* § 1447(c) (now filling that vacuum). Our reasoning, in that pre-§ 1367 era, focused on the values served by supplemental jurisdiction, as set out in *Gibbs*. "[E]conomy, convenience, fairness, and comity," we stated, "support[] giving a district court discretion to remand when the exercise of [supplemental] jurisdiction is inappropriate." *Cohill*, 484 U.S. at 351, 108 S. Ct. 614. So when a plaintiff cuts her federal claims, the court should have a choice about how best to get rid of the case.

In one spot, though, the *Cohill* Court intimated a view on whether the District Court also had discretion to retain the suit. The sentence, pressed by Royal Canin, comes just before the Court's statement of the question presented, quoted above. *See* Brief for Petitioners 10–11, 19. It reads: "When the single federal-law claim in the action was eliminated at an early stage of the litigation, the District Court had a powerful reason to choose not to continue to exercise jurisdiction." *Cohill*, 484 U.S. at 351, 108 S. Ct. 614. In using the word "choose," *Cohill* suggested that the court, though having strong cause to dismiss or remand, likewise had authority to decide the case.

But that slender (and somewhat backhanded) dictum cannot make us stop in our tracks. Nowhere did *Cohill* analyze why a federal court could retain jurisdiction once an amendment excised all federal-law claims. *Cohill* simply supposed the court could and asserted as much, without pausing to consider the matter. And that lack of scrutiny reflected the issue's lack of importance — not in today's case of course, but in that earlier one. As just explained, the District Court in *Cohill* never thought to exercise jurisdiction after the amendment; the issue in dispute was only how to get rid of the action. So *Cohill*'s view about keeping jurisdiction was gratuitous, and no sooner noted than dropped. It supported neither the decision's result nor its values-based reasoning. And anyway, our own analysis is based mainly on legal authorities post-dating *Cohill* — most notably, § 1367 and our *Rockwell* decision. Those later materials supersede whatever *Cohill* presumed about exercising federal jurisdiction in a case like this one. So by virtue of both what it decided and when it arose, *Cohill* does not matter to the question before us.

That leaves the *Rockwell* footnote Royal Canin cites. As earlier explained, the body of *Rockwell* examines what happens in an original case when a plaintiff amends a complaint to expunge federal claims. The federal court, *Rockwell* held, loses jurisdiction. *See* 549 U.S. at 473–474, 127 S. Ct. 1397. But in a two-sentence footnote, the *Rockwell* Court said that the opposite rule applies in removed cases. "[W]hen a defendant removes a case to federal court based on the presence of a federal claim," the footnote stated, "an amendment eliminating the original basis for federal jurisdiction generally does not defeat jurisdiction." *Id.*, at 474, n. 6, 127 S. Ct. 1397. That is because "removal cases raise forum-manipulation concerns that simply do not exist when it is the plaintiff who chooses a federal forum and then pleads away jurisdiction through amendment." *Ibid.* (emphasis in original). The footnote thus sets out exactly the rule Royal Canin wants — and, in so doing, gives the company its best argument.

But still, the footnote is dictum, and does not control the outcome here. *Rockwell* was an original federal case, not a removed one. So the footnote's assertion of a special rule for removed cases was outside the issue being decided — or more colloquially put, beside the point. The statement had no bearing on the Court's conclusion about jurisdiction in original cases. Nor did it relate to the rationale supporting that result. And to top it off, the footnote was itself barely reasoned.[9] This Court has often stated that "drive-by jurisdictional rulings" — asserting or denying jurisdiction "without elaboration," or analysis of whether anything "turn[ed] on" the ruling — should be accorded "no precedential effect." *Wilkins v. United States*, 598 U.S. 152, 160, 143 S. Ct. 870, 215 L.Ed.2d 116 (2023) (*quoting Arbaugh v. Y & H Corp.*, 546 U.S. 500, 511, 512, 126 S. Ct. 1235, 163 L.Ed.2d 1097 (2006); alteration in original; *Henderson v. Shinseki*, 562 U.S. 428, 437, 131 S. Ct. 1197, 179 L.Ed.2d 159 (2011)). The admonition goes double for throwaway footnotes about jurisdictional issues neither raised in nor conceivably relevant to a case. We therefore need not follow the *Rockwell* footnote just because it exists; our adherence instead depends on whether it withstands analysis.[10]

And it does not, for all the reasons already given. A recap here fittingly begins with *Rockwell*'s own core insight, which points the opposite way. Federal courts, *Rockwell* stated, "look to the amended complaint to determine jurisdiction." 549 U.S. at 474, 127 S. Ct. 1397. That rule, as earlier described, explains a host of jurisdictional outcomes. It operates in federal-question cases and diversity cases, both to destroy and to create jurisdiction. And it cannot give way, in a case like this one, just because the case was removed from state to federal court. When, as here, a complaint asserts both federal and state claims, and an amendment strips out the federal ones, a district court's jurisdiction depends on § 1367. And § 1367, as earlier shown, makes no distinction between cases beginning in federal court and cases removed there. If in the former the amendment "defeat[s] jurisdiction," as *Rockwell* rightly held, 549 U.S. at 473, 127 S. Ct. 1397, then so too in the latter. Regardless of removal, the plaintiff 's excision of her federal-law claims deprives the district court of its authority to decide the state-law claims remaining.

---

9. The footnote's cursory reference to "forum-manipulation concerns" fails on multiple levels. First, and most practically, plaintiffs can usually forum shop without any resort to amendments. Except when a statute of limitations has expired, a plaintiff need only voluntarily dismiss her federal suit and file a new state-claim-only action in state court. So the forum-manipulation benefit of the *Rockwell* footnote's approach to removed federal-question cases is likely quite marginal. Second, that approach conflicts with the one taken in the most comparable situation: when in a removed diversity case, a plaintiff seeks a remand to state court by means of adding a non-diverse party. As noted earlier, the rule in that context is the standard one: Jurisdiction follows the amended pleading — regardless of any (probably minor) forum-manipulation concerns. *See* § 1447(e); supra, at ——. Third and most important, those policy-based concerns, even if significant, cannot trump a federal statute. And as we elsewhere discuss — including in the next paragraph — § 1367 offers no basis for treating original and removed cases differently, as the *Rockwell* footnote proposes. *See supra*, at —— - ——.

10. It is of course a much different thing for this Court to reach that conclusion than for a lower court to do so. We do not at all fault any court that relied on the *Rockwell* footnote to find jurisdiction in a case like this one. Courts that did so simply took us at our word, in a way both understandable and appropriate.

III

For those reasons, the District Court here should have remanded Wullschleger's suit to state court. The earliest version of that suit contained federal-law claims and therefore was properly removed to federal court. The additional state-law claims were sufficiently related to the federal ones to come within that court's supplemental jurisdiction. But when Wullschleger amended her complaint, the jurisdictional analysis also changed. Her deletion of all federal claims deprived the District Court of federal-question jurisdiction. And once that was gone, the court's supplemental jurisdiction over the state claims dissolved too. Wullschleger had reconfigured her suit to make it only about state law. And so the suit became one for a state court.

We accordingly affirm the judgment of the Court of Appeals for the Eighth Circuit.

It is so ordered.

USCOURTS.GOV
FORMS AND STATISTICS

JS 44 (Rev. 03/24)

CIVIL COVER SHEET

The JS 44 civil cover sheet and the information contained herein neither replace nor supplement the filing and service of pleadings or other papers as required by law, except as provided by local rules of court. This form, approved by the Judicial Conference of the United States in September 1974, is required for the use of the Clerk of Court for the purpose of initiating the civil docket sheet. *(SEE INSTRUCTIONS ON NEXT PAGE OF THIS FORM.)*

I. (a) PLAINTIFFS	DEFENDANTS
(b) County of Residence of First Listed Plaintiff ______ *(EXCEPT IN U.S. PLAINTIFF CASES)*	County of Residence of First Listed Defendant ______ *(IN U.S. PLAINTIFF CASES ONLY)* NOTE: IN LAND CONDEMNATION CASES, USE THE LOCATION OF THE TRACT OF LAND INVOLVED.
(c) Attorneys *(Firm Name, Address, and Telephone Number)*	Attorneys *(If Known)*

II. BASIS OF JURISDICTION *(Place an "X" in One Box Only)*

☐ 1 U.S. Government Plaintiff
☐ 3 Federal Question *(U.S. Government Not a Party)*
☐ 2 U.S. Government Defendant
☐ 4 Diversity *(Indicate Citizenship of Parties in Item III)*

III. CITIZENSHIP OF PRINCIPAL PARTIES *(Place an "X" in One Box for Plaintiff and One Box for Defendant)*
(For Diversity Cases Only)

	PTF	DEF		PTF	DEF
Citizen of This State	☐ 1	☐ 1	Incorporated *or* Principal Place of Business In This State	☐ 4	☐ 4
Citizen of Another State	☐ 2	☐ 2	Incorporated *and* Principal Place of Business In Another State	☐ 5	☐ 5
Citizen or Subject of a Foreign Country	☐ 3	☐ 3	Foreign Nation	☐ 6	☐ 6

IV. NATURE OF SUIT *(Place an "X" in One Box Only)* Click here for: Nature of Suit Code Descriptions.

CONTRACT
☐ 110 Insurance
☐ 120 Marine
☐ 130 Miller Act
☐ 140 Negotiable Instrument
☐ 150 Recovery of Overpayment & Enforcement of Judgment
☐ 151 Medicare Act
☐ 152 Recovery of Defaulted Student Loans (Excludes Veterans)
☐ 153 Recovery of Overpayment of Veteran's Benefits
☐ 160 Stockholders' Suits
☐ 190 Other Contract
☐ 195 Contract Product Liability
☐ 196 Franchise

REAL PROPERTY
☐ 210 Land Condemnation
☐ 220 Foreclosure
☐ 230 Rent Lease & Ejectment
☐ 240 Torts to Land
☐ 245 Tort Product Liability
☐ 290 All Other Real Property

TORTS

PERSONAL INJURY
☐ 310 Airplane
☐ 315 Airplane Product Liability
☐ 320 Assault, Libel & Slander
☐ 330 Federal Employers' Liability
☐ 340 Marine
☐ 345 Marine Product Liability
☐ 350 Motor Vehicle
☐ 355 Motor Vehicle Product Liability
☐ 360 Other Personal Injury
☐ 362 Personal Injury - Medical Malpractice

PERSONAL INJURY
☐ 365 Personal Injury - Product Liability
☐ 367 Health Care/ Pharmaceutical Personal Injury Product Liability
☐ 368 Asbestos Personal Injury Product Liability

PERSONAL PROPERTY
☐ 370 Other Fraud
☐ 371 Truth in Lending
☐ 380 Other Personal Property Damage
☐ 385 Property Damage Product Liability

CIVIL RIGHTS
☐ 440 Other Civil Rights
☐ 441 Voting
☐ 442 Employment
☐ 443 Housing/ Accommodations
☐ 445 Amer. w/Disabilities - Employment
☐ 446 Amer. w/Disabilities - Other
☐ 448 Education

PRISONER PETITIONS
Habeas Corpus:
☐ 463 Alien Detainee
☐ 510 Motions to Vacate Sentence
☐ 530 General
☐ 535 Death Penalty
Other:
☐ 540 Mandamus & Other
☐ 550 Civil Rights
☐ 555 Prison Condition
☐ 560 Civil Detainee - Conditions of Confinement

FORFEITURE/PENALTY
☐ 625 Drug Related Seizure of Property 21 USC 881
☐ 690 Other

LABOR
☐ 710 Fair Labor Standards Act
☐ 720 Labor/Management Relations
☐ 740 Railway Labor Act
☐ 751 Family and Medical Leave Act
☐ 790 Other Labor Litigation
☐ 791 Employee Retirement Income Security Act

IMMIGRATION
☐ 462 Naturalization Application
☐ 465 Other Immigration Actions

BANKRUPTCY
☐ 422 Appeal 28 USC 158
☐ 423 Withdrawal 28 USC 157

INTELLECTUAL PROPERTY RIGHTS
☐ 820 Copyrights
☐ 830 Patent
☐ 835 Patent - Abbreviated New Drug Application
☐ 840 Trademark
☐ 880 Defend Trade Secrets Act of 2016

SOCIAL SECURITY
☐ 861 HIA (1395ff)
☐ 862 Black Lung (923)
☐ 863 DIWC/DIWW (405(g))
☐ 864 SSID Title XVI
☐ 865 RSI (405(g))

FEDERAL TAX SUITS
☐ 870 Taxes (U.S. Plaintiff or Defendant)
☐ 871 IRS—Third Party 26 USC 7609

OTHER STATUTES
☐ 375 False Claims Act
☐ 376 Qui Tam (31 USC 3729(a))
☐ 400 State Reapportionment
☐ 410 Antitrust
☐ 430 Banks and Banking
☐ 450 Commerce
☐ 460 Deportation
☐ 470 Racketeer Influenced and Corrupt Organizations
☐ 480 Consumer Credit (15 USC 1681 or 1692)
☐ 485 Telephone Consumer Protection Act
☐ 490 Cable/Sat TV
☐ 850 Securities/Commodities/ Exchange
☐ 890 Other Statutory Actions
☐ 891 Agricultural Acts
☐ 893 Environmental Matters
☐ 895 Freedom of Information Act
☐ 896 Arbitration
☐ 899 Administrative Procedure Act/Review or Appeal of Agency Decision
☐ 950 Constitutionality of State Statutes

V. ORIGIN *(Place an "X" in One Box Only)*

☐ 1 Original Proceeding ☐ 2 Removed from State Court ☐ 3 Remanded from Appellate Court ☐ 4 Reinstated or Reopened ☐ 5 Transferred from Another District *(specify)* ☐ 6 Multidistrict Litigation - Transfer ☐ 8 Multidistrict Litigation - Direct File

VI. CAUSE OF ACTION
Cite the U.S. Civil Statute under which you are filing *(Do not cite jurisdictional statutes unless diversity)*:
Brief description of cause:

VII. REQUESTED IN COMPLAINT: ☐ CHECK IF THIS IS A **CLASS ACTION** UNDER RULE 23, F.R.Cv.P. **DEMAND $** CHECK YES only if demanded in complaint: **JURY DEMAND:** ☐ Yes ☐ No

VIII. RELATED CASE(S) IF ANY *(See instructions):* JUDGE ______ DOCKET NUMBER ______

DATE SIGNATURE OF ATTORNEY OF RECORD

FOR OFFICE USE ONLY

RECEIPT # ______ AMOUNT ______ APPLYING IFP ______ JUDGE ______ MAG. JUDGE ______

AO 450 (Rev. 11/11) Judgment in a Civil Action

UNITED STATES DISTRICT COURT

for the

______________________)
Plaintiff)
v.) Civil Action No.
______________________)
Defendant)

JUDGMENT IN A CIVIL ACTION

The court has ordered that *(check one)*:

❒ the plaintiff *(name)* ______________________ recover from the defendant *(name)* ______________________ the amount of ______________________ dollars ($ ________), which includes prejudgment interest at the rate of ________ %, plus post judgment interest at the rate of ________ % per annum, along with costs.

❒ the plaintiff recover nothing, the action be dismissed on the merits, and the defendant *(name)* ______________________ recover costs from the plaintiff *(name)* ______________________ .

❒ other: .

This action was *(check one)*:

❒ tried by a jury with Judge ______________________ presiding, and the jury has rendered a verdict.

❒ tried by Judge ______________________ without a jury and the above decision was reached.

❒ decided by Judge ______________________ on a motion for .

Date: ______________________ *CLERK OF COURT*

____
Signature of Clerk or Deputy Clerk

Table C-2.
U.S. District Courts—Civil Cases Commenced, by Basis of Jurisdiction and Nature of Suit, During the 12-Month Periods Ending September 30, 2023 and 2024

Nature of Suit	2023	2024 Total	U.S. Cases Plaintiff	U.S. Cases Defendant	Private Cases Federal Question	Private Cases Diversity of Citizenship	Private Cases Local Jurisdiction
Total Cases	339,731	290,896	3,069	42,567	141,000	104,254	6
Contract Actions, Total	31,372	29,102	224	243	4,303	24,332	0
Franchise	175	222	0	0	50	172	0
Insurance	17,620	13,488	18	39	1,098	12,333	0
Marine	701	562	1	3	493	65	0
Miller Act	195	185	52	1	132	0	0
Negotiable Instruments	425	544	29	3	164	348	0
Recovery of Overpayments and Enforcement of Judgments	614	604	75	95	108	326	0
Defaulted Student Loans	10	13	11	1	1	0	0
Veterans' Overpayment	8	3	2	1	0	0	0
Other	596	588	62	93	107	326	0
Other Contract Actions	11,642	13,497	49	102	2,258	11,088	0
Real Property Actions, Total	4,515	4,787	110	195	2,253	2,229	0
Condemnation of Land	79	150	31	2	111	6	0
Foreclosure	1,353	1,215	43	70	353	749	0
Rent, Lease, and Ejectment	742	1,046	19	9	896	122	0
Torts to Land, Including Product Liability	1,249	1,162	5	31	448	678	0
Other Real Property Actions	1,092	1,214	12	83	445	674	0
Tort Actions, Total	131,770	80,982	37	2,981	5,104	72,858	2
Personal Injury, Total	127,437	76,390	21	2,810	4,051	69,506	2
Personal Injury/Product Liability, Total	104,060	54,192	0	48	461	53,683	0
Airplane	44	27	0	1	4	22	0
Marine	12	9	0	0	1	8	0
Motor Vehicle	306	277	0	4	21	252	0
Asbestos	128	88	0	1	58	29	0
Health Care/Pharma	37,797	17,276	0	10	121	17,145	0
Other	65,773	36,515	0	32	256	36,227	0
Other Personal Injury, Total	23,377	22,198	21	2,762	3,590	15,823	2

Nature of Suit	2023	2024					
		Total	U.S. Cases		Private Cases		
			Plaintiff	Defendant	Federal Question	Diversity of Citizenship	Local Jurisdiction
Airplane	158	181	0	7	85	89	0
Marine	1,042	1,167	0	14	627	526	0
Motor Vehicle	5,836	6,394	5	927	395	5,067	0
Assault, Libel, and Slander	650	718	0	38	203	477	0
Federal Employers Liability Act	340	328	0	34	294	0	0
Medical Malpractice	1,022	783	0	295	201	287	0
Other	14,329	12,627	16	1,447	1,785	9,377	2
Personal Property Damage, Total	**4,333**	**4,592**	**16**	**171**	**1,053**	**3,352**	**0**
Fraud, Including Truth in Lending	2,495	2,624	13	38	764	1,809	0
Other Personal Property Damage	1,838	1,968	3	133	289	1,543	0
Actions Under Statutes, Total	**172,074**	**176,025**	**2,698**	**39,148**	**129,340**	**4,835**	**4**
Antitrust	**400**	**800**	**14**	**4**	**782**	**0**	**0**
Bankruptcy, Total	**1,486**	**1,387**	**1**	**6**	**1,380**	**0**	**0**
Appeal (28 U.S.C. 158)	1,346	1,248	1	6	1,241	0	0
Withdrawal (28 U.S.C. 157)	140	139	0	0	139	0	0
Banks and Banking	**225**	**229**	**2**	**5**	**222**	**0**	**0**
Civil Rights, Total	**41,404**	**45,781**	**222**	**1,601**	**40,719**	**3,239**	**0**
Voting	109	159	3	8	147	1	0
Employment	12,152	13,526	103	427	10,513	2,483	0
Housing and Accommodations	977	922	23	9	875	15	0
Welfare	0	0	0	0	0	0	0
ADA–Employment	2,566	3,018	30	59	2,849	80	0
ADA–Other	8,776	9,030	12	37	8,942	39	0
Education	744	932	2	3	917	10	0
Other Civil Rights	16,080	18,194	49	1,058	16,476	611	0
Environmental Matters	**411**	**452**	**78**	**122**	**252**	**0**	**0**
Deportation	**18**	**9**	**0**	**5**	**4**	**0**	**0**
Prisoner Petitions, Total	**50,353**	**49,182**	**0**	**8,341**	**40,841**	**0**	**0**
Motions to Vacate Sentence	3,763	3,764	0	3,764	0	0	0
Habeas Corpus–General	14,224	12,825	0	2,450	10,375	0	0

Nature of Suit	2023	2024					
		Total	U.S. Cases		Private Cases		
			Plaintiff	Defendant	Federal Question	Diversity of Citizenship	Local Jurisdiction
Habeas Corpus–Death Penalty	123	121	0	5	116	0	0
Mandamus and Other	1,614	1,848	0	720	1,128	0	0
Civil Rights	19,618	19,386	0	633	18,753	0	0
Prison Condition	10,476	10,599	0	321	10,278	0	0
Habeas Corpus–Alien Detainees	356	432	0	432	0	0	0
Civil Detainee–Conditions of Confinement	179	207	0	16	191	0	0
Forfeiture and Penalty, Total	**842**	**786**	**747**	**39**	**0**	**0**	**0**
Agricultural Acts	0	0	0	0	0	0	0
Food and Drug Act	0	0	0	0	0	0	0
Drug-Related Seizure of Property	345	301	299	2	0	0	0
Air Traffic Regulations	0	0	0	0	0	0	0
Occupational Safety and Health Act	0	0	0	0	0	0	0
Other Forfeiture and Penalty Suits	497	485	448	37	0	0	0
Labor Laws, Total	**13,287**	**12,869**	**202**	**40**	**11,680**	**947**	**0**
Fair Labor Standards Act	5,794	5,252	144	10	5,098	0	0
Labor Management Relations Act	382	423	7	6	410	0	0
Labor Management Reporting and Disclosure Act	0	0	0	0	0	0	0
Railway Labor Act	38	43	0	1	42	0	0
Employee Retirement Income Security Act	4,716	4,758	31	5	4,722	0	0
Family and Medical Leave Act	851	945	0	3	942	0	0
Other Labor Litigation	1,506	1,448	20	15	466	947	0
Immigration, Totall	**11,134**	**12,218**	**35**	**12,183**	**0**	**0**	**0**
Naturalization Applications	442	340	0	340	0	0	0
Other Immigration Actions	10,692	11,878	35	11,843	0	0	0
Intellectual Property Rights, Total	**13,839**	**14,959**	**3**	**36**	**14,872**	**48**	**0**

		2024					
			U.S. Cases		Private Cases		
Nature of Suit	2023	Total	Plaintiff	Defendant	Federal Question	Diversity of Citizenship	Local Jurisdiction
Copyright	6,237	7,250	0	0	7,250	0	0
Patent	3,016	3,356	3	36	3,317	0	0
Patent–Abbreviated New Drug Application	243	282	0	0	282	0	0
Trademark	3,678	3,363	0	0	3,363	0	0
Defend Trade Secrets Act	665	708	0	0	660	48	0
Securities, Commodities, and Exchanges	**1,566**	**1,202**	**199**	**6**	**997**	**0**	**0**
Social Security Laws, Total	**15,017**	**13,881**	**36**	**13,845**	**0**	**0**	**0**
Disability Insurance	7,745	7,285	36	7,249	0	0	0
Supplemental Security Income	6,556	5,962	0	5,962	0	0	0
Retirement and Survivors Benefits	628	547	0	547	0	0	0
Other	88	87	0	87	0	0	0
Racketeer Influenced and Corrupt Organization Act	**1,220**	**881**	**2**	**0**	**808**	**71**	**0**
State Reapportionment Suits	**1**	**5**	**0**	**0**	**5**	**0**	**0**
Tax Suits	**543**	**517**	**258**	**255**	**0**	**0**	**4**
Customer Challenge	**0**	**0**	**0**	**0**	**0**	**0**	**0**
Consumer Credit	**8,108**	**8,731**	**4**	**8**	**8,525**	**194**	**0**
Cable/Sat. TV	**380**	**471**	**0**	**0**	**452**	**19**	**0**
Freedom of Information Act	**846**	**959**	**0**	**831**	**128**	**0**	**0**
Constitutionality of State Statutes	**414**	**424**	**3**	**16**	**364**	**41**	**0**
Other Statutory Actions	**10,580**	**10,282**	**892**	**1,805**	**7,309**	**276**	**0**
Other Actions, Total	**0**	**0**	**0**	**0**	**0**	**0**	**0**

Note: Data collection for the categories of health care/pharmaceuticals, education, civil detainee — conditions of confinement, and Family and Medical Leave Act began on October 1, 2011.

[1] Data collection for these categories began in December 2007.

Table C-4.
U.S. District Courts–Civil Cases Terminated, by Nature of Suit and Action Taken, During the 12-Month Period Ending September 30, 2024

			Court Action						
						During or After Trial			
Nature of Suit	Total	No Court Action	Total Court Action	Before Trial	During or After Pretrial	Total	Non-Jury	Jury	Percent Reaching Trial
Total Cases	396,486	76,961	319,525	294,724	22,986	1,815	571	1,244	0.5
United States Cases	46,396	11,152	35,244	34,015	1,078	151	114	37	0.3
Contract Actions									
Franchise	-	-	-	-	-	-	-	-	-
Negotiable Instruments	24	6	18	18	-	-	-	-	-
Recovery of Overpayments and Enforcement of Judgments	106	26	80	78	2	-	-	-	-
Other Contracts	254	61	193	171	20	2	2	-	0.8
Real Property	**272**	**64**	**208**	**183**	**22**	**3**	**3**	-	**1.1**
Tort Actions									
Marine Personal Injury	26	5	21	9	12	-	-	-	-
Motor Vehicle Personal Injury	790	220	570	417	133	20	20	-	2.5
Health Care/Pharma	7	-	7	5	2	-	-	-	-
Other Personal Injury	1,076	203	873	692	152	29	27	2	2.7
Other Torts	152	45	107	96	9	2	2	-	1.3
Actions Under Statutes									
Consumer Credit	4	2	2	2	-	-	-	-	-
Cable/Satellite TV	1	-	1	-	1	-	-	-	-
Antitrust	9	2	7	5	1	1	1	-	11.1
Consumer Credit	7	1	6	4	2	-	-	-	-
Telephone Consumer Protection Act	-	-	-	-	-	-	-	-	-
Cable/Satellite TV	-	-	-	-	-	-	-	-	-
Antitrust	5	-	5	5	-	-	-	-	-
Civil Rights									
ADA–Employment	113	13	100	86	10	4	1	3	3.5
ADA–Other	40	8	32	30	2	-	-	-	-
Employment	552	84	468	381	79	8	1	7	1.4
Education	4	-	4	4	-	-	-	-	-
Other Civil Rights	1,067	157	910	868	34	8	5	3	0.7
Deportation	5	2	3	2	-	1	1	-	20.0

Nature of Suit	Total	No Court Action	Court Action						
			Total Court Action	Before Trial	During or After Pretrial	During or After Trial			
						Total	Non-Jury	Jury	Percent Reaching Trial
Prisoner Petitions									
Motions to Vacate Sentence	4,137	666	3,471	3,461	6	4	1	3	0.1
Habeas Corpus–General	2,541	357	2,184	2,177	4	3	3	-	0.1
Habeas Corpus–Death Penalty	4	-	4	4	-	-	-	-	-
Mandamus and Other	654	258	396	377	3	16	16	-	2.4
Civil Rights	659	77	582	570	12	-	-	-	-
Prison Condition	300	24	276	270	3	3	3	-	1.0
Habeas Corpus–Alien Detainee	419	106	313	311	1	1	1	-	0.2
Civil Detainee–Conditions of Confinement	20	2	18	17	1	-	-	-	-
Liquor Forfeitures	-	-	-	-	-	-	-	-	-
Other Forfeiture and Penalty Suits	841	155	686	657	25	4	1	3	0.5
Fair Labor Standards Act	164	29	135	109	25	1	1	-	0.6
Family and Medical Leave Act	7	-	7	4	3	-	-	-	-
Other Labor Litigation	116	28	88	74	12	2	2	-	1.7
Selective Service	-	-	-	-	-	-	-	-	-
Social Security Laws									
Disability Insurance	8,411	843	7,568	7,456	108	4	3	1	-
Supplemental Security Income	6,912	687	6,225	6,139	82	4	1	3	0.1
Retirement and Services Benefits	652	52	600	596	3	1	-	1	0.2
Other	82	12	70	67	3	-	-	-	-
Tax Suits	531	126	405	341	57	7	6	1	1.3
Immigration									
Naturalization Applications	391	108	283	278	3	2	2	-	0.5
Other Immigration Actions	11,372	5,712	5,660	5,597	57	6	5	1	0.1
All Other U.S. Actions	3,669	1,011	2,658	2,454	189	15	6	9	0.4
Federal Question	**137,040**	**29,862**	**107,178**	**93,519**	**12,533**	**1,126**	**289**	**837**	**0.8**
Contract Actions									
Franchise	47	7	40	32	8	-	-	-	-

Nature of Suit	Total	No Court Action	Court Action						
			Total Court Action	Before Trial	During or After Pretrial	During or After Trial			
						Total	Non-Jury	Jury	Percent Reaching Trial
Marine	581	146	435	348	77	10	9	1	1.7
Miller Act	145	57	88	72	15	1	1	-	0.7
Recovery of Defaulted Student Loans	2	2	-	-	-	-	-	-	-
Other Contracts	3,287	685	2,602	2,218	359	25	10	15	0.8
Real Property	**1,982**	**363**	**1,619**	**1,560**	**56**	**3**	**-**	**3**	**0.2**
Tort Actions									
Employers Liability Act	338	49	289	157	125	7	1	6	2.1
Marine Personal Injury	691	125	566	403	151	12	8	4	1.7
Medical Malpractice	215	32	183	157	23	3	-	3	1.4
Health Care/Pharma	134	29	105	67	38	-	-	-	-
Other Personal Injury	2,846	722	2,124	1,786	317	21	5	16	0.7
Other Torts	1,003	184	819	720	90	9	7	2	0.9
Actions Under Statutes									
Consumer Credit	8,611	2,117	6,494	5,380	1,097	17	4	13	0.2
Telephone Consumer Protection Act	1,289	451	838	728	109	1	-	1	0.1
Cable/Satellite TV	320	84	236	202	33	1	-	1	0.3
Bankruptcy Suits	1,455	274	1,181	1,143	30	8	3	5	0.5
Antitrust	518	204	314	260	42	12	2	10	2.3
Civil Rights									
ADA–Employment	2,436	527	1,909	1,292	588	29	5	24	1.2
ADA–Other	9,168	3,366	5,802	5,268	520	14	6	8	0.2
Employment	9,630	1,761	7,869	5,520	2,226	123	11	112	1.3
Education	846	123	723	574	140	9	3	6	1.1
Other Civil Rights	16,537	2,687	13,850	11,843	1,755	252	46	206	1.5
Prisoner Petitions									
Habeas Corpus–General	10,900	1,765	9,135	9,087	46	2	1	1	-
Habeas Corpus–Death Penalty	134	17	117	112	5	-	-	-	-
Mandamus and Other	1,063	284	779	772	7	-	-	-	-
Civil Rights	18,389	2,706	15,683	14,891	665	127	13	114	0.7
Prison Condition	9,626	1,096	8,530	8,143	301	86	8	78	0.9
Civil Detainee–Conditions of Confinement	167	34	133	124	8	1	-	1	0.6

Nature of Suit	Total	No Court Action	Court Action						
			Total Court Action	Before Trial	During or After Pretrial	During or After Trial			
						Total	Non-Jury	Jury	Percent Reaching Trial
Fair Labor Standards Act	5,470	875	4,595	3,461	1,076	58	19	39	1.1
Family and Medical Leave Act	844	142	702	471	224	7	-	7	0.8
Labor Management Relations Act	437	80	357	311	44	2	1	1	0.5
Other Labor Litigation	5,141	1,443	3,698	2,919	751	28	21	7	0.5
Copyright	6,737	3,073	3,664	3,394	249	21	2	19	0.3
Patent	3,171	1,106	2,065	1,752	243	70	6	64	2.2
Patent–Abbreviated New Drug Application	276	30	246	149	75	22	22	-	8.0
Trademark	3,427	798	2,629	2,263	314	52	21	31	1.5
Defend Trade Secrets Act	540	114	426	317	102	7	2	5	1.3
Constitutionality of State Statutes	1,056	182	874	820	50	4	3	1	0.4
All Other Federal Question	**7,581**	**2,122**	**5,459**	**4,803**	**574**	**82**	**49**	**33**	**1.1**
Diversity of Citizenship	**213,050**	**35,947**	**177,103**	**167,190**	**9,375**	**538**	**168**	**370**	**0.3**
Contract Actions									
Franchise	143	26	117	79	37	1	1	-	0.7
Insurance	16,747	3,283	13,464	11,181	2,204	79	16	63	0.5
Negotiable Instruments	317	68	249	203	43	3	2	1	0.9
Other Contracts	10,704	2,305	8,399	6,555	1,642	202	104	98	1.9
Real Property	**2,154**	**554**	**1,600**	**1,356**	**224**	**20**	**12**	**8**	**0.9**
Tort Actions									
Marine Personal Injury	517	70	447	416	26	5	3	2	1.0
Motor Vehicle Personal Injury	5,108	975	4,133	2,758	1,321	54	6	48	1.1
Health Care/Pharma	8,106	1,440	6,666	6,280	381	5	1	4	0.1
Other Personal Injury	161,623	25,427	136,196	133,677	2,403	116	10	106	0.1
Other Torts	3,144	773	2,371	1,875	466	30	9	21	1.0
Actions Under Statutes									
Consumer Credit	168	39	129	115	14	-	-	-	-
Telephone Consumer Protection Act	40	11	29	27	1	1	-	1	2.5
Cable/Satellite TV	14	2	12	11	1	-	-	-	-
Civil Rights									
ADA–Employment	71	18	53	42	11	-	-	-	-

Nature of Suit	Total	No Court Action	Court Action						
			Total Court Action	Before Trial	During or After Pretrial	During or After Trial			
						Total	Non-Jury	Jury	Percent Reaching Trial
ADA–Other	42	13	29	27	2	-	-	-	-
Employment	2,110	399	1,711	1,359	340	12	1	11	0.6
Education	6	1	5	5	-	-	-	-	-
Other Civil Rights	526	100	426	376	48	2	1	1	0.4
Prison Condition	-	-	-	-	-	-	-	-	-
All Other Diversity	1,510	443	1,067	848	211	8	2	6	0.5
Local Jurisdiction	-	-	-	-	-	-	-	-	-
Contract Actions	-	-	-	-	-	-	-	-	-
Real Property	-	-	-	-	-	-	-	-	-
Tort Actions									-
Motor Vehicle Personal Injury	-	-	-	-	-	-	-	-	-
Other Personal Injury	-	-	-	-	-	-	-	-	-
Other Torts	-	-	-	-	-	-	-	-	-
Prisoner Petitions									-
Habeas Corpus–General	-	-	-	-	-	-	-	-	-
Habeas Corpus–Death Penalty	-	-	-	-	-	-	-	-	-
Mandamus and Other	-	-	-	-	-	-	-	-	-
Prison Condition	-	-	-	-	-	-	-	-	-
Civil Rights	-	-	-	-	-	-	-	-	-
All Other Local	-	-	-	-	-	-	-	-	-

Note: Land condemnation cases omitted

Table C-5.
U.S. District Courts–Median Time Intervals From Filing to Disposition of Civil Cases Terminated, by District and Method of Disposition, During the 12-Month Period Ending September 30, 2024

Circuit and District	Total Cases		No Court Action		Court Action					
					Before Pretrial		During or After Pretrial		During Trial	
	Number of Cases	Median Time Interval in Months	Number of Cases	Median Time Interval in Months	Number of Cases	Median Time Interval in Months	Number of Cases	Median Time Interval in Months	Number of Cases	Median Time Interval in Months
Total	346,938	13.7	69,436	8.3	254,080	16.0	21,861	13.5	1,561	31.6
DC	3,290	6.2	1,023	5.2	2,244	6.9	9	-	14	51.5
1st	6,536	20.1	1,654	5.5	4,081	35.9	737	19.2	64	34.7
ME	409	8.0	99	6.6	290	8.0	15	25.6	5	-
MA	2,439	7.2	1,180	4.8	590	4.6	633	18.8	36	36.4
NH	2,499	49.7	47	4.4	2,386	50.7	61	17.8	5	-
RI	483	8.7	249	9.6	218	6.8	7	-	9	-
PR	706	13.6	79	8.1	597	13.9	21	16.3	9	-
2nd	24,572	6.0	5,618	2.8	15,711	6.5	3,076	14.1	167	43.1
CT	1,501	8.1	295	3.9	771	6.1	417	15.5	18	38.4
NY,N	1,393	7.7	304	3.9	819	7.6	259	17.0	11	37.3
NY,E	7,879	5.8	1,987	2.6	5,083	6.7	759	13.3	50	55.2
NY,S	10,695	6.4	1,853	3.2	7,188	6.0	1,581	13.2	73	37.4
NY,W	1,783	7.9	123	5.2	1,599	7.7	49	27.7	12	61.2
VT	1,321	2.4	1,056	2.3	251	5.6	11	30.6	3	-
3rd	18,996	6.7	4,110	3.2	10,619	5.7	4,111	12.2	156	33.6
DE	1,331	8.5	317	2.5	878	10.1	92	20.3	44	39.2
NJ	7,921	8.1	295	2.0	5,298	5.4	2,293	13.6	35	54.4
PA,E	6,200	4.6	2,166	2.9	2,989	3.9	996	10.2	49	17.0
PA,M	1,535	8.7	681	6.8	824	9.7	19	34.7	11	33.0
PA,W	1,871	6.3	575	3.0	613	7.2	670	9.1	13	31.4
VI	138	16.0	76	13.6	17	17.3	41	15.5	4	-
4th	15,730	8.3	6,006	9.5	8,271	6.6	1,349	12.6	104	27.3
MD	3,119	7.5	140	7.8	2,356	6.0	595	18.7	28	35.9
NC,E	1,093	7.1	549	6.0	530	8.5	9	-	5	-
NC,M	679	7.8	451	6.6	215	10.9	7	-	6	-
NC,W	1,154	5.5	225	2.9	649	4.9	266	12.3	14	26.5
SC	5,800	12.2	3,681	14.1	2,069	8.7	36	9.6	14	30.6
VA,E	2,613	5.3	870	4.9	1,327	4.6	396	8.6	20	14.3

Circuit and District	Total Cases		No Court Action		Court Action					
					Before Pretrial		During or After Pretrial		During Trial	
	Number of Cases	Median Time Interval in Months	Number of Cases	Median Time Interval in Months	Number of Cases	Median Time Interval in Months	Number of Cases	Median Time Interval in Months	Number of Cases	Median Time Interval in Months
VA,W	535	9.5	49	3.7	470	10.0	10	12.5	6	-
WV,N	268	10.1	14	2.2	227	9.7	21	19.0	6	-
WV,S	469	10.6	27	2.3	428	11.0	9	-	5	-
5th	**27,192**	**9.4**	**7,281**	**6.9**	**16,879**	**9.5**	**2,824**	**14.0**	**208**	**26.5**
LA,E	6,506	10.7	757	11.1	4,764	10.1	965	14.0	20	16.5
LA,M	1,251	9.1	349	8.4	878	10.1	15	29.6	9	-
LA,W	3,194	16.5	409	13.2	2,234	17.0	525	16.4	26	25.8
MS,N	734	5.5	152	3.7	337	3.2	238	10.9	7	-
MS,S	988	8.7	487	8.0	467	8.7	27	19.0	7	-
TX,N	3,648	5.6	604	3.3	3,007	6.1	12	9.7	25	18.2
TX,E	2,345	7.5	766	5.6	1,526	8.1	22	57.1	31	23.3
TX,S	5,086	7.5	2,523	5.6	1,804	7.6	712	11.9	47	30.6
TX,W	3,440	7.8	1,234	6.7	1,862	7.5	308	13.8	36	34.4
6th	**12,129**	**8.3**	**3,049**	**4.7**	**6,400**	**7.6**	**2,572**	**14.1**	**108**	**32.7**
KY,E	653	8.5	146	5.7	495	8.9	6	-	6	-
KY,W	966	9.9	154	5.0	791	10.6	16	19.8	5	-
MI,E	2,615	7.9	315	2.7	1,164	4.4	1,116	15.4	20	41.7
MI,W	906	6.8	87	2.6	583	5.5	229	12.9	7	-
OH,N	2,008	7.4	406	3.5	942	7.0	650	11.5	10	22.3
OH,S	2,137	8.2	842	5.0	957	9.3	322	15.4	16	41.1
TN,E	845	10.4	247	8.5	513	9.9	62	19.0	23	32.0
TN,M	1,262	7.6	536	5.3	554	7.6	165	13.2	7	-
TN,W	737	9.4	316	7.9	401	10.9	6	-	14	28.2
7th	**16,880**	**7.6**	**5,744**	**7.5**	**9,331**	**6.9**	**1,720**	**13.3**	**85**	**43.0**
IL,N	9,700	6.8	4,003	7.3	5,335	6.2	322	12.7	40	61.3
IL,C	704	8.0	298	6.6	387	9.3	9	-	10	53.2
IL,S	1,389	10.4	1,031	9.9	349	11.2	4	-	5	-
IN,N	1,336	8.5	58	3.0	930	7.4	342	14.6	6	-
IN,S	2,243	9.9	34	2.2	1,386	6.9	816	12.9	7	-
WI,E	982	6.4	149	3.0	794	7.3	28	14.2	11	43.0
WI,W	526	6.6	171	2.9	150	4.7	199	12.8	6	-
8th	**8,449**	**7.8**	**3,226**	**5.7**	**4,564**	**8.3**	**588**	**13.0**	**71**	**28.8**
AR,E	787	10.1	348	13.8	427	7.6	1	-	11	28.8

Circuit and District	Total Cases		No Court Action		Court Action					
					Before Pretrial		During or After Pretrial		During Trial	
	Number of Cases	Median Time Interval in Months	Number of Cases	Median Time Interval in Months	Number of Cases	Median Time Interval in Months	Number of Cases	Median Time Interval in Months	Number of Cases	Median Time Interval in Months
AR,W	465	9.4	33	4.4	389	8.9	36	12.4	7	-
IA,N	259	6.9	84	8.4	170	5.8	0	-	5	-
IA,S	360	7.6	159	8.3	189	6.5	3	-	9	-
MN	2,636	8.3	1,448	4.7	654	11.5	523	12.9	11	47.6
MO,E	1,525	6.6	412	3.2	1,099	7.7	7	-	7	-
MO,W	1,461	6.9	524	5.7	919	7.6	8	-	10	27.5
NE	522	7.8	121	3.8	385	8.4	9	-	7	-
ND	186	11.6	5	-	179	11.7	0	-	2	-
SD	248	11.5	92	12.3	153	10.1	1	-	2	-
9th	**40,426**	**7.1**	**14,553**	**7.5**	**23,551**	**6.2**	**2,008**	**15.8**	**314**	**31.6**
AK	230	9.0	10	4.4	216	9.0	2	-	2	-
AZ	2,278	6.7	97	2.0	1,795	5.6	352	15.8	34	26.8
CA,N	9,248	20.6	6,752	23.4	1,671	8.5	792	15.7	33	36.3
CA,E	2,575	9.2	890	7.1	1,616	9.9	54	23.0	15	67.7
CA,C	15,348	3.9	4,459	3.0	10,689	4.3	73	25.8	127	27.5
CA,S	2,146	6.6	644	3.7	1,019	6.4	469	12.7	14	32.7
HI	624	4.8	215	4.2	384	4.8	10	29.5	15	26.1
ID	389	10.4	36	4.5	294	9.5	55	24.5	4	-
MT	385	10.9	132	6.0	125	7.6	122	14.0	6	-
NV	2,177	8.5	398	6.8	1,710	8.6	50	14.1	19	54.2
OR	1,633	10.2	290	4.9	1,319	11.2	6	-	18	39.4
WA,E	700	7.2	100	5.5	596	7.2	1	-	3	-
WA,W	2,639	6.5	514	3.6	2,088	7.1	14	24.2	23	30.5
GU	41	34.9	5	-	28	60.0	7	-	1	-
NMI	13	8.3	11	5.7	1	-	1	-	0	-
10th	**7,787**	**7.8**	**1,798**	**5.7**	**5,243**	**7.6**	**660**	**15.7**	**86**	**30.4**
CO	2,704	7.4	529	7.1	2,058	6.5	74	25.4	43	31.8
KS	912	7.3	226	5.5	601	7.1	70	19.1	15	22.1
NM	918	8.0	138	4.4	524	6.8	253	13.6	3	-
OK,N	491	7.5	48	3.5	441	8.6	1	-	1	-
OK,E	375	9.6	13	2.7	355	9.6	3	-	4	-
OK,W	1,062	7.3	460	5.1	414	8.5	183	11.6	5	-
UT	1,141	9.3	314	7.6	806	9.4	10	50.1	11	33.4

Circuit and District	Total Cases		No Court Action		Court Action					
					Before Pretrial		During or After Pretrial		During Trial	
	Number of Cases	Median Time Interval in Months	Number of Cases	Median Time Interval in Months	Number of Cases	Median Time Interval in Months	Number of Cases	Median Time Interval in Months	Number of Cases	Median Time Interval in Months
WY	184	9.0	70	4.5	44	4.1	66	13.8	4	-
11th	164,951	39.1	15,374	41.9	147,186	39.0	2,207	11.3	184	25.2
AL,N	1,290	8.6	113	2.8	1,155	9.4	7	-	15	33.5
AL,M	485	9.0	27	2.7	444	9.2	12	16.5	2	-
AL,S	424	9.1	74	6.3	333	9.2	6	-	11	31.7
FL,N	140,479	43.4	13,394	42.9	127,072	43.5	2	-	11	18.2
FL,M	7,115	5.6	88	4.7	6,658	5.2	334	14.1	35	27.0
FL,S	7,755	3.6	745	3.2	6,903	3.5	50	10.0	57	16.8
GA,N	6,190	5.3	690	2.9	3,669	3.5	1,782	10.8	49	29.6
GA,M	648	8.0	226	6.9	406	8.0	12	38.2	4	-
GA,S	565	6.8	17	10.1	546	6.6	2	-	0	-

Note: Median time intervals are not computed when fewer than 10 cases reported. This table excludes land condemnations, prisoner petitions, deportation reviews, recovery of overpayments, and enforcement of judgments. Includes cases filed in previous years as consolidated cases that thereafter were severed into individual cases. For fiscal years prior to 2001, this table included data on recovery of overpayments and enforcement of judgments.

UNITED STATES CONSTITUTION

Preamble

We the people of the United States, in order to form a more perfect union, establish justice, insure domestic tranquility, provide for the common defense, promote the general welfare, and secure the blessings of liberty to ourselves and our posterity, do ordain and establish this Constitution for the United States of America.

Article I

Section 1. All legislative Powers herein granted shall be vested in a Congress of the United States, which shall consist of a Senate and House of Representatives.

Section 2. The House of Representatives shall be composed of Members chosen every second Year by the People of the several States, and the Electors in each State shall have the Qualifications requisite for Electors of the most numerous Branch of the State Legislature.

No Person shall be a Representative who shall not have attained to the Age of twenty five Years, and been seven Years a Citizen of the United States, and who shall not, when elected, be an Inhabitant of that State in which he shall be chosen.

Representatives and direct Taxes shall be apportioned among the several States which may be included within this Union, according to their respective Numbers, which shall be determined by adding to the whole Number of free Persons, including those bound to Service for a Term of Years, and excluding Indians not taxed, three fifths of all other Persons.

The actual Enumeration shall be made within three Years after the first Meeting of the Congress of the United States, and within every subsequent Term of ten Years, in such Manner as they shall by Law direct. The Number of Representatives shall not exceed one for every thirty Thousand, but each State shall have at Least one Representative; and until such enumeration shall be made, the State of New Hampshire shall be entitled to chuse three, Massachusetts eight, Rhode Island and Providence Plantations one, Connecticut five, New York six, New Jersey four, Pennsylvania eight, Delaware one, Maryland six, Virginia ten, North Carolina five, South Carolina five and Georgia three.

When vacancies happen in the Representation from any State, the Executive Authority thereof shall issue Writs of Election to fill such Vacancies.

The House of Representatives shall chuse their Speaker and other Officers; and shall have the sole Power of Impeachment.

Section 3. The Senate of the United States shall be composed of two Senators from each State, chosen by the Legislature thereof, for six Years; and each Senator shall have one Vote.

Immediately after they shall be assembled in Consequence of the first Election, they shall be divided as equally as may be into three Classes. The Seats of the Senators of the first Class shall be vacated at the Expiration of the second Year, of the second Class at the Expiration of the fourth Year, and of the third Class at the Expiration of the sixth Year, so that one third may be chosen every second Year; and if Vacancies happen by Resignation, or otherwise, during the Recess of the Legislature of any State, the Executive thereof may make temporary Appointments until the next Meeting of the Legislature, which shall then fill such Vacancies.

No person shall be a Senator who shall not have attained to the Age of thirty Years, and been nine Years a Citizen of the United States, and who shall not, when elected, be an Inhabitant of that State for which he shall be chosen.

The Vice President of the United States shall be President of the Senate, but shall have no Vote, unless they be equally divided.

The Senate shall chuse their other Officers, and also a President pro tempore, in the absence of the Vice President, or when he shall exercise the Office of President of the United States.

The Senate shall have the sole Power to try all Impeachments. When sitting for that Purpose, they shall be on Oath or Affirmation. When the President of the United States is tried, the Chief Justice shall preside: And no Person shall be convicted without the Concurrence of two thirds of the Members present.

Judgment in Cases of Impeachment shall not extend further than to removal from Office, and disqualification to hold and enjoy any Office of honor, Trust or Profit under the United States: but the Party convicted shall nevertheless be liable and subject to Indictment, Trial, Judgment and Punishment, according to Law.

Section 4. The Times, Places and Manner of holding Elections for Senators and Representatives, shall be prescribed in each State by the Legislature thereof; but the Congress may at any time by Law make or alter such Regulations, except as to the Place of Chusing Senators.

The Congress shall assemble at least once in every Year, and such Meeting shall be on the first Monday in December, unless they shall by Law appoint a different Day.

Section 5. Each House shall be the Judge of the Elections, Returns and Qualifications of its own Members, and a Majority of each shall constitute a Quorum to do Business; but a smaller number may adjourn from day to day, and may be authorized to compel the Attendance of absent Members, in such Manner, and under such Penalties as each House may provide.

Each House may determine the Rules of its Proceedings, punish its Members for disorderly Behavior, and, with the Concurrence of two-thirds, expel a Member.

Each House shall keep a Journal of its Proceedings, and from time to time publish the same, excepting such Parts as may in their Judgment require Secrecy; and the Yeas and Nays of the Members of either House on any question shall, at the Desire of one fifth of those Present, be entered on the Journal.

Neither House, during the Session of Congress, shall, without the Consent of the other, adjourn for more than three days, nor to any other Place than that in which the two Houses shall be sitting.

Section 6. The Senators and Representatives shall receive a Compensation for their Services, to be ascertained by Law, and paid out of the Treasury of the United States. They shall in all Cases, except Treason, Felony and Breach of the Peace, be privileged from Arrest during their Attendance at the Session of their respective Houses, and in going to and returning from the same; and for any Speech or Debate in either House, they shall not be questioned in any other Place.

No Senator or Representative shall, during the Time for which he was elected, be appointed to any civil Office under the Authority of the United States which shall have been created, or the Emoluments whereof shall have been increased during such time; and no Person holding any Office under the United States, shall be a Member of either House during his Continuance in Office.

Section 7. All bills for raising Revenue shall originate in the House of Representatives; but the Senate may propose or concur with Amendments as on other Bills.

Every Bill which shall have passed the House of Representatives and the Senate, shall, before it become a Law, be presented to the President of the United States; If he approve he shall sign it, but if not he shall return it, with his Objections to that House in which it shall have originated, who shall enter the Objections at large on their Journal, and proceed to reconsider it. If after such Reconsideration two thirds of that House shall agree to pass the Bill, it shall be sent, together with the Objections, to the other House, by which it shall likewise be reconsidered, and if approved by two thirds of that House, it shall become a Law. But in all such Cases the Votes of both Houses shall be determined by Yeas and Nays, and the Names of the Persons voting for and against the Bill shall be entered on the Journal of each House respectively. If any Bill shall not be returned by the President within ten Days (Sundays excepted) after it shall have been presented to him, the Same shall be a Law, in like Manner as if he had signed it, unless the Congress by their Adjournment prevent its Return, in which Case it shall not be a Law.

Every Order, Resolution, or Vote to which the Concurrence of the Senate and House of Representatives may be necessary (except on a question of Adjournment) shall be presented to the President of the United States; and before the Same shall take Effect, shall be approved by him, or being disapproved by him, shall be repassed by two thirds of the Senate and House of Representatives, according to the Rules and Limitations prescribed in the Case of a Bill.

***Section** 8*. The Congress shall have Power To lay and collect Taxes, Duties, Imposts and Excises, to pay the Debts and provide for the common Defence and general Welfare of the United States; but all Duties, Imposts and Excises shall be uniform throughout the United States;

To borrow money on the credit of the United States;

To regulate Commerce with foreign Nations, and among the several States, and with the Indian Tribes;

To establish an uniform Rule of Naturalization, and uniform Laws on the subject of Bankruptcies throughout the United States;

To coin Money, regulate the Value thereof, and of foreign Coin, and fix the Standard of Weights and Measures; To provide for the Punishment of counterfeiting the Securities and current Coin of the United States;

To establish Post Offices and Post Roads;

To promote the Progress of Science and useful Arts, by securing for limited Times to Authors and Inventors the exclusive Right to their respective Writings and Discoveries;

To constitute Tribunals inferior to the supreme Court;

To define and punish Piracies and Felonies committed on the high Seas, and Offenses against the Law of Nations;

To declare War, grant Letters of Marque and Reprisal, and make Rules concerning Captures on Land and Water;

To raise and support Armies, but no Appropriation of Money to that Use shall be for a longer Term than two Years;

To provide and maintain a Navy;

To make Rules for the Government and Regulation of the land and naval Forces;

To provide for calling forth the Militia to execute the Laws of the Union, suppress Insurrections and repel Invasions;

To provide for organizing, arming, and disciplining the Militia, and for governing such Part of them as may be employed in the Service of the United States, reserving to the States respectively, the Appointment of the Officers, and the Authority of training the Militia according to the discipline prescribed by Congress;

To exercise exclusive Legislation in all Cases whatsoever, over such District (not exceeding ten Miles square) as may, by Cession of particular States, and the acceptance of Congress, become the Seat of the Government of the United States, and to exercise like Authority over all Places purchased by the Consent of the Legislature of the State in which the Same shall be, for the Erection of Forts, Magazines, Arsenals, dock-Yards, and other needful Buildings; And

To make all Laws which shall be necessary and proper for carrying into Execution the foregoing Powers, and all other Powers vested by this Constitution in the Government of the United States, or in any Department or Officer thereof.

Section 9. The Migration or Importation of such Persons as any of the States now existing shall think proper to admit, shall not be prohibited by the Congress prior to the Year one thousand eight hundred and eight, but a tax or duty may be imposed on such Importation, not exceeding ten dollars for each Person.

The privilege of the Writ of Habeas Corpus shall not be suspended, unless when in Cases of Rebellion or Invasion the public Safety may require it.

No Bill of Attainder or ex post facto Law shall be passed.

No capitation, or other direct, Tax shall be laid, unless in Proportion to the Census or Enumeration herein before directed to be taken.

No Tax or Duty shall be laid on Articles exported from any State.

No Preference shall be given by any Regulation of Commerce or Revenue to the Ports of one State over those of another: nor shall Vessels bound to, or from, one State, be obliged to enter, clear, or pay Duties in another.

No Money shall be drawn from the Treasury, but in Consequence of Appropriations made by Law; and a regular Statement and Account of the Receipts and Expenditures of all public Money shall be published from time to time.

No Title of Nobility shall be granted by the United States: And no Person holding any Office of Profit or Trust under them, shall, without the Consent of the Congress, accept of any present, Emolument, Office, or Title, of any kind whatever, from any King, Prince or foreign State.

Section 10. No State shall enter into any Treaty, Alliance, or Confederation; grant Letters of Marque and Reprisal; coin Money; emit Bills of Credit; make any Thing but gold and silver Coin a Tender in Payment of Debts; pass any Bill of Attainder, ex post facto Law, or Law impairing the Obligation of Contracts, or grant any Title of Nobility.

No State shall, without the Consent of the Congress, lay any Imposts or Duties on Imports or Exports, except what may be absolutely necessary for executing it's inspection Laws: and the net Produce of all Duties and Imposts, laid by any State on Imports or Exports, shall be for the Use of the Treasury of the United States; and all such Laws shall be subject to the Revision and Controul of the Congress.

No State shall, without the Consent of Congress, lay any duty of Tonnage, keep Troops, or Ships of War in time of Peace, enter into any Agreement or Compact with another State, or with a foreign Power, or engage in War, unless actually invaded, or in such imminent Danger as will not admit of delay.

Article II

Section 1. The executive Power shall be vested in a President of the United States of America. He shall hold his Office during the Term of four Years, and, together with the Vice-President chosen for the same Term, be elected, as follows:

Each State shall appoint, in such Manner as the Legislature thereof may direct, a Number of Electors, equal to the whole Number of Senators and Representatives to which the State may be entitled in the Congress: but no Senator or Representative, or Person holding an Office of Trust or Profit under the United States, shall be appointed an Elector.

The Electors shall meet in their respective States, and vote by Ballot for two persons, of whom one at least shall not lie an Inhabitant of the same State with themselves. And they shall make a List of all the Persons voted for, and of the Number of Votes for each; which List they shall sign and certify, and transmit sealed to the Seat of the Government of the United States, directed to the President of the Senate. The President of the Senate shall, in the Presence of the Senate and House of Representatives, open all the Certificates, and the Votes shall then be counted. The Person having the greatest Number of Votes shall be the President, if such Number be a Majority of the whole Number of Electors appointed; and if there be more than one who have such Majority, and have an equal Number of Votes, then the House of Representatives shall immediately chuse by Ballot one of them for President; and if no Person have a Majority, then from the five highest on the List the said House shall in like Manner chuse the President. But in chusing the President, the Votes shall be taken by States, the Representation from each State having one Vote; a quorum for this Purpose shall consist of a Member or Members from two- thirds of the States, and a Majority of all the States shall be necessary to a Choice. In every Case, after the Choice of the President, the Person having the greatest Number of Votes of the Electors shall be the Vice President. But if there should remain two or more who have equal Votes, the Senate shall chuse from them by Ballot the Vice-President.

The Congress may determine the Time of chusing the Electors, and the Day on which they shall give their Votes; which Day shall be the same throughout the United States.

No person except a natural born Citizen, or a Citizen of the United States, at the time of the Adoption of this Constitution, shall be eligible to the Office of President; neither shall any Person be eligible to that Office who shall not have attained to the Age of thirty-five Years, and been fourteen Years a Resident within the United States.

In Case of the Removal of the President from Office, or of his Death, Resignation, or Inability to discharge the Powers and Duties of the said Office, the same shall devolve on the Vice President, and the Congress may by Law provide for the Case of Removal, Death, Resignation or Inability, both of the President and Vice President, declaring what Officer shall then act as President, and such

Officer shall act accordingly, until the Disability be removed, or a President shall be elected.

The President shall, at stated Times, receive for his Services, a Compensation, which shall neither be increased nor diminished during the Period for which he shall have been elected, and he shall not receive within that Period any other Emolument from the United States, or any of them.

Before he enter on the Execution of his Office, he shall take the following Oath or Affirmation:

"I do solemnly swear (or affirm) that I will faithfully execute the Office of President of the United States, and will to the best of my Ability, preserve, protect and defend the Constitution of the United States."

Section 2. The President shall be Commander in Chief of the Army and Navy of the United States, and of the Militia of the several States, when called into the actual Service of the United States; he may require the Opinion, in writing, of the principal Officer in each of the executive Departments, upon any subject relating to the Duties of their respective Offices, and he shall have Power to Grant Reprieves and Pardons for Offenses against the United States, except in Cases of Impeachment.

He shall have Power, by and with the Advice and Consent of the Senate, to make Treaties, provided two thirds of the Senators present concur; and he shall nominate, and by and with the Advice and Consent of the Senate, shall appoint Ambassadors, other public Ministers and Consuls, Judges of the supreme Court, and all other Officers of the United States, whose Appointments are not herein otherwise provided for, and which shall be established by Law: but the Congress may by Law vest the Appointment of such inferior Officers, as they think proper, in the President alone, in the Courts of Law, or in the Heads of Departments.

The President shall have Power to fill up all Vacancies that may happen during the Recess of the Senate, by granting Commissions which shall expire at the End of their next Session.

Section 3. He shall from time to time give to the Congress Information of the State of the Union, and recommend to their Consideration such Measures as he shall judge necessary and expedient; he may, on extraordinary Occasions, convene both Houses, or either of them, and in Case of Disagreement between them, with Respect to the Time of Adjournment, he may adjourn them to such Time as he shall think proper; he shall receive Ambassadors and other public Ministers; he shall take Care that the Laws be faithfully executed, and shall Commission all the Officers of the United States.

Section 4. The President, Vice President and all civil Officers of the United States, shall be removed from Office on Impeachment for, and Conviction of, Treason, Bribery, or other high Crimes and Misdemeanors.

Article III

Section 1. The judicial Power of the United States, shall be vested in one supreme Court, and in such inferior Courts as the Congress may from time to time ordain and establish. The Judges, both of the supreme and inferior Courts, shall hold their Offices during good Behavior, and shall, at stated Times, receive for their Services a Compensation which shall not be diminished during their Continuance in Office.

Section 2. The judicial Power shall extend to all Cases, in Law and Equity, arising under this Constitution, the Laws of the United States, and Treaties made, or which shall be made, under their Authority; to all Cases affecting Ambassadors, other public Ministers and Consuls; to all Cases of admiralty and maritime Jurisdiction; to Controversies to which the United States shall be a Party; to Controversies between two or more States; between a State and Citizens of another State; between Citizens of different States; between Citizens of the same State claiming Lands under Grants of different States, and between a State, or the Citizens thereof, and foreign States, Citizens or Subjects.

In all Cases affecting Ambassadors, other public Ministers and Consuls, and those in which a State shall be Party, the supreme Court shall have original Jurisdiction. In all the other Cases before mentioned, the supreme Court shall have appellate Jurisdiction, both as to Law and Fact, with such Exceptions, and under such Regulations as the Congress shall make.

The Trial of all Crimes, except in Cases of Impeachment, shall be by Jury; and such Trial shall be held in the State where the said Crimes shall have been committed; but when not committed within any State, the Trial shall be at such Place or Places as the Congress may by Law have directed.

Section 3. Treason against the United States, shall consist only in levying War against them, or in adhering to their Enemies, giving them Aid and Comfort. No Person shall be convicted of Treason unless on the Testimony of two Witnesses to the same overt Act, or on Confession in open Court.

The Congress shall have power to declare the Punishment of Treason, but no Attainder of Treason shall work Corruption of Blood, or Forfeiture except during the Life of the Person attainted.

Article IV

Section 1. Full Faith and Credit shall be given in each State to the public Acts, Records, and judicial Proceedings of every other State. And the Congress may by general Laws prescribe the Manner in which such Acts, Records and Proceedings shall be proved, and the Effect thereof.

Section 2. The Citizens of each State shall be entitled to all Privileges and Immunities of Citizens in the several States.

A Person charged in any State with Treason, Felony, or other Crime, who shall flee from Justice, and be found in another State, shall on demand of the executive Authority of the State from which he fled, be delivered up, to be removed to the State having Jurisdiction of the Crime.

No Person held to Service or Labour in one State, under the Laws thereof, escaping into another, shall, in Consequence of any Law or Regulation therein, be discharged from such Service or Labour, But shall be delivered up on Claim of the Party to whom such Service or Labour may be due.

Section 3. New States may be admitted by the Congress into this Union; but no new States shall be formed or erected within the Jurisdiction of any other State; nor any State be formed by the Junction of two or more States, or parts of States, without the Consent of the Legislatures of the States concerned as well as of the Congress.

The Congress shall have Power to dispose of and make all needful Rules and Regulations respecting the Territory or other Property belonging to the United States; and nothing in this Constitution shall be so construed as to Prejudice any Claims of the United States, or of any particular State.

Section 4. The United States shall guarantee to every State in this Union a Republican Form of Government, and shall protect each of them against Invasion; and on Application of the Legislature, or of the Executive (when the Legislature cannot be convened) against domestic Violence.

Article V

The Congress, whenever two thirds of both Houses shall deem it necessary, shall propose Amendments to this Constitution, or, on the Application of the Legislatures of two thirds of the several States, shall call a Convention for proposing Amendments, which, in either Case, shall be valid to all Intents and Purposes, as part of this Constitution, when ratified by the Legislatures of three fourths of the several States, or by Conventions in three fourths thereof, as the one or the other Mode of Ratification may be proposed by the Congress; Provided that no Amendment which may be made prior to the Year One thousand eight hundred and eight shall in any Manner affect the first and fourth Clauses in the Ninth Section of the first Article; and that no State, without its Consent, shall be deprived of its equal Suffrage in the Senate.

Article VI

All Debts contracted and Engagements entered into, before the Adoption of this Constitution, shall be as valid against the United States under this Constitution, as under the Confederation.

This Constitution, and the Laws of the United States which shall be made in Pursuance thereof; and all Treaties made, or which shall be made, under the Authority of the United States, shall be the supreme Law of the Land; and the Judges in every State shall be bound thereby, any Thing in the Constitution or Laws of any State to the Contrary notwithstanding.

The Senators and Representatives before mentioned, and the Members of the several State Legislatures, and all executive and judicial Officers, both of the United States and of the several States, shall be bound by Oath or Affirmation, to support this Constitution; but no religious Test shall ever be required as a Qualification to any Office or public Trust under the United States.

Article VII

The Ratification of the Conventions of nine States, shall be sufficient for the Establishment of this Constitution between the States so ratifying the Same.

Done in Convention by the Unanimous Consent of the States present the Seventeenth Day of September in the Year of our Lord one thousand seven hundred and Eighty seven and of the Independence of the United States of America the Twelfth. In Witness whereof We have hereunto subscribed our Names.

Amendment I

Congress shall make no law respecting an establishment of religion, or prohibiting the free exercise thereof; or abridging the freedom of speech, or of the press; or the right of the people peaceably to assemble, and to petition the Government for a redress of grievances.

Amendment II

A well regulated Militia, being necessary to the security of a free State, the right of the people to keep and bear Arms, shall not be infringed.

Amendment III

No Soldier shall, in time of peace be quartered in any house, without the consent of the Owner, nor in time of war, but in a manner to be prescribed by law.

Amendment IV

The right of the people to be secure in their persons, houses, papers, and effects, against unreasonable searches and seizures, shall not be violated, and no Warrants shall issue, but upon probable cause, supported by Oath or affirmation, and particularly describing the place to be searched, and the persons or things to be seized.

Amendment V

No person shall be held to answer for a capital, or otherwise infamous crime, unless on a presentment or indictment of a Grand Jury, except in cases arising in the land or naval forces, or in the Militia, when in actual service in time of War or public danger; nor shall any person be subject for the same offense to be twice put in jeopardy of life or limb; nor shall be compelled in any criminal case to be a witness against himself, nor be deprived of life, liberty, or property, without due process of law; nor shall private property be taken for public use, without just compensation.

Amendment VI

In all criminal prosecutions, the accused shall enjoy the right to a speedy and public trial, by an impartial jury of the State and district wherein the crime shall have been committed, which district shall have been previously ascertained by law, and to be informed of the nature and cause of the accusation; to be confronted with the witnesses against him; to have compulsory process for obtaining witnesses in his favor, and to have the Assistance of Counsel for his defence.

Amendment VII

In Suits at common law, where the value in controversy shall exceed twenty dollars, the right of trial by jury shall be preserved, and no fact tried by a jury, shall be otherwise re-examined in any Court of the United States, than according to the rules of the common law.

Amendment VIII

Excessive bail shall not be required, nor excessive fines imposed, nor cruel and unusual punishments inflicted.

Amendment IX

The enumeration in the Constitution, of certain rights, shall not be construed to deny or disparage others retained by the people.

Amendment X

The powers not delegated to the United States by the Constitution, nor prohibited by it to the States, are reserved to the States respectively, or to the people.

Amendment XI

The Judicial power of the United States shall not be construed to extend to any suit in law or equity, commenced or prosecuted against one of the United States by Citizens of another State, or by Citizens or Subjects of any Foreign State.

Amendment XII

The Electors shall meet in their respective states, and vote by ballot for President and Vice-President, one of whom, at least, shall not be an inhabitant of the same state with themselves; they shall name in their ballots the person voted for as President, and in distinct ballots the person voted for as Vice-President, and they shall make distinct lists of all persons voted for as President, and of all persons voted for as Vice-President and of the number of votes for each, which lists they shall sign and certify, and transmit sealed to the seat of the government of the United States, directed to the President of the Senate;

The President of the Senate shall, in the presence of the Senate and House of Representatives, open all the certificates and the votes shall then be counted;

The person having the greatest Number of votes for President, shall be the President, if such number be a majority of the whole number of Electors appointed; and if no person have such majority, then from the persons having the highest numbers not exceeding three on the list of those voted for as President, the House of Representatives shall choose immediately, by ballot, the President. But in choosing the President, the votes shall be taken by states, the representation from each state having one vote; a quorum for this purpose shall consist of a member or members from two-thirds of the states, and a majority of all the states shall be necessary to a choice. And if the House of Representatives shall not choose a President whenever the right of choice shall devolve upon them, before the fourth day of March next following, then the Vice-President shall act as President, as in the case of the death or other constitutional disability of the President.

The person having the greatest number of votes as Vice-President, shall be the Vice-President, if such number be a majority of the whole number of Electors appointed, and if no person have a majority, then from the two highest numbers on the list, the Senate shall choose the Vice-President; a quorum for the purpose shall consist of two-thirds of the whole number of Senators, and a majority of the whole number shall be necessary to a choice. But no person constitutionally ineligible to the office of President shall be eligible to that of Vice- President of the United States.

Amendment XIII

1. Neither slavery nor involuntary servitude, except as a punishment for crime whereof the party shall have been duly convicted, shall exist within the United States, or any place subject to their jurisdiction.

2. Congress shall have power to enforce this article by appropriate legislation.

Amendment XIV

1. All persons born or naturalized in the United States, and subject to the jurisdiction thereof, are citizens of the United States and of the State wherein they reside. No State shall make or enforce any law which shall abridge the privileges or immunities of citizens of the United States; nor shall any State deprive any person of life, liberty, or property, without due process of law; nor deny to any person within its jurisdiction the equal protection of the laws.

2. Representatives shall be apportioned among the several States according to their respective numbers, counting the whole number of persons in each State, excluding Indians not taxed. But when the right to vote at any election for the choice of electors for President and Vice-President of the United States, Representatives in Congress, the Executive and Judicial officers of a State, or the members of the Legislature thereof, is denied to any of the male inhabitants of such State, being twenty-one years of age, and citizens of the United States, or in any way abridged, except for participation in rebellion, or other crime, the basis of representation therein shall be reduced in the proportion which the number of such male citizens shall bear to the whole number of male citizens twenty-one years of age in such State.

3. No person shall be a Senator or Representative in Congress, or elector of President and Vice-President, or hold any office, civil or military, under the United States, or under any State, who, having previously taken an oath, as a member of Congress, or as an officer of the United States, or as a member of any State legislature, or as an executive or judicial officer of any State, to support the Constitution of the United States, shall have engaged in insurrection or rebellion against the same, or given aid or comfort to the enemies thereof. But Congress may by a vote of two-thirds of each House, remove such disability.

4. The validity of the public debt of the United States, authorized by law, including debts incurred for payment of pensions and bounties for services in suppressing insurrection or rebellion, shall not be questioned. But neither the United States nor any State shall assume or pay any debt or obligation incurred

in aid of insurrection or rebellion against the United States, or any claim for the loss or emancipation of any slave; but all such debts, obligations and claims shall be held illegal and void.

5. The Congress shall have power to enforce, by appropriate legislation, the provisions of this article.

Amendment XV

1. The right of citizens of the United States to vote shall not be denied or abridged by the United States or by any State on account of race, color, or previous condition of servitude.

2. The Congress shall have power to enforce this article by appropriate legislation.

Amendment XVI

The Congress shall have power to lay and collect taxes on incomes, from whatever source derived, without apportionment among the several States, and without regard to any census or enumeration.

Amendment XVII

The Senate of the United States shall be composed of two Senators from each State, elected by the people thereof, for six years; and each Senator shall have one vote. The electors in each State shall have the qualifications requisite for electors of the most numerous branch of the State legislatures.

When vacancies happen in the representation of any State in the Senate, the executive authority of such State shall issue writs of election to fill such vacancies: Provided, That the legislature of any State may empower the executive thereof to make temporary appointments until the people fill the vacancies by election as the legislature may direct.

This amendment shall not be so construed as to affect the election or term of any Senator chosen before it becomes valid as part of the Constitution.

Amendment XVIII

1. After one year from the ratification of this article the manufacture, sale, or transportation of intoxicating liquors within, the importation thereof into, or the exportation thereof from the United States and all territory subject to the jurisdiction thereof for beverage purposes is hereby prohibited.

2. The Congress and the several States shall have concurrent power to enforce this article by appropriate legislation.

3. This article shall be inoperative unless it shall have been ratified as an amendment to the Constitution by the legislatures of the several States, as provided in the Constitution, within seven years from the date of the submission hereof to the States by the Congress.

Amendment XIX

The right of citizens of the United States to vote shall not be denied or abridged by the United States or by any State on account of sex.

Congress shall have power to enforce this article by appropriate legislation.

Amendment XX

1. The terms of the President and Vice President shall end at noon on the 20th day of January, and the terms of Senators and Representatives at noon on the 3d day of January, of the years in which such terms would have ended if this article had not been ratified; and the terms of their successors shall then begin.

2. The Congress shall assemble at least once in every year, and such meeting shall begin at noon on the 3d day of January, unless they shall by law appoint a different day.

3. If, at the time fixed for the beginning of the term of the President, the President elect shall have died, the Vice President elect shall become President. If a President shall not have been chosen before the time fixed for the beginning of his term, or if the President elect shall have failed to qualify, then the Vice President elect shall act as President until a President shall have qualified; and the Congress may by law provide for the case wherein neither a President elect nor a Vice President elect shall have qualified, declaring who shall then act as President, or the manner in which one who is to act shall be selected, and such person shall act accordingly until a President or Vice President shall have qualified.

4. The Congress may by law provide for the case of the death of any of the persons from whom the House of Representatives may choose a President whenever the right of choice shall have devolved upon them, and for the case of the death of any of the persons from whom the Senate may choose a Vice President whenever the right of choice shall have devolved upon them.

5. Sections 1 and 2 shall take effect on the 15th day of October following the ratification of this article.

6. This article shall be inoperative unless it shall have been ratified as an amendment to the Constitution by the legislatures of three-fourths of the several States within seven years from the date of its submission.

Amendment XXI

1. The eighteenth article of amendment to the Constitution of the United States is hereby repealed.

2. The transportation or importation into any State, Territory, or possession of the United States for delivery or use therein of intoxicating liquors, in violation of the laws thereof, is hereby prohibited.

3. The article shall be inoperative unless it shall have been ratified as an amendment to the Constitution by conventions in the several States, as provided in the Constitution, within seven years from the date of the submission hereof to the States by the Congress.

Amendment XXII

1. No person shall be elected to the office of the President more than twice, and no person who has held the office of President, or acted as President, for more than two years of a term to which some other person was elected President shall be elected to the office of the President more than once. But this Article shall not apply to any person holding the office of President, when this Article was proposed by the Congress, and shall not prevent any person who may be holding the office of President, or acting as President, during the term within which this Article becomes operative from holding the office of President or acting as President during the remainder of such term.

2. This article shall be inoperative unless it shall have been ratified as an amendment to the Constitution by the legislatures of three-fourths of the several States within seven years from the date of its submission to the States by the Congress.

Amendment XXIII

1. The District constituting the seat of Government of the United States shall appoint in such manner as the Congress may direct: A number of electors of President and Vice President equal to the whole number of Senators and Representatives in Congress to which the District would be entitled if it were a State, but in no event more than the least populous State; they shall be in addition to those appointed by the States, but they shall be considered, for the purposes of the election of President and Vice President, to be electors appointed by a State; and they shall meet in the District and perform such duties as provided by the twelfth article of amendment.

2. The Congress shall have power to enforce this article by appropriate legislation.

Amendment XXIV

1. The right of citizens of the United States to vote in any primary or other election for President or Vice President, for electors for President or Vice President, or for Senator or Representative in Congress, shall not be denied or abridged by the United States or any State by reason of failure to pay any poll tax or other tax.

2. The Congress shall have power to enforce this article by appropriate legislation.

Amendment XXV

1. In case of the removal of the President from office or of his death or resignation, the Vice President shall become President.

2. Whenever there is a vacancy in the office of the Vice President, the President shall nominate a Vice President who shall take office upon confirmation by a majority vote of both Houses of Congress.

3. Whenever the President transmits to the President pro tempore of the Senate and the Speaker of the House of Representatives his written declaration that he is unable to discharge the powers and duties of his office, and until he transmits to them a written declaration to the contrary, such powers and duties shall be discharged by the Vice President as Acting President.

4. Whenever the Vice President and a majority of either the principal officers of the executive departments or of such other body as Congress may by law provide, transmit to the President pro tempore of the Senate and the Speaker of the House of Representatives their written declaration that the President is unable to discharge the powers and duties of his office, the Vice President shall immediately assume the powers and duties of the office as Acting President.

Thereafter, when the President transmits to the President pro tempore of the Senate and the Speaker of the House of Representatives his written declaration that no inability exists, he shall resume the powers and duties of his office unless the Vice President and a majority of either the principal officers of the executive department or of such other body as Congress may by law provide, transmit within four days to the President pro tempore of the Senate and the Speaker of the House of Representatives their written declaration that the President is unable to discharge the powers and duties of his office. Thereupon Congress shall decide the issue, assembling within forty eight hours for that purpose if not in session. If the Congress, within twenty one days after receipt of the latter written declaration, or, if Congress is not in session, within twenty one days after Congress is required to assemble, determines by two thirds vote of both Houses that the President is unable to discharge the powers and duties of his office, the Vice President shall continue to discharge the same as Acting President; otherwise, the President shall resume the powers and duties of his office.

Amendment XXVI

1. The right of citizens of the United States, who are eighteen years of age or older, to vote shall not be denied or abridged by the United States or by any State on account of age.

2. The Congress shall have power to enforce this article by appropriate legislation.

Amendment XXVII

No law, varying the compensation for the services of the Senators and Representatives, shall take effect, until an election of Representatives shall have intervened.

UNITED STATES CODE

(Selected Provisions)

Title 28, Judiciary and Judicial Procedure

Chapter 83 — Courts of Appeals

§ 1291. Final Decisions of District Courts

The courts of appeals (other than the United States Court of Appeals for the Federal Circuit) shall have jurisdiction of appeals from all final decisions of the district courts of the United States, the United States District Court for the District of the Canal Zone, the District Court of Guam, and the District Court of the Virgin Islands, except where a direct review may be had in the Supreme Court. The jurisdiction of the United States Court of Appeals for the Federal Circuit shall be limited to the jurisdiction described in sections 1292(c) and (d) and 1295 of this title.

§ 1292. Interlocutory Decisions

(a) Except as provided in subsections (c) and (d) of this section, the courts of appeals shall have jurisdiction of appeals from:

(1) Interlocutory orders of the district courts of the United States, the United States District Court for the District of the Canal Zone, the District Court of Guam, and the District Court of the Virgin Islands, or of the judges thereof, granting, continuing, modifying, refusing or dissolving injunctions, or refusing to dissolve or modify injunctions, except where a direct review may be had in the Supreme Court;

(2) Interlocutory orders appointing receivers, or refusing orders to wind up receiverships or to take steps to accomplish the purposes thereof, such as directing sales or other disposals of property;

(3) Interlocutory decrees of such district courts or the judges thereof determining the rights and liabilities of the parties to admiralty cases in which appeals from final decrees are allowed.

(b) When a district judge, in making in a civil action an order not otherwise appealable under this section, shall be of the opinion that such order involves a controlling question of law as to which there is substantial ground for difference of opinion and that an immediate appeal from the order may materially advance the ultimate termination of the litigation, he shall so state in writing in such order. The Court of Appeals which would have jurisdiction of an appeal of such action may thereupon, in its discretion, permit an appeal to be taken from such order, if application is made to it within ten days after the entry of the order: Provided, however, That application for an appeal hereunder shall not stay proceedings in the district court unless the district judge or the Court of Appeals or a judge thereof shall so order.

(c) The United States Court of Appeals for the Federal Circuit shall have exclusive jurisdiction:

(1) of an appeal from an interlocutory order or decree described in subsection (a) or (b) of this section in any case over which the court would have jurisdiction of an appeal under section 1295 of this title; and

(2) of an appeal from a judgment in a civil action for patent infringement which would otherwise be appealable to the United States Court of Appeals for the Federal Circuit and is final except for an accounting.

(d) (1) When the chief judge of the Court of International Trade issues an order under the provisions of section 256(b) of this title, or when any judge of the Court of International Trade, in issuing any other interlocutory order, includes in the order a statement that a controlling question of law is involved with respect to which there is a substantial ground for difference of opinion and that an immediate appeal from that order may materially advance the ultimate termination of the litigation, the United States Court of Appeals for the Federal Circuit may, in its discretion, permit an appeal to be taken from such order, if application is made to that Court within ten days after the entry of such order.

(2) When the chief judge of the United States Court of Federal Claims issues an order under section 798(b) of this title, or when any judge of the United States Court of Federal Claims, in issuing an interlocutory order, includes in the order a statement that a controlling question of law is involved with respect to which there is a substantial ground for difference of opinion and that an immediate appeal from that order may materially advance the ultimate termination of the litigation, the United States Court of Appeals for the Federal Circuit may, in its discretion, permit an appeal to be taken from such order, if application is made to that Court within ten days after the entry of such order.

(3) Neither the application for nor the granting of an appeal under this subsection shall stay proceedings in the Court of International Trade or in the Court of Federal Claims, as the case may be, unless a stay is ordered by a judge of the Court of International Trade or of the Court of Federal Claims or by the United States Court of Appeals for the Federal Circuit or a judge of that court.

(4) (A) The United States Court of Appeals for the Federal Circuit shall have exclusive jurisdiction of an appeal from an interlocutory order of a district court of the United States, the District Court of Guam, the District Court of the Virgin Islands, or the District Court for the Northern Mariana Islands,

granting or denying, in whole or in part, a motion to transfer an action to the United States Court of Federal Claims under section 1631 of this title.

(B) When a motion to transfer an action to the Court of Federal Claims is filed in a district court, no further proceedings shall be taken in the district court until 60 days after the court has ruled upon the motion. If an appeal is taken from the district court's grant or denial of the motion, proceedings shall be further stayed until the appeal has been decided by the Court of Appeals for the Federal Circuit. The stay of proceedings in the district court shall not bar the granting of preliminary or injunctive relief, where appropriate and where expedition is reasonably necessary. However, during the period in which proceedings are stayed as provided in this subparagraph, no transfer to the Court of Federal Claims pursuant to the motion shall be carried out.

(e) The Supreme Court may prescribe rules, in accordance with section 2072 of this title, to provide for an appeal of an interlocutory decision to the courts of appeals that is not otherwise provided for under subsection (a), (b), (c), or (d).

Chapter 85 — District Courts; Jurisdiction

§ 1331. Federal Question

The district courts shall have original jurisdiction of all civil actions arising under the Constitution, laws, or treaties of the United States.

§ 1332. Diversity of Citizenship; Amount in Controversy; Costs

(a) The district courts shall have original jurisdiction of all civil actions where the matter in controversy exceeds the sum or value of $75,000, exclusive of interest and costs, and is between:

(1) citizens of different States;

(2) citizens of a State and citizens or subjects of a foreign state, except that the district courts shall not have original jurisdiction under this subsection of an action between citizens of a State and citizens or subjects of a foreign state who are lawfully admitted for permanent residence in the United States and are domiciled in the same State;

(3) citizens of different States and in which citizens or subjects of a foreign state are additional parties; and

(4) a foreign state, defined in section 1603(a) of this title, as plaintiff and citizens of a State or of different States.

(b) Except when express provision therefor is otherwise made in a statute of the United States, where the plaintiff who files the case originally in the Federal courts is finally adjudged to be entitled to recover less than the sum or value of $75,000, computed without regard to any setoff or counterclaim to which the defendant may be adjudged to be entitled, and exclusive of interest and costs, the district court may deny costs to the plaintiff and, in addition, may impose costs on the plaintiff.

(c) For the purposes of this section and section 1441 of this title:

(1) a corporation shall be deemed to be a citizen of every State and foreign state by which it has been incorporated and of the State or foreign state where it has its principal place of business, except that in any direct action against the insurer of a policy or contract of liability insurance, whether incorporated or unincorporated, to which action the insured is not joined as a party-defendant, such insurer shall be deemed a citizen of—

(A) every State and foreign state of which the insured is a citizen;

(B) every State and foreign state by which the insurer has been incorporated; and

(C) the State or foreign state where the insurer has its principal place of business; and

(2) the legal representative of the estate of a decedent shall be deemed to be a citizen only of the same State as the decedent, and the legal representative of an infant or incompetent shall be deemed to be a citizen only of the same State as the infant or incompetent.

(d) (1) In this subsection—

(A) the term "class" means all of the class members in a class action;

(B) the term "class action" means any civil action filed under rule 23 of the Federal Rules of Civil Procedure or similar State statute or rule of judicial procedure authorizing an action to be brought by 1 or more representative persons as a class action;

(C) the term "class certification order" means an order issued by a court approving the treatment of some or all aspects of a civil action as a class action; and

(D) the term "class members" means the persons (named or unnamed) who fall within the definition of the proposed or certified class in a class action.

(2) The district courts shall have original jurisdiction of any civil action in which the matter in controversy exceeds the sum or value of $5,000,000, exclusive of interest and costs, and is a class action in which—

(A) any member of a class of plaintiffs is a citizen of a State different from any defendant;

(B) any member of a class of plaintiffs is a foreign state or a citizen or subject of a foreign state and any defendant is a citizen of a State; or

(C) any member of a class of plaintiffs is a citizen of a State and any defendant is a foreign state or a citizen or subject of a foreign state.

(3) A district court may, in the interests of justice and looking at the totality of the circumstances, decline to exercise jurisdiction under paragraph

(2) over a class action in which greater than one-third but less than two-thirds of the members of all proposed plaintiff classes in the aggregate and the primary defendants are citizens of the State in which the action was originally filed based on consideration of—

(A) whether the claims asserted involve matters of national or interstate interest;

(B) whether the claims asserted will be governed by laws of the State in which the action was originally filed or by the laws of other States;

(C) whether the class action has been pleaded in a manner that seeks to avoid Federal jurisdiction;

(D) whether the action was brought in a forum with a distinct nexus with the class members, the alleged harm, or the defendants;

(E) whether the number of citizens of the State in which the action was originally filed in all proposed plaintiff classes in the aggregate is substantially larger than the number of citizens from any other State, and the citizenship of the other members of the proposed class is dispersed among a substantial number of States; and

(F) whether, during the 3-year period preceding the filing of that class action, 1 or more other class actions asserting the same or similar claims on behalf of the same or other persons have been filed.

(4) A district court shall decline to exercise jurisdiction under paragraph (2)

(A) (i) over a class action in which—

(I) greater than two-thirds of the members of all proposed plaintiff classes in the aggregate are citizens of the State in which the action was originally filed;

(II) at least 1 defendant is a defendant—

(aa) from whom significant relief is sought by members of the plaintiff class;

(bb) whose alleged conduct forms a significant basis for the claims asserted by the proposed plaintiff class; and

(cc) who is a citizen of the State in which the action was originally filed; and

(III) principal injuries resulting from the alleged conduct or any related conduct of each defendant were incurred in the State in which the action was originally filed; and

(ii) during the 3-year period preceding the filing of that class action, no other class action has been filed asserting the same or similar factual allegations against any of the defendants on behalf of the same or other persons; or

(B) two-thirds or more of the members of all proposed plaintiff classes in the aggregate, and the primary defendants, are citizens of the State in which the action was originally filed.

(5) Paragraphs (2) through (4) shall not apply to any class action in which—

(A) the primary defendants are States, State officials, or other governmental entities against whom the district court may be foreclosed from ordering relief; or

(B) the number of members of all proposed plaintiff classes in the aggregate is less than 100.

(6) In any class action, the claims of the individual class members shall be aggregated to determine whether the matter in controversy exceeds the sum or value of $5,000,000, exclusive of interest and costs.

(7) Citizenship of the members of the proposed plaintiff classes shall be determined for purposes of paragraphs (2) through (6) as of the date of filing of the complaint or amended complaint, or, if the case stated by the initial pleading is not subject to Federal jurisdiction, as of the date of service by plaintiffs of an amended pleading, motion, or other paper, indicating the existence of Federal jurisdiction.

(8) This subsection shall apply to any class action before or after the entry of a class certification order by the court with respect to that action.

(9) Paragraph (2) shall not apply to any class action that solely involves a claim —

(A) concerning a covered security as defined under 16(f)(3) of the Securities Act of 1933 (15 U.S.C. 78p(f)(3)) and section 28(f)(5)(E) of the Securities Exchange Act of 1934 (15 U.S.C. 78bb(f)(5)(E));

(B) that relates to the internal affairs or governance of a corporation or other form of business enterprise and that arises under or by virtue of the laws of the State in which such corporation or business enterprise is incorporated or organized; or

(C) that relates to the rights, duties (including fiduciary duties), and obligations relating to or created by or pursuant to any security (as defined under section 2(a)(1) of the Securities Act of 1933 (15 U.S.C. 77b(a)(1)) and the regulations issued thereunder).

(10) For purposes of this subsection and section 1453, an unincorporated association shall be deemed to be a citizen of the State where it has its principal place of business and the State under whose laws it is is organized.

(11) (A) For purposes of this subsection and section 1453, a mass action shall be deemed to be a class action removable under paragraphs (2) through (10) if it otherwise meets the provisions of those paragraphs.

(B) (i) As used in subparagraph (A), the term "mass action" means any civil action (except a civil action within the scope of section 1711(2)) in which monetary relief claims of 100 or more persons are proposed to be tried jointly on the ground that the plaintiffs' claims involve common questions of law or fact, except that jurisdiction shall exist only over those plaintiffs whose claims in a mass action satisfy the jurisdictional amount requirements under subsection (a).

(ii) As used in subparagraph (A), the term "mass action" shall not include any civil action in which —

(I) all of the claims in the action arise from an event or occurrence in the State in which the action was filed, and that allegedly resulted in injuries in that State or in States contiguous to that State;

(II) the claims are joined upon motion of a defendant;

(III) all of the claims in the action are asserted on behalf of the general public (and not on behalf of individual claimants or members of a purported class) pursuant to a State statute specifically authorizing such action; or

(IV) the claims have been consolidated or coordinated solely for pretrial proceedings.

(C) (i) Any action(s) removed to Federal court pursuant to this subsection shall not thereafter be transferred to any other court pursuant to section 1407, or the rules promulgated thereunder, unless a majority of the plaintiffs in the action request transfer pursuant to section 1407.

(ii) This subparagraph will not apply —

(I) to cases certified pursuant to rule 23 of the Federal Rules of Civil Procedure; or

(II) if plaintiffs propose that the action proceed as a class action pursuant to rule 23 of the Federal Rules of Civil Procedure.

(D) The limitations periods on any claims asserted in a mass action that is removed to Federal court pursuant to this subsection shall be deemed tolled during the period that the action is pending in Federal court.

(e) The word "States", as used in this section, includes the Territories, the District of Columbia, and the Commonwealth of Puerto Rico.

§ 1333. Admiralty, Maritime and Prize Cases

The district courts shall have original jurisdiction, exclusive of the courts of the States, of:

(1) Any civil case of admiralty or maritime jurisdiction, saving to suitors in all cases all other remedies to which they are otherwise entitled.

(2) Any prize brought into the United States and all proceedings for the condemnation of property taken as prize.

§ 1335. Interpleader

(a) The district courts shall have original jurisdiction of any civil action of interpleader or in the nature of interpleader filed by any person, firm, or corporation, association, or society having in his or its custody or possession money or property of the value of $500 or more, or having issued a note, bond, certificate, policy of insurance, or other instrument of value or amount of $500 or more, or providing for the delivery or payment or the loan of money or property of such amount or value, or being under any obligation written or unwritten to the amount of $500 or more, if

(1) Two or more adverse claimants, of diverse citizenship as defined in subsection (a) or (d) of section 1332 of this title, are claiming or may claim to be entitled to such money or property, or to any one or more of the benefits arising by virtue of any note, bond, certificate, policy or other instrument, or arising by virtue of any such obligation; and if

(2) the plaintiff has deposited such money or property or has paid the amount of or the loan or other value of such instrument or the amount due under such obligation into the registry of the court, there to abide the judgment of the court, or has given bond payable to the clerk of the court in such amount and with such surety as the court or judge may deem proper, conditioned upon the compliance by the plaintiff with the future order or judgment of the court with respect to the subject matter of the controversy.

(b) Such an action may be entertained although the titles or claims of the conflicting claimants do not have a common origin, or are not identical, but are adverse to and independent of one another.

§ 1343. Civil Rights and Elective Franchise

(a) The district courts shall have original jurisdiction of any civil action authorized by law to be commenced by any person:

(1) To recover damages for injury to his person or property, or because of the deprivation of any right or privilege of a citizen of the United States, by any act done in furtherance of any conspiracy mentioned in section 1985 of Title 42;

(2) To recover damages from any person who fails to prevent or to aid in preventing any wrongs mentioned in section 1985 of Title 42 which he had knowledge were about to occur and power to prevent;

(3) To redress the deprivation, under color of any State law, statute, ordinance, regulation, custom or usage, of any right, privilege or immunity secured by the Constitution of the United States or by any Act of Congress providing for equal rights of citizens or of all persons within the jurisdiction of the United States;

(4) To recover damages or to secure equitable or other relief under any Act of Congress providing for the protection of civil rights, including the right to vote.

(b) For purposes of this section:

(1) the District of Columbia shall be considered to be a State; and

(2) any Act of Congress applicable exclusively to the District of Columbia shall be considered to be a statute of the District of Columbia.

§ 1344. Election Disputes

The district courts shall have original jurisdiction of any civil action to recover possession of any office, except that of elector of President or Vice President, United States Senator, Representative in or delegate to Congress, or member of a state legislature, authorized by law to be commenced, wherein it appears that the sole question touching the title to office arises out of denial of the right to vote, to any citizen offering to vote, on account of race, color or previous condition of servitude.

The jurisdiction under this section shall extend only so far as to determine the rights of the parties to office by reason of the denial of the right, guaranteed by the Constitution of the United States and secured by any law, to enforce the right of citizens of the United States to vote in all the States.

§ 1345. United States as Plaintiff

Except as otherwise provided by Act of Congress, the district courts shall have original jurisdiction of all civil actions, suits or proceedings commenced by the United States, or by any agency or officer thereof expressly authorized to sue by Act of Congress

§ 1346. United States as Defendant

(a) The district courts shall have original jurisdiction, concurrent with the United States Court of Federal Claims, of:

(1) Any civil action against the United States for the recovery of any internal-revenue tax alleged to have been erroneously or illegally assessed or collected, or any penalty claimed to have been collected without authority or any sum alleged to have been excessive or in any manner wrongfully collected under the internal- revenue laws;

(2) Any other civil action or claim against the United States, not exceeding $10,000 in amount, founded either upon the Constitution, or any Act of Congress, or any regulation of an executive department, or upon any express or implied contract with the United States, or for liquidated or unliquidated damages in cases not sounding in tort, except that the district courts shall not have jurisdiction of any civil action or claim against the United States founded

upon any express or implied contract with the United States or for liquidated or unliquidated damages in cases not sounding in tort which are subject to sections 7107(b)(1) and 7107(a)(1) of title 41. For the purpose of this paragraph, an express or implied contract with the Army and Air Force Exchange Service, Navy Exchanges, Marine Corps Exchanges, Coast Guard Exchanges, or Exchange Councils of the National Aeronautics and Space Administration shall be considered an express or implied contract with the United States.

(b) (1) Subject to the provisions of chapter 171 of this title, the district courts, together with the United States District Court for the District of the Canal Zone and the District Court of the Virgin Islands, shall have exclusive jurisdiction of civil actions on claims against the United States, for money damages, accruing on and after January 1, 1945, for injury or loss of property, or personal injury or death caused by the negligent or wrongful act or omission of any employee of the Government while acting within the scope of his office or employment, under circumstances where the United States, if a private person, would be liable to the claimant in accordance with the law of the place where the act or omission occurred.

(2) No person convicted of a felony who is incarcerated while awaiting sentencing or while serving a sentence may bring a civil action against the United States or an agency, officer, or employee of the Government, for mental or emotional injury suffered while in custody without a prior showing of physical injury or the commission of a sexual act (as defined in section 2246 of Title 18).

(c) The jurisdiction conferred by this section includes jurisdiction of any set-off, counterclaim, or other claim or demand whatever on the part of the United States against any plaintiff commencing an action under this section.

(d) The district courts shall not have jurisdiction under this section of any civil action or claim for a pension.

(e) The district courts shall have original jurisdiction of any civil action against the United States provided in section 6226, 6228(a), 7426, or 7428 (in the case of the United States district court for the District of Columbia) or section 7429 of the Internal Revenue Code of 1986.

(f) The district courts shall have exclusive original jurisdiction of civil actions under section 2409a to quiet title to an estate or interest in real property in which an interest is claimed by the United States.

(g) Subject to the provisions of chapter 179, the district courts of the United States shall have exclusive jurisdiction over any civil action commenced under section 453(2) of title 3, by a covered employee under chapter 5 of such title.

§ 1350. Alien's Action for Tort

The district courts shall have original jurisdiction of any civil action by an alien for a tort only, committed in violation of the law of nations or a treaty of the United States.

§ 1359. Parties Collusively Joined or Made

A district court shall not have jurisdiction of a civil action in which any party, by assignment or otherwise, has been improperly or collusively made or joined to invoke the jurisdiction of such court.

§ 1361. Action to Compel an Officer of the United States to Perform his Duty

The district courts shall have original jurisdiction of any action in the nature of mandamus to compel an officer or employee of the United States or any agency thereof to perform a duty owed to the plaintiff.

§ 1362. Indian Tribes

The district courts shall have original jurisdiction of all civil actions, brought by any Indian tribe or band with a governing body duly recognized by the Secretary of the Interior, wherein the matter in controversy arises under the Constitution, laws, or treaties of the United States.

§ 1367. Supplemental Jurisdiction

(a) Except as provided in subsections (b) and (c) or as expressly provided otherwise by Federal statute, in any civil action of which the district courts have original jurisdiction, the district courts shall have supplemental jurisdiction over all other claims that are so related to claims in the action within such original jurisdiction that they form part of the same case or controversy under Article III of the United States Constitution. Such supplemental jurisdiction shall include claims that involve the joinder or intervention of additional parties.

(b) In any civil action of which the district courts have original jurisdiction founded solely on section 1332 of this title, the district courts shall not have supplemental jurisdiction under subsection (a) over claims by plaintiffs against persons made parties under Rule 14, 19, 20, or 24 of the Federal Rules of Civil Procedure, or over claims by persons proposed to be joined as plaintiffs under Rule 19 of such rules, or seeking to intervene as plaintiffs under Rule 24 of such rules, when exercising supplemental jurisdiction over such claims would be inconsistent with the jurisdictional requirements of section 1332.

(c) The district courts may decline to exercise supplemental jurisdiction over a claim under subsection (a) if:

(1) the claim raises a novel or complex issue of State law,

(2) the claim substantially predominates over the claim or claims over which the district court has original jurisdiction,

(3) the district court has dismissed all claims over which it has original jurisdiction, or

(4) in exceptional circumstances, there are other compelling reasons for declining jurisdiction.

(d) The period of limitations for any claim asserted under subsection (a), and for any other claim in the same action that is voluntarily dismissed at the same time as or after the dismissal of the claim under subsection (a), shall be tolled while the claim is pending and for a period of 30 days after it is dismissed unless State law provides for a longer tolling period.

(e) As used in this section, the term "State" includes the District of Columbia, the Commonwealth of Puerto Rico, and any territory or possession of the United States.

§ 1369. Multiparty, Multiforum Jurisdiction

(a) In general. The district courts shall have original jurisdiction of any civil action involving minimal diversity between adverse parties that arises from a single accident, where at least 75 natural persons have died in the accident at a discrete location, if:

(1) a defendant resides in a State and a substantial part of the accident took place in another State or other location, regardless of whether that defendant is also a resident of the State where a substantial part of the accident took place;

(2) any two defendants reside in different States, regardless of whether such defendants are also residents of the same State or States; or

(3) substantial parts of the accident took place in different States.

(b) Limitation of jurisdiction of district courts. The district court shall abstain from hearing any civil action described in subsection (a) in which:

(1) the substantial majority of all plaintiffs are citizens of a single State of which the primary defendants are also citizens; and

(2) the claims asserted will be governed primarily by the laws of that State.

(c) Special rules and definitions. For purposes of this section:

(1) minimal diversity exists between adverse parties if any party is a citizen of a State and any adverse party is a citizen of another State, a citizen or subject of a foreign state, or a foreign state as defined in section 1603(a) of this title;

(2) a corporation is deemed to be a citizen of any State, and a citizen or subject of any foreign state, in which it is incorporated or has its principal place of business, and is deemed to be a resident of any State in which it is incorporated or licensed to do business or is doing business;

(3) the term "injury" means:

(A) physical harm to a natural person; and

(B) physical damage to or destruction of tangible property, but only if physical harm described in subparagraph (A) exists;

(4) the term "accident" means a sudden accident, or a natural event culminating in an accident, that results in death incurred at a discrete location by at least 75 natural persons; and

(5) the term "State" includes the District of Columbia, the Commonwealth of Puerto Rico, and any territory or possession of the United States.

(d) Intervening parties. In any action in a district court which is or could have been brought, in whole or in part, under this section, any person with a claim arising from the accident described in subsection (a) shall be permitted to intervene as a party plaintiff in the action, even if that person could not have brought an action in a district court as an original matter.

(e) Notification of judicial panel on multidistrict litigation. A district court in which an action under this section is pending shall promptly notify the judicial panel on multidistrict litigation of the pendency of the action.

Chapter 87 — District Courts; Venue

§ 1390. Venue: Scope

(a) Venue defined. As used in this chapter, the term "venue" refers to the geographic specification of the proper court or courts for the litigation of a civil action that is within the subject-matter jurisdiction of the district courts in general, and does not refer to any grant or restriction of subject-matter jurisdiction providing for a civil action to be adjudicated only by the district court for a particular district or districts.

(b) Exclusion of certain cases. Except as otherwise provided by law, this chapter shall not govern the venue of a civil action in which the district court exercises the jurisdiction conferred by section 1333, except that such civil actions may be transferred between district courts as provided in this chapter.

(c) Clarification regarding cases removed from State courts. This chapter shall not determine the district court to which a civil action pending in a State court may be removed, but shall govern the transfer of an action so removed as between districts and divisions of the United States district courts.

§ 1391. Venue Generally

(a) Applicability of section. Except as otherwise provided by law —

(1) this section shall govern the venue of all civil actions brought in district courts of the United States; and

(2) the proper venue for a civil action shall be determined without regard to whether the action is local or transitory in nature.

(b) Venue in general. A civil action may be brought in —

(1) a judicial district in which any defendant resides, if all defendants are residents of the State in which the district is located;

(2) a judicial district in which a substantial part of the events or omissions giving rise to the claim occurred, or a substantial part of property that is the subject of the action is situated; or

(3) if there is no district in which an action may otherwise be brought as provided in this section, any judicial district in which any defendant is subject to the court's personal jurisdiction with respect to such action.

(c) Residency. For all venue purposes —

(1) a natural person, including an alien lawfully admitted for permanent residence in the United States, shall be deemed to reside in the judicial district in which that person is domiciled;

(2) an entity with the capacity to sue and be sued in its common name under applicable law, whether or not incorporated, shall be deemed to reside, if a defendant, in any judicial district in which such defendant is subject to the court's personal jurisdiction with respect to the civil action in question and, if a plaintiff, only in the judicial district in which it maintains its principal place of business; and

(3) a defendant not resident in the United States may be sued in any judicial district, and the joinder of such a defendant shall be disregarded in determining where the action may be brought with respect to other defendants.

(d) Residency of corporations in States with multiple districts. For purposes of venue under this chapter, in a State which has more than one judicial district and in which a defendant that is a corporation is subject to personal jurisdiction at the time an action is commenced, such corporation shall be deemed to reside in any district in that State within which its contacts would be sufficient to subject it to personal jurisdiction if that district were a separate State, and, if there is no such district, the corporation shall be deemed to reside in the district within which it has the most significant contacts.

(e) Actions where defendant is officer or employee of the United States.

(1) In general. A civil action in which a defendant is an officer or employee of the United States or any agency thereof acting in his official capacity or under color of legal authority, or an agency of the United States, or the United States, may, except as otherwise provided by law, be brought in any judicial district in which (A) a defendant in the action resides, (B) a substantial part of the events or omissions giving rise to the claim occurred, or a substantial part of property that is the subject of the action is situated, or (C) the plaintiff resides if no real property is involved in the action. Additional persons may be joined as parties to any such action in accordance with the Federal Rules of Civil

Procedure and with such other venue requirements as would be applicable if the United States or one of its officers, employees, or agencies were not a party.

(2) Service. The summons and complaint in such an action shall be served as provided by the Federal Rules of Civil Procedure except that the delivery of the summons and complaint to the officer or agency as required by the rules may be made by certified mail beyond the territorial limits of the district in which the action is brought.

(f) Civil actions against a foreign state. A civil action against a foreign state as defined in section 1603(a) of this title may be brought:

(1) in any judicial district in which a substantial part of the events or omissions giving rise to the claim occurred, or a substantial part of property that is the subject of the action is situated;

(2) in any judicial district in which the vessel or cargo of a foreign state is situated, if the claim is asserted under section 1605(b) of this title;

(3) in any judicial district in which the agency or instrumentality is licensed to do business or is doing business, if the action is brought against an agency or instrumentality of a foreign state as defined in section 1603(b) of this title; or

(4) in the United States District Court for the District of Columbia if the action is brought against a foreign state or political subdivision thereof.

(g) Multiparty, multiforum litigation. A civil action in which jurisdiction of the district court is based upon section 1369 of this title may be brought in any district in which any defendant resides or in which a substantial part of the accident giving rise to the action took place.

§ 1397. Interpleader

Any civil action of interpleader or in the nature of interpleader under section 1335 of this title may be brought in the judicial district in which one or more of the claimants reside.

§ 1404. Change of Venue

(a) For the convenience of parties and witnesses, in the interest of justice, a district court may transfer any civil action to any other district or division where it might have been brought or to any district or division to which all parties have consented.

(b) Upon motion, consent or stipulation of all parties, any action, suit or proceeding of a civil nature or any motion or hearing thereof, may be transferred, in the discretion of the court, from the division in which pending to any other division in the same district. Transfer of proceedings in rem brought by or on behalf of the United States may be transferred under this section without the consent of the United States where all other parties request transfer.

(c) A district court may order any civil action to be tried at any place within the division in which it is pending.

(d) Transfers from a district court of the United States to the District Court of Guam, the District Court for the Northern Mariana Islands, or the District Court of the Virgin Islands shall not be permitted under this section. As otherwise used in this section, the term "district court" includes the District Court of Guam, the District Court for the Northern Mariana Islands, and the District Court of the Virgin Islands, and the term "district" includes the territorial jurisdiction of each such court.

§ 1406. Cure or Waiver of Defects

(a) The district court of a district in which is filed a case laying venue in the wrong division or district shall dismiss, or if it be in the interest of justice, transfer such case to any district or division in which it could have been brought.

(b) Nothing in this chapter shall impair the jurisdiction of a district court of any matter involving a party who does not interpose timely and sufficient objection to the venue.

(c) As used in this section, the term "district court" includes the District Court of Guam, the District Court for the Northern Mariana Islands, and the District Court of the Virgin Islands, and the term "district" includes the territorial jurisdiction of each such court.

§ 1407. Multidistrict Litigation

(a) When civil actions involving one or more common questions of fact are pending in different districts, such actions may be transferred to any district for coordinated or consolidated pretrial proceedings. Such transfers shall be made by the judicial panel on multidistrict litigation authorized by this section upon its determination that transfers for such proceedings will be for the convenience of parties and witnesses and will promote the just and efficient conduct of such actions. Each action so transferred shall be remanded by the panel at or before the conclusion of such pretrial proceedings to the district from which it was transferred unless it shall have been previously terminated: Provided, however, That the panel may separate any claim, cross-claim, counter-claim, or third-party claim and remand any of such claims before the remainder of the action is remanded.

(b) Such coordinated or consolidated pretrial proceedings shall be conducted by a judge or judges to whom such actions are assigned by the judicial panel on multidistrict litigation. For this purpose, upon request of the panel, a circuit judge or a district judge may be designated and assigned temporarily for service in the transferee district by the Chief Justice of the United States or the chief judge of the circuit, as may be required, in accordance with the provisions of chapter 13 of this title. With the consent of the transferee district court, such actions may be assigned by the panel to a judge or judges of such district. The judge or judges to whom such actions are assigned, the members of the judicial panel on multidistrict litigation, and other circuit and district judges designated when needed by the panel may exercise the powers of a district judge in any district for the purpose of conducting pretrial depositions in such coordinated or consolidated pretrial proceedings.

(c) Proceedings for the transfer of an action under this section may be initiated by:

(i) the judicial panel on multidistrict litigation upon its own initiative, or

(ii) motion filed with the panel by a party in any action in which transfer for coordinated or consolidated pretrial proceedings under this section may be appropriate. A copy of such motion shall be filed in the district court in which the moving party's action is pending.

The panel shall give notice to the parties in all actions in which transfers for coordinated or consolidated pretrial proceedings are contemplated, and such notice shall specify the time and place of any hearing to determine whether such transfer shall be made. Orders of the panel to set a hearing and other orders of the panel issued prior to the order either directing or denying transfer shall be filed in the office of the clerk of the district court in which a transfer hearing is to be or has been held. The panel's order of transfer shall be based upon a record of such hearing at which material evidence may be offered by any party to an action pending in any district that would be affected by the proceedings under this section, and shall be supported by findings of fact and conclusions of law based upon such record. Orders of transfer and such other orders as the panel may make thereafter shall be filed in the office of the clerk of the district court of the transferee district and shall be effective when thus filed. The clerk of the transferee district court shall forthwith transmit a certified copy of the panel's order to transfer to the clerk of the district court from which the action is being transferred. An order denying transfer shall be filed in each district wherein there is a case pending in which the motion for transfer has been made.

(d) The judicial panel on multidistrict litigation shall consist of seven circuit and district judges designated from time to time by the Chief Justice of the United States, no two of whom shall be from the same circuit. The concurrence of four members shall be necessary to any action by the panel.

(e) No proceedings for review of any order of the panel may be permitted except by extraordinary writ pursuant to the provisions of title 28, section 1651, United States Code. Petitions for an extraordinary writ to review an order of the panel to set a transfer hearing and other orders of the panel issued prior to the order either directing or denying transfer shall be filed only in the court of appeals having jurisdiction over the district in which a hearing is to be or has been held. Petitions for an extraordinary writ to review an order to transfer or orders subsequent to transfer shall be filed only in the court of appeals having jurisdiction over the transferee district. There shall be no appeal or review of an order of the panel denying a motion to transfer for consolidated or coordinated proceedings.

(f) The panel may prescribe rules for the conduct of its business not inconsistent with Acts of Congress and the Federal Rules of Civil Procedure.

(g) Nothing in this section shall apply to any action in which the United States or a State is a complainant arising under the antitrust laws. "Antitrust laws" as used herein include those acts referred to in the Act of October 15, 1914, as amended (38 Stat. 730; 15 U.S.C. 12), and also include the Act of June 19, 1936 (49 Stat. 1526; 15 U.S.C. 13, 13a, and 13b) and the Act of September 26, 1914, as added March 21, 1938 (52 Stat. 116, 117; 15 U.S.C. 56).

Chapter 89 — District Courts; Removal of Cases from State Courts

§ 1441. Actions Removable Generally

(a) Generally. Except as otherwise expressly provided by Act of Congress, any civil action brought in a State court of which the district courts of the United States have original jurisdiction, may be removed by the defendant or the defendants, to the district court of the United States for the district and division embracing the place where such action is pending.

(b) Removal based on diversity of citizenship.

(1) In determining whether a civil action is removable on the basis of the jurisdiction under section 1332(a) of this title, the citizenship of defendants sued under fictitious names shall be disregarded.

(2) A civil action otherwise removable solely on the basis of the jurisdiction under section 1332(a) of this title may not be removed if any of the parties in interest properly joined and served as defendants is a citizen of the State in which such action is brought.

(c) Joinder of Federal law claims and State law claims.

(1) If a civil action includes —

(A) a claim arising under the Constitution, laws, or treaties of the United States (within the meaning of section 1331 of this title), and

(B) a claim not within the original or supplemental jurisdiction of the district court or a claim that has been made nonremovable by statute, the entire action may be removed if the action would be removable without the inclusion of the claim described in subparagraph (B).

(2) Upon removal of an action described in paragraph (1), the district court shall sever from the action all claims described in paragraph (1)(B) and shall remand the severed claims to the State court from which the action was removed. Only defendants against whom a claim described in paragraph (1)(A) has been asserted are required to join in or consent to the removal under paragraph (1).

(d) Actions against foreign States. Any civil action brought in a State court against a foreign state as defined in section 1603(a) of this title may be removed by the foreign state to the district court of the United States for the district and division embracing the place where such action is pending. Upon removal the action shall be tried by the court without jury. Where removal is based upon this subsection, the time limitations of section 1446(b) of this chapter may be enlarged at any time for cause shown.

(e) Multiparty, multiforum jurisdiction.

(1) Notwithstanding the provisions of subsection (b) of this section, a defendant in a civil action in a State court may remove the action to the district court of the United States for the district and division embracing the place where the action is pending if:

(A) the action could have been brought in a United States district court under section 1369 of this title; or

(B) the defendant is a party to an action which is or could have been brought, in whole or in part, under section 1369 in a United States district court and arises from the same accident as the action in State court, even if the action to be removed could not have been brought in a district court as an original matter.

The removal of an action under this subsection shall be made in accordance with section 1446 of this title, except that a notice of removal may also be filed before trial of the action in State court within 30 days after the date on which the defendant first becomes a party to an action under section 1369 in a United States district court that arises from the same accident as the action in State court, or at a later time with leave of the district court.

(2) Whenever an action is removed under this subsection and the district court to which it is removed or transferred under section 1407(j) has made a liability determination requiring further proceedings as to damages, the district court shall remand the action to the State court from which it had been removed for the determination of damages, unless the court finds that, for the convenience of parties and witnesses and in the interest of justice, the action should be retained for the determination of damages.

(3) Any remand under paragraph (2) shall not be effective until 60 days after the district court has issued an order determining liability and has certified its intention to remand the removed action for the determination of damages.

An appeal with respect to the liability determination of the district court may be taken during that 60-day period to the court of appeals with appellate jurisdiction over the district court. In the event a party files such an appeal, the remand shall not be effective until the appeal has been finally disposed of. Once the remand has become effective, the liability determination shall not be subject to further review by appeal or otherwise.

(4) Any decision under this subsection concerning remand for the determination of damages shall not be reviewable by appeal or otherwise.

(5) An action removed under this subsection shall be deemed to be an action under section 1369 and an action in which jurisdiction is based on section 1369 of this title for purposes of this section and sections 1407, 1697, and 1785 of this title.

(6) Nothing in this subsection shall restrict the authority of the district court to transfer or dismiss an action on the ground of inconvenient forum.

(f) Derivative removal jurisdiction. The court to which a civil action is removed under this section is not precluded from hearing and determining any claim in such civil action because the State court from which such civil action is removed did not have jurisdiction over that claim.

§ 1443. Civil Rights Cases

Any of the following civil actions or criminal prosecutions, commenced in a State court may be removed by the defendant to the district court of the United States for the district and division embracing the place wherein it is pending:

(1) Against any person who is denied or cannot enforce in the courts of such State a right under any law providing for the equal civil rights of citizens of the United States, or of all persons within the jurisdiction thereof;

(2) For any act under color of authority derived from any law providing for equal rights, or for refusing to do any act on the ground that it would be inconsistent with such law.

§ 1445. Nonremovable Actions

(a) A civil action in any State court against a railroad or its receivers or trustees, arising under sections 1-4 and 5-10 of the Act of April 22, 1908 (45 U.S.C. 51-54, 55-60), may not be removed to any district court of the United States.

(b) A civil action in any State court against a carrier or its receivers or trustees to recover damages for delay, loss, or injury of shipments, arising under section 11706 or 14706 of title 49, may not be removed to any district court of the United States unless the matter in controversy exceeds $10,000, exclusive of interest and costs.

(c) A civil action in any State court arising under the workmen's compensation laws of such State may not be removed to any district court of the United States.

(d) A civil action in any State court arising under section 40302 of the Violence Against Women Act of 1994 may not be removed to any district court of the United States.

§ 1446. Procedure for Removal of Civil Actions

(a) Generally. A defendant or defendants desiring to remove any civil action from a State court shall file in the district court of the United States for the district and division within which such action is pending a notice of removal signed pursuant to Rule 11 of the Federal Rules of Civil Procedure and containing a short and plain statement of the grounds for removal, together with a copy of all process, pleadings, and orders served upon such defendant or defendants in such action.

(b) Requirements; generally.

(1) The notice of removal of a civil action or proceeding shall be filed within 30 days after the receipt by the defendant, through service or otherwise, of a copy of the initial pleading setting forth the claim for relief upon which such action or proceeding is based, or within 30 days after the service of summons upon the defendant if such initial pleading has then been filed in court and is not required to be served on the defendant, whichever period is shorter.

(2) (A) When a civil action is removed solely under section 1441(a), all defendants who have been properly joined and served must join in or consent to the removal of the action.

(B) Each defendant shall have 30 days after receipt by or service on that defendant of the initial pleading or summons described in paragraph (1) to file the notice of removal.

(C) If defendants are served at different times, and a later-served defendant files a notice of removal, any earlier-served defendant may consent to the removal even though that earlier-served defendant did not previously initiate or consent to removal.

(3) Except as provided in subsection (c), if the case stated by the initial pleading is not removable, a notice of removal may be filed within 30 days after receipt by the defendant, through service or otherwise, of a copy of an amended pleading, motion, order or other paper from which it may first be ascertained that the case is one which is or has become removable.

(c) Requirements; removal based on diversity of citizenship.

(1) A case may not be removed under subsection (b)(3) on the basis of jurisdiction conferred by section 1332 more than 1 year after commencement of the action, unless the district court finds that the plaintiff has acted in bad faith in order to prevent a defendant from removing the action.

(2) If removal of a civil action is sought on the basis of the jurisdiction conferrred by section 1332(a), the sum demanded in good faith in the initial pleading shall be deemed to be the amount in controversy, except that—

(A) the notice of removal may assert the amount in controversy if the initial pleading seeks—

(i) nonmonetary relief; or

(ii) a money judgment, but the State practice either does not permit demand for a specific sum or permits recovery of damages in excess of the amount demanded; and

(B) removal of the action is proper on the basis of an amount in controversy asserted under subparagraph (A) if the district court finds, by the preponderance of the evidence, that the amount in controversy exceeds the amount specified in section 1332(a).

(3) (A) If the case stated by the initial pleading is not removable solely because the amount in controversy does not exceed the amount specified in section 1332(a), information relating to the amount in controversy in the record of the State proceeding, or in responses to discovery, shall be treated as an "other paper" under subsection (b)(3).

(B) If the notice of removal is filed more than 1 year after commencement of the action and the district court finds that the plaintiff deliberately failed to disclose the actual amount in controversy to prevent removal, that finding shall be deemed bad faith under paragraph (1).

(d) Notice to adverse parties and State court. Promptly after the filing of such notice of removal of a civil action the defendant or defendants shall give written notice thereof to all adverse parties and shall file a copy of the notice with the clerk of such State court, which shall effect the removal and the State court shall proceed no further unless and until the case is remanded.

(e) Counterclaim in 337 proceeding. With respect to any counterclaim removed to a district court pursuant to section 337(c) of the Tariff Act of 1930, the district court shall resolve such counterclaim in the same manner as an original complaint under the Federal Rules of Civil Procedure, except that the payment of a filing fee shall not be required in such cases and the counterclaim shall relate back to the date of the original complaint in the proceeding before the International Trade Commission under section 337 of that Act.

[(f) Redesignated (e)]

(g) Where the civil action or criminal prosecution that is removable under section 1442(a) is a proceeding in which a judicial order for testimony or documents is sought or issued or sought to be enforced, the 30-day requirement of subsection (b) of this section and paragraph (1) of section 1455(b)) is satisfied if the person or entity desiring to remove the proceeding files the notice of removal not later than 30 days after receiving, through service, notice of any such proceeding.

§ 1447. Procedure After Removal Generally

(a) In any case removed from a State court, the district court may issue all necessary orders and process to bring before it all proper parties whether served by process issued by the State court or otherwise.

(b) It may require the removing party to file with its clerk copies of all records and proceedings in such State court or may cause the same to be brought before it by writ of certiorari issued to such State court.

(c) A motion to remand the case on the basis of any defect other than lack of subject matter jurisdiction must be made within 30 days after the filing of the notice of removal under section 1446(a). If at any time before final judgment it appears that the district court lacks subject matter jurisdiction, the case shall be remanded. An order remanding the case may require payment of just costs and any actual expenses, including attorney fees, incurred as a result of the removal. A certified copy of the order of remand shall be mailed by the clerk to the clerk of the State court. The State court may thereupon proceed with such case.

(d) An order remanding a case to the State court from which it was removed is not reviewable on appeal or otherwise, except that an order remanding a case to the State court from which it was removed pursuant to section 1442 or 1443 of this title shall be reviewable by appeal or otherwise.

(e) If after removal the plaintiff seeks to join additional defendants whose joinder would destroy subject matter jurisdiction, the court may deny joinder, or permit joinder and remand the action to the State court.

§ 1448. Process After Removal

In all cases removed from any State court to any district court of the United States in which any one or more of the defendants has not been served with process or in which the service has not been perfected prior to removal, or in which process served proves to be defective, such process or service may be completed or new process issued in the same manner as in cases originally filed in such district court.

This section shall not deprive any defendant upon whom process is served after removal of his right to move to remand the case.

§ 1453. Removal of Class Actions

(a) Definitions. In this section, the terms "class," "class action," "class certification order," and "class member" shall have the meanings given such terms under section 1332(d)(1).

(b) In general. A class action may be removed to a district court of the United States in accordance with section 1446 (except that the 1-year limitation under section 1446(c)(1) shall not apply), without regard to whether any defendant is a citizen of the State in which the action is brought, except that such action may be removed by any defendant without the consent of all defendants.

(c) Review of remand orders.

(1) In general. Section 1447 shall apply to any removal of a case under this section, except that notwithstanding section 1447(d), a court of appeals may accept an appeal from an order of a district court granting or denying a motion to remand a class action to the State court from which it was removed if application is made to the court of appeals not more than 10 days after entry of the order.

(2) Time period for judgment. — If the court of appeals accepts an appeal under paragraph (1), the court shall complete all action on such appeal, including rendering judgment, not later than 60 days after the date on which such appeal was filed, unless an extension is granted under paragraph (3).

(3) Extension of time period. — The court of appeals may grant an extension of the 60-day period described in paragraph (2) if —

(A) all parties to the proceeding agree to such extension, for any period of time; or

(B) such extension is for good cause shown and in the interests of justice, for a period not to exceed 10 days.

(4) Denial of appeal. If a final judgment on the appeal under paragraph (1) is not issued before the end of the period described in paragraph (2), including any extension under paragraph (3), the appeal shall be denied.

(d) Exception. This section shall not apply to any class action that solely involves —

(1) a claim concerning a covered security as defined under section 16(f)(3) of the Securities Act of 1933 (15 U.S.C. 78p(f)(3)) and section 28(f)(5)(E) of the Securities Exchange Act of 1934 (15 U.S.C. 78bb(f)(5)(E));

(2) a claim that relates to the internal affairs or governance of a corporation or other form of business enterprise and arises under or by virtue of the laws of the State in which such corporation or business enterprise is incorporated or organized; or

(3) a claim that relates to the rights, duties (including fiduciary duties), and obligations relating to or created by or pursuant to any security (as defined under section 2(a)(1) of the Securities Act of 1933 (15 U.S.C. 77b(a)(1)) and the regulations issued thereunder).

Chapter 99 — General Provisions

§ 1631. Transfer to Cure Want of Jurisdiction

Whenever a civil action is filed in a court as defined in section 610 of this title or an appeal, including a petition for review of administrative action, is noticed for or filed with such a court and that court finds that there is a want of jurisdiction, the court shall, if it is in the interest of justice, transfer such action or appeal to any other such court (or, for cases within the jurisdiction of the United States Tax Court, to that court) in which the action or appeal could have been brought at the time it was filed or noticed, and the action or appeal shall proceed as if it had been filed in or noticed for the court to which it is transferred on the date upon which it was actually filed in or noticed for the court from which it is transferred.

Chapter 111 — General Provisions

§ 1651. Writs

(a) The Supreme Court and all courts established by Act of Congress may issue all writs necessary or appropriate in aid of their respective jurisdictions and agreeable to the usages and principles of law.

(b) An alternative writ or rule nisi may be issued by a justice or judge of a court which has jurisdiction.

§ 1652. State Laws as Rules of Decision

The laws of the several states, except where the Constitution or treaties of the United States or Acts of Congress otherwise require or provide, shall be regarded as rules of decision in civil actions in the courts of the United States, in cases where they apply.

§ 1658. Time Limitations on the Commencement of Civil Actions Arising Under Acts of Congress

(a) Except as otherwise provided by law, a civil action arising under an Act of Congress enacted after the date of the enactment of this section may not be commenced later than 4 years after the cause of action accrues.

(b) Notwithstanding subsection (a), a private right of action that involves a claim of fraud, deceit, manipulation, or contrivance in contravention of a regulatory requirement concerning the securities laws, as defined in section 3(a)(47) of the Securities Exchange Act of 1934 (15 U.S.C. 78c(a)(47)), may be brought not later than the earlier of:

(1) 2 years after the discovery of the facts constituting the violation; or

(2) 5 years after such violation.

Chapter 114 — Class Actions

§ 1711. Definitions

In this chapter:

(1) Class. The term "class" means all of the class members in a class action.

(2) Class action. The term "class action" means any civil action filed in a district court of the United States under rule 23 of the Federal Rules of Civil Procedure or any civil action that is removed to a district court of the United States that was originally filed under a State statute or rule of judicial procedure authorizing an action to be brought by 1 or more representatives as a class action.

(3) Class counsel. The term "class counsel" means the persons who serve as the attorneys for the class members in a proposed or certified class action.

(4) Class members. The term "class members" means the persons (named or unnamed) who fall within the definition of the proposed or certified class in a class action.

(5) Plaintiff class action. The term "plaintiff class action" means a class action in which class members are plaintiffs.

(6) Proposed settlement. The term "proposed settlement" means an agreement regarding a class action that is subject to court approval and that, if approved, would be binding on some or all class members.

§ 1712. Coupon Settlements

(a) Contingent fees in coupon settlements. If a proposed settlement in a class action provides for a recovery of coupons to a class member, the portion of any attorney's fee award to class counsel that is attributable to the award of the coupons shall be based on the value to class members of the coupons that are redeemed.

(b) Other attorney's fee awards in coupon settlements.

(1) In general. If a proposed settlement in a class action provides for a recovery of coupons to class members, and a portion of the recovery of the coupons is not used to determine the attorney's fee to be paid to class counsel, any attorney's fee award shall be based upon the amount of time class counsel reasonably expended working on the action.

(2) Court approval. Any attorney's fee under this subsection shall be subject to approval by the court and shall include an appropriate attorney's fee, if any, for obtaining equitable relief, including an injunction, if applicable. Nothing in this subsection shall be construed to prohibit application of a lodestar with a multiplier method of determining attorney's fees.

(c) Attorney's fee awards calculated on a mixed basis in coupon settlements. — If a proposed settlement in a class action provides for an award of coupons to class members and also provides for equitable relief, including injunctive relief —

(1) that portion of the attorney's fee to be paid to class counsel that is based upon a portion of the recovery of the coupons shall be calculated in accordance with subsection (a); and

(2) that portion of the attorney's fee to be paid to class counsel that is not based upon a portion of the recovery of the coupons shall be calculated in accordance with subsection (b).

(d) Settlement valuation expertise. In a class action involving the awarding of coupons, the court may, in its discretion upon the motion of a party, receive expert testimony from a witness qualified to provide information on the actual value to the class members of the coupons that are redeemed.

(e) Judicial scrutiny of coupon settlements. In a proposed settlement under which class members would be awarded coupons, the court may approve the proposed settlement only after a hearing to determine whether, and making a written finding that, the settlement is fair, reasonable, and adequate for class members. The court, in its discretion, may also require that a proposed settlement agreement provide for the distribution of a portion of the value of unclaimed coupons to 1 or more charitable or governmental organizations, as agreed to by the parties. The distribution and redemption of any proceeds under this subsection shall not be used to calculate attorneys' fees under this section.

§ 1713. Protection Against Loss By Class Members

The court may approve a proposed settlement under which any class member is obligated to pay sums to class counsel that would result in a net loss to the class member only if the court makes a written finding that nonmonetary benefits to the class member substantially outweigh the monetary loss.

§ 1714. Protection Against Discrimination Based on Geographic Location

The court may not approve a proposed settlement that provides for the payment of greater sums to some class members than to others solely on the basis that the class members to whom the greater sums are to be paid are located in closer geographic proximity to the court.

§ 1715. Notifications to Appropriate Federal and State Officials

(a) Definitions

(1) Appropriate Federal official. In this section, the term "appropriate Federal official" means

(A) the Attorney General of the United States; or

(B) in any case in which the defendant is a Federal depository institution, a State depository institution, a depository institution holding company, a foreign bank, or a nondepository institution subsidiary of the foregoing (as such terms are defined in section 3 of the Federal Deposit Insurance Act (12 U.S.C. 1813)), the person who has the primary Federal regulatory or supervisory responsibility with respect to the defendant, if some or all of the matters alleged in the class action are subject to regulation or supervision by that person.

(2) Appropriate State official. In this section, the term "appropriate State official" means the person in the State who has the primary regulatory or supervisory responsibility with respect to the defendant, or who licenses or otherwise authorizes the defendant to conduct business in the State, if some or all of the matters alleged in the class action are subject to regulation by that person. If there is no primary regulator, supervisor, or licensing authority, or the matters alleged in the class action are not subject to regulation or supervision by that person, then the appropriate State official shall be the State attorney general.

(b) In general. Not later than 10 days after a proposed settlement of a class action is filed in court, each defendant that is participating in the proposed settlement shall serve upon the appropriate State official of each State in which a class member resides and the appropriate Federal official, a notice of the proposed settlement consisting of—

(1) a copy of the complaint and any materials filed with the complaint and any amended complaints (except such materials shall not be required to be served if such materials are made electronically available through the Internet and such service includes notice of how to electronically access such material);

(2) notice of any scheduled judicial hearing in the class action;

(3) any proposed or final notification to class members of—

(A) (i) the members' rights to request exclusion from the class action; or

(ii) if no right to request exclusion exists, a statement that no such right exists; and

(B) a proposed settlement of a class action;

(4) any proposed or final class action settlement;

(5) any settlement or other agreement contemporaneously made between class counsel and counsel for the defendants;

(6) any final judgment or notice of dismissal;

(7) (A) if feasible, the names of class members who reside in each State and the estimated proportionate share of the claims of such members to the entire settlement to that State's appropriate State official; or

(B) if the provision of information under subparagraph (A) is not feasible, a reasonable estimate of the number of class members residing in each State and the estimated proportionate share of the claims of such members to the entire settlement; and

(8) any written judicial opinion relating to the materials described under subparagraphs (3) through (6).

(c) Depository institutions notification.

(1) Federal and other depository institutions. In any case in which the defendant is a Federal depository institution, a depository institution holding company, a foreign bank, or a non-depository institution subsidiary of the foregoing, the notice requirements of this section are satisfied by serving the notice required under subsection (b) upon the person who has the primary Federal regulatory or supervisory responsibility with respect to the defendant, if some or all of the matters alleged in the class action are subject to regulation or supervision by that person.

(2) State depository institutions. In any case in which the defendant is a State depository institution (as that term is defined in section 3 of the Federal Deposit Insurance Act (12 U.S.C. 1813)), the notice requirements of this section are satisfied by serving the notice required under subsection (b) upon the State bank supervisor (as that term is defined in section 3 of the Federal Deposit Insurance Act (12 U.S.C. 1813)) of the State in which the defendant is incorporated or chartered, if some or all of the matters alleged in the class action are subject to regulation or supervision by that person, and upon the appropriate Federal official.

(d) Final approval. An order giving final approval of a proposed settlement may not be issued earlier than 90 days after the later of the dates on which the appropriate Federal official and the appropriate State official are served with the notice required under subsection (b).

(e) Noncompliance if notice not provided

(1) In general. A class member may refuse to comply with and may choose not to be bound by a settlement agreement or consent decree in a class action if the class member demonstrates that the notice required under subsection (b) has not been provided.

(2) Limitation. A class member may not refuse to comply with or to be bound by a settlement agreement or consent decree under paragraph (1) if the notice required under subsection (b) was directed to the appropriate Federal official and to either the State attorney general or the person that has primary regulatory, supervisory, or licensing authority over the defendant.

(3) Application of rights. The rights created by this subsection shall apply only to class members or any person acting on a class member's behalf, and shall not be construed to limit any other rights affecting a class member's participation in the settlement.

(f) Rule of construction. Nothing in this section shall be construed to expand the authority of, or impose any obligations, duties, or responsibilities upon, Federal or State officials.

Chapter 115 — Evidence; Documentary

§ 1738. State and Territorial Statutes and Judicial Proceedings; Full Faith and Credit

The Acts of the legislature of any State, Territory, or Possession of the United States, or copies thereof, shall be authenticated by affixing the seal of such State, Territory or Possession thereto.

The records and judicial proceedings of any court of any such State, Territory or Possession, or copies thereof, shall be proved or admitted in other courts within the United States and its Territories and Possessions by the attestation of the clerk and seal of the court annexed, if a seal exists, together with a certificate of a judge of the court that the said attestation is in proper form.

Such Acts, records and judicial proceedings or copies thereof, so authenticated, shall have the same full faith and credit in every court within the United States and its Territories and Possessions as they have by law or usage in the courts of such State, Territory or Possession from which they are taken.

Chapter 123 — Fees and Costs

§ 1914. District Court; Filing and Miscellaneous Fees; Rules of Court

(a) The clerk of each district court shall require the parties instituting any civil action, suit or proceeding in such court, whether by original process, removal or otherwise, to pay a filing fee of $350, except that on application for a writ of habeas corpus the filing fee shall be $5.

(b) The clerk shall collect from the parties such additional fees only as are prescribed by the Judicial Conference of the United States.

(c) Each district court by rule or standing order may require advance payment of fees.

§ 1915. Proceedings in Forma Pauperis

(a) (1) Subject to subsection (b), any court of the United States may authorize the commencement, prosecution or defense of any suit, action or proceeding, civil or criminal, or appeal therein, without prepayment of fees or security therefor, by a person who submits an affidavit that includes a statement of all assets such prisoner possesses that the person is unable to pay such fees or give security therefor. Such affidavit shall state the nature of the action, defense or appeal and affiant's belief that the person is entitled to redress.

(2) A prisoner seeking to bring a civil action or appeal a judgment in a civil action or proceeding without prepayment of fees or security therefor, in addition to filing the affidavit filed under paragraph (1), shall submit a certified copy of the trust fund account statement (or institutional equivalent) for the prisoner for the 6-month period immediately preceding the filing of the complaint or notice of appeal, obtained from the appropriate official of each prison at which the prisoner is or was confined.

(3) An appeal may not be taken in forma pauperis if the trial court certifies in writing that it is not taken in good faith.

(b) (1) Notwithstanding subsection (a), if a prisoner brings a civil action or files an appeal in forma pauperis, the prisoner shall be required to pay the full amount of a filing fee. The court shall assess and, when funds exist, collect, as a partial payment of any court fees required by law, an initial partial filing fee of 20 percent of the greater of:

(A) the average monthly deposits to the prisoner's account; or

(B) the average monthly balance in the prisoner's account for the 6-month period immediately preceding the filing of the complaint or notice of appeal.

(2) After payment of the initial partial filing fee, the prisoner shall be required to make monthly payments of 20 percent of the preceding month's income credited to the prisoner's account. The agency having custody of the prisoner shall forward payments from the prisoner's account to the clerk of the court each time the amount in the account exceeds $10 until the filing fees are paid.

(3) In no event shall the filing fee collected exceed the amount of fees permitted by statute for the commencement of a civil action or an appeal of a civil action or criminal judgment.

(4) In no event shall a prisoner be prohibited from bringing a civil action or appealing a civil or criminal judgment for the reason that the prisoner has no assets and no means by which to pay the initial partial filing fee.

(c) Upon the filing of an affidavit in accordance with subsections (a) and (b) and the prepayment of any partial filing fee as may be required under subsection (b), the court may direct payment by the United States of the expenses of (1) printing the record on appeal in any civil or criminal case, if such printing is required by the appellate court; (2) preparing a transcript of proceedings before a United States magistrate judge in any civil or criminal case, if such transcript is required by the district court, in the case of proceedings conducted under section 636(b) of this title or under section 3401(b) of title 18, United States Code; and (3) printing the record on appeal if such printing is required by the appellate court, in the case of proceedings conducted pursuant to section 636(c) of this title. Such expenses shall be paid when authorized by the Director of the Administrative Office of the United States Courts.

(d) The officers of the court shall issue and serve all process, and perform all duties in such cases. Witnesses shall attend as in other cases, and the same remedies shall be available as are provided for by law in other cases.

(e) (1) The court may request an attorney to represent any person unable to afford counsel.

(2) Notwithstanding any filing fee, or any portion thereof, that may have been paid, the court shall dismiss the case at any time if the court determines that:

(A) the allegation of poverty is untrue; or

(B) the action or appeal:

(i) is frivolous or malicious;

(ii) fails to state a claim on which relief may be granted; or

(iii) seeks monetary relief against a defendant who is immune from such relief.

(f) (1) Judgment may be rendered for costs at the conclusion of the suit or action as in other proceedings, but the United States shall not be liable for any of the costs thus incurred. If the United States has paid the cost of a stenographic transcript or printed record for the prevailing party, the same shall be taxed in favor of the United States.

(2) (A) If the judgment against a prisoner includes the payment of costs under this subsection, the prisoner shall be required to pay the full amount of the costs ordered.

(B) The prisoner shall be required to make payments for costs under this subsection in the same manner as is provided for filing fees under subsection (a)(2).

(C) In no event shall the costs collected exceed the amount of the costs ordered by the court.

(g) In no event shall a prisoner bring a civil action or appeal a judgment in a civil action or proceeding under this section if the prisoner has, on 3 or more prior occasions, while incarcerated or detained in any facility, brought an action or appeal in a court of the United States that was dismissed on the grounds that it is frivolous, malicious, or fails to state a claim upon which relief may be granted, unless the prisoner is under imminent danger of serious physical injury.

(h) As used in this section, the term "prisoner" means any person incarcerated or detained in any facility who is accused of, convicted of, sentenced for, or adjudicated delinquent for, violations of criminal law or the terms and conditions of parole, probation, pretrial release, or diversionary program.

§ 1915A. Screening

(a) Screening. The court shall review, before docketing, if feasible or, in any event, as soon as practicable after docketing, a complaint in a civil action in which a prisoner seeks redress from a governmental entity or officer or employee of a governmental entity.

(b) Grounds for dismissal. On review, the court shall identify cognizable claims or dismiss the complaint, or any portion of the complaint, if the complaint:

(1) is frivolous, malicious, or fails to state a claim upon which relief may be granted; or

(2) seeks monetary relief from a defendant who is immune from such relief.

(c) Definition. As used in this section, the term "prisoner" means any person incarcerated or detained in any facility who is accused of, convicted of, sentenced for, or adjudicated delinquent for, violations of criminal law or the terms and conditions of parole, probation, pretrial release, or diversionary program.

§ 1920. Taxation of Costs

A judge or clerk of any court of the United States may tax as costs the following:

(1) Fees of the clerk and marshal;

(2) Fees for printed or electronically recorded transcripts necessarily obtained for use in the case;

(3) Fees and disbursements for printing and witnesses;

(4) Fees for exemplification and the costs of making copies of any materials where the copies are necessarily obtained for use in the case;

(5) Docket fees under section 1923 of this title;

(6) Compensation of court appointed experts, compensation of interpreters, and salaries, fees, expenses, and costs of special interpretation services under section 1828 of this title.

A bill of costs shall be filed in the case and, upon allowance, included in the judgment or decree.

Chapter 131 — Rules of Courts

§ 2071. Rule-Making Power Generally

(a) The Supreme Court and all courts established by Act of Congress may from time to time prescribe rules for the conduct of their business. Such rules shall be consistent with Acts of Congress and rules of practice and procedure prescribed under section 2072 of this title.

(b) Any rule prescribed by a court, other than the Supreme Court, under subsection (a) shall be prescribed only after giving appropriate public notice and an opportunity for comment. Such rule shall take effect upon the date specified by the prescribing court and shall have such effect on pending proceedings as the prescribing court may order.

(c) (1) A rule of a district court prescribed under subsection (a) shall remain in effect unless modified or abrogated by the judicial council of the relevant circuit.

(2) Any other rule prescribed by a court other than the Supreme Court under subsection (a) shall remain in effect unless modified or abrogated by the Judicial Conference.

(d) Copies of rules prescribed under subsection (a) by a district court shall be furnished to the judicial council, and copies of all rules prescribed by a court other than the Supreme Court under subsection (a) shall be furnished to the Director of the Administrative Office of the United States Courts and made available to the public.

(e) If the prescribing court determines that there is an immediate need for a rule, such court may proceed under this section without public notice and opportunity for comment, but such court shall promptly thereafter afford such notice and opportunity for comment.

(f) No rule may be prescribed by a district court other than under this section.

§ 2072. Rules of Procedure and Evidence; Power to Prescribe

(a) The Supreme Court shall have the power to prescribe general rules of practice and procedure and rules of evidence for cases in the United States district courts (including proceedings before magistrate judges thereof) and courts of appeals.

(b) Such rules shall not abridge, enlarge or modify any substantive right. All laws in conflict with such rules shall be of no further force or effect after such rules have taken effect.

(c) Such rules may define when a ruling of a district court is final for the purposes of appeal under section 1291 of this title.

§ 2073. Rules of Procedure and Evidence; Method of Prescribing

(a) (1) The Judicial Conference shall prescribe and publish the procedures for the consideration of proposed rules under this section.

(2) The Judicial Conference may authorize the appointment of committees to assist the Conference by recommending rules to be prescribed under sections 2072 and 2075 of this title. Each such committee shall consist of members of the bench and the professional bar, and trial and appellate judges.

(b) The Judicial Conference shall authorize the appointment of a standing committee on rules of practice, procedure, and evidence under subsection (a) of this section. Such standing committee shall review each recommendation of any other committees so appointed and recommend to the Judicial Conference rules of practice, procedure, and evidence and such changes in rules proposed by a committee appointed under subsection (a)(2) of this section as may be necessary to maintain consistency and otherwise promote the interest of justice.

(c) (1) Each meeting for the transaction of business under this chapter by any committee appointed under this section shall be open to the public, except when the committee so meeting, in open session and with a majority present, determines that it is in the public interest that all or part of the remainder of the meeting on that day shall be closed to the public, and states the reason for so closing the meeting. Minutes of each meeting for the transaction of business under this chapter shall be maintained by the committee and made available to the public, except that any portion of such minutes, relating to a closed meeting and made available to the public, may contain such deletions as may be necessary to avoid frustrating the purposes of closing the meeting.

(2) Any meeting for the transaction of business under this chapter, by a committee appointed under this section, shall be preceded by sufficient notice to enable all interested persons to attend.

(d) In making a recommendation under this section or under section 2072 or 2075, the body making that recommendation shall provide a proposed rule, an explanatory note on the rule, and a written report explaining the body's action, including any minority or other separate views.

(e) Failure to comply with this section does not invalidate a rule prescribed under section 2072 or 2075 of this title.

§ 2074. Rules of Procedure and Evidence; Submission to Congress; Effective Date

(a) The Supreme Court shall transmit to the Congress not later than May 1 of the year in which a rule prescribed under section 2072 is to become effective a copy of the proposed rule. Such rule shall take effect no earlier than December 1 of the year in which such rule is so transmitted unless otherwise provided by law. The Supreme Court may fix the extent such rule shall apply to proceedings then pending, except that the Supreme Court shall not require the application of such rule to further proceedings then pending to the extent that, in the opinion of the court in which such proceedings are pending, the application of such rule in such proceedings would not be feasible or would work injustice, in which event the former rule applies.

(b) Any such rule creating, abolishing, or modifying an evidentiary privilege shall have no force or effect unless approved by Act of Congress.

§ 2077. Publication of Rules; Advisory Committees

(a) The rules for the conduct of the business of each court of appeals, including the operating procedures of such court, shall be published. Each court of appeals shall print or cause to be printed necessary copies of the rules. The Judicial Conference shall prescribe the fees for sales of copies under section 1913 of this title, but the Judicial Conference may provide for free distribution of copies to members of the bar of each court and to other interested persons.

(b) Each court, except the Supreme Court, that is authorized to prescribe rules of the conduct of such court's business under section 2071 of this title shall appoint an advisory committee for the study of the rules of practice and internal operating procedures of such court and, in the case of an advisory committee appointed by a court of appeals, of the rules of the judicial council of the circuit. The advisory committee shall make recommendations to the court concerning such rules and procedures. Members of the committee shall serve without compensation, but the Director may pay travel and transportation expenses in accordance with section 5703 of title 5.

Chapter 151 — Declaratory Judgments

§ 2201. Creation of Remedy

(a) In a case of actual controversy within its jurisdiction, except with respect to Federal taxes other than actions brought under section 7428 of the Internal Revenue Code of 1986, a proceeding under section 505 or 1146 of title 11, or in any civil action involving an antidumping or countervailing duty proceeding regarding a class or kind of merchandise of a free trade area country (as defined in section 516A(f)(9) of the Tariff Act of 1930), as determined by the administering authority, any court of the United States, upon the filing of an appropriate pleading, may declare the rights and other legal relations of any interested party seeking such declaration, whether or not further relief is or could be sought. Any such declaration shall have the force and effect of a final judgment or decree and shall be reviewable as such.

(b) For limitations on actions brought with respect to drug patents see section 505 or 512 of the Federal Food, Drug, and Cosmetic Act, or section 351 of the Public Health Service Act.

§ 2202. Further Relief

Further necessary or proper relief based on a declaratory judgment or decree may be granted, after reasonable notice and hearing, against any adverse party whose rights have been determined by such judgment.

Chapter 159 — Interpleader

§ 2361. Process and Procedure

In any civil action of interpleader or in the nature of interpleader under section 1335 of this title, a district court may issue its process for all claimants and enter its order restraining them from instituting or prosecuting any proceeding in any State or United States court affecting the property, instrument or obligation involved in the interpleader action until further order of the court. Such process and order shall be returnable at such time as the court or judge thereof directs, and shall be addressed to and served by the United States marshals for the respective districts where the claimants reside or may be found.

Such district court shall hear and determine the case, and may discharge the plaintiff from further liability, make the injunction permanent, and make all appropriate orders to enforce its judgment.

Chapter 161 — United States as Party Generally

§ 2401. Time for Commencing Action Against United States

(a) Except as provided by chapter 71 of title 41, every civil action commenced against the United States shall be barred unless the complaint is filed within six years after the right of action first accrues. The action of any person under legal disability or beyond the seas at the time the claim accrues may be commenced within three years after the disability ceases.

(b) A tort claim against the United States shall be forever barred unless it is presented in writing to the appropriate Federal agency within two years after such claim accrues or unless action is begun within six months after the date of mailing, by certified or registered mail, of notice of final denial of the claim by the agency to which it was presented.

Title 42, The Public Health and Welfare

Chapter 21 — Civil Rights

§ 1981. Equal Rights Under the Law

(a) Statement of equal rights. All persons within the jurisdiction of the United States shall have the same right in every State and Territory to make and enforce contracts, to sue, be parties, give evidence, and to the full and equal benefit of all laws and proceedings for the security of persons and property as is enjoyed by white citizens, and shall be subject to like punishment, pains, penalties, taxes, licenses, and exactions of every kind, and to no other.

(b) "Make and enforce contracts" defined. For purposes of this section, the term "make and enforce contracts" includes the making, performance, modification, and termination of contracts, and the enjoyment of all benefits, privileges, terms, and conditions of the contractual relationship.

(c) Protection against impairment. The rights protected by this section are protected against impairment by nongovernmental discrimination and impairment under color of State law.

§ 1982. Property Rights of Citizens

All citizens of the United States shall have the same right, in every State and Territory, as is enjoyed by white citizens thereof to inherit, purchase, lease, sell, hold, and convey real and personal property.

§ 1983. Civil Action for Deprivation of Rights

Every person who, under color of any statute, ordinance, regulation, custom, or usage, of any State or Territory or the District of Columbia, subjects, or causes to be subjected, any citizen of the United States or other person within the jurisdiction thereof to the deprivation of any rights, privileges, or immunities secured by the Constitution and laws, shall be liable to the party injured in an action at law, suit in equity, or other proper proceeding for redress, except that in any action brought against a judicial officer for an act or omission taken in such officer's judicial capacity, injunctive relief shall not be granted unless a declaratory decree was violated or declaratory relief was unavailable. For the purposes of this section, any Act of Congress applicable exclusively to the District of Columbia shall be considered to be a statute of the District of Columbia.

§ 1985. Conspiracy to Interfere With Civil Rights

(1) Preventing officer from performing duties. If two or more persons in any State or Territory conspire to prevent, by force, intimidation, or threat, any person from accepting or holding any office, trust, or place of confidence under the United States, or from discharging any duties thereof; or to induce by like means any officer of the United States to leave any State, district, or place, where his duties as an officer are required to be performed, or to injure him in his person or property on account of his lawful discharge of the duties of his office, or while engaged in the lawful discharge thereof, or to injure his property so as to molest, interrupt, hinder, or impede him in the discharge of his official duties;

(2) Obstructing justice; intimidating party, witness, or juror. If two or more persons in any State or Territory conspire to deter, by force, intimidation, or threat, any party or witness in any court of the United States from attending such court, or from testifying to any matter pending therein, freely, fully, and truthfully, or to injure such party or witness in his person or property on account of his having so attended or testified, or to influence the verdict, presentment, or indictment of any grand or petit juror in any such court, or to injure such juror in his person or property on account of any verdict, presentment, or indictment lawfully assented to by him, or of his being or having been such juror; or if two or more persons conspire for the purpose of impeding, hindering, obstructing, or defeating, in any manner, the due course of justice in any State or Territory, with intent to deny to any citizen the equal protection of the laws, or to injure him or his property for lawfully enforcing, or attempting to enforce, the right of any person, or class of persons, to the equal protection of the laws;

(3) Depriving persons of rights or privileges. If two or more persons in any State or Territory conspire or go in disguise on the highway or on the premises of another, for the purpose of depriving, either directly or indirectly, any person or class of persons of the equal protection of the laws, or of equal privileges and immunities under the laws; or for the purpose of preventing or hindering the constituted authorities of any State or Territory from giving or securing to all persons within such State or Territory the equal protection of the laws; or if two or more persons conspire to prevent by force, intimidation, or threat, any citizen who is lawfully entitled to vote, from giving his support or advocacy in a legal manner, toward or in favor of the election of any lawfully qualified person as an elector for President or Vice President, or as a Member of Congress of the United States; or to injure any citizen in person or property on account of such support or advocacy; in any case of conspiracy set forth in this section, if one or more persons engaged therein do, or cause to be done, any act in furtherance of the object of such conspiracy, whereby another is injured in his person or property, or deprived of having and exercising any right or privilege of a citizen of the United States, the party so injured or deprived may have an action for the recovery of damages occasioned by such injury or deprivation, against any one or more of the conspirators.

§ 1986. Action for Neglect to Prevent

Every person who, having knowledge that any of the wrongs conspired to be done, and mentioned in section 1985 of this title, are about to be committed, and having power to prevent or aid in preventing the commission of the same, neglects or refuses so to do, if such wrongful act be committed, shall be liable to the party injured, or his legal representatives, for all damages caused by such wrongful act, which such person by reasonable diligence could have prevented; and such damages may be recovered in an action on the case; and any number of persons guilty of such wrongful neglect or refusal may be joined as defendants in the action; and if the death of any party be caused by any such wrongful act and neglect, the legal representatives of the deceased shall have such action therefor, and may recover not exceeding $5,000 damages therein, for the benefit of the widow of the deceased, if there be one, and if there be no widow, then for the benefit of the next of kin of the deceased. But no action under the provisions of this section shall be sustained which is not commenced within one year after the cause of action has accrued.

§ 1987. Prosecution of Violation of Certain Laws

The United States attorneys, marshals, and deputy marshals, the United States magistrate judges appointed by the district and territorial courts, with power to arrest, imprison, or bail offenders, and every other officer who is especially empowered by the President, are authorized and required, at the expense of the United States, to institute prosecutions against all persons violating any of the provisions of section 1990 of this title or of sections 5506 to 5516 and 5518 to 5532 of the Revised Statutes, and to cause such persons to be arrested, and imprisoned or bailed, for trial before the court of the United States or the territorial court having cognizance of the offense.

§ 1988. Proceedings in Vindication of Civil Rights

(a) Applicability of statutory and common law. The jurisdiction in civil and criminal matters conferred on the district courts by the provisions of titles 13, 24, and 70 of the Revised Statutes for the protection of all persons in the United States in their civil rights, and for their vindication, shall be exercised and enforced in conformity with the laws of the United States, so far as such laws are suitable to carry the same into effect; but in all cases where they are not adapted to the object, or are deficient in the provisions necessary to furnish suitable remedies and punish offenses against law, the common law, as modified and changed by the constitution and statutes of the State wherein the court having jurisdiction of such civil or criminal cause is held, so far as the same is not inconsistent with the Constitution and laws of the United States, shall be extended to and govern the said courts in the trial and disposition of the cause, and, if it is of a criminal nature, in the infliction of punishment on the party found guilty.

(b) Attorney's fees. In any action or proceeding to enforce a provision of sections 1981, 1981a, 1982, 1983, 1985, and 1986 of this title, title IX of Public Law 92-318 [20 U.S.C.A. § 1681 et seq.], the Religious Freedom Restoration Act of 1993 [42 U.S.C.A. § 2000bb et seq.], the Religious Land Use and Institutionalized Persons Act of 2000 [42 U.S.C.A. § 2000cc et seq.], title VI of the Civil Rights Act of 1964 [42 U.S.C.A. § 2000d et seq.], or section 13981 of this title, the court, in its discretion, may allow the prevailing party, other than the United States, a reasonable attorney's fee as part of the costs, except that in any action brought against a judicial officer for an act or omission taken in such officer's judicial capacity such officer shall not be held liable for any costs, including attorney's fees, unless such action was clearly in excess of such officer's jurisdiction.

(c) Expert fees. In awarding an attorney's fee under subsection (b) of this section in any action or proceeding to enforce a provision of section 1981 or 1981a of this title, the court, in its discretion, may include expert fees as part of the attorney's fee.

FEDERAL RULES OF APPELLATE PROCEDURE

(Selected Rules)

I. Applicability of Rules

Rule 1. Scope of Rules; Definition; Title

(a) Scope of Rules

(1) These rules govern procedure in the United States courts of appeals.

(2) When these rules provide for filing a motion or other document in the district court, the procedure must comply with the practice of the district court.

(b) Definition. In these rules, "state" includes the District of Columbia and any United States commonwealth or territory.

(c) Title. These rules are to be known as the Federal Rules of Appellate Procedure.

II. Appeal from a Judgment or Order of a District Court

Rule 3. Appeal as of Right — How Taken

(a) Filing the Notice of Appeal

(1) An appeal permitted by law as of right from a district court to a court of appeals may be taken only by filing a notice of appeal with the district clerk within the time allowed by Rule 4. At the time of filing, the appellant must furnish the clerk with enough copies of the notice to enable the clerk to comply with Rule 3(d).

(2) An appellant's failure to take any step other than the timely filing of a notice of appeal does not affect the validity of the appeal, but is ground only for the court of appeals to act as it considers appropriate, including dismissing the appeal.

(3) An appeal from a judgment by a magistrate judge in a civil case is taken in the same way as an appeal from any other district court judgment.

(4) An appeal by permission under 28 U.S.C. § 1292(b) or an appeal in a bankruptcy case may be taken only in the manner prescribed by Rules 5 and 6, respectively.

(b) Joint or Consolidated Appeals

(1) When two or more parties are entitled to appeal from a district-court judgment or order, and their interests make joinder practicable, they may file a joint notice of appeal. They may then proceed on appeal as a single appellant.

(2) When the parties have filed separate timely notices of appeal, the appeals may be joined or consolidated by the court of appeals.

(c) Contents of the Notice of Appeal

(1) The notice of appeal must:

(A) specify the party or parties taking the appeal by naming each one in the caption or body of the notice, but an attorney representing more than one party may describe those parties with such terms as "all plaintiffs," "the defendants," "the plaintiffs A, B, et al.," or "all defendants except X";

(B) designate the judgment — or the appealable order — from which the appeal is taken; and

(C) name the court to which the appeal is taken.

(2) A pro se notice of appeal is considered filed on behalf of the signer and the signer's spouse and minor children (if they are parties), unless the notice clearly indicates otherwise.

(3) In a class action, whether or not the class has been certified, the notice of appeal is sufficient if it names one person qualified to bring the appeal as representative of the class.

(4) The notice of appeal encompasses all orders that, for purposes of appeal, merge into the designated judgment or appealable order. It is not necessary to designate those orders in the notice of appeal.

(5) In a civil case, a notice of appeal encompasses the final judgment, whether or not that judgment is set out in a separate document under Federal Rule of Civil Procedure 58, if the notice designates:

(A) an order that adjudicates all remaining claims and the rights and liabilities of all remaining parties; or

(B) an order described in Rule 4(a)(4)(A).

(6) An appellant may designate only part of a judgment or appealable order by expressly stating that the notice of appeal is so limited. Without such an express statement, specific designations do not limit the scope of the notice of appeal.

(7) An appeal must not be dismissed for informality of form or title of the notice of appeal, for failure to name a party whose intent to appeal is otherwise

clear from the notice, or for failure to properly designate the judgment if the notice of appeal was filed after entry of the judgment and designates an order that merged into that judgment.

(8) Forms 1A and 1B in the Appendix of Forms are suggested forms of notices of appeal.

(d) Serving the Notice of Appeal

(1) The district clerk must serve notice of the filing of a notice of appeal by sending a copy to each party's counsel of record — excluding the appellant's — or, if a party is proceeding pro se, to the party's last known address. When a defendant in a criminal case appeals, the clerk must also serve a copy of the notice of appeal on the defendant. The clerk must promptly send a copy of the notice of appeal and of the docket entries — and any later docket entries — to the clerk of the court of appeals named in the notice. The district clerk must note, on each copy, the date when the notice of appeal was filed.

(2) If an inmate confined in an institution files a notice of appeal in the manner provided by Rule 4(c), the district clerk must also note the date when the clerk docketed the notice.

(3) The district clerk's failure to serve notice does not affect the validity of the appeal. The clerk must note on the docket the names of the parties to whom the clerk sends copies, with the date of sending. Service is sufficient despite the death of a party or the party's counsel.

(e) Payment of Fees. Upon filing a notice of appeal, the appellant must pay the district clerk all required fees. The district clerk receives the appellate docket fee on behalf of the court of appeals.

Rule 4. Appeal as of Right — When Taken

(a) Appeal in a Civil Case

(1) Time for Filing a Notice of Appeal

(A) In a civil case, except as provided in Rules 4(a)(1)(B), 4(a)(4), and 4(c), the notice of appeal required by Rule 3 must be filed with the district clerk within 30 days after entry of the judgment or order appealed from.

(B) The notice of appeal may be filed by any party within 60 days after entry of the judgment or order appealed from if one of the parties is:

(i) the United States;

(ii) a United States agency;

(iii) a United States officer or employee sued in an official capacity; or

(iv) a current or former United States officer or employee sued in an individual capacity for an act or omission occurring in connection with duties performed on the United States' behalf — including all instances in which the United States represents that person when the judgment or order is entered or files the appeal for that person.

(C) An appeal from an order granting or denying an application for a writ of error coram nobis is an appeal in a civil case for purposes of Rule 4(a).

(2) Filing Before Entry of Judgment. A notice of appeal filed after the court announces a decision or order — but before the entry of the judgment or order — is treated as filed on the date of and after the entry.

(3) Multiple Appeals. If one party timely files a notice of appeal, any other party may file a notice of appeal within 14 days after the date when the first notice was filed, or within the time otherwise prescribed by this Rule 4(a), whichever period ends later.

(4) Effect of a Motion on a Notice of Appeal

(A) If a party files in the district court any of the following motions under the Federal Rules of Civil Procedure — and does so within the time allowed by those rules — the time to file an appeal runs for all parties from the entry of the order disposing of the last such remaining motion:

(i) for judgment under Rule 50(b);

(ii) to amend or make additional factual findings under Rule 52(b), whether or not granting the motion would alter the judgment;

(iii) for attorney's fees under Rule 54 if the district court extends the time to appeal under Rule 58;

(iv) to alter or amend the judgment under Rule 59;

(v) for a new trial under Rule 59; or

(vi) for relief under Rule 60 if the motion is filed within the time allowed for filing a motion under Rule 59.

(B) (i) If a party files a notice of appeal after the court announces or enters a judgment — but before it disposes of any motion listed in Rule 4(a)(4)(A) — the notice becomes effective to appeal a judgment or order, in whole or in part, when the order disposing of the last such remaining motion is entered.

(ii) A party intending to challenge an order disposing of any motion listed in Rule 4(a)(4)(A), or a judgment's alteration or amendment upon such a motion, must file a notice of appeal, or an amended notice of appeal — in compliance with Rule 3(c) — within the time prescribed by this Rule measured from the entry of the order disposing of the last such remaining motion.

(iii) No additional fee is required to file an amended notice.

(5) Motion for Extension of Time

(A) The district court may extend the time to file a notice of appeal if:

(i) a party so moves no later than 30 days after the time prescribed by this Rule 4(a) expires; and

(ii) regardless of whether its motion is filed before or during the 30 days after the time prescribed by this Rule 4(a) expires, that party shows excusable neglect or good cause.

(B) A motion filed before the expiration of the time prescribed in Rule 4(a)(1) or (3) may be ex parte unless the court requires otherwise. If the motion is filed after the expiration of the prescribed time, notice must be given to the other parties in accordance with local rules.

(C) No extension under this Rule 4(a)(5) may exceed 30 days after the prescribed time or 14 days after the date when the order granting the motion is entered, whichever is later.

(6) Reopening the Time to File an Appeal. The district court may reopen the time to file an appeal for a period of 14 days after the date when its order to reopen is entered, but only if all the following conditions are satisfied:

(A) the court finds that the moving party did not receive notice under Federal Rule of Civil Procedure 77(d) of the entry of the judgment or order sought to be appealed within 21 days after entry;

(B) the motion is filed within 180 days after the judgment or order is entered or within 14 days after the moving party receives notice under Federal Rule of Civil Procedure 77(d) of the entry, whichever is earlier; and

(C) the court finds that no party would be prejudiced.

(7) Entry Defined

(A) A judgment or order is entered for purposes of this Rule 4(a):

(i) if Federal Rule of Civil Procedure 58(a) does not require a separate document, when the judgment or order is entered in the civil docket under Federal Rule of Civil Procedure 79(a); or

(ii) if Federal Rule of Civil Procedure 58(a) requires a separate document, when the judgment or order is entered in the civil docket under Federal Rule of Civil Procedure 79(a) and when the earlier of these events occurs:

- the judgment or order is set forth on a separate document, or
- 150 days have run from entry of the judgment or order in the civil docket under Federal Rule of Civil Procedure 79(a).

(B) A failure to set forth a judgment or order on a separate document when required by Federal Rule of Civil Procedure 58(a) does not affect the validity of an appeal from that judgment or order.

(b) Appeal in a Criminal Case

(1) Time for Filing a Notice of Appeal

(A) In a criminal case, a defendant's notice of appeal must be filed in the district court within 14 days after the later of:

(i) the entry of either the judgment or the order being appealed; or

(ii) the filing of the government's notice of appeal.

(B) When the government is entitled to appeal, its notice of appeal must be filed in the district court within 30 days after the later of:

(i) the entry of the judgment or order being appealed; or

(ii) the filing of a notice of appeal by any defendant.

(2) Filing Before Entry of Judgment. A notice of appeal filed after the court announces a decision, sentence, or order — but before the entry of the judgment or order — is treated as filed on the date of and after the entry.

(3) Effect of a Motion on a Notice of Appeal

(A) If a defendant timely makes any of the following motions under the Federal Rules of Criminal Procedure, the notice of appeal from a judgment of conviction must be filed within 14 days after the entry of the order disposing of the last such remaining motion, or within 14 days after the entry of the judgment of conviction, whichever period ends later. This provision applies to a timely motion:

(i) for judgment of acquittal under Rule 29;

(ii) for a new trial under Rule 33, but if based on newly discovered evidence, only if the motion is made no later than 14 days after the entry of the judgment; or

(iii) for arrest of judgment under Rule 34.

(B) A notice of appeal filed after the court announces a decision, sentence, or order — but before it disposes of any of the motions referred to in Rule 4(b)(3)(A) — becomes effective upon the later of the following:

(i) the entry of the order disposing of the last such remaining motion; or

(ii) the entry of the judgment of conviction.

(C) A valid notice of appeal is effective — without amendment — to appeal from an order disposing of any of the motions referred to in Rule 4(b)(3)(A).

(4) Motion for Extension of Time. Upon a finding of excusable neglect or good cause, the district court may — before or after the time has expired, with or without motion and notice — extend the time to file a notice of appeal for a period not to exceed 30 days from the expiration of the time otherwise prescribed by this Rule 4(b).

(5) Jurisdiction. The filing of a notice of appeal under this Rule 4(b) does not divest a district court of jurisdiction to correct a sentence under Federal Rule of Criminal Procedure 35(a), nor does the filing of a motion under 35(a) affect the validity of a notice of appeal filed before entry of the order disposing of the motion. The filing of a motion under Federal Rule of Criminal Procedure 35(a) does not suspend the time for filing a notice of appeal from a judgment of conviction.

(6) Entry Defined. A judgment or order is entered for purposes of this Rule 4(b) when it is entered on the criminal docket.

(c) Appeal by an Inmate Confined in an Institution

(1) If an institution has a system designed for legal mail, an inmate confined there must use that system to receive the benefit of this Rule 4(c)(1). If an inmate files a notice of appeal in either a civil or a criminal case, the notice is timely if it is deposited in the institution's internal mail system on or before the last day for filing and:

(A) it is accompanied by:

(i) a declaration in compliance with 28 U.S.C. § 1746 — or a notarized statement — setting out the date of deposit and stating that first-class postage is being prepaid; or

(ii) evidence (such as a postmark or date stamp) showing that the notice was so deposited and that postage was prepaid; or

(B) the court of appeals exercises its discretion to permit the later filing of a declaration or notarized statement that satisfies Rule 4(c)(1)(A)(i).

(2) If an inmate files the first notice of appeal in a civil case under this Rule 4(c), the 14-day period provided in Rule 4(a)(3) for another party to file a notice of appeal runs from the date when the district court dockets the first notice.

(3) When a defendant in a criminal case files a notice of appeal under this Rule 4(c), the 30-day period for the government to file its notice of appeal runs from the entry of the judgment or order appealed from or from the district court's docketing of the defendant's notice of appeal, whichever is later.

(d) Mistaken Filing in the Court of Appeals. If a notice of appeal in either a civil or a criminal case is mistakenly filed in the court of appeals, the clerk of that court must note on the notice the date when it was received and send it to the district clerk. The notice is then considered filed in the district court on the date so noted.

Rule 5. Appeal by Permission

(a) Petition for Permission to Appeal

(1) To request permission to appeal when an appeal is within the court of appeals' discretion, a party must file a petition with the circuit clerk and serve it on all other parties to the district-court action.

(2) The petition must be filed within the time specified by the statute or rule authorizing the appeal or, if no such time is specified, within the time provided by Rule 4(a) for filing a notice of appeal.

(3) If a party cannot petition for appeal unless the district court first enters an order granting permission to do so or stating that the necessary conditions are met, the district court may amend its order, either on its own or in response to a party's motion, to include the required permission or statement. In that event, the time to petition runs from entry of the amended order.

(b) Contents of the Petition; Answer or Cross-Petition; Oral Argument

(1) The petition must include the following:

(A) the facts necessary to understand the question presented;

(B) the question itself;

(C) the relief sought;

(D) the reasons why the appeal should be allowed and is authorized by a statute or rule; and

(E) an attached copy of:

(i) the order, decree, or judgment complained of and any related opinion or memorandum, and

(ii) any order stating the district court's permission to appeal or finding that the necessary conditions are met.

(2) A party may file an answer in opposition or a cross-petition within 10 days after the petition is served.

(3) The petition and answer will be submitted without oral argument unless the court of appeals orders otherwise.

(c) Form of Papers; Number of Copies; Length Limits. All papers must conform to Rule 32(c)(2). An original and 3 copies must be filed unless the court requires a different number by local rule or by order in a particular case. Except by the court's permission, and excluding the accompanying documents required by Rule 5(b)(1)(E):

(1) a paper produced using a computer must not exceed 5,200 words; and

(2) a handwritten or typewritten paper must not exceed 20 pages.

(d) Grant of Permission; Fees; Cost Bond; Filing the Record

(1) Within 14 days after the entry of the order granting permission to appeal, the appellant must:

(A) pay the district clerk all required fees; and

(B) file a cost bond if required under Rule 7.

(2) A notice of appeal need not be filed. The date when the order granting permission to appeal is entered serves as the date of the notice of appeal for calculating time under these rules.

(3) The district clerk must notify the circuit clerk once the petitioner has paid the fees. Upon receiving this notice, the circuit clerk must enter the appeal on the docket. The record must be forwarded and filed in accordance with Rules 11 and 12(c).

Rule 7. Bond for Costs on Appeal in a Civil Case

In a civil case, the district court may require an appellant to file a bond or provide other security in any form and amount necessary to ensure payment of costs on appeal. Rule 8(b) applies to a surety on a bond given under this rule.

Rule 8. Stay or Injunction Pending Appeal

(a) Motion for Stay

(1) Initial Motion in the District Court. A party must ordinarily move first in the district court for the following relief:

(A) a stay of the judgment or order of a district court pending appeal;

(B) approval of a bond or other security provided to obtain a stay of judgment; or

(C) an order suspending, modifying, restoring, or granting an injunction while an appeal is pending.

(2) Motion in the Court of Appeals; Conditions on Relief. A motion for the relief mentioned in Rule 8(a)(1) may be made to the court of appeals or to one of its judges.

(A) The motion must:

(i) show that moving first in the district court would be impracticable; or

(ii) state that, a motion having been made, the district court denied the motion or failed to afford the relief requested and state any reasons given by the district court for its action.

(B) The motion must also include:

(i) the reasons for granting the relief requested and the facts relied on;

(ii) originals or copies of affidavits or other sworn statements supporting facts subject to dispute; and

(iii) relevant parts of the record.

(C) The moving party must give reasonable notice of the motion to all parties.

(D) A motion under this Rule 8(a)(2) must be filed with the circuit clerk and normally will be considered by a panel of the court. But in an exceptional case in which time requirements make that procedure impracticable, the motion may be made to and considered by a single judge.

(E) The court may condition relief on a party's filing a bond or other security in the district court.

(b) Proceeding Against a Security Provider. If a party gives security with one or more security providers, each provider submits to the jurisdiction of the district court and irrevocably appoints the district clerk as its agent on whom any papers affecting its liability on the security may be served. On motion, a security provider's liability may be enforced in the district court without the necessity of an independent action. The motion and any notice that the district court prescribes may be served on the district clerk, who must promptly send a copy to each security provider whose address is known.

(c) Stay in a Criminal Case. Rule 38 of the Federal Rules of Criminal Procedure governs a stay in a criminal case.

Rule 10. The Record on Appeal

(a) Composition of the Record on Appeal. The following items constitute the record on appeal:

(1) the original papers and exhibits filed in the district court;

(2) the transcript of proceedings, if any; and

(3) a certified copy of the docket entries prepared by the district clerk.

(b) The Transcript of Proceedings

(1) Appellant's Duty to Order. Within 14 days after filing the notice of appeal or entry of an order disposing of the last timely remaining motion of a type specified in Rule 4(a)(4)(A), whichever is later, the appellant must do either of the following:

(A) order from the reporter a transcript of such parts of the proceedings not already on file as the appellant considers necessary, subject to a local rule of the court of appeals and with the following qualifications:

(i) the order must be in writing;

(ii) if the cost of the transcript is to be paid by the United States under the Criminal Justice Act, the order must so state; and

(iii) the appellant must, within the same period, file a copy of the order with the district clerk; or

(B) file a certificate stating that no transcript will be ordered.

(2) Unsupported Finding or Conclusion. If the appellant intends to urge on appeal that a finding or conclusion is unsupported by the evidence or is contrary to the evidence, the appellant must include in the record a transcript of all evidence relevant to that finding or conclusion.

(3) Partial Transcript. Unless the entire transcript is ordered:

(A) the appellant must — within the 14 days provided in Rule 10(b)(1) — file a statement of the issues that the appellant intends to present on the appeal and must serve on the appellee a copy of both the order or certificate and the statement;

(B) if the appellee considers it necessary to have a transcript of other parts of the proceedings, the appellee must, within 14 days after the service of the order or certificate and the statement of the issues, file and serve on the appellant a designation of additional parts to be ordered; and

(C) unless within 14 days after service of that designation the appellant has ordered all such parts, and has so notified the appellee, the appellee may within the following 14 days either order the parts or move in the district court for an order requiring the appellant to do so.

(4) Payment. At the time of ordering, a party must make satisfactory arrangements with the reporter for paying the cost of the transcript.

(c) Statement of the Evidence When the Proceedings Were Not Recorded or When a Transcript Is Unavailable. If the transcript of a hearing or trial is unavailable, the appellant may prepare a statement of the evidence or proceedings from the best available means, including the appellant's recollection. The statement must be served on the appellee, who may serve objections or proposed amendments within 14 days after being served. The statement and any objections or proposed amendments must then be submitted to the district court for settlement and approval. As settled and approved, the statement must be included by the district clerk in the record on appeal.

(d) Agreed Statement as the Record on Appeal. In place of the record on appeal as defined in Rule 10(a), the parties may prepare, sign, and submit to the district court a statement of the case showing how the issues presented by the appeal arose and were decided in the district court. The statement must set forth only those facts averred and proved or sought to be proved that are essential to the court's resolution of the issues. If the statement is truthful, it — together with any additions that the district court may consider necessary to a full presentation of the issues on appeal — must be approved by the district court and must then be certified to the court of appeals as the record on appeal. The district clerk must then send it to the circuit clerk within the time provided by Rule 11. A copy of the agreed statement may be filed in place of the appendix required by Rule 30.

(e) Correction or Modification of the Record

(1) If any difference arises about whether the record truly discloses what occurred in the district court, the difference must be submitted to and settled by that court and the record conformed accordingly.

(2) If anything material to either party is omitted from or misstated in the record by error or accident, the omission or misstatement may be corrected and a supplemental record may be certified and forwarded:

(A) on stipulation of the parties;

(B) by the district court before or after the record has been forwarded; or

(C) by the court of appeals.

(3) All other questions as to the form and content of the record must be presented to the court of appeals.

Rule 12. Docketing the Appeal; Filing a Representation Statement; Filing the Record

(a) **Docketing the Appeal.** Upon receiving the copy of the notice of appeal and the docket entries from the district clerk under Rule 3(d), the circuit clerk must docket the appeal under the title of the district-court action and must identify the appellant, adding the appellant's name if necessary.

(b) **Filing a Representation Statement.** Unless the court of appeals designates another time, the attorney who filed the notice of appeal must, within 14 days after filing the notice, file a statement with the circuit clerk naming the parties that the attorney represents on appeal.

(c) **Filing the Record, Partial Record, or Certificate.** Upon receiving the record, partial record, or district clerk's certificate as provided in Rule 11, the circuit clerk must file it and immediately notify all parties of the filing date.

VI. Habeas Corpus; Proceedings in Forma Pauperis

Rule 22. Habeas Corpus and Section 2255 Proceedings

(a) **Application for the Original Writ.** An application for a writ of habeas corpus must be made to the appropriate district court. If made to a circuit judge, the application must be transferred to the appropriate district court. If a district court denies an application made or transferred to it, renewal of the application before a circuit judge is not permitted. The applicant may, under 28 U.S.C. § 2253, appeal to the court of appeals from the district court's order denying the application.

(b) **Certificate of Appealability**

(1) In a habeas corpus proceeding in which the detention complained of arises from process issued by a state court, or in a 28 U.S.C. § 2255 proceeding, the applicant cannot take an appeal unless a circuit justice or a circuit or district judge issues a certificate of appealability under 28 U.S.C. § 2253(c). If an applicant files a notice of appeal, the district clerk must send to the court of appeals the certificate (if any) and the statement described in Rule 11(a) of the Rules Governing Proceedings Under 28 U.S.C. § 2254 or § 2255 (if any), along with the notice of appeal and the file of the district-court proceedings. If the district judge has denied the certificate, the applicant may request a circuit judge to issue it.

(2) A request addressed to the court of appeals may be considered by a circuit judge or judges, as the court prescribes. If no express request for a certificate

is filed, the notice of appeal constitutes a request addressed to the judges of the court of appeals.

(3) A certificate of appealability is not required when a state or its representative or the United States or its representative appeals.

VII. General Provisions

Rule 28. Briefs

(a) Appellant's Brief. The appellant's brief must contain, under appropriate headings and in the order indicated:

(1) a disclosure statement if required by Rule 26.1;

(2) a table of contents, with page references;

(3) a table of authorities — cases (alphabetically arranged), statutes, and other authorities — with references to the pages of the brief where they are cited;

(4) a jurisdictional statement, including:

(A) the basis for the district court's or agency's subject-matter jurisdiction, with citations to applicable statutory provisions and stating relevant facts establishing jurisdiction;

(B) the basis for the court of appeals' jurisdiction, with citations to applicable statutory provisions and stating relevant facts establishing jurisdiction;

(C) the filing dates establishing the timeliness of the appeal or petition for review; and

(D) an assertion that the appeal is from a final order or judgment that disposes of all parties' claims, or information establishing the court of appeals' jurisdiction on some other basis;

(5) a statement of the issues presented for review;

(6) a concise statement of the case setting out the facts relevant to the issues submitted for review, describing the relevant procedural history, and identifying the rulings presented for review, with appropriate references to the record (see Rule 28(e));

(7) a summary of the argument, which must contain a succinct, clear, and accurate statement of the arguments made in the body of the brief, and which must not merely repeat the argument headings;

(8) the argument, which must contain:

(A) appellant's contentions and the reasons for them, with citations to the authorities and parts of the record on which the appellant relies; and

(B) for each issue, a concise statement of the applicable standard of review (which may appear in the discussion of the issue or under a separate heading placed before the discussion of the issues);

(9) a short conclusion stating the precise relief sought; and

(10) the certificate of compliance, if required by Rule 32(g)(1).

(b) Appellee's Brief. The appellee's brief must conform to the requirements of Rule 28(a)(1)-(8) and (10), except that none of the following need appear unless the appellee is dissatisfied with the appellant's statement:

(1) the jurisdictional statement;
(2) the statement of the issues;
(3) the statement of the case; and
(4) the statement of the standard of review.

(c) Reply Brief. The appellant may file a brief in reply to the appellee's brief. Unless the court permits, no further briefs may be filed. A reply brief must contain a table of contents, with page references, and a table of authorities — cases (alphabetically arranged), statutes, and other authorities — with references to the pages of the reply brief where they are cited.

(d) References to Parties. In briefs and at oral argument, counsel should minimize use of the terms "appellant" and "appellee." To make briefs clear, counsel should use the parties' actual names or the designations used in the lower court or agency proceeding, or such descriptive terms as "the employee," "the injured person," "the taxpayer," "the ship," "the stevedore."

(e) References to the Record. References to the parts of the record contained in the appendix filed with the appellant's brief must be to the pages of the appendix. If the appendix is prepared after the briefs are filed, a party referring to the record must follow one of the methods detailed in Rule 30(c). If the original record is used under Rule 30(f) and is not consecutively paginated, or if the brief refers to an unreproduced part of the record, any reference must be to the page of the original document. For example:

- Answer p. 7;
- Motion for Judgment p. 2;
- Transcript p. 231.

Only clear abbreviations may be used. A party referring to evidence whose admissibility is in controversy must cite the pages of the appendix or of the transcript at which the evidence was identified, offered, and received or rejected.

(f) Reproduction of Statutes, Rules, Regulations, etc. If the court's determination of the issues presented requires the study of statutes, rules, regulations, etc., the relevant parts must be set out in the brief or in an addendum at the end, or may be supplied to the court in pamphlet form.

(g) [Reserved]

(h) [Reserved]

(i) Briefs in a Case Involving Multiple Appellants or Appellees. In a case involving more than one appellant or appellee, including consolidated cases, any number of appellants or appellees may join in a brief, and any party may adopt by reference a part of another's brief. Parties may also join in reply briefs.

(j) Citation of Supplemental Authorities. If pertinent and significant authorities come to a party's attention after the party's brief has been filed — or after oral argument but before decision — a party may promptly advise the circuit clerk by letter, with a copy to all other parties, setting forth the citations. The letter must state the reasons for the supplemental citations, referring either to the page of the brief or to a point argued orally. The body of the letter must not exceed 350 words. Any response must be made promptly and must be similarly limited.

Rule 29. Brief of an Amicus Curiae

(a) During Initial Consideration of a Case on the Merits

(1) Applicability. This Rule 29(a) governs amicus filings during a court's initial consideration of a case on the merits.

(2) When Permitted. The United States or its officer or agency or a state may file an amicus brief without the consent of the parties or leave of court. Any other amicus curiae may file a brief only by leave of court or if the brief states that all parties have consented to its filing, but a court of appeals may prohibit the filing of or may strike an amicus brief that would result in a judge's disqualification.

(3) Motion for Leave to File. The motion must be accompanied by the proposed brief and state:

(A) the movant's interest; and

(B) the reason why an amicus brief is desirable and why the matters asserted are relevant to the disposition of the case.

(4) Contents and Form. An amicus brief must comply with Rule 32. In addition to the requirements of Rule 32, the cover must identify the party or parties supported and indicate whether the brief supports affirmance or reversal. An amicus brief need not comply with Rule 28, but must include the following:

(A) if the amicus curiae is a corporation, a disclosure statement like that required of parties by Rule 26.1;

(B) a table of contents, with page references;

(C) a table of authorities — cases (alphabetically arranged), statutes, and other authorities — with references to the pages of the brief where they are cited;

(D) a concise statement of the identity of the amicus curiae, its interest in the case, and the source of its authority to file;

(E) unless the amicus curiae is one listed in the first sentence of Rule 29(a)(2), a statement that indicates whether:

(i) a party's counsel authored the brief in whole or in part;

(ii) a party or a party's counsel contributed money that was intended to fund preparing or submitting the brief; and

(iii) a person — other than the amicus curiae, its members, or its counsel — contributed money that was intended to fund preparing or submitting the brief and, if so, identifies each such person;

(F) an argument, which may be preceded by a summary and which need not include a statement of the applicable standard of review; and

(G) a certificate of compliance under Rule 32(g)(1), if length is computed using a word or line limit.

(5) Length. Except by the court's permission, an amicus brief may be no more than one-half the maximum length authorized by these rules for a party's principal brief. If the court grants a party permission to file a longer brief, that extension does not affect the length of an amicus brief.

(6) Time for Filing. An amicus curiae must file its brief, accompanied by a motion for filing when necessary, no later than 7 days after the principal brief of the party being supported is filed. An amicus curiae that does not support either party must file its brief no later than 7 days after the appellant's or petitioner's principal brief is filed. A court may grant leave for later filing, specifying the time within which an opposing party may answer.

(7) Reply Brief. Except by the court's permission, an amicus curiae may not file a reply brief.

(8) Oral Argument. An amicus curiae may participate in oral argument only with the court's permission.

(b) During Consideration of Whether to Grant Rehearing

(1) Applicability. This Rule 29(b) governs amicus filings during a court's consideration of whether to grant panel rehearing or rehearing en banc, unless a local rule or order in a case provides otherwise.

(2) When Permitted. The United States or its officer or agency or a state may file an amicus brief without the consent of the parties or leave of court. Any other amicus curiae may file a brief only by leave of court.

(3) Motion for Leave to File. Rule 29(a)(3) applies to a motion for leave.

(4) Contents, Form, and Length. Rule 29(a)(4) applies to the amicus brief. The brief must not exceed 2,600 words.

(5) Time for Filing. An amicus curiae supporting the petition for rehearing or supporting neither party must file its brief, accompanied by a motion for filing when necessary, no later than 7 days after the petition is filed. An amicus curiae opposing the petition must file its brief, accompanied by a motion for filing when necessary, no later than the date set by the court for the response.

Rule 30. Appendix to the Briefs

(a) Appellant's Responsibility

(1) Contents of the Appendix. The appellant must prepare and file an appendix to the briefs containing:

(A) the relevant docket entries in the proceeding below;

(B) the relevant portions of the pleadings, charge, findings, or opinion;

(C) the judgment, order, or decision in question; and

(D) other parts of the record to which the parties wish to direct the court's attention.

(2) Excluded Material. Memoranda of law in the district court should not be included in the appendix unless they have independent relevance. Parts of the record may be relied on by the court or the parties even though not included in the appendix.

(3) Time to File; Number of Copies. Unless filing is deferred under Rule 30(c), the appellant must file 10 copies of the appendix with the brief and must serve one copy on counsel for each party separately represented. An unrepresented party proceeding in forma pauperis must file 4 legible copies with the clerk, and one copy must be served on counsel for each separately represented party. The court may by local rule or by order in a particular case require the filing or service of a different number.

(b) All Parties' Responsibilities

(1) Determining the Contents of the Appendix. The parties are encouraged to agree on the contents of the appendix. In the absence of an agreement, the appellant must, within 14 days after the record is filed, serve on the appellee a designation of the parts of the record the appellant intends to include in the appendix and a statement of the issues the appellant intends to present for review. The appellee may, within 14 days after receiving the designation, serve on the appellant a designation of additional parts to which it wishes to direct the court's attention. The appellant must include the designated parts in the appendix. The parties must not engage in unnecessary designation of parts of the record, because the entire record is available to the court. This paragraph applies also to a cross-appellant and a cross-appellee.

(2) Costs of Appendix. Unless the parties agree otherwise, the appellant must pay the cost of the appendix. If the appellant considers parts of the record designated by the appellee to be unnecessary, the appellant may advise the appellee, who must then advance the cost of including those parts. The cost of the appendix is a taxable cost. But if any party causes unnecessary parts of the record to be included in the appendix, the court may impose the cost of those parts on that party. Each circuit must, by local rule, provide for sanctions against attorneys who unreasonably and vexatiously increase litigation costs by including unnecessary material in the appendix.

(c) Deferred Appendix

(1) Deferral Until After Briefs Are Filed. The court may provide by rule for classes of cases or by order in a particular case that preparation of the appendix may be deferred until after the briefs have been filed and that the appendix may be filed 21 days after the appellee's brief is served. Even though the filing of the appendix may be deferred, Rule 30(b) applies; except that a party must designate the parts of the record it wants included in the appendix when it serves its brief, and need not include a statement of the issues presented.

(2) References to the Record.

(A) If the deferred appendix is used, the parties may cite in their briefs the pertinent pages of the record. When the appendix is prepared, the record pages cited in the briefs must be indicated by inserting record page numbers, in brackets, at places in the appendix where those pages of the record appear.

(B) A party who wants to refer directly to pages of the appendix may serve and file copies of the brief within the time required by Rule 31(a), containing appropriate references to pertinent pages of the record. In that event, within 14 days after the appendix is filed, the party must serve and file copies of the brief, containing references to the pages of the appendix in place of or in addition to the references to the pertinent pages of the record. Except for the correction of typographical errors, no other changes may be made to the brief.

(d) Format of the Appendix. The appendix must begin with a table of contents identifying the page at which each part begins. The relevant docket entries must follow the table of contents. Other parts of the record must follow chronologically. When pages from the transcript of proceedings are placed in the appendix, the transcript page numbers must be shown in brackets immediately before the included pages. Omissions in the text of papers or of the transcript must be indicated by asterisks. Immaterial formal matters (captions, subscriptions, acknowledgments, etc.) should be omitted.

(e) Reproduction of Exhibits. Exhibits designated for inclusion in the appendix may be reproduced in a separate volume, or volumes, suitably indexed. Four copies must be filed with the appendix, and one copy must be served on counsel for each separately represented party. If a transcript of a proceeding before an administrative agency, board, commission, or officer was used in a district-court action and has been designated for inclusion in the appendix, the transcript must be placed in the appendix as an exhibit.

(f) Appeal on the Original Record Without an Appendix. The court may, either by rule for all cases or classes of cases or by order in a particular case, dispense with the appendix and permit an appeal to proceed on the original record with any copies of the record, or relevant parts, that the court may order the parties to file.

Rule 31. Serving and Filing Briefs

(a) Time to Serve and File a Brief

(1) The appellant must serve and file a brief within 40 days after the record is filed. The appellee must serve and file a brief within 30 days after the appellant's brief is served. The appellant may serve and file a reply brief within 21 days after service of the appellee's brief but a reply brief must be filed at least 7 days before argument, unless the court, for good cause, allows a later filing.

(2) A court of appeals that routinely considers cases on the merits promptly after the briefs are filed may shorten the time to serve and file briefs, either by local rule or by order in a particular case.

(b) Number of Copies. Twenty-five copies of each brief must be filed with the clerk and 2 copies must be served on each unrepresented party and on counsel for each separately represented party. An unrepresented party proceeding in forma pauperis must file 4 legible copies with the clerk, and one copy must be served on each unrepresented party and on counsel for each separately represented party. The court may by local rule or by order in a particular case require the filing or service of a different number.

(c) Consequence of Failure to File. If an appellant fails to file a brief within the time provided by this rule, or within an extended time, an appellee may move to dismiss the appeal. An appellee who fails to file a brief will not be heard at oral argument unless the court grants permission.

Rule 32. Form of Briefs, Appendices, and Other Papers

(a) Form of a Brief

(1) Reproduction

(A) A brief may be reproduced by any process that yields a clear black image on light paper. The paper must be opaque and unglazed. Only one side of the paper may be used.

(B) Text must be reproduced with a clarity that equals or exceeds the output of a laser printer.

(C) Photographs, illustrations, and tables may be reproduced by any method that results in a good copy of the original; a glossy finish is acceptable if the original is glossy.

(2) Cover. Except for filings by unrepresented parties, the cover of the appellant's brief must be blue; the appellee's, red; an intervenor's or amicus curiae's, green; any reply brief, gray; and any supplemental brief, tan. The front cover of a brief must contain:

(A) the number of the case centered at the top;

(B) the name of the court;

(C) the title of the case (see Rule 12(a));

(D) the nature of the proceeding (e.g., Appeal, Petition for Review) and the name of the court, agency, or board below;

(E) the title of the brief, identifying the party or parties for whom the brief is filed; and

(F) the name, office address, and telephone number of counsel representing the party for whom the brief is filed.

(3) Binding. The brief must be bound in any manner that is secure, does not obscure the text, and permits the brief to lie reasonably flat when open.

(4) Paper Size, Line Spacing, and Margins. The brief must be on 8½ by 11 inch paper. The text must be double-spaced, but quotations more than two lines long may be indented and single-spaced. Headings and footnotes may be single-spaced. Margins must be at least one inch on all four sides. Page numbers may be placed in the margins, but no text may appear there.

(5) Typeface. Either a proportionally spaced or a monospaced face may be used.

(A) A proportionally spaced face must include serifs, but sans-serif type may be used in headings and captions. A proportionally spaced face must be 14-point or larger.

(B) A monospaced face may not contain more than 10 ½ characters per inch.

(6) Type Styles. A brief must be set in a plain, roman style, although italics or boldface may be used for emphasis. Case names must be italicized or underlined.

(7) Length

(A) Page Limitation. A principal brief may not exceed 30 pages, or a reply brief 15 pages, unless it complies with Rule 32(a)(7)(B).

(B) Type-Volume Limitation.

(i) A principal brief is acceptable if it:

- contains no more than 13,000 words; or
- uses a monospaced face and contains no more than 1,300 lines of text.

(ii) A reply brief is acceptable if it contains no more than half of the type volume specified in Rule 32(a)(7)(B)(i).

(b) Form of an Appendix. An appendix must comply with Rule 32(a)(1), (2), (3), and (4), with the following exceptions:

(1) The cover of a separately bound appendix must be white.

(2) An appendix may include a legible photocopy of any document found in the record or of a printed judicial or agency decision.

(3) When necessary to facilitate inclusion of odd-sized documents such as technical drawings, an appendix may be a size other than 8 ½ by 11 inches, and need not lie reasonably flat when opened.

(c) Form of Other Papers

(1) Motion. The form of a motion is governed by Rule 27(d).

(2) Other Papers. Any other paper, including a petition for panel rehearing and a petition for hearing or rehearing en banc, and any response to such a petition, must be reproduced in the manner prescribed by Rule 32(a), with the following exceptions:

(A) A cover is not necessary if the caption and signature page of the paper together contain the information required by Rule 32(a)(2). If a cover is used, it must be white.

(B) Rule 32(a)(7) does not apply.

(d) Signature. Every brief, motion, or other paper filed with the court must be signed by the party filing the paper or, if the party is represented, by one of the party's attorneys.

(e) Local Variation. Every court of appeals must accept documents that comply with the form requirements of this rule and the length limits set by these rules. By local rule or order in a particular case, a court of appeals may accept documents that do not meet all the form requirements of this rule or the length limits set by these rules.

(f) Items Excluded from Length. In computing any length limit, headings, footnotes, and quotations count toward the limit but the following items do not:

- cover page;
- disclosure statement;
- table of contents;
- table of citations;
- statement regarding oral argument;
- addendum containing statutes, rules, or regulations;
- certificate of counsel;
- signature block;
- proof of service; and
- any item specifically excluded by these rules or by local rule.

(g) Certificate of Compliance

(1) Briefs and Papers That Require a Certificate. A brief submitted under Rules 28.1(e)(2), 29(b)(4), or 32(a)(7)(B) — and a paper submitted under Rules 5(c)(1), 21(d)(1), 27(d)(2)(A), 27(d)(2)(C), or 40(d)(3)(A) — must include a certificate by the attorney, or an unrepresented party, that the document complies with the type-volume limitation. The person preparing the certificate may rely on the word or line count of the word-processing system used to prepare the document. The certificate must state the number of words — or the number of lines of monospaced type — in the document.

(2) Acceptable Form. Form 6 in the Appendix of Forms meets the requirements for a certificate of compliance.

Rule 32.1 Citing Judicial Dispositions

(a) Citation Permitted. A court may not prohibit or restrict the citation of federal judicial opinions, orders, judgments, or other written dispositions that have been:

(i) designated as "unpublished," "not for publication," "non-precedential," "not precedent," or the like; and

(ii) issued on or after January 1, 2007.

(b) Copies Required. If a party cites a federal judicial opinion, order, judgment, or other written disposition that is not available in a publicly accessible electronic database, the party must file and serve a copy of that opinion, order, judgment, or disposition with the brief or other paper in which it is cited.

Rule 33. Appeal Conferences

The court may direct the attorneys — and, when appropriate, the parties — to participate in one or more conferences to address any matter that may aid in disposing of the proceedings, including simplifying the issues and discussing settlement. A judge or other person designated by the court may preside over the conference, which may be conducted in person or by telephone. Before a settlement conference, the attorneys must consult with their clients and obtain as much authority as feasible to settle the case. The court may, as a result of the conference, enter an order controlling the course of the proceedings or implementing any settlement agreement.

Rule 34. Oral Argument

(a) In General

(1) Party's Statement. Any party may file, or a court may require by local rule, a statement explaining why oral argument should, or need not, be permitted.

(2) Standards. Oral argument must be allowed in every case unless a panel of three judges who have examined the briefs and record unanimously agrees that oral argument is unnecessary for any of the following reasons:

(A) the appeal is frivolous;

(B) the dispositive issue or issues have been authoritatively decided; or

(C) the facts and legal arguments are adequately presented in the briefs and record, and the decisional process would not be significantly aided by oral argument.

(b) Notice of Argument; Postponement. The clerk must advise all parties whether oral argument will be scheduled, and, if so, the date, time, and place for it, and the time allowed for each side. A motion to postpone the argument or to allow longer argument must be filed reasonably in advance of the hearing date.

(c) Order and Contents of Argument. The appellant opens and concludes the argument. Counsel must not read at length from briefs, records, or authorities.

(d) Cross-Appeals and Separate Appeals. If there is a cross-appeal, Rule 28.1(b) determines which party is the appellant and which is the appellee for purposes of oral argument. Unless the court directs otherwise, a cross-appeal or separate appeal must be argued when the initial appeal is argued. Separate parties should avoid duplicative argument.

(e) Nonappearance of a Party. If the appellee fails to appear for argument, the court must hear appellant's argument. If the appellant fails to appear for argument, the court may hear the appellee's argument. If neither party appears, the case will be decided on the briefs, unless the court orders otherwise.

(f) Submission on Briefs. The parties may agree to submit a case for decision on the briefs, but the court may direct that the case be argued.

(g) Use of Physical Exhibits at Argument; Removal. Counsel intending to use physical exhibits other than documents at the argument must arrange to place them in the courtroom on the day of the argument before the court convenes. After the argument, counsel must remove the exhibits from the courtroom, unless the court directs otherwise. The clerk may destroy or dispose of the exhibits if counsel does not reclaim them within a reasonable time after the clerk gives notice to remove them.

Rule 35. En Banc Determination

(a) When Hearing or Rehearing En Banc May Be Ordered. A majority of the circuit judges who are in regular active service and who are not disqualified may order that an appeal or other proceeding be heard or reheard by the court of appeals en banc. An en banc hearing or rehearing is not favored and ordinarily will not be ordered unless:

(1) en banc consideration is necessary to secure or maintain uniformity of the court's decisions; or

(2) the proceeding involves a question of exceptional importance.

(b) Petition for Hearing or Rehearing En Banc. A party may petition for a hearing or rehearing en banc.

(1) The petition must begin with a statement that either:

(A) the panel decision conflicts with a decision of the United States Supreme Court or of the court to which the petition is addressed (with citation to the conflicting case or cases) and consideration by the full court is therefore necessary to secure and maintain uniformity of the court's decisions; or

(B) the proceeding involves one or more questions of exceptional importance, each of which must be concisely stated; for example, a petition may assert that a proceeding presents a question of exceptional importance if it involves an issue on which the panel decision conflicts with the authoritative decisions of other United States Courts of Appeals that have addressed the issue.

(2) Except by the court's permission:

(A) a petition for an en banc hearing or rehearing produced using a computer must not exceed 3,900 words; and

(B) a handwritten or typewritten petition for an en banc hearing or rehearing must not exceed 15 pages.

(3) For purposes of the limits in Rule 35(b)(2), if a party files both a petition for panel rehearing and a petition for rehearing en banc, they are considered a single document even if they are filed separately, unless separate filing is required by local rule.

(c) Time for Petition for Hearing or Rehearing En Banc. A petition that an appeal be heard initially en banc must be filed by the date when the appellee's brief is due. A petition for a rehearing en banc must be filed within the time prescribed by Rule 40 for filing a petition for rehearing.

(d) Number of Copies. The number of copies to be filed must be prescribed by local rule and may be altered by order in a particular case.

(e) Response. No response may be filed to a petition for an en banc consideration unless the court orders a response. The length limits in Rule 35(b)(2) apply to a response.

(f) Call for a Vote. A vote need not be taken to determine whether the case will be heard or reheard en banc unless a judge calls for a vote.

Rule 36. Entry of Judgment; Notice

(a) **Entry.** A judgment is entered when it is noted on the docket. The clerk must prepare, sign, and enter the judgment:

(1) after receiving the court's opinion — but if settlement of the judgment's form is required, after final settlement; or

(2) if a judgment is rendered without an opinion, as the court instructs.

(b) **Notice.** On the date when judgment is entered, the clerk must serve on all parties a copy of the opinion — or the judgment, if no opinion was written — and a notice of the date when the judgment was entered.

Rule 38. Frivolous Appeal — Damages and Costs

If a court of appeals determines that an appeal is frivolous, it may, after a separately filed motion or notice from the court and reasonable opportunity to respond, award just damages and single or double costs to the appellee.

Rule 39. Costs[1]

(a) **Against Whom Assessed.** The following rules apply unless the law provides or the court orders otherwise:

(1) if an appeal is dismissed, costs are taxed against the appellant, unless the parties agree otherwise;

(2) if a judgment is affirmed, costs are taxed against the appellant;

(3) if a judgment is reversed, costs are taxed against the appellee;

(4) if a judgment is affirmed in part, reversed in part, modified, or vacated, costs are taxed only as the court orders.

(b) **Costs For and Against the United States.** Costs for or against the United States, its agency, or officer will be assessed under Rule 39(a) only if authorized by law.

(c) **Costs of Copies.** Each court of appeals must, by local rule, fix the maximum rate for taxing the cost of producing necessary copies of a brief or appendix, or copies of records authorized by Rule 30(f). The rate must not exceed that

1. Pending amendment to Rule 39 may take effect December 1, 2025. See details, *infra*.

generally charged for such work in the area where the clerk's office is located and should encourage economical methods of copying.

(d) Bill of Costs: Objections; Insertion in Mandate

(1) A party who wants costs taxed must — within 14 days after entry of judgment — file with the circuit clerk and serve an itemized and verified bill of costs.

(2) Objections must be filed within 14 days after service of the bill of costs, unless the court extends the time.

(3) The clerk must prepare and certify an itemized statement of costs for insertion in the mandate, but issuance of the mandate must not be delayed for taxing costs. If the mandate issues before costs are finally determined, the district clerk must — upon the circuit clerk's request — add the statement of costs, or any amendment of it, to the mandate.

(e) Costs on Appeal Taxable in the District Court. The following costs on appeal are taxable in the district court for the benefit of the party entitled to costs under this rule:

(1) the preparation and transmission of the record;

(2) the reporter's transcript, if needed to determine the appeal;

(3) premiums paid for a bond or other security to preserve rights pending appeal; and

(4) the fee for filing the notice of appeal.

Pending Amendment to Rule 39 that may take effect December 1, 2025

Rule 39. Costs

(a) Allocating Costs Among the Parties. The following rules apply to allocating taxable costs among the parties unless the law provides, the parties agree, or the court orders otherwise:

(1) if an appeal is dismissed, costs are allocated against the appellant;

(2) if a judgment is affirmed, costs are allocated against the appellant;

(3) if a judgment is reversed, costs are allocated against the appellee;

(4) if a judgment is affirmed in part, reversed in part, modified, or vacated, each party bears its own costs.

(b) Reconsideration. Once the allocation of costs is established by the entry of judgment, a party may seek reconsideration of that allocation by filing a motion in the court of appeals within 14 days after the entry of judgment. But issuance of the mandate under Rule 41 must not be delayed awaiting a determination of the motion. The court of appeals retains jurisdiction to decide the motion after the mandate issues.

(c) Costs Governed by Allocation Determination. The allocation of costs applies both to costs taxable in the court of appeals under Rule 39(e) and to costs taxable in district court under Rule 39(f).

(d) Costs For and Against the United States. Costs for or against the United States, its agency, or officer will be allocated under Rule 39(a) only if authorized by law.

(e) Costs on Appeal Taxable in the Court of Appeals

(1) Costs Taxable. The following costs on appeal are taxable in the court of appeals for the benefit of the party entitled to costs:

(A) the production of necessary copies of brief or appendix, or copies of records authorized by Rule 30(f);

(B) the docketing fee; and

(C) a filing fee paid in the court of appeals.

(2) Costs of Copies. Each court of appeals must, by local rule, set the maximum rate for taxing the cost of producing necessary copies of a brief or appendix, or copies of records authorized by Rule 30(f). The rate must not exceed that generally charged for such work in the area where the clerk's office is located and should encourage economical methods of copying.

(3) Bill of Costs: Objections; Insertion in Mandate

(A) A party who wants costs taxed in the court of appeals must — within 14 days after judgment is entered — file with the circuit clerk and serve an itemized and verified bill of costs.

(B) Objections must be filed within 14 days after the bill of costs is served, unless the court extends the time.

(C) The clerk must prepare and certify an itemized statement of costs for insertion in the mandate, but issuance of the mandate must not be delayed for taxing costs. If the mandate issues before costs are finally determined, the district clerk must — upon the circuit clerk's request — add the statement of costs, or any amendment of it, to the mandate.

(f) Costs on Appeal Taxable in the District Court. The following costs on appeal are taxable in the district court for the benefit of the party entitled to costs:

(1) the preparation and transmission of the record;

(2) the reporter's transcript, if needed to determine the appeal;

(3) premiums paid for a bond or other security to preserve rights pending appeal; and

(4) the fee for filing the notice of appeal.

Rule 40. Panel Rehearing; En Banc Determination

(a) **A Party's Options.** A party may seek rehearing of a decision through a petition for panel rehearing, a petition for rehearing en banc, or both. Unless a local rule provides otherwise, a party seeking both forms of rehearing must file the petitions as a single document. Panel rehearing is the ordinary means of reconsidering a panel decision; rehearing en banc is not favored.

(b) **Content of a Petition**

(1) Petition for Panel Rehearing. A petition for panel rehearing must:

(A) state with particularity each point of law or fact that the petitioner believes the court has overlooked or misapprehended; and

(B) argue in support of the petition.

(2) Petition for Rehearing En Banc. A petition for rehearing en banc must begin with a statement that:

(A) the panel decision conflicts with a decision of the court to which the petition is addressed (with citation to the conflicting case or cases) and the full court's consideration is therefore necessary to secure or maintain uniformity of the court's decisions;

(B) the panel decision conflicts with a decision of the United States Supreme Court (with citation to the conflicting case or cases);

(C) the panel decision conflicts with an authoritative decision of another United States court of appeals (with citation to the conflicting case or cases); or

(D) the proceeding involves one or more questions of exceptional importance, each concisely stated.

(c) **When Rehearing En Banc May Be Ordered.** On their own or in response to a party's petition, a majority of the circuit judges who are in regular active service and who are not disqualified may order that an appeal or other proceeding be reheard en banc. Unless a judge calls for a vote, a vote need not be taken to determine whether the case will be so reheard. Rehearing en banc is not favored and ordinarily will be allowed only if one of the criteria in Rule 40(b)(2)(A)-(D) is met.

(d) **Time to File; Form; Length; Response; Oral Argument**

(1) Time. Unless the time is shortened or extended by order or local rule, any petition for panel rehearing or rehearing en banc must be filed within 14 days after judgment is entered — or, if the panel later amends its decision (on rehearing or otherwise), within 14 days after the amended decision is entered. But in a civil case, unless an order shortens or extends the time, the petition may be filed by any party within 45 days after entry of judgment or of an amended decision if one of the parties is:

(A) the United States;

(B) a United States agency;

(C) a United States officer or employee sued in an official capacity; or

(D) a current or former United States officer or employee sued in an individual capacity for an act or omission occurring in connection with duties performed on the United States' behalf — including all instances in which the United States represents that person when the court of appeals' judgment is entered or files that person's petition.

(2) Form of the Petition. The petition must comply in form with Rule 32. Copies must be filed and served as Rule 31 prescribes, except that the number of filed copies may be prescribed by local rule or altered by order in a particular case.

(3) Length. Unless the court or a local rule allows otherwise, the petition (or a single document containing a petition for panel rehearing and a petition for rehearing en banc) must not exceed:

(A) 3,900 words if produced using a computer; or

(B) 15 pages if handwritten or typewritten.

(4) Response. Unless the court so requests, no response to the petition is permitted. Ordinarily, the petition will not be granted without such a request. If a response is requested, the requirements of Rule 40(d)(2)-(3) apply to the response.

(5) Oral Argument. Oral argument on whether to grant the petition is not permitted.

(e) **If a Petition Is Granted.** If a petition for panel rehearing or rehearing en banc is granted, the court may:

(1) dispose of the case without further briefing or argument;

(2) order additional briefing or argument; or

(3) issue any other appropriate order.

(f) **Panel's Authority After a Petition for Rehearing En Banc.** The filing of a petition for rehearing en banc does not limit the panel's authority to take action described in Rule 40(e).

(g) **Initial Hearing En Banc.** On its own or in response to a party's petition, a court may hear an appeal or other proceeding initially en banc. A party's petition must be filed no later than the date when its principal brief is due. The provisions of Rule 40(b)(2), (c), and (d)(2)-(5) apply to an initial hearing en banc. But initial hearing en banc is not favored and ordinarily will not be ordered.

Rule 41. Mandate: Contents; Issuance and Effective Date; Stay

(a) **Contents.** Unless the court directs that a formal mandate issue, the mandate consists of a certified copy of the judgment, a copy of the court's opinion, if any, and any direction about costs.

(b) When Issued. The court's mandate must issue 7 days after the time to file a petition for rehearing expires, or 7 days after entry of an order denying a timely petition for panel rehearing, petition for rehearing en banc, or motion for stay of mandate, whichever is later. The court may shorten or extend the time by order.

(c) Effective Date. The mandate is effective when issued.

(d) Staying the Mandate Pending a Petition for Certiorari

(1) Motion to Stay. A party may move to stay the mandate pending the filing of a petition for a writ of certiorari in the Supreme Court. The motion must be served on all parties and must show that the petition would present a substantial question and that there is good cause for a stay.

(2) Duration of Stay; Extensions. The stay must not exceed 90 days, unless:

(A) the period is extended for good cause; or

(B) the party who obtained the stay notifies the circuit clerk in writing within the period of the stay:

(i) that the time for filing a petition has been extended, in which case the stay continues for the extended period; or

(ii) that the petition has been filed, in which case the stay continues until the Supreme Court's final disposition.

(3) Security. The court may require a bond or other security as a condition to granting or continuing a stay of the mandate.

(4) Issuance of Mandate. The court of appeals must issue the mandate immediately on receiving a copy of a Supreme Court order denying the petition, unless extraordinary circumstances exist.

STATE PROVISIONS REGARDING RELATION-BACK OF AMENDMENTS

(EXCERPTS FROM SELECTED STATES)

CALIFORNIA

Cal. Civ. Proc. Code § 474. Defendant designated by fictitious name; amendment; requirements for default judgment; notice to person served

When the plaintiff is ignorant of the name of a defendant, he must state that fact in the complaint, or the affidavit if the action is commenced by affidavit, and such defendant may be designated in any pleading or proceeding by any name, and when his true name is discovered, the pleading or proceeding must be amended accordingly; provided, that no default or default judgment shall be entered against a defendant so designated, unless it appears that the copy of the summons or other process, or, if there be no summons or process, the copy of the first pleading or notice served upon such defendant bore on the face thereof a notice stating in substance: "To the person served: You are hereby served in the within action (or proceedings) as (or on behalf of) the person sued under the fictitious name of (designating it)." The certificate or affidavit of service must state the fictitious name under which such defendant was served and the fact that notice of identity was given by endorsement upon the document served as required by this section. The foregoing requirements for entry of a default or default judgment shall be applicable only as to fictitious names designated pursuant to this section and not in the event the plaintiff has sued the defendant by an erroneous name and shall not be applicable to entry of a default or default judgment based upon service, in the manner otherwise provided by law, of an amended pleading, process or notice designating defendant by his true name.

Organizacion Comunidad De Alviso v. City of San Jose

60 Cal. App. 5th 783, 794–95, 275 Cal. Rptr. 3d 99, 108–09 (2021)

GROVER, J.

. . .

Plaintiff argues the trial court erred by not applying the relation back doctrine of Code of Civil Procedure section to allow it to substitute Microsoft in place of one of the fictitiously named Doe real parties in interest. "When the plaintiff is ignorant of the name of a defendant, he must state that fact in the complaint, or the affidavit if the action is commenced by affidavit, and such defendant may be designated in any pleading or proceeding by any name, and when his true name is discovered, the pleading or proceeding must be amended accordingly." (Code Civ. Proc., § 474.) A plaintiff's ignorance must be genuine and based on a lack of knowledge of the defendant's connection with the case. (*General Motors Corp. v. Superior Court* (1996) 48 Cal.App.4th 580, 594.) If a plaintiff satisfies those requirements, the amendment relates back to the filing of the original petition or complaint such that the "statute of limitations stops running as of the date the original complaint was filed." (*Id.* at p. 589.) Trial courts also have discretion, "in furtherance of justice, and on any terms as may be proper, [to] allow a party to amend any pleading or proceeding by adding or striking out the name of any party." (Code Civ. Proc., § 473, subd. (a)(1).)

. . .

FLORIDA

Fla. R. Civ. P. 1.190. Amended and Supplemental Pleadings

(a) Amendments. A party may amend a pleading once as a matter of course at any time before a responsive pleading is served or, if the pleading is one to which no responsive pleading is permitted and the action has not been placed on the trial calendar, may so amend it at any time within 20 days after it is served. Otherwise a party may amend a pleading only by leave of court or by written consent of the adverse party. If a party files a motion to amend a pleading, the party shall attach the proposed amended pleading to the motion. Leave of court shall be given freely when justice so requires. A party shall plead in response to an amended pleading within 10 days after service of the amended pleading unless the court otherwise orders.

(b) Amendments to Conform with the Evidence. When issues not raised by the pleadings are tried by express or implied consent of the parties, they shall be treated in all respects as if they had been raised in the pleadings. Such amendment of the pleadings as may be necessary to cause them to conform to the evidence and to raise these issues may be made upon motion of any party at any time, even after judgment, but failure so to amend shall not affect the result of the trial of these issues. If the evidence is objected to at the trial on the ground that it is not within the issues made by the pleadings, the court may allow the pleadings to be amended to conform with the evidence and shall do so freely when the merits of the cause are more effectually presented thereby and the objecting party fails to satisfy the court that the admission of such evidence will prejudice the objecting party in maintaining an action or defense upon the merits.

(c) Relation Back of Amendments. When the claim or defense asserted in the amended pleading arose out of the conduct, transaction, or occurrence set forth or attempted to be set forth in the original pleading, the amendment shall relate back to the date of the original pleading.

(d) Supplemental Pleadings. Upon motion of a party the court may permit that party, upon reasonable notice and upon such terms as are just, to serve a supplemental pleading setting forth transactions or occurrences or events which have happened since the date of the pleading sought to be supplemented. If the court deems it advisable that the adverse party plead thereto, it shall so order, specifying the time therefor.

(e) Amendments Generally. At any time in furtherance of justice, upon such terms as may be just, the court may permit any process, proceeding, pleading, or record to be amended or material supplemental matter to be set forth in an amended or supplemental pleading. At every stage of the action the court must disregard any error or defect in the proceedings which does not affect the substantial rights of the parties.

(f) Claims for Punitive Damages. A motion for leave to amend a pleading to assert a claim for punitive damages shall make a reasonable showing, by evidence in the record or evidence to be proffered by the claimant, that provides a reasonable basis for recovery of such damages. The motion to amend can be filed separately and before the supporting evidence or proffer, but each shall be served on all parties at least 20 days before the hearing.

Friedel v. Edwards

327 So.3d 1242 (Fla. Dist. Ct. App. 2021)

LUCAS, Judge.

. . .

"It is well-settled that the rule permitting amendments to pleadings, and the relation-back doctrine, are to be liberally construed and applied." *Est. of Eisen*, 126 So. 3d at 328-329 (collecting cases). As we explained in *Sorenson v. Bank of New York Mellon as Trustee for Certificate Holders CWALT, Inc.*, 261 So. 3d 660, 663 (Fla. 2d DCA 2018),

> Florida Rule of Civil Procedure 1.190(a) provides that "[l]eave of court [to amend pleadings] shall be given freely when justice so requires." Behind this rule is a "[p]ublic policy favor[ing] the liberal amendment of pleadings, and courts should resolve all doubts in favor of allowing the amendment of pleadings to allow cases to be decided on their merit." *Laurencio v. Deutsche Bank Nat'l Trust Co.*, 65 So. 3d 1190, 1193 (Fla. 2d DCA 2011) (*citing S. Developers & Earthmoving, Inc. v. Caterpillar Fin. Servs. Corp.*, 56 So. 3d 56, 62 (Fla. 2d DCA 2011)). "A trial court's refusal to permit an amendment of a pleading is an abuse of discretion unless it is clear that: (1) the amendment would prejudice the opposing party, (2) the privilege to amend has been abused, or (3) the amendment would be futile." *Id.*

Moreover, in *May v. HCA Health Services of Florida, Inc.*, our court held that amendments should relate back to the original date of filing if the new party "knew or should have known that the plaintiff had made a mistake or was guilty of a misnomer as concerns the correct identity of the defendant so that the added party was deemed to have suffered no prejudice by being tardily brought in or substituted as a party." 166 So. 3d 850, 854 (Fla. 2d DCA 2015) (*quoting Arnwine v. Huntington Nat'l Bank, N.A.*, 818 So. 2d 621, 624 (Fla. 2d DCA 2002)). We observed that "[t]he relation back doctrine is in accordance with the policies that [the rule] permitting the amendment of pleadings[] 'should be liberally construed' and that 'cases should be resolved on the merits whenever possible.'" *Id.* at 854 n.2 (*quoting Caduceus Props., LLC v. Graney*, 137 So. 3d 987, 993 (Fla. 2014)).

. . .

ILLINOIS

735 Ill. Comp. Stat. 5/2-616. Amendments

(a) At any time before final judgment amendments may be allowed on just and reasonable terms, introducing any party who ought to have been joined as plaintiff or defendant, dismissing any party, changing the cause of action or defense or adding new causes of action or defenses, and in any matter, either of form or substance, in any process, pleading, bill of particulars or proceedings, which may enable the plaintiff to sustain the claim for which it was intended to be brought or the defendant to make a defense or assert a cross claim.

(b) The cause of action, cross claim or defense set up in any amended pleading shall not be barred by lapse of time under any statute or contract prescribing or limiting the time within which an action may be brought or right asserted, if the time prescribed or limited had not expired when the original pleading was filed, and if it shall appear from the original and amended pleadings that the cause of action asserted, or the defense or cross claim interposed in the amended pleading grew out of the same transaction or occurrence set up in the original pleading, even though the original pleading was defective in that it failed to allege the performance of some act or the existence of some fact or some other matter which is a necessary condition precedent to the right of recovery or defense asserted, if the condition precedent has in fact been performed, and for the purpose of preserving the cause of action, cross claim or defense set up in the amended pleading, and for that purpose only, an amendment to any pleading shall be held to relate back to the date of the filing of the original pleading so amended.

(c) A pleading may be amended at any time, before or after judgment, to conform the pleadings to the proofs, upon terms as to costs and continuance that may be just.

(d) A cause of action against a person not originally named a defendant is not barred by lapse of time under any statute or contract prescribing or limiting the time within which an action may be brought or right asserted, if all the following terms and conditions are met: (1) the time prescribed or limited had not expired when the original action was commenced; (2) the person, within the time that the action might have been brought or the right asserted against him or her plus the time for service permitted under Supreme Court Rule 103(b), received such notice of the commencement of the action that the person will not be prejudiced in maintaining a defense on the merits and knew or should have known that, but for a mistake concerning the identity of the proper party, the action would have been brought against him or her; and (3) it appears from the original and amended pleadings that the cause of action asserted in the amended pleading grew out of the same transaction or occurrence set up in the original pleading, even though the original pleading was defective in that it failed to allege the performance of some act or the existence of some fact or some other matter which is a necessary condition precedent to the right of recovery when the condition precedent has in fact been performed, and even though the person was not named originally as a defendant. For the purpose of preserving the cause of action under those conditions, an amendment adding the person as a defendant relates back to the date of the filing of the original pleading so amended.

(e) A cause of action against a beneficiary of a land trust not originally named a defendant is not barred by lapse of time under any statute or contract prescribing or limiting the time within which an action may be brought or right asserted, if all the following terms and conditions are met: (1) the cause of action arises from the ownership, use or possession of real estate, record title whereto is held by a land trustee; (2) the time prescribed or limited had not expired when the original action was commenced; (3) the land trustee of record is named as a defendant; and (4) the plaintiff proceeds with reasonable diligence subsequent to the commencement of the action to serve process upon the land trustee, to determine the identity of the beneficiary, and to amend the complaint to name the beneficiary as a defendant.

(f) The changes made by this amendatory Act of the 92nd General Assembly apply to all complaints filed on or after the effective date of this amendatory Act, and to complaints filed before the effective date of this amendatory Act if the limitation period has not ended before the effective date.

MASSACHUSETTS

Mass. R. Civ. P. 15. Amended and Supplemental Pleadings

(a) Amendments. A party may amend his pleading once as a matter of course at any time before a responsive pleading is served and prior to entry of an order of dismissal or, if the pleading is one to which no responsive pleading is permitted and the action has not been placed upon the trial calendar, he may so amend it at any time within 20 days after it is served. Otherwise a party may amend his pleading only by leave of court or by written consent of the adverse party; and leave shall be freely given when justice so requires. A party shall plead in response to an amended pleading within the time remaining for response to the original pleading or within 10 days after service of the amended pleading, whichever period may be the longer, unless the court otherwise orders.

(b) Amendments to Conform to the Evidence. When issues not raised by the pleadings are tried by express or implied consent of the parties, they shall be treated in all respects as if they had been raised in the pleadings. Such amendment of the pleadings as may be necessary to cause them to conform to the evidence and to raise these issues may be made upon motion of any party at any time, even after judgment; but failure so to amend does not affect the result of the trial of these issues. If evidence is objected to at the trial on the ground that it is not within the issues made by the pleadings, the court may allow the pleadings to be amended and shall do so freely when the presentation of the merits of the action will be subserved thereby and the objecting party fails to satisfy the court that the admission of such evidence would prejudice him in maintaining his action or defense upon the merits. The court may grant a continuance to enable the objecting party to meet such evidence.

(c) Relation Back of Amendments. Whenever the claim or defense asserted in the amended pleading arose out of the conduct, transaction, or occurrence set forth or attempted to be set forth in the original pleading, the amendment (including an amendment changing a party) relates back to the original pleading.

(d) Supplemental Pleadings. Upon motion of a party the court may, upon reasonable notice and upon such terms as are just, permit him to serve a supplemental pleading setting forth transactions or occurrences or events which have happened since the date of the pleading sought to be supplemented. Permission may be granted even though the original pleading is defective in its statement of a claim for relief or defense. If the court deems it advisable that the adverse party plead to the supplemental pleading it shall so order, specifying the time therefor.

NEW YORK

N.Y. CPLR § 203. Method of Computing Periods of Limitation Generally

(a) Accrual of cause of action and interposition of claim. The time within which an action must be commenced, except as otherwise expressly prescribed, shall be computed from the time the cause of action accrued to the time the claim is interposed.

. . .

(c) Claim in complain where action commenced by filing. In an action which is commenced by filing, a claim asserted in the complaint is interposed against the defendant or a co-defendant united in interest with such defendant when the action is commenced.

. . .

(f) Claim in amended pleading. A claim asserted in an amended pleading is deemed to have been interposed at the time the claims in the original pleading were interposed, unless the original pleading does not give notice of the transactions, occurrences, or series of transactions or occurrences, to be proved pursuant to the amended pleading.

. . .

N.Y. CPLR Rule 3025. Amended and Supplemental Pleadings

(a) Amendments without leave. A party may amend his pleading once without leave of court within twenty days after its service, or at any time before the period for responding to it expires, or within twenty days after service of a pleading responding to it.

(b) Amendments and supplemental pleadings by leave. A party may amend his or her pleading, or supplement it by setting forth additional or subsequent transactions or occurrences, at any time by leave of court or by stipulation of all parties. Leave shall be freely given upon such terms as may be just including the granting of costs and continuances. Any motion to amend or supplement pleadings shall be accompanied by the proposed amended or supplemental pleading clearly showing the changes or additions to be made to the pleading.

(c) Amendment to conform to the evidence. The court may permit pleadings to be amended before or after judgment to conform them to the evidence, upon such terms as may be just including the granting of costs and continuances.

(d) Responses to amended or supplemental pleadings. Except where otherwise prescribed by law or order of the court, there shall be an answer or reply to an amended or supplemental pleading if an answer or reply is required to the pleading being amended or supplemented. Service of such an answer or reply shall be made within twenty days after service of the amended or supplemental pleading to which it responds.

Bisono v. Mist Enterprises, Inc.
231 A.D.3d 134 (App.2d) (2024)

DILLON, J.P.

. . .

Generally speaking, leave to amend a pleading shall be freely granted upon terms as may be just (*see* CPLR 3025[b]; *Edenwald Contr. Co. v. City of NewYork*, 60 N.Y.2d 957, 959). Leave may be denied if the proposed amendment is palpably insufficient or patently devoid of merit, or if it would cause undue prejudice to a party (*see e.g. Watkins–Bey v. MTA Bus Co.*, 174 A.D.3d 553, 554). Amendments that seek to add a time-barred claim or party will be found to be patently devoid of merit (*see Schwartz v. Walter*, 171 A.D.3d 969, 970, 95 N.Y.S.3d 879; *Roco G.C. Corp. v. Bridge View Tower, LLC*, 166 A.D.3d 1031, 1033; *Grant v. Brooklyn Ctr. for Rehabilitation & Residential Health Care, LLC*, 153 A.D.3d 798; *Jenal v. Brown*, 80 A.D.3d 727; Ricca v. Valenti, 24 A.D.3d 647, 648, unless the untimeliness can be saved by application of the relation-back doctrine (*see e.g. Catnap, LLC v. Cammeby's Mgt. Co., LLC*, 170 A.D.3d 1103, 1106; *Myung Hwa Jang v. Mang*, 164 A.D.3d 803, 804–805; *Marrone v. Miloscio*, 145 A.D.3d 996, 999; *Rodriguez v. Paramount Dev. Assoc., LLC*, 67 A.D.3d 767, 768).

The statutory basis for the relation-back doctrine is found in CPLR 203(c) and (f) (*see Matter of Red Hook/Gowanus Chamber of Commerce v. New York City Bd. of Stds. & Appeals*, 5 N.Y.3d 452, 457; *Ortega v. New York City Tr. Auth.*, 170 A.D.3d 872, 873; *Martin v. City of New York*, 153 A.D.3d 693, 694; *Moezinia v. Ashkenazi*, 136 A.D.3d 990, 992). CPLR 203(c) provides that "[i]n an action which is commenced by filing, a claim asserted in the complaint is interposed against the defendant or a co-defendant united in interest with such defendant when the action is commenced." CPLR 203(f) provides that "a claim asserted in an amended pleading is deemed to have been interposed at the time the claims in the original pleading were interposed, unless the original pleading does not give notice of the transactions, occurrences, or series of transactions or occurrences to be proved pursuant to the amended pleading." Built upon those provisions, the relation-back doctrine permits, under certain defined circumstances, the commencement of claims against a party that has not been timely sued, but which relate back to the original timely complaint. The doctrine also permits the addition of untimely claims against an original defendant under some of those same defined conditions.

The leading case on the relation-back doctrine is (*Buran v. Coupal*, 87 N.Y.2d 173). In *Buran*, the relation-back doctrine was defined as requiring that the plaintiff establish all three prongs of a three-part test for the addition of untimely claims or parties. The first prong is that the new claims arise out of the same conduct, transaction, or occurrence as that alleged in the original complaint. Second, if a new party is to be added, it must be united in interest with one or more of the original defendants, and by reason of that relationship can be charged with such notice of the institution of the action that he or she will not be prejudiced in defending the action on the merits. Third, if a new party is to be added, the newly-added defendant must have known, or should have known, that the action would have been timely commenced against him or her but for a mistake by the plaintiff as to the identity of the proper parties (*see id.* at 178–179; *see also Wilson v. Rye Family Realty, LLC*, 218 A.D.3d 836, 838; *Estate of Stengel v. Good Samaritan Hosp.*, 214 A.D.3d 954; *Sanders v. Guida*, 213 A.D.3d 712, 715; *Marcotrigiano v. Dental Specialty Assoc., P.C.*, 209 A.D.3d 850, 851–852; *OneWest Bank N.A. v. Muller*, 189 A.D.3d 853, 855).

. . .

TEXAS

Tex. R. Civ. P. 63. Amendments and Responsive Pleadings

Parties may amend their pleadings, respond to pleadings on file of other parties, file suggestions of death and make representative parties, and file such other pleas as they may desire by filing such pleas with the clerk at such time as not to operate as a surprise to the opposite party; provided, that any pleadings, responses or pleas offered for filing within seven days of the date of trial or thereafter, or after as such time as may be ordered by the judge under Rule 166, shall be filed only after leave of the judge is obtained, which leave shall be granted by the judge unless there is a showing that such filing will operate as a surprise to the opposite party.

Tex. Civ. Prac. & Rem § 16.068. Amended and Supplemental Pleadings

If a filed pleading relates to a cause of action, cross action, counterclaim, or defense that is not subject to a plea limitation when the pleading is filed, a subsequent amendment or supplement to the pleading that changes the facts or grounds of liability or defense is not subject to a plea of limitation unless the amendment or supplement is wholly based on a new, distinct, or different transaction or occurrence.

Salazar v. Pena

No. 08-23-00298-CV (Tex. App. Oct. 17, 2024)

Jeff Alley, Chief Justice

. . .

Generally, an amended pleading adding a new party does not relate back to the original pleading. *Univ. of Texas Health Sci. Ctr. v. Bailey*, 332 S.W.3d 395, 400 (Tex. 2011). This is because, with limited exceptions, § 16.068 "addresses adding claims, not parties." *Brown v. Enter. Recovery Sys., Inc.*, No. 02-11-00436-CV, 2013 WL 4506582, at *11 (Tex. App. — Fort Worth Aug. 22, 2013, pet. denied) (mem. op.); *Pfister v. De La Rosa*, No. 04-11-00475-CV, 2012 WL 2834762, at *2–3 (Tex. App. — San Antonio July 11, 2012, no pet.) (mem. op.)(affirming summary judgment where correct defendant served after four-year statute of limitations expired).

The "misnomer" and "misidentification" doctrines represent limited exceptions under the "relation-back" rule. *University of Texas Health*, 332 S.W.3d at 400. Misnomer occurs when a plaintiff serves the correct defendant under an incorrect name. *Chilkewitz v. Hyson*, 22 S.W.3d 825, 828 (Tex. 1999). Said another way, misnomer occurs when the plaintiff misnames the correct defendant, and the correct defendant is actually served. *See Enserch Corp. v. Parker*, 794 S.W.2d 2, 4–5 (Tex. 1990). In that circumstance, the limitations period is tolled, and a subsequent amendment of the petition (correcting the defendant's name) will "relate back" to the date of the original petition/service. Id. But here, the record confirms Salazar did not mis-name and serve the correct party; instead, she named and served the wrong party.

Thus, under § 16.068, Salazar's post-limitations amended answer naming Daniel as a new party does not relate back to the timely filed and served Original petition. *See Nolan v. Hughes*, 349 S.W.3d 209, 214 (Tex. App. — Dallas 2011, no pet.) (rejecting argument that § 16.068 permits relation-back when the amended pleading names a new party as defendant after expiration of limitations).

The point of error arguing Salazar's late-filing against Daniel represents a misnomer scenario in which the limitations period is tolled is overruled.

Misidentification occurs when two separate legal entities exist, and a plaintiff mistakenly sues an "entity with a name similar to that of the correct entity." *Benevides v, QQ Delight, LLC*, 666 S.W.3d 793, 797 (Tex. App. — Texarkana 2023, no pet.) (citing *In re Greater Houston Orthopaedic Specialists, Inc.*, 295 S.W.3d 323, 325 (Tex. 2009) (per curiam) (orig. proceeding)). "[A] suit mistakenly filed against the wrong defendant imposes no duty on the correct defendant to intervene and point out plaintiff's error." *Matthews Trucking Co. v. Smith*, 682 S.W.2d 237, 239 (Tex. 1984). That "no duty" applies even if the correct defendant may have known of the suit. Id.

While the limitations period is generally not tolled in misidentification cases, the Texas Supreme Court has carved out a limited equitable exception. *Cont'l S. Lines, Inc. v. Hilland*, 528 S.W.2d 828, 830–831 (Tex. 1975). In *Hilland*, the plaintiff, who was injured while stepping off a bus marked "Continental Trailways" in large letters, timely served a bus company under the same name. *Id.* at 829. After limitations expired, the plaintiff amended her petition to correctly name the proper corporate entity, Continental Southern Lines, Inc. *Id.* Continental Southern Lines asserted a limitations defense. *Id.* Confirming the general "misidentification" rule that the institution of suit against one corporation will not toll the running of limitations as to a different corporation, the Court allowed limitations to be "equitably" tolled because the evidence demonstrated Continental Southern Lines, Inc. "made a conscious effort" to mislead the public about its true corporate name. *Id.* at 829–31. In fact, Continental Southern Lines, Inc. operated under the trade name "Continental Trailways." *Id.* at 831. Under those circumstances, the Court allowed the plaintiff an opportunity to demonstrate that the later-sued entity was aware of the facts, was not misled, and was not placed at a disadvantage in obtaining relevant evidence for its defense. *Id.*; *see also Chilkewitz*, 22 S.W.3d at 828 (clarifying limitations may be tolled in misidentification cases where incorrect entity "use[s] a similar trade name and the correct entity had notice of the suit and was not misled or disadvantaged by the mistake.").

The *Hilland* exception to the misidentification rule applies only where the intended defendant and the mis-identified defendant are corporate entities with a business relationship or connection. *See McCord v. Dodds*, 69 S.W.3d 230, 234–235 (Tex. App. — Corpus Christi 2001, pet. denied) (citing *Matthews Trucking Co. v. Smith*, 682 S.W.2d 237, 238 (Tex. 1984)). Similarly, "prejudice" is a relevant issue only when the intended corporate or business-entity defendant and the defendant actually named have a business relationship. *See Cortinas v. Wilson*, 851 S.W.2d 324, 327 (Tex. App. — Dallas 1993, no pet.). Thus, Salazar's arguments that equitable tolling applies or that a fact question exists because Daniel was not "prejudiced" by his late entry into the case are mistaken. Because Salazar misidentified the proper individual, her case factually falls outside the scope of the *Hilland* exception. *See Chavez v. Andersen*, 525 S.W.3d 382, 386, 388 (Tex. App. — Houston [14th Dist.] 2017, no pet.) (confirming *Hilland* exception does not apply where plaintiff in vehicular incident mistakenly names and sues wrong individual as driver and later adds correct party outside limitations period).

Texas courts have consistently held that suits for personal injuries sustained in vehicular collisions are barred by limitations where, as here, the plaintiff timely sues a particular person believed to be the driver, the person served is not the actual driver, and the plaintiff does not amend to name the proper defendant until after limitations expires. *See id.* at 389 (affirming summary judgment where plaintiff sued wrong person and then added correct driver six months post-limitations); *Brown v. Valiyaparampil*, 507 S.W.3d 773, 776–77 (Tex. App. — El Paso 2015, pet. denied) (affirming summary judgment where plaintiff originally sued son instead of father who actually drove vehicle); *Cortinas*, 851 S.W.2d at 326–28 (affirming summary judgment on limitations where plaintiff originally sued parents instead of daughter who was actually driving the vehicle); *Marez v. Moeck*, 608 S.W.2d 740, 741–42 (Tex. App. — Corpus Christi 1980, no writ) (affirming limitations bar where plaintiff originally sued father instead of son actually driving the vehicle). "In cases involving a vehicular accident, as here, suing a party, believed to have been the driver, but who was not the actual driver [and then failing to sue/serve the correct driver prior to the expiration of limitations] constitutes misidentification." *Chavez*, 525 S.W.3d at 387.

. . .

WEST VIRGINIA

W. Va. R. Civ. P. 15. Amended and Supplemental Pleadings

(a) Amendments. A party may amend the party's pleading once as a matter of course at any time before a responsive pleading is served or, if the pleading is one to which no responsive pleading is permitted and the action has not been placed upon the trial calendar, the party may so amend it at any time within 20 days after it is served. Otherwise a party may amend the party's pleading only by leave of court or by written consent of the adverse party; and leave shall be freely given when justice so requires. A party shall plead in response to an amended pleading within the time remaining for response to the original pleading or within 10 days after service of the amended pleading, whichever period may be the longer, unless the court otherwise orders.

(b) Amendments to Conform to the Evidence. When issues not raised by the pleadings are tried by express or implied consent of the parties, they shall be treated in all respects as if they had been raised in the pleadings. Such amendment of the pleadings as may be necessary to cause them to conform to the evidence and to raise these issues may be made upon motion of any party at any time, even after judgment; but failure so to amend does not affect the result of the trial of these issues. If evidence is objected to at the trial on the ground that it is not within the issues made by the pleadings, the court may allow the pleadings to be amended and shall do so freely when the presentation of the merits of the action will be subserved thereby and the objecting party fails to satisfy the court that the admission of such evidence would prejudice the party in maintaining the party's action or defense upon the merits. The court may grant a continuance to enable the objecting party to meet such evidence.

(c) Relation Back of Amendments. An amendment of a pleading relates back to the date of the original pleading when:

(1) relation back is permitted by the law that provides the statute of limitations applicable to the action; or

(2) the claim or defense asserted in the amended pleading arose out of the conduct, transaction, or occurrence set forth or attempted to be set forth in the original pleading; or

(3) the amendment changes the party or the naming of the party against whom a claim is asserted if the foregoing paragraph (2) is satisfied and, within the period provided by Rule 4(k) for service of the summons and complaint, the party to be brought in by amendment (A) has received such notice of the institution of the action that the party will not be prejudiced in maintaining a defense on the merits, and (B) knew or should have known that, but for a mistake concerning the identity of the proper party, the action would have brought against the party.

(d) Supplemental Pleadings. Upon motion of a party the court may, upon reasonable notice and upon such terms as are just, permit the party to serve a supplemental pleading setting forth transactions or occurrences or events which have happened since the date of the pleading sought to be supplemented. Permission may be granted even though the original pleading is defective in its statement of a claim for relief or defense. If the court deems it advisable that the adverse party plead to the supplemental pleading, it shall so order, specifying the time therefor.

Muto ex rel. Muto v. Scott

224 W. Va. 350 (2008)

MAYNARD, Chief Justice.

. . .

[W]e believe that construing the term "mistake" in Rule 15(c)(3)(B) to include circumstances where a "John Doe" complaint is filed due to failure to identify the proper defendants is consistent with our prior expansive construction of Rule 15(c). For example, in *Brooks v. Isinghood*, 213 W.Va. 675 (2003), this Court confronted the issue of whether "a mistake concerning the identity of the proper party" is limited to the common situation where the wrong party is named or whether it can also include mistakes of law. This Court held in Syllabus Point 7:

> Under Rule 15(c)(3)(B) of the West Virginia Rules of Civil Procedure [1998], a "mistake concerning the identity of the proper party" can include a mistake by a plaintiff of either law or fact, so long as the plaintiff's mistake resulted in a failure to identify, and assert a claim against, the proper defendant. A court considering

> whether a mistake has occurred should focus on whether the failure to include the proper defendant was an error and not a deliberate strategy.

The appellees assert that the appellant's failure to identify them in her original complaint does not constitute a "mistake" under Rule 15(c)(3)(B). According to the appellees, the great majority of federal courts that have examined this issue have concluded that lack of knowledge of the true identity of a party does not qualify as a "mistake" under Rule 15(c)(3), so that an amended complaint which substitutes the proper defendants for a "John Doe" defendant does not relate back on the grounds of mistake.

While we recognize the position taken by the majority of federal courts, we are not persuaded to adopt this position in this instance.

> We have previously noted that we give substantial weight to federal cases in determining the meaning and scope of our rules. This does not mean that our legal analysis in this area should amount to nothing more that Pavlovian responses to federal decisional law. Rather, a federal case interpreting a federal counterpart to a West Virginia rule of procedure may be persuasive, but it is not binding or controlling.

Brooks, 213 W.Va. at 682, 584 S.E.2d at 538 (citations, quotations, and parentheticals omitted). In circumstances like the instant case in which a plaintiff, through no fault of her own, is unable to identify the defendants prior to the expiration of the statute of limitations, and where the remaining requirements of Rule 15(c) are met, this Court believes that both justice and common sense require that a plaintiff's lack of knowledge should constitute a "mistake" under Rule 15(c)(3)(B). Such a finding is wholly consistent with a liberal reading of Rule 15(c) in order to promote the adjudication of cases on their merits.

Accordingly, we now hold that under Rule 15(c)(3)(B) of the West Virginia Rules of Civil Procedure, a "mistake concerning the identity of the proper party" may include the circumstance where the original complaint names a "John Doe" defendant due to the plaintiff's lack of knowledge of the proper defendant where the filing of the "John Doe" complaint is not part of a deliberate strategy in order to achieve an advantage and the plaintiff's lack of knowledge is not due to the plaintiff's dilatory conduct in identifying the proper defendant prior to the expiration of the applicable statute of limitations.

STATE LONG-ARM STATUTES

(EXCERPTS FROM SELECTED STATES)

CALIFORNIA

Cal. Civ. Proc. Code § 410.10. Jurisdiction. Basis

A court of this state may exercise jurisdiction on any basis not inconsistent with the Constitution of this state or of the United States.

CONNECTICUT

Conn. Gen. Stat. § 52-59b. Jurisdiction of Courts Over Nonresident Individuals, Foreign Partnerships and Foreign Voluntary Associations. Service of Process

(a) As to a cause of action arising from any of the acts enumerated in this section, a court may exercise personal jurisdiction over any nonresident individual, foreign partnership or foreign voluntary association, or over the executor or administrator of such nonresident individual, foreign partnership or foreign voluntary association, who in person or through an agent:

(1) transacts any business within the state;

(2) commits a tortious act within the state, except as to a cause of action for defamation of character arising from the act;

(3) commits a tortious act outside the state causing injury to person or property within the state, except as to a cause of action for defamation of character arising from the act, if such person or agent (A) regularly does or solicits business, or engages in any other persistent course of conduct, or derives substantial revenue from goods used or consumed or services rendered, in the state, or (B) expects or should reasonably expect the act to have consequences in the state and derives substantial revenue from interstate or international commerce;

(4) owns, uses or possesses any real property situated within the state; or

(5) uses a computer, as defined in subdivision (1) of subsection (a) of section 53-451, or a computer network, as defined in subdivision (3) of subsection (a) of said section, located within the state.

(b) Where personal jurisdiction is based solely upon this section, an appearance does not confer personal jurisdiction with respect to causes of action not arising from an act enumerated in this section.

(c) Any nonresident individual, foreign partnership or foreign voluntary association, or the executor or administrator of such nonresident individual, foreign partnership or foreign voluntary association, over whom a court may exercise personal jurisdiction, as provided in subsection (a) of this section, shall be deemed to have appointed the Secretary of the State as its attorney and to have agreed that any process in any civil action brought against the nonresident individual, foreign partnership or foreign voluntary association, or the executor or administrator of such nonresident individual, foreign partnership or foreign voluntary association, may be served upon the Secretary of the State and shall have the same validity as if served upon the nonresident individual, foreign partnership or foreign voluntary association personally. The process shall be served by the officer to whom the same is directed upon the Secretary of the State by leaving with or at the office of the Secretary of the State, at least twelve days before the return day of such process, a true and attested copy thereof, and by sending to the defendant at the defendant's last-known address, by registered or certified mail, postage prepaid, return receipt requested, a like true and attested copy with an endorsement thereon of the service upon the Secretary of the State. The officer serving such process upon the Secretary of the State shall leave with the Secretary of the State, at the time of service, a fee of fifty dollars, which fee shall be taxed in favor of the plaintiff in the plaintiff's costs if the plaintiff prevails in any such action. The Secretary of the State shall keep a record of each such process and the day and hour of service.

FLORIDA

Fla. Stat. § 48.193. Acts Subjecting Person to Jurisdiction of Courts of State

(1)

(a) A person, whether or not a citizen or resident of this state, who personally or through an agent does any of the acts enumerated in this subsection thereby submits himself or herself and, if he or she is a natural person, his or her personal representative to the jurisdiction of the courts of this state for any cause of action arising from the doing of any of the following acts:

1. Operating, conducting, engaging in, or carrying on a business or business venture in this state or having an office or agency in this state.

2. Committing a tortious act within this state.

3. Owning, using, possessing, or holding a mortgage or other lien on any real property within this state.

4. Contracting to insure a person, property or risk located within this state at the time of contracting.

5. With respect to a proceeding for alimony, child support, or division of property in connection with an action to dissolve a marriage or with respect to an independent action for support of dependents, maintaining a matrimonial domicile in this state at the time of the commencement of this action or, if the defendant resided in this state preceding the commencement of the action, whether cohabiting during that time or not. This paragraph does not change the residency requirement for filing an action for dissolution of marriage.

6. Causing injury to persons or property within this state arising out of an act or omission by the defendant outside this state, if, at or about the time of the injury, either:

a. The defendant was engaged in solicitation or service activities within this state; or

b. Products, materials, or things processed, serviced, or manufactured by the defendant anywhere were used or consumed within this state in the ordinary course of commerce, trade, or use.

7. Breaching a contract in this state by failing to perform acts required by the contract to be performed in this state.

8. With respect to a proceeding for paternity, engaging in the act of sexual intercourse within this state with respect to which a child may have been conceived.

9. Entering into a contract that complies with Section 685.102.

(b) Notwithstanding any other provision of this subsection, an order issued, or a penalty or fine imposed by an agency of another state is not enforceable against any person or entity incorporated or having its principal place of business in this state if the other state does not provide a mandatory right of review of the agency decision in a state court of competent jurisdiction.

(2) A defendant who is engaged in substantial and not isolated activity within this state, whether such activity is wholly interstate, intrastate, or otherwise, is subject to the jurisdiction of the courts of this state, whether or not the claim arises from that activity.

(3) Service of process upon any person who is subject to the jurisdiction of the courts of this state as provided in this section may be made by personally serving the process upon the defendant outside this state, as provided in Section 48.194. The service shall have the same effect as if it had been personally served within this state.

(4) If a defendant in his or her pleadings demands affirmative relief on causes of action unrelated to the transaction forming the basis of the plaintiff's claim, the defendant shall thereafter in that action be subject to the jurisdiction of the court for any cause of action, regardless of its basis, which the plaintiff may by amendment assert against the defendant.

(5) Nothing contained in this section limits or affects the right to serve any process in any other manner now or hereinafter provided by law.

ILLINOIS

735 Ill. Comp. Stat. 5/2-209. Act Submitting to Jurisdiction — Process

(a) Any person, whether or not a citizen or resident of this state, who in person or through an agent does any of the acts hereinafter enumerated, thereby submits such person, and, if an individual, his or her personal representative, to the jurisdiction of the courts of this State as to any cause of action arising from the doing of any such acts:

(1) The transaction of any business within this State;

(2) The commission of a tortious act within this State;

(3) The ownership, use or possession of any real estate situated in this State;

(4) Contracting to insure any person, property or risk located within this State at the time of contracting;

(5) With respect to actions of dissolution of marriage, declaration of invalidity of marriage and legal separation, the maintenance in this State of a matrimonial domicile at the time this cause of action arose or the commission in this State of any act giving rise to the cause of action;

(6) With respect to actions brought under the Illinois Parentage Act of 1984, as now or hereafter amended, or under the Illinois Parentage Act of 2015 on and after the effective date of that Act, the performance of an act of sexual intercourse within this State during the possible period of conception;

(7) The making or performance of any contract or promise substantially connected with this State;

(8) The performance of sexual intercourse within this State which is claimed to have resulted in a the conception of a child who resides in this State;

(9) The failure to support a child, spouse or former spouse who has continued to reside in this State since the person either formerly resided with them in this State or directed them to reside in this State;

(10) The acquisition of ownership, possession or control of any asset or thing of value present within this State when ownership, possession or control was acquired;

(11) The breach of any fiduciary duty within this State;

(12) The performance of duties as a director or officer of a corporation organized under the laws of this State or having its principal place of business within this State;

(13) The ownership of an interest in any trust administered within this State; or

(14) The exercise of powers granted under the authority of this State as a fiduciary.

(b) A court may exercise jurisdiction in any action arising within or without this State against any person who:

(1) Is a natural person present within this State when served;

(2) Is a natural person domiciled or resident within this State when the cause of action arose, the action was commenced, or process was served;

(3) Is a corporation organized under the laws of this State; or

(4) Is a natural person or corporation doing business within this State.

(5) Foreign defamation judgment. The courts of this state shall have personal jurisdiction over any person who obtains a judgment in a defamation proceeding outside the United States against any person who is a resident of Illinois or, if not a natural person, has its principal place of business in Illinois, for the purposes of rendering declaratory relief with respect to that resident's liability for the judgment, or for the purpose of determining whether said judgment should be deemed non-recognizable pursuant to this Code, to the fullest extent permitted by the United States Constitution, provided:

(1) the publication at issue was published in Illinois, and

(2) that resident (i) has assets in Illinois which might be used to satisfy the foreign defamation judgment, or (ii) may have to take actions in Illinois to comply with the foreign defamation judgment.

The provisions of this subsection (b-5) shall apply to persons who obtained judgments in defamation proceedings outside the United States prior to, on, or after the effective date of this amendatory Act of the 95th General Assembly.

(c) A court may also exercise jurisdiction on any other basis now or hereafter permitted by the Illinois Constitution and the Constitution of the United States.

(d) Service of process upon any person who is subject to the jurisdiction of the courts of this State, as provided in this Section, may be made by personally serving the summons upon the defendant outside this State, as provided in this Act, with the same force and effect as though summons had been personally served within this State.

(e) Service of process upon any person who resides or whose business address is outside the United States and who is subject to the jurisdiction of the courts of this State, as provided in this Section, in any action based upon product liability may be made by serving a copy of the summons with a copy of the complaint attached upon the Secretary of State. The summons shall be accompanied by a $5 fee payable to the Secretary of State. The plaintiff shall forthwith mail a copy of the summons, upon which the date of service upon the Secretary is clearly shown, together with a copy of the complaint to the defendant at his or her last known place of residence or business address. Plaintiff shall file with the circuit clerk an affidavit of the plaintiff or his or her attorney stating the last known place of residence or the last known business address of the defendant and a certificate of mailing a copy of the summons and complaint to the defendant at such address as required by this subsection (e). The certificate of mailing shall be prima facie evidence that the plaintiff or his or her attorney mailed a copy of the summons and complaint to the defendant as required. Service of the summons shall be deemed to have been made upon the defendant on the date it is served upon the Secretary and shall have the same force and effect as though summons had been personally served upon the defendant within this State.

(f) Only causes of action arising from acts enumerated herein may be asserted against a defendant in an action in which jurisdiction over him or her is based upon subsection (a).

(g) Nothing herein contained limits or affects the right to serve any process in any other manner now or hereafter provided by law.

LOUISIANA

La. Rev. Stat. Ann. § 13:3201. Personal Jurisdiction Over Nonresidents

A. A court may exercise jurisdiction over a nonresident, who acts directly or by an agent, as to a cause of action arising from any one of the following activities performed by the nonresident:

(1) Transacting any business in this state.

(2) Contracting to supply services or things in this state.

(3) Causing injury or damage by an offense or quasi offense committed through an act or omission in this state.

(4) Causing injury or damage in this state by an offense or quasi offense committed through an act or omission outside of this state if he regularly does or solicits business, or engages in any other persistent course of conduct, or derives revenue from goods used or consumed or services rendered in this state.

(5) Having an interest in, using or possessing a real right on immovable property in this state.

(6) Non-support of a child, parent, or spouse or a former spouse domiciled in this state to whom an obligation of support is owed and with whom the nonresident formerly resided in this state.

(7) Oarentage and support of a child who was conceived by the nonresident while he resided in or was in this state.

(8) Manufacturing of a product or component thereof which caused damage or injury in this state, if at the time of placing the product into the stream of commerce, the manufacturer could have foreseen, realized, expected, or anticipated that the product may eventually be found in this state by reason of its nature and the manufacturer's marketing practices.

B. In addition to the provisions of Subsection A, a court of this state may exercise personal jurisdiction over a nonresident on any basis consistent with the constitution of this state and of the Constitution of the United States.

MASSACHUSETTS

Mass. Gen. Laws ch. 223a, § 3. Transactions or Conduct for Personal Jurisdiction

A court may exercise personal jurisdiction over a person, who acts directly or by an agent, as to a cause of action in law or equity arising from the person's

(a) transacting any business in this commonwealth;

(b) contracting to supply services or things in this commonwealth;

(c) causing tortious injury by an act or omission in this commonwealth;

(d) causing tortious injury in this commonwealth by an act or omission outside this commonwealth if he regularly does or solicits business, or engages in any other persistent course of conduct, or derives substantial revenue from goods used or consumed or services rendered, in this commonwealth;

(e) having an interest in, using or possessing real property in this commonwealth;

(f) contracting to insure any person, property or risk located within this commonwealth at the time of contracting;

(g) maintaining a domicile in this commonwealth while a party to a personal or marital relationship out of which arises a claim for divorce, alimony, property settlement, parentage of a child, child support or child custody; or the commission of any act giving rise to such a claim; or

(h) having been subject to the exercise of personal jurisdiction of a court of the commonwealth which has resulted in an order of alimony, custody, child support or property settlement, notwithstanding the subsequent departure of one of the original parties from the commonwealth, if the action involves modification of such order or orders and the moving party resides in the commonwealth, or if the action involves enforcement of such order notwithstanding the domicile of the moving party.

NEVADA

N.R.S. § 14.065. Exercise of Jurisdiction on Any Basis Consistent with State and Federal Constitutions; Service of Summons to Confer Jurisdiction

1. A court of this state may exercise jurisdiction over a party to a civil action on any basis not inconsistent with the Constitution of this state or the Constitution of the United States.

2. Personal service of summons upon a party outside this state is sufficient to confer upon a court of this state jurisdiction over the party so served if the service is made by delivering a copy of the summons, together with a copy of the complaint, to the party served in the manner provided by statute or rule of court for service upon a person of like kind within this state.

3. The method of service provided in this section is cumulative, and may be utilized with, after or independently of other methods of service.

NEW YORK

N.Y. CPLR § 302. Personal Jurisdiction by Acts of Non-Domiciliaries

(a) Acts which are the basis of jurisdiction. As to a cause of action arising from any of the acts enumerated in this section, a court may exercise personal jurisdiction over any non-domiciliary, or his executor or administrator, who in person or through an agent:

1. transacts any business within the state or contracts anywhere to supply goods or services in the state; or
2. commits a tortious act within the state, except as to a cause of action for defamation of character arising from the act; or
3. commits a tortious act without the state causing injury to person or property within the state, except as to a cause of action for defamation of character arising from the act, if he

(i) regularly does or solicits business, or engages in any other persistent course of conduct, or derives substantial revenue from goods used or consumed or services rendered, in the state, or

(ii) expects or should reasonably expect the act to have consequences in the state and derives substantial revenue from interstate or international commerce; or

4. owns, uses, or possesses any real property situated within the state.

(b) Personal jurisdiction over non-resident defendant in matrimonial actions or family court proceedings. A court in any matrimonial action or family court proceeding involving a demand for support, alimony, maintenance, distributive awards or special relief in matrimonial actions may exercise personal jurisdiction over the respondent or defendant notwithstanding the fact that he or she no longer is a resident or domiciliary of this state, or over his or her executor or administrator, if the party seeking support is a resident of or domiciled in this state at the time such demand is made, provided that this state was the matrimonial domicile of the parties before their separation, or the defendant abandoned the plaintiff in this state, or the claim for support, alimony, maintenance, distributive awards or special relief in matrimonial actions accrued under the laws of this state or under an agreement executed in this state. The family court may exercise personal jurisdiction over a non-resident respondent to the extent provided in sections one hundred fifty-four and one thousand thirty-six and article five-B of the family court act and article five-A of the domestic relations law.

(c) Effect of appearance. Where personal jurisdiction is based solely upon this section, an appearance does not confer such jurisdiction with respect to causes of action not arising from an act enumerated in this section.

(d) Foreign defamation judgment. The courts of this state shall have personal jurisdiction over any person who obtains a judgment in a defamation proceeding outside the United States against any person who is a resident of New York or is a person or entity amenable to jurisdiction in New York who has assets in New York or may have to take actions in New York to comply with the judgment, for the purposes of rendering declaratory relief with respect to that person's liability for the judgment, and/or for the purpose of determining whether said judgment should be deemed non-recognizable pursuant to section fifty-three hundred four of this chapter, to the fullest extent permitted by the United States constitution, provided:

(1) the publication at issue was published in New York, and

(2) that resident or person amenable to jurisdiction in New York (i) has assets in New York which might be used to satisfy the foreign defamation judgment, or (ii) may have to take actions in New York to comply with the foreign defamation judgment.

The provisions of this subdivision shall apply to persons who obtained judgments in defamation proceedings outside the United States prior to and/or after the effective date of this subdivision.

OHIO

Ohio R. Civ. P. 4.3. Process: Out-of-State Service

(a) When service permitted. Service of process may be made outside of this state, as provided in this rule, in any action in this state, upon a person who, at the time of service of process, is a nonresident of this state or is a resident of this state who is absent from this state. "Person" includes an individual, an individual's executor, administrator, or other personal representative, or a corporation, partnership, association, or any other legal or commercial entity, who, acting directly or by an agent, has caused an event to occur out of which the claim that is the subject of the complaint arose, from the person's:

(1) Transacting any business in this state;

(2) Contracting to supply services or goods in this state;

(3) Causing tortious injury by an act or omission in this state, including, but not limited to, actions arising out of the ownership, operation, or use of a motor vehicle or aircraft in this state;

(4) Causing tortious injury in this state by an act or omission outside this state if the person regularly does or solicits business, engages in any other persistent course of conduct, or derives substantial revenue from goods used or consumed or services rendered in this state;

(5) Causing injury in this state to any person by breach of warranty expressly or impliedly made in the sale of goods outside this state when the person to be served might reasonably have expected the person who was injured to use, consume, or be affected by the goods in this state, provided that the person to be served also regularly does or solicits business, engages in any other persistent course of conduct, or derives substantial revenue from goods used or consumed or services rendered in this state;

(6) Having an interest in, using, or possessing real property in this state;

(7) Contracting to insure any person, property, or risk located within this state at the time of contracting;

(8) Living in the marital relationship within this state notwithstanding subsequent departure from this state, as to all obligations arising for spousal support, custody, child support, or property settlement, if the other party to the marital relationship continues to reside in this state;

(9) Causing tortious injury in this state to any person by an act outside this state committed with the purpose of injuring persons, when the person to be served might reasonably have expected that some person would be injured by the act in this state;

(10) Causing tortious injury to any person by a criminal act, any element of which takes place in this state, that the person to be served commits or in the commission of which the person to be served is guilty of complicity.

(b) Methods of service

(1) Service by clerk. The clerk may make service of process or other documents to be served outside the state in the same manner as provided in Civ. R. 4.1(A)(1) through Civ. R. 4.1(A)(3).

(2) Personal service. When ordered by the court, a "person" as defined in division (A) of this rule may be personally served with a copy of the process and complaint or other document to be served. Service under this division may be made by any person not less than eighteen years of age who is not a party and who has been designated by order of the court to make personal service of process. On request, the clerk shall deliver the summons to the plaintiff for transmission to the person who will make the service. The person serving process shall locate the person to be served and shall tender a copy of the process and accompanying documents to the person to be served.

Proof of service may be made as prescribed by Civ. R. 4.1(B) or by order of the court. Failure to make service within the twenty-eight-day period and failure to make proof of service do not affect the validity of service.

STATE VENUE STATUTES

(EXCERPTS FROM SELECTED STATES)

CALIFORNIA

Cal. Civ. Proc. Code § 392. Real Property Actions; Proper Court

(a) Subject to the power of the court to transfer actions and proceedings as provided in this title, the superior court in the county where the real property that is the subject of the action, or some part thereof, is situated, is the proper court for the trial of the following actions:

(1) For the recovery of real property, or of an estate or interest therein, or for the determination in any form, of that right or interest, and for injuries to real property.

(2) For the foreclosure of all liens and mortgages on real property.

(b) In the court designated as the proper court in subdivision (a), the proper court location for trial of a proceeding for an unlawful detainer, as defined in Section 1161, is the location where the court tries that type of proceeding that is nearest or most accessible to where the real property that is the subject of the action, or some part thereof, is situated. Otherwise any location of the superior court designated as the proper court in subdivision (a) is a proper court location for the trial. The court may specify by local rule the nearest or most accessible court location where the court tries that type of case.

Cal. Civ. Proc. Code § 393. Actions to Recover Penalty or Forfeiture; Actions Against Public Officers; Proper Court

Subject to the power of the court to transfer actions and proceedings as provided in this title, the county in which the cause, or some part of the cause, arose, is the proper county for the trial of the following actions:

(a) For the recovery of a penalty or forfeiture imposed by statute, except, that when it is imposed for an offense committed on a lake, river, or other stream of water, situated in two or more counties, the action may be tried in any county bordering on the lake, river, or stream, and opposite to the place where the offense was committed.

(b) Against a public officer or person especially appointed to execute the duties of a public officer, for an act done by the officer or person in virtue of the office, or against a person who, by the officer's command or in the officer's aid, does anything touching the duties of the officer.

Cal. Civ. Proc. Code § 394. Actions by or Against a City, County, City and County or Local Agency; Transfer of Cases; Proper Court

(a) An action or proceeding against a county, or city and county, a city, or local agency, may be tried in the county, or city and county, or the county in which the city or local agency is situated, unless the action or proceeding is brought by a county, or city and county, a city, or local agency, in which case it may be tried in any county, or city and county, not a party thereto and in which the city or local agency is not situated. Except for actions initiated by the local child support agency pursuant to Section 17400, 17402, 17404, or 17416 of the Family Code, any action or proceeding brought by a county, city and county, city, or local agency within a certain county, or city and county, against a resident of another county, city and county, or city, or a corporation doing business in the latter, shall be, on motion of either party, transferred for trial to a county, or city and county, other than the plaintiff, if the plaintiff is a county, or city and county, and other than that in which the plaintiff is situated, if the plaintiff is a city, or a local agency, and other than that in which the defendant resides, or is doing business, or is situated. Whenever an action or proceeding is brought against a county, city and county, city, or local agency, in any county, or city and county, other than the defendant, if the defendant is a county, or city and county, or, if the defendant is a city, or local agency, other than that in which the defendant is situated, the action or proceeding must be, on motion of that defendant, transferred for trial to a county, or city and county, other than that in which the plaintiff, or any of the plaintiffs, resides, or is doing business, or is situated, and other than the plaintiff county, or city and county, or county in which that plaintiff city or local agency is situated, and other than the defendant county, or city and county, or county in which the defendant city or local agency is situated; provided, however, that any action or proceeding against the city, county, city and county, or local agency for injury occurring within the city, county, or city and county, or within the county in which the local agency is situated, to person or property or person and property caused by the negligence or alleged negligence of the city, county, city and county, local agency, or its agents or employees, shall be tried in that county, or city and county, or if a city is a defendant, in the city or in the county in which the city is situated, or if a local agency is a defendant, in the county in which the local agency is situated. In that action or proceeding, the parties thereto may, by stipulation in writing, or made in open court, and entered in the minutes, agree upon any county, or city and county, for the place of trial thereof. When the action or proceeding is one in which a jury is not of right, or in case a jury is waived, then in lieu of transferring the cause, the court in the original county may request the chairperson of the Judicial Council to assign a disinterested judge from a neutral county to hear that cause and all proceedings in connection therewith. When the action or proceeding is transferred to another county for trial, a witness required to respond to a subpoena for a hearing within the original county shall be compelled to attend hearings in the county to which the cause is transferred. If the demand for transfer is made by one party and the opposing party does not consent thereto, the additional costs of the nonconsenting party occasioned by the transfer of the cause, including living and traveling expenses of the nonconsenting party and material witnesses, found by the court to be material, and called by the nonconsenting party, not to exceed five dollars ($5) per day each in excess of witness fees and mileage otherwise allowed by law, shall be assessed by the court hearing the cause against the party requesting the transfer. To the extent of that excess, those costs shall be awarded to the nonconsenting party regardless of the outcome of the trial. This section shall apply to actions or proceedings now pending or hereafter brought.

(b) For the purposes of this section, "local agency" shall mean any governmental district, board, or agency, or any other local governmental body or corporation, but shall not include the State of California or any of its agencies, departments, commissions, or boards.

Cal. Civ. Proc. Code § 395. Actions Generally; Proper Court; Waiver

(a) Except as otherwise provided by law and subject to the power of the court to transfer actions or proceedings as provided in this title, the superior court in the county where the defendants or some of them reside at the commencement of the action is the proper court for the trial of the action. If the action is for injury to person or personal property or for death from wrongful act or negligence, the superior court in either the county where the injury occurs or the injury causing death occurs or the county where the defendants, or some of them reside at the commencement of the action, is a proper court for the trial of the action. In a proceeding for dissolution of marriage, the superior court in the county where either the petitioner or respondent has been a resident for three months next preceding the commencement of the proceeding is the proper court for the trial of the proceeding. In a proceeding for nullity of marriage or legal separation of the parties, the superior court in the county where either the petitioner or the respondent resides at the commencement of the proceeding is the proper court for the trial of the proceeding. In a proceeding to enforce an obligation of support under Section 3900 of the Family Code, the superior court in the county where the child resides is the proper court for the trial of the action. In a proceeding to establish and enforce a foreign judgment or court order for the support of a minor child, the superior court in the county where the child resides is the proper court for the trial of the action. Subject to subdivision (b), if a defendant has contracted to perform an obligation in a particular county, the superior court in the county where the obligation is to be performed, where the contract in fact was entered into, or where the defendant or any defendant resides at the commencement of the action is a proper court for the trial of an action founded on that obligation, and the county where the obligation is incurred is the county where it is to be performed, unless there is a special contract in writing to the contrary. If none of the defendants reside in the state or if they reside in the state and the county where they reside is unknown to the plaintiff, the action may be tried in the superior court in any county that the plaintiff may designate in his or her complaint, and, if the defendant is about to depart from the state, the action may be tried in the superior court in any county where either of the parties reside or service is made. If any person is improperly joined as a defendant or has been made a defendant solely for the purpose of having the action tried in the superior court in the county where he or she resides, his or her residence shall not be considered in determining the proper place for the trial of the action.

(b) Subject to the power of the court to transfer actions or proceedings as provided in this title, in an action arising from an offer or provision of goods, services, loans or extensions of credit intended primarily for personal, family or household use, other than an obligation described in Section 1812.10 or Section 2984.4 of the Civil Code, or an action arising from a transaction consummated as a proximate result of either an unsolicited telephone call made by a seller engaged in the business of consummating transactions of that kind or a telephone call or electronic transmission made by the buyer or lessee in response to a solicitation by the seller, the superior court in the county where the buyer or lessee in fact signed the contract, where the buyer or lessee resided at the time the contract was entered into, or where the buyer or lessee resides at the commencement of the action is the proper court for the trial of the action. In the superior court designated in this subdivision as the proper court, the proper court location for trial of a case is the location where the court tries that type of case that is nearest or most accessible to where the buyer or lessee resides, where the buyer or lessee in fact signed the contract, where the buyer or lessee resided at the time the contract was entered into, or where the buyer or lessee resides at the commencement of the action. Otherwise, any location of the superior court designated as the proper court in this subdivision is a proper court location for the trial. The court may specify by local rule the nearest or most accessible court location where the court tries that type of case.

(c) Any provision of an obligation described in subdivision (b) waiving that subdivision is void and unenforceable.

Cal. Civ. Proc. Code § 395.1. Executor; Administrator, Guardian, Conservator, or Trustee in Official or Representative Capacity

Except as otherwise provided in Section 17005 of the Probate Code pertaining to trustees, when a defendant is sued in an official or representative capacity as executor, administrator, guardian, conservator, or trustee on a claim for the payment of money or for the recovery of personal property, the county which has jurisdiction of the estate which the defendant represents shall be the proper county for the trial of the action.

Cal. Civ. Proc. Code § 395.2. Unincorporated Associations

If an unincorporated association has filed a statement with the Secretary of State pursuant to statute, designating its principal office in this state, the proper county for the trial of an action against the unincorporated association is the same as it would be if the unincorporated association were a corporation and, for the purpose of determining the proper county, the principal place of business of the unincorporated association shall be deemed to be the principal office in this state listed in the statement.

Cal. Civ. Proc. Code § 395.5. Actions Against Corporations or Associations; Place of Trial

A corporation or association may be sued in the county where the contract is made or is to be performed, or where the obligation or liability arises, or the breach occurs; or in the county where the principal place of business of such corporation is situated, subject to the power of the court to change the place of trial as in other cases.

MASSACHUSETTS

Mass. Gen. L. ch. 223, § 1. Transitory Actions; General Provisions

A transitory action shall, except as otherwise provided, if any one of the parties thereto lives in the commonwealth, be brought in the county where one of them lives or has his usual place of business; provided, however, that if the instrument of the crime is a forged check, credit card, or other negotiable instrument, intending on its face to be presented for payment at another place in another county and the value of the money, goods or services involved is in excess of one hundred dollars, the action may be brought in the county where the instrument was presented or at the place where the instrument was presented for payment, if such place of payment is located in the commonwealth; and provided, further, that except in actions upon negotiable instruments if the plaintiff is an assignee of the cause of action, it shall be brought only in a county where it might have been brought by the assignor thereof. If neither party lives in the commonwealth, the action may be brought in any county. If an action is dismissed because the defendant has raised timely objection to venue, the defendant shall be allowed double costs.

Mass. Gen. L. ch. 223, § 2. Transitory Actions; District Courts

Except as provided in section twenty-one of chapter two hundred and eighteen, a transitory action in a district court shall be brought in a court in the judicial district where one of the parties lives or has his usual place of business or in a court, the judicial district of which is adjacent to the judicial district where one of the parties lives or has his usual place of business or, if in connection with the commencement of such an action the approval of trustee process is sought, that action shall be brought in a court in the judicial district where one of the parties or any person alleged to be trustee lives or has a usual place of business, or in a court the judicial district of which adjoins the judicial district where one of the parties or one of the alleged trustees lives or has a usual place of business; provided, however, that an action may be brought in the municipal court of the city of Boston as provided in section fifty-four of chapter two hundred and eighteen.

Said courts shall have jurisdiction of a transitory action against a defendant who is not an inhabitant of the commonwealth, if personal service or an effectual attachment of property is made within the commonwealth; and such action may be brought in any of said courts in the county where the service or attachment was made.

Mass. Gen. L. ch. 223, § 3. Transitory Actions; Enumeration

Every action for rent, use and occupation or breach of covenant shall be considered a transitory action.

Mass. Gen. L. ch. 223, § 4. Replevin Actions

An action brought pursuant to chapter two hundred and forty-seven shall be brought in the county where the goods or beasts are detained.

Mass. Gen. L. ch. 223, § 5. Actions by the Commonwealth

A civil action in which the commonwealth is plaintiff or in which money due to the commonwealth is sought to be recovered may be brought in the county where the defendant lives or has his usual place of business, or in Suffolk county.

Mass. Gen. L. ch. 223, § 6. Counties; Actions by or Against

A local or transitory action by a county shall be brought in the county where the defendant lives or in a county adjoining the plaintiff county. If the defendant lives in the plaintiff county, it shall be brought in an adjoining county. Such action against a county shall, at the election of the plaintiff, be brought in the county where he lives, in the defendant county or in an adjoining county.

Mass. Gen. L. ch. 223, § 7. Defective Ways, Etc.; Negligence Actions

An action against a town or person to recover for injury or damage received by reason of a defect, want of repair or of an insufficient railing in or upon a public way shall be brought in the county where said town is situated or in the county where the plaintiff lives, except that such action against the city of Boston may be brought in Middlesex county, in Norfolk county or in the county where the plaintiff lives, and such action against the town of Nantucket or against any town in Dukes county may be brought in Bristol county. An action against a town or person to recover for injury or damage received in the commonwealth by reason of negligence other than that relating to such defect, want of repair or insufficient railing shall be brought in the county where the plaintiff lives or has his usual place of business, or in the county where the alleged injury or damage was received. This section shall not apply to actions that may be brought in a district court.

Mass. Gen. L. ch. 223, § 8. Corporations; Actions by or Against

Transitory actions, except those mentioned in the preceding section, to which a corporation, other than a county or the city of Boston, is a party, may be brought as follows:

(1) If both parties are cities, towns or parishes, in the county where either party is situated.

(2) If both parties are corporations, other than a city, town or parish, in any county in which either corporation has a usual place of business, or in which it held its last annual meeting, or usually holds its meetings.

(3) If one party is a city, town or parish, and the other a corporation named in clause (2), in any county in which either party might sue or be sued.

(4) If one party is a corporation named in clause (1) or (2), and the other an individual, in any county in which the corporation might sue or be sued, or in the county in which the individual lives or has a usual place of business.

Mass. Gen. L. ch. 223, § 9. Transitory Actions by or Against City of Boston

An action by or against the city of Boston, except actions mentioned in section seven and actions by the collector of said city under sections thirty-five and thirty-six of chapter sixty, may be brought in Suffolk, Essex, Middlesex or Norfolk county, or in the county in which the plaintiff lives.

Mass. Gen. L. ch. 223, § 11. Executors or Administrators; Transitory Actions by or Against

A transitory action by or against an executor or administrator may be brought in a county in which it might have been brought by or against the testator or intestate at the time of his decease.

Mass. Gen. L. ch. 223, § 12. Land Title Actions

If a tract of land lies in two or more counties, an action relative to it, to which neither a county, the city of Boston nor any corporation named in section eight is a party, may be brought in any of said counties, and the complaint shall be so drawn as to include the whole tract.

NEVADA

N.R.S. § 13.010. Where Actions are to be Commenced

1. When a person has contracted to perform an obligation at a particular place, and resides in another county, the action must be commenced, and, subject to the power of the court to change the place of trial as provided in this

chapter, must be tried in the county in which such obligation is to be performed or in which the person resides; and the county in which the obligation is incurred shall be deemed to be the county in which it is to be performed, unless there is a special contract to the contrary.

2. Actions for the following causes shall be tried in the county in which the subject of the action, or some part thereof, is situated, subject to the power of the court to change the place of trial as provided in this chapter:

(a) For the recovery of real property, or an estate, or interest therein, or for the determination in any form of such right or interest, and for injuries to real property.

(b) For the partition of real property.

(c) For the foreclosure of all liens and mortgages on real property. Where the real property is situated partly in one county and partly in another the plaintiff may select either of the counties, and the county so selected is the proper county for the trial of such action; but, in the case mentioned in this paragraph, if the plaintiff prays in the complaint for an injunction pending the action, or applies pending the action for an injunction, the proper county for the trial shall be the county in which the defendant resides or a majority of the defendants reside at the commencement of the action.

N.R.S. § 13.020. Venue of Actions for Recovery of Penalties and Forfeitures; Actions Against Public Officers; Actions Against State of Nevada

Actions for the following causes must be tried in the county where the cause, or some part thereof, arose, subject to the power of the court to change the place of trial:

1. For the recovery of a penalty or forfeiture imposed by statute; except, that when it is imposed for an offense committed on a lake, river or other stream of water, situated in two or more counties, the action may be brought in any county bordering on such lake, river or stream, and opposite to the place where the offense was committed.
2. Against a public officer, or person especially appointed to execute the duties of a public officer, for an act done by him or her in virtue of the office, or against a person who, by his or her command, or in his or her aid, does anything touching the duties of the officer.
3. Against the State of Nevada or any agency of the State for any tort action, except that any such tort action may also be brought in Carson City.

N.R.S. § 13.030. Venue of Actions By or Against Counties

1. Actions against a county may be commenced in the district court of the judicial district embracing the county; but actions between counties shall be commenced in a court of competent jurisdiction in any county not a party to the action.

2. Immediately on the service of process, the officer served shall deliver such process and all papers accompanying such service to the district attorney for the county.

3. Actions brought for or against the county shall be in the name of the county.

N.R.S. § 13.040. Venue in Other Cases

In all other cases, the action shall be tried in the county in which the defendants, or any one of them, may reside at the commencement of the action; or, if none of the defendants reside in the State, or if residing in the State the county in which they so reside be unknown to the plaintiff, the same may be tried in any county which the plaintiff may designate in the complaint; and if any defendant, or defendants, may be about to depart from the State, such action may be tried in any county where either of the parties may reside or service be had, subject, however, to the power of the court to change the place of trial as provided in this chapter.

N.R.S. § 13.050. Cases in Which Venue May be Changed

1. If the county designated for that purpose in the complaint, petition or motion is not the proper county, the proceeding may, notwithstanding, be tried or heard therein, unless:

(a) After the filing of a complaint or petition, the defendant demands in writing, before the time for answering expires, that the trial be had in the proper county, and the place of trial be thereupon changed by consent of the parties, or by order of the court, as provided in this section.

(b) In a proceeding in which the court has continuing jurisdiction after the issuance of a final order, judgment or decree, including, without limitation, any proceeding for divorce, annulment, separate maintenance or parentage or custody of a child and where no party currently resides in the county in which the order, judgment or decree was entered, the respondent demands in writing, before the time for filing a response expires, that the petition or motion be heard in the county of residence of either party to the proceeding or in the county where the child who is the subject of the proceeding resides, or by order of the court, as provided in this section.

2. The court may, on motion or stipulation, change the place of the proceeding in the following cases:

(a) When the county designated in the complaint, petition or motion is not the proper county.

(b) When there is reason to believe that an impartial proceeding cannot be had therein.

(c) When the convenience of the witnesses and the ends of justice would be promoted by the change.

(d) When any defendant in a case commenced in a county without a business court requests a change to a county:

(1) With a business court; and

(2) In which the case, if originally commenced in such county, would be eligible for assignment to the business court.

(e) When each of the parties consent to the change.

3. When the place of the proceeding is changed, all matters relating to the proceeding shall be had in the county to which the place of proceeding is changed, unless otherwise provided by the consent of the parties in writing duly filed, or by order of the court, and the papers shall be filed or transferred accordingly.

4. As used in this section, "business court" means, as designated pursuant to the rules of the applicable district court:

(a) A business court docket;

(b) A business matter designation; or

(c) At least one business court judge.

NEW YORK

N.Y. CPLR § 501. Contractual Provisions Fixing Venue

Subject to the provisions of subdivision two of section five hundred ten and section five hundred fourteen of this article, written agreement fixing place of trial, made before an action is commenced, shall be enforced upon a motion for change of place of trial.

N.Y. CPLR § 502. Conflicting Venue Provisions

Where, because of joinder of claims or parties, there is a conflict of provisions under this article, the court, upon motion, shall order as the place of trial one proper under this article as to at least one of the parties or claims.

N.Y. CPLR § 503. Venue Based on Residence

(a) Generally. Except where otherwise prescribed by law, the place of trial shall be in the county in which one of the parties resided when it was commenced; the county in which a substantial part of the events or omissions giving rise to the claim occurred; or, if none of the parties then resided in the state, in any county designated by the plaintiff. A party resident in more than one county shall be deemed a resident of each such county.

(b) Executor, administrator, trustee, committee, conservator, general or testamentary guardian, or receiver. An executor, administrator, trustee, committee, conservator, general or testamentary guardian, or receiver shall be deemed a resident of the county of his appointment as well as the county in which he actually resides.

(c) Corporation. A domestic corporation, or a foreign corporation authorized to transact business in the state, shall be deemed a resident of the county in which its principal office is located; except that such a corporation, if a railroad or other common carrier, shall also be deemed a resident of the county where the cause of action arose.

(d) Unincorporated association, partnership, or individually-owned business. A president or treasurer of an unincorporated association, suing or being sued on behalf of the association, shall be deemed a resident of any county in which the association has its principal office, as well as the county in which he actually resides. A partnership or an individually-owned business shall be deemed a resident of any county in which it has its principal office, as well as the county in which the partner or individual owner suing or being sued actually resides.

(e) Assignee. In an action for a sum of money only, brought by an assignee other than an assignee for the benefit of creditors or a holder in due course of a negotiable instrument, the assignee's residence shall be deemed the same as that of the original assignor at the time of the original assignment.

(f) Consumer credit transaction. In an action arising out of a consumer credit transaction where a purchaser, borrower or debtor is a defendant, the place of trial shall be the residence of a defendant, if one resides within the state or the county where such transaction took place, if it is within the state, or, in other cases, as set forth in subdivision (a).

(g) Student debt. In an action to recover tuition, fees, room and board, educational benefit payments, student loans, or other such charges incurred by a student in furtherance of such student's education owed to the state of New York, the place of trial shall be the residence of the defendant, if one resides within the state, or in other cases, as set forth in this article.

N.Y. CPLR § 504. Actions Against Counties, Cities, Towns, Villages, School Districts and District Corporations

Notwithstanding the provisions of any charter heretofore granted by the state and subject to the provisions of subdivision (b) of section 506, the place of trial of all actions against counties, cities, towns, villages, school districts and district corporations or any of their officers, boards or departments shall be, for:

1. a county, in such county;
2. a city, except the city of New York, town, village, school district or district corporation, in the county in which such city, town, village, school district or district corporation is situated, or if such school district or district corporation is situated in more than one county, in either county; and
3. the city of New York, in the county within the city in which the cause of action arose, or if it arose outside of the city, in the county of New York.

N.Y. CPLR § 505. Actions Involving Public Authorities

(a) Generally. The place of trial of an action by or against a public authority constituted under the laws of the state shall be in the county in which the authority has its principal office or where it has facilities involved in the action.

(b) Against New York city transit authority. The place of trial of an action against the New York city transit authority shall be in the county within the city of New York in which the cause of action arose, or, if it arose outside of the city, in the county of New York.

N.Y. CPLR § 506. Where Special Proceeding Commenced

(a) Generally. Unless otherwise prescribed in subdivision (b) or in the law authorizing the proceeding, a special proceeding may be commenced in any county within the judicial district where the proceeding is triable.

(b) Proceeding against body or officer. A proceeding against a body or officer shall be commenced in any county within the judicial district where the respondent made the determination complained of or refused to perform the duty specifically enjoined upon him by law, or where the proceedings were brought or taken in the course of which the matter sought to be restrained originated, or where the material events otherwise took place, or where the principal office of the respondent is located, except that

1. a proceeding against a justice of the supreme court or a judge of a county court or the court of general sessions shall be commenced in the appellate

division in the judicial department where the action, in the course of which the matter sought to be enforced or restrained originated, is triable, unless a term of the appellate division in that department is not in session, in which case the proceeding may be commenced in the appellate division in an adjoining judicial department; and

2. a proceeding against the regents of the university of the state of New York, the commissioner of education, the commissioner of taxation and finance, the tax appeals tribunal except as provided in section two thousand sixteen of the tax law, the public service commission, the commissioner or the department of transportation relating to articles three, four, five, six, seven, eight, nine or ten of the transportation law or to the railroad law, the water resources board, the comptroller or the department of agriculture and markets, shall be commenced in the supreme court, Albany county.

3. notwithstanding the provisions of paragraph two of this subdivision, a proceeding against the commissioner of education pursuant to section forty-four hundred four of the education law may be commenced in the supreme court in the county of residence of the petitioner.

4. a proceeding against the New York city tax appeals tribunal established by section one hundred sixty-eight of the New York city charter shall be commenced in the appellate division of the supreme court, first department.

5. a proceeding challenging apportionment by the legislature shall be commenced in the supreme court in any of the following designated counties in a judicial department where at least one petitioner resides:

(i) first judicial department: New York county;
(ii) second judicial department: Westchester county;
(iii) third judicial department: Albany county; or
(iv) fourth judicial department: Erie county.

N.Y. CPLR § 507. Real Property Actions

The place of trial of an action in which the judgment demanded would affect the title to, or the possession, use or enjoyment of, real property shall be in the county in which any part of the subject of the action is situated.

N.Y. CPLR § 508. Actions to Recover a Chattel

The place of trial of an action to recover a chattel may be in the county in which any part of the subject of the action is situated at the time of the commencement of the action.

NORTH CAROLINA

N.C. G.S.A. § 1-76. Where Subject of Action Situated

Actions for the following causes must be tried in the county in which the subject of the action, or some part thereof, is situated, subject to the power of the court to change the place of trial in the cases provided by law:

(1) Recovery of real property, or of an estate or interest therein, or for the determination in any form of such right or interest, and for injuries to real property.

(2) Partition of real property.

(3) Foreclosure of a mortgage of real property.

(4) Recovery of personal property when the recovery of the property itself is the sole or primary relief demanded.

N.C. G.S.A. § 1-76.1. Where Deficiency Debtor Resides or Where Loan was Negotiated

Subject to the power of the court to change the place of trial as provided by law, actions to recover a deficiency, which remains owing on a debt after secured personal property has been sold to partially satisfy the debt, must be brought in the county in which the debtor or debtor's agent resides or in the county where the loan was negotiated.

N.C. G.S.A. § 1-77. Where Cause of Action Arose

Actions for the following causes must be tried in the county where the cause, or some part thereof, arose, subject to the power of the court to change the place of trial, in the cases provided by law:

(1) Recovery of a penalty or forfeiture, imposed by statute; except that, when it is imposed for an offense committed on a sound, bay, river, or other body of water, situated in two or more counties, the action may be brought in any county bordering on such body of water, and opposite to the place where the offense was committed.

(2) Against a public officer or person especially appointed to execute his duties, for an act done by him by virtue of his office; or against a person who by his command or in his aid does anything touching the duties of such officer.

N.C. G.S.A. § 1-78. Official Bonds, Executors and Administrators

All actions against executors and administrators in their official capacity, except where otherwise provided by statute, and all actions upon official bonds must be instituted in the county where the bonds were given, if the principal or any surety on the bond is in the county; if not, then in the plaintiff's county.

N.C. G.S.A. § 1-79. Domestic Corporations, Limited Partnerships, Limited Liability Companies, and Registered Limited Liability Partnerships

(a) For the purpose of suing and being sued the residence of a domestic corporation, limited partnership, limited liability company, or registered limited liability partnership is as follows:

(1) Where the registered or principal office of the corporation, limited partnership, limited liability company, or registered limited liability partnership is located, or

(2) Where the corporation, limited partnership, limited liability company, or registered limited liability partnership maintains a place of business, or

(3) If no registered or principal office is in existence, and no place of business is currently maintained or can reasonably be found, the term "residence" shall include any place where the corporation, limited partnership, limited liability company, or registered limited liability partnership is regularly engaged in carrying on business.

(b) For purposes of this section, the term "domestic" when applied to an entity means:

(1) An entity formed under the laws of this State, or

(2) An entity that (i) is formed under the laws of any jurisdiction other than this State, and (ii) maintains a registered office in this State pursuant to a certificate of authority from the Secretary of State.

N.C. G.S.A. § 1-80. Foreign Corporations

An action against a corporation created by or under the law of any other state or government may be brought in the appropriate trial court division of any county in which the cause of action arose, or in which the corporation usually did business, or has property, or in which the plaintiffs, or either of them, reside, in the following cases:

(1) By a resident of this State, for any cause of action.

(2) By a nonresident of this State in any county where he or they are regularly engaged in carrying on business.

(3) By a plaintiff, not a resident of this State, when the cause of action arose or the subject of the action is situated in this State.

N.C. G.S.A. § 1-81. Actions Against Railroads

In all actions against railroads the action must be tried either in the county where the cause of action arose or where the plaintiff resided at that time or in some county adjoining that in which the cause of action arose, subject to the power of the court to change the place of trial as provided by statute.

N.C. G.S.A. § 1-81.2. Venue in Complex Business Cases

(a) To facilitate the effective administration in the State's statewide electronic filing system of mandatory complex business cases and those cases assigned to a business court judge, and subject to subsection (e) of this section, venue shall lie exclusively in Wake County in any action designated by the Chief Justice of the Supreme Court of North Carolina as a mandatory complex business case pursuant to G.S. 7A-45.4 or otherwise assigned to a business court judge by the Chief Justice pursuant to the General Rules of Practice for the Superior and District Courts.

(b) When a Notice of Designation filed pursuant to G.S. 7A-45.4(c) is filed contemporaneously with the initiation of an action, the action shall be brought in Wake County. If the Chief Justice or the Chief Business Court Judge enters an order declining to designate an action filed pursuant to this subsection as a mandatory complex business case, that order shall direct the clerk of superior court to transfer the action to the county of origin identified in the Notice of Designation.

(c) When a Notice of Designation filed pursuant to G.S. 7A-45.4(c) is filed in an action instituted outside of Wake County, the clerk of superior court in the county of origin shall transfer the action to Wake County after the issuance of summons in accordance with G.S. 1A-1, Rule 4. If the Chief Justice or the Chief Business Court Judge subsequently enters an order declining to designate an action filed pursuant to this subsection as a mandatory complex business case or declines to otherwise assign the matter to a business court judge pursuant to the General Rules of Practice for the Superior and District Courts, the order shall direct the clerk of superior court to transfer the action to the county of origin identified in the Notice of Designation.

(d) No later than five days after an action is transferred to or from Wake County pursuant to subsection (b) or (c) of this section, the Wake County Clerk of Superior Court shall serve the party that filed the Notice of Designation with a notice of transfer. The notice shall be on a form promulgated by the Administrative Office of the Courts. No later than five days after being served with the notice of transfer, the party that filed the Notice of Designation shall serve a copy of the notice of transfer on all parties in the action not served by the Wake County Clerk of Superior Court.

(e) Notwithstanding the provisions of this Article or any other General Statute concerning venue, trials in mandatory complex business cases and cases assigned to a business court judge pursuant to the General Rules of Practice for Superior and District Courts shall be held in the county of origin identified in the Notice of Designation. The presiding business court judge may conduct trials outside the county of origin in any superior court or business court facility with the consent of the parties, or upon the motion of a party or the judge and an order finding that the convenience of witnesses and the ends of justice would be promoted by the change. The presiding business court judge may conduct trials remotely pursuant to G.S. 7A-49.6. The presiding business court judge may conduct pretrial proceedings outside the county of origin in any superior court or business court facility, or remotely pursuant to G.S. 7A-49.6, in the judge's discretion.

N.C. G.S.A. § 1-82. Venue in All Other Cases

In all other cases the action must be tried in the county in which the plaintiffs or the defendants, or any of them, reside at its commencement, or if none of the defendants reside in the State, then in the county in which the plaintiffs, or any of them, reside; and if none of the parties reside in the State, then the action may be tried in any county which the plaintiff designates in the plaintiff 's summons and complaint, subject to the power of the court to change the place of trial, in the cases provided by statute; provided that any person who has resided on or been stationed in a United States army, navy, marine corps, coast guard or air force installation or reservation within this State for a period of one (1) year or more next preceding the institution of an action shall be deemed a resident of the county within which such installation or reservation, or part thereof, is situated and of any county adjacent to such county where such person stationed at such installation or reservation lives in such adjacent county, for the purposes of this section. The term person shall include military personnel and the spouses and dependents of such personnel.

STATE SERVICE STATUTES AND RULES

(EXCERPTS FROM SELECTED STATES)

CALIFORNIA

Cal. Civ. Proc. Code § 415.10. Personal Delivery of Copy of Summons and Complaint; Date

A summons may be served by personal delivery of a copy of the summons and of the complaint to the person to be served. Service of a summons in this manner is deemed complete at the time of such delivery.

The date upon which personal delivery is made shall be entered on or affixed to the face of the copy of the summons at the time of its delivery. However, service of a summons without such date shall be valid and effective.

Cal. Civ. Proc. Code § 415.20. Leaving Copy of Summons and Complaint at Office, Dwelling House, Usual Place of Abode or Business, or Usual Mailing Address; Mailing Copy; Private Mailboxes

(a) In lieu of personal delivery of a copy of the summons and complaint to the person to be served as specified in Section 416.10, 416.20, 416.30, 416.40, or 416.50, a summons may be served by leaving a copy of the summons and complaint during usual office hours in his or her office or, if no physical address is known, at his or her usual mailing address, other than a United States Postal Service post office box, with the person who is apparently in charge thereof, and by thereafter mailing a copy of the summons and complaint by first-class mail, postage prepaid to the person to be served at the place where a copy of the summons and complaint were left. When service is effected by leaving a copy of the summons and complaint at a mailing address, it shall be left with a person at least 18 years of age, who shall be informed of the contents thereof. Service of a summons in this manner is deemed complete on the 10th day after the mailing.

(b) If a copy of the summons and complaint cannot with reasonable diligence be personally delivered to the person to be served, as specified in Section 416.60,

416.70, 416.80, or 416.90, a summons may be served by leaving a copy of the summons and complaint at the person's dwelling house, usual place of abode, usual place of business, or usual mailing address other than a United States Postal Service post office box, in the presence of a competent member of the household or a person apparently in charge of his or her office, place of business, or usual mailing address other than a United States Postal Service post office box, at least 18 years of age, who shall be informed of the contents thereof, and by thereafter mailing a copy of the summons and of the complaint by first-class mail, postage prepaid to the person to be served at the place where a copy of the summons and complaint were left. Service of a summons in this manner is deemed complete on the 10th day after the mailing.

(c) Notwithstanding subdivision (b), if the only address reasonably known for the person to be served is a private mailbox obtained through a commercial mail receiving agency, service of process may be effected on the first delivery attempt by leaving a copy of the summons and complaint with the commercial mail receiving agency in the manner described in subdivision (d) of Section 17538.5 of the Business and Professions Code.

Cal. Civ. Proc. Code § 415.21. Access to Gated Community or Covered Multifamily Dwelling; Identification

(a) Notwithstanding any other law, any person shall be granted access to a gated community or a covered multifamily dwelling for a reasonable period of time for the sole purpose of performing lawful service of process or service of a subpoena upon displaying a current driver's license or other identification, and one of the following:

(1) A badge or other confirmation that the individual is acting in the individual's capacity as a representative of a county sheriff or marshal, or as an investigator employed by an office of the Attorney General, a county counsel, a city attorney, a district attorney, or a public defender.

(2) Evidence of current registration as a process server pursuant to Chapter 16 (commencing with Section 22350) of Division 8 of the Business and Professions Code or of licensure as a private investigator pursuant to Chapter 11.3 (commencing with Section 7512) of Division 3 of the Business and Professions Code.

(b) This section shall only apply to a gated community or a covered multifamily dwelling that is staffed at the time service of process is attempted by a guard or other security personnel assigned to control access to the community or dwelling.

(c) For purposes of this section, "covered multifamily dwelling" means either of the following:

(1) An apartment building, including a timeshare apartment building not considered a place of public accommodation or transient lodging, with three or more dwelling units.

(2) A condominium, including a timeshare condominium not considered a place of public accommodation or transient lodging, with four or more dwelling units.

Cal. Civ. Proc. Code § 415.30. Service by Mail

(a) A summons may be served by mail as provided in this section. A copy of the summons and of the complaint shall be mailed (by first-class mail or airmail, postage prepaid) to the person to be served, together with two copies of the notice and acknowledgment provided for in subdivision (b) and a return envelope, postage prepaid, addressed to the sender.

(b) The notice specified in subdivision (a) shall be in substantially the following form:

(Title of court and cause, with action number, to be inserted by the sender prior to mailing)

NOTICE

To: (Here state the name of the person to be served.)

This summons is served pursuant to Section 415.30 of the California Code of Civil Procedure. Failure to complete this form and return it to the sender within 20 days may subject you (or the party on whose behalf you are being served) to liability for the payment of any expenses incurred in serving a summons upon you in any other manner permitted by law. If you are served on behalf of a corporation, unincorporated association (including a partnership), or other entity, this form must be signed in the name of such entity by you or by a person authorized to receive service of process on behalf of such entity. In all other cases, this form must be signed by you personally or by a person authorized by you to acknowledge receipt of summons. Section 415.30 provides that this summons is deemed served on the date of execution of an acknowledgment of receipt of summons.

____
Signature of sender

ACKNOWLEDGMENT OF RECEIPT OF SUMMONS

This acknowledges receipt on (insert date) of a copy of the summons and of the complaint at (insert address).

Date: ____
(Date this acknowledgement is executed)

Signature:____
(Signature of person acknowledging receipt, with title if acknowledgment is made on behalf of another person)

(c) Service of a summons pursuant to this section is deemed complete on the date a written acknowledgment of receipt of summons is executed, if such acknowledgment thereafter is returned to the sender.

(d) If the person to whom a copy of the summons and of the complaint are mailed pursuant to this section fails to complete and return the acknowledgment form set forth in subdivision (b) within 20 days from the date of such mailing, the party to whom the summons was mailed shall be liable for reasonable expenses thereafter incurred in serving or attempting to serve the party by another method permitted by this chapter, and, except for good cause shown, the court in which the action is pending, upon motion, with or without notice, shall award the party such expenses whether or not he is otherwise entitled to recover his costs in the action.

(e) A notice or acknowledgment of receipt in form approved by the Judicial Council is deemed to comply with this section.

Cal. Civ. Proc. Code § 415.40. Service on Person Outside State

A summons may be served on a person outside this state in any manner provided by this article or by sending a copy of the summons and of the complaint to the person to be served by first-class mail, postage prepaid, requiring a return receipt. Service of a summons by this form of mail is deemed complete on the 10th day after such mailing.

Cal. Civ. Proc. Code § 415.45. Unlawful Detainer; Service by Posting and Mailing or Other Manner

(a) A summons in an action for unlawful detainer of real property may be served by posting if upon affidavit it appears to the satisfaction of the court in which the action is pending that the party to be served cannot with reasonable diligence be served in any manner specified in this article other than publication and that:

(1) A cause of action exists against the party upon whom service is to be made or he is a necessary or proper party to the action; or

(2) The party to be served has or claims an interest in real property in this state that is subject to the jurisdiction of the court or the relief demanded in the action consists wholly or in part in excluding such party from any interest in such property.

(b) The court shall order the summons to be posted on the premises in a manner most likely to give actual notice to the party to be served and direct that a copy of the summons and of the complaint be forthwith mailed by certified mail to such party at his last known address.

(c) Service of summons in this manner is deemed complete on the 10th day after posting and mailing.

(d) Notwithstanding an order for posting of the summons, a summons may be served in any other manner authorized by this article, except publication, in which event such service shall supersede any posted summons.

Cal. Civ. Proc. Code § 415.50. Service by Publication

(a) A summons may be served by publication if upon affidavit it appears to the satisfaction of the court in which the action is pending that the party to be served cannot with reasonable diligence be served in another manner specified in this article and that either:

(1) A cause of action exists against the party upon whom service is to be made or he or she is a necessary or proper party to the action.

(2) The party to be served has or claims an interest in real or personal property in this state that is subject to the jurisdiction of the court or the relief demanded in the action consists wholly or in part in excluding the party from any interest in the property.

(b) The court shall order the summons to be published in a named newspaper, published in this state, that is most likely to give actual notice to the party to be served. If the party to be served resides or is located out of this state, the court may also order the summons to be published in a named newspaper outside this state that is most likely to give actual notice to that party. The order shall direct that a copy of the summons, the complaint, and the order for publication be forthwith mailed to the party if his or her address is ascertained before expiration of the time prescribed for publication of the summons. Except as otherwise provided by statute, the publication shall be made as provided by Section 6064 of the Government Code unless the court, in its discretion, orders publication for a longer period.

(c) Service of a summons in this manner is deemed complete as provided in Section 6064 of the Government Code.

(d) Notwithstanding an order for publication of the summons, a summons may be served in another manner authorized by this chapter, in which event the service shall supersede any published summons.

(e) As a condition of establishing that the party to be served cannot with reasonable diligence be served in another manner specified in this article, the court may not require that a search be conducted of public databases where access by a registered process server to residential addresses is prohibited by law or by published policy of the agency providing the database, including, but not limited to, voter registration rolls and records of the Department of Motor Vehicles.

Cal. Civ. Proc. Code § 415.95. Service of Summons on a Business Organization, Form Unknown

(a) A summons may be served on a business organization, form unknown, by leaving a copy of the summons and complaint during usual office hours with the person who is apparently in charge of the office of that business organization, and by thereafter mailing a copy of the summons and complaint by first-class mail, postage prepaid, to the person to be served at the place where a copy of the summons and complaint was left. Service of a summons in this manner is deemed complete on the 10th day after the mailing.

(b) Service of a summons pursuant to this section is not valid for a corporation with a registered agent for service of process listed with the Secretary of State.

FLORIDA

Fla. Stat. § 48.031. Service of Process Generally; Service of Witness Subpoenas

(1)

(a) Service of original process is made by delivering a copy of it to the person to be served with a copy of the complaint, petition, or other initial pleading or paper or by leaving the copies at his or her usual place of abode with any person residing therein who is 15 years of age or older and informing the person of their contents. Minors who are or have been married shall be served as provided in this section.

(b) An employer, when contacted by an individual authorized to serve process, shall allow the authorized individual to serve an employee in a private area designated by the employer. An employer who fails to comply with this paragraph commits a noncriminal violation, punishable by a fine of up to $1,000.

(2)

(a) Substituted service on the spouse of the person to be served may be made at any place in a county by an individual authorized under s. 48.021 or s. 48.27 to serve process in that county, if the cause of action is not an adversarial proceeding between the spouse and the person to be served, if the spouse requests such service or the spouse is also a party to the action, and if the spouse and person to be served reside together in the same dwelling, regardless of whether such dwelling is located in the county where substituted service is made.

(b) Substituted service may be made on an individual doing business as a sole proprietorship at his or her place of business, during regular business hours, by serving the person in charge of the business at the time of service if two attempts to serve the owner are made at the place of business.

(3)

(a) The service of process of witness subpoenas, whether in criminal cases or civil actions, shall be made as provided in subsection (1). However, service of a subpoena on a witness in a civil traffic case, a criminal traffic case, a misdemeanor case, or a second degree or third degree felony may be made by United States mail directed to the witness at the last known address, and the service must be mailed at least 7 days prior to the date of the witness's required appearance. Failure of a witness to appear in response to a subpoena served by United States mail that is not certified may not be grounds for finding the witness in contempt of court.

(b) A criminal witness subpoena commanding the witness to appear for a court appearance may be posted by a person authorized to serve process at the witness's residence if three attempts to serve the subpoena, made at different times of the day or night on different dates, have failed. A criminal witness subpoena commanding the witness to appear for a deposition may be posted by a person authorized to serve process at the witness's residence if one attempt to serve the subpoena has failed. The subpoena must be posted at least 5 days before the date of the witness's required appearance.

(4)

(a) Service of a criminal witness subpoena upon a law enforcement officer or upon any federal, state, or municipal employee called to testify in an official capacity in a criminal case may be made as provided in subsection (1) or by delivery to a designated supervisory or administrative employee at the witness's place of employment if the agency head or highest ranking official at the witness's place of employment has designated such employee to accept such service. However, no such designated employee is required to accept service:

1. For a witness who is no longer employed by the agency at that place of employment;

2. If the witness is not scheduled to work prior to the date the witness is required to appear; or

3. If the appearance date is less than 5 days from the date of service.

The agency head or highest ranking official at the witness's place of employment may determine the days of the week and the hours that service may be made at the witness's place of employment.

(b) Service may also be made in accordance with subsection (3) provided that the person who requests the issuance of the criminal witness subpoena shall be responsible for mailing the subpoena in accordance with that subsection and for making the proper return of service to the court.

(5) A person serving process shall place, on the first page only of at least one of the processes served, the date and time of service, his or her initials or signature, and, if applicable, his or her identification number. The person requesting service or the person authorized to serve the process shall file the return-of-service form with the court.

(6)

(a) If the only address for a person to be served which is discoverable through public records is a private mailbox, a virtual office, or an executive office or mini suite, substituted service may be made by leaving a copy of the process with the person in charge of the private mailbox, virtual office, or executive office or mini suite, but only if the process server determines that the person to be served maintains a mailbox, a virtual office, or an executive office or mini suite at that location.

(b) For purposes of this subsection, the term "virtual office" means an office that provides communications services, such as telephone or facsimile services, and address services without providing dedicated office space, and where all communications are routed through a common receptionist. The term "executive office or mini suite" means an office that provides communications services, such as telephone and facsimile services, a dedicated office space, and other supportive services, and where all communications are routed through a common receptionist.

(7) A gated residential community, including a condominium association or a cooperative, shall grant unannounced entry into the community, including its common areas and common elements, to a person who is attempting to serve process on a defendant or witness who resides within or is known to be within the community.

Fla. Stat. § 48.041. Service on Minor

(1) Process against a minor who has never been married shall be served:

(a) By serving a parent or guardian of the minor as provided for in s. 48.031 or, when there is a legal guardian appointed for the minor, by serving the guardian as provided for in s. 48.031.

(b) By serving the guardian ad litem or other person, if one is appointed by the court to represent the minor. Service on the guardian ad litem is unnecessary when he or she appears voluntarily or when the court orders the appearance without service of process on him or her.

(2) In all cases heretofore adjudicated in which process was served on a minor as prescribed by any law heretofore existing, the service was lawfully made, and no proceeding shall be declared irregular or illegal if a guardian ad litem appeared for the minor.

Fla. Stat. § 48.061. Service on Partnerships, Limited Liability Partnerships, and Limited Partnerships

(1)

(a) Process against a partnership that is not a limited liability partnership or a limited partnership, including a limited liability limited partnership, must be served on any partner and is as valid for service on the partnership as if served on each individual partner.

1. If a partner is not available during regular business hours to accept service on behalf of the partnership, he or she may designate an employee or agent to accept such service.

2. After one attempt to serve a partner or designated employee or agent for service of process has been made, process may be served on a person in charge of the partnership during regular business hours.

(b) If the partnership designated an agent when registering as a general partnership with the Department of State, service on the agent is as valid for service on the partnership as if served on each individual partner; however, unless individual partners are served, the plaintiff may only proceed to judgment and execution against the assets of the partnership.

(2)

(a) Process against a domestic limited liability partnership must first be served on the then-current registered agent for service of process specified in its statement of qualification, in its statement of qualification as amended or restated, or as redesignated in its annual report or change of agent filing and is as valid for service on the limited liability partnership as if served on each individual partner. If service cannot be made on the registered agent because the domestic limited liability partnership ceases to have a registered agent, or if the registered agent cannot otherwise be served after one good faith attempt because of a failure to comply with this chapter or chapter 620, the process may be served on any partner.

1. If a partner is not available during regular business hours to accept service on behalf of the partnership, he or she may designate an employee to accept such service.

2. After one attempt to serve a partner or designated employee has been made, process may be served on a person in charge of the partnership during regular business hours.

(b) If, after due diligence, the process cannot be completed under paragraph (a), the process may be served as provided in § 48.161 on the Secretary of State as an agent of the domestic limited liability partnership or by order of the court under § 48.102.

(3)

(a)

1. Process against a domestic limited partnership, including a domestic limited liability limited partnership, must first be served on the then-current agent for service of process specified in its certificate of limited partnership, in its certificate as amended or restated, or as redesignated in its annual report or change of agent filing and is as valid for service on the domestic limited partnership as if served on each individual general partner of the partnership.

2. If service cannot be made on the registered agent because the domestic limited partnership or domestic limited liability limited partnership ceases to have a registered agent, or if the registered agent cannot otherwise be served following one good faith attempt because of a failure to comply with this chapter or chapter 620, the process may be served on any general partner.

3. After service on a general partner or the registered agent, the plaintiff may proceed to judgment and execution against the assets of the domestic limited partnership or of that general partner, unless the domestic limited partnership is a limited liability limited partnership.

(b) If, after due diligence, the process cannot be completed under paragraph (a), then process may be served as provided in § 48.161 on the Secretary of State as an agent of the limited partnership or by order of the court under § 48.102.

(4)

(a) Process against a foreign limited liability partnership that was required to comply with § 620.9102 may be served as prescribed under subsection (2).

(b) A foreign limited liability partnership engaging in business in this state but not registered is considered, for purposes of service of process, a nonresident engaging in business in this state and may be served pursuant to § 48.181 or by order of the court under § 48.102.

(5)

(a) Process against a foreign limited partnership that was required to comply with § 620.1902 may be served as prescribed under subsection (3).

(b) A foreign limited partnership engaging in business in this state but not registered is considered, for purposes of service of process, a nonresident engaging in business in this state and may be served pursuant to § 48.181 or by order of the court under § 48.102.

Fla. Stat. § 48.081. Service on a Domestic Corporation or Registered Foreign Corporation

(1) As used in this section, the term "registered foreign corporation" means a foreign corporation that has an active certificate of authority to transact business in this state pursuant to a record filed with the Department of State.

(2) A domestic corporation or registered foreign corporation may be served with process required or authorized by law by service on its registered agent designated by the corporation under chapter 607 or chapter 617, as applicable.

(3) If service cannot be made on a registered agent of the domestic corporation or registered foreign corporation because the domestic corporation or registered foreign corporation ceases to have a registered agent, or if the registered agent of the domestic corporation or registered foreign corporation cannot otherwise be served after one good faith attempt because of a failure to comply with this chapter, chapter 607, or chapter 617, as applicable, the process may be served on either of the following:

(a) The chair of the board of directors, the president, any vice president, the secretary, or the treasurer of the domestic corporation or registered foreign corporation.

(b) Any person listed publicly by the domestic corporation or registered foreign corporation on its latest annual report, as most recently amended.

(4) If, after due diligence, the process cannot be completed under subsection (2) and if either:

(a) The only person listed publicly by the domestic corporation or registered foreign corporation on its latest annual report, as most recently amended, is also the registered agent on whom service was attempted under subsection (2); or

(b) After due diligence, service was attempted on at least one person listed publicly by the domestic corporation or registered foreign corporation on its latest annual report, as most recently amended, and cannot be completed on such person under subsection (3),

the process may be served as provided in s. 48.161 on the Secretary of State as an agent of the domestic corporation or registered foreign corporation or by order of the court under s. 48.102.

(5) If the address for the registered agent or any person listed publicly by the domestic corporation or registered foreign corporation on its latest annual report, as most recently amended, is a residence, a private mailbox, a virtual office, or an executive office or mini suite, service on the domestic corporation or registered foreign corporation may be made by serving any of the following:

(a) The registered agent of the domestic corporation or registered foreign corporation, in accordance with § 48.031.

(b) Any person listed publicly by the domestic corporation or registered foreign corporation on its latest annual report, as most recently amended, in accordance with § 48.031.

(c) Any person serving in one of the positions specified in paragraph (3)(a), in accordance with § 48.031.

(6) A foreign corporation engaging in business in this state which is not registered is considered, for purposes of service of process, a nonresident engaging in business in this state and may be served pursuant to § 48.181 or by order of the court under § 48.102.

(7) This section does not apply to service of process on insurance companies.

Fla. Stat. § 48.101. Service on Dissolved Corporations, Dissolved Limited Liability Companies, Dissolved Limited Partnerships, and Dissolved Limited Liability Partnerships

(1) Process against the directors of any corporation that was dissolved before July 1, 1990, as trustees of the dissolved corporation must be served on one or

more of the directors of the dissolved corporation as trustees thereof and binds all of the directors of the dissolved corporation as trustees thereof.

(2)

(a) Process against any other dissolved domestic corporation must be served in accordance with § 48.081.

(b) In addition, provided that service was first properly attempted on the registered agent pursuant to § 48.081(2), but was not successful, service may then be attempted as required under § 48.081(3). In addition to the persons listed in § 48.081(3), service may then be attempted on the person appointed by the circuit court as the trustee, custodian, or receiver under § 607.1405(6).

(c) A party attempting to serve a dissolved domestic for-profit corporation under this section may petition the court to appoint one of the persons specified in § 607.1405(6) to receive service of process on behalf of the corporation.

(3)

(a) Process against any dissolved domestic limited liability company must be served in accordance with § 48.062.

(b) In addition, provided that service was first properly attempted on the registered agent pursuant to § 48.062(2), but was not successful, service may then be attempted as required under § 48.062(3). In addition to the persons listed in § 48.062(3), service on a dissolved domestic limited liability company may be made on the person appointed as the liquidator, trustee, or receiver under § 605.0709.

(c) A party attempting to serve a dissolved domestic limited liability company under this section may petition the court to appoint one of the persons specified in § 605.0709(5) to receive service of process on behalf of the limited liability company.

(4) Process against any dissolved domestic limited partnership must be served in accordance with § 48.061.

Fla. Stat. § 48.102. Service by Other Means

If, after due diligence, a party seeking to effectuate service is unable to effectuate personal service of process on a domestic or foreign corporation; a domestic or foreign general partnership, including a limited liability partnership; a domestic or foreign limited partnership, including a limited liability limited partnership; or a domestic or foreign limited liability company, the court, upon motion and a showing of such inability, may authorize service in any other manner that the party seeking to effectuate service shows will be reasonably effective to give the entity on which service is sought to be effectuated actual notice of the suit. Such other manners of service may include service electronically by e-mail or other technology by any person authorized to serve process in accordance with this chapter, or by an attorney. The court may authorize other methods of service consistent with the principles of due process. In suits involving a breach of contract, the court may consider authorizing the parties to effectuate service in the manner provided for in the contractual notice provision of the subject contract.

NEW YORK

N.Y. CPLR § 305. Summons; Supplemental Summons, Amendment

(a) Summons; supplemental summons. A summons shall specify the basis of the venue designated and if based upon the residence of the plaintiff it shall specify the plaintiff's address, and also shall bear the index number assigned and the date of filing with the clerk of the court. A third-party summons shall also specify the date of filing of the third-party summons with the clerk of the court. The summons in an action arising out of a consumer credit transaction shall prominently display at the top of the summons the words "consumer credit transaction" and, where a purchaser, borrower or debtor is a defendant, shall specify the county of residence of a defendant, if one resides within the state, and the county where the consumer credit transaction took place, if it is within the state. Where, upon order of the court or by stipulation of all parties or as of right pursuant to section 1003, a new party is joined in the action and the joinder is not made upon the new party's motion, a supplemental summons specifying the pleading which the new party must answer shall be filed with the clerk of the court and served upon such party.

(b) Summons and notice. If the complaint is not served with the summons, the summons shall contain or have attached thereto a notice stating the nature of the action and the relief sought, and, except in an action for medical malpractice, the sum of money for which judgment may be taken in case of default.

(c) Amendment. At any time, in its discretion and upon such terms as it deems just, the court may allow any summons or proof of service of a summons to be amended, if a substantial right of a party against whom the summons issued is not prejudiced.

N.Y. CPLR § 306. Proof of Service

(a) Generally. Proof of service shall specify the papers served, the person who was served and the date, time, address, or, in the event there is no address, place and manner of service, and set forth facts showing that the service was made by an authorized person and in an authorized manner.

(b) Personal service. Whenever service is made pursuant to this article by delivery of the summons to an individual, proof of service shall also include, in addition to any other requirement, a description of the person to whom it was so delivered, including, but not limited to, the process server's perception of the person's: gender, race, hair color, approximate age, approximate weight and height, and other identifying features.

(c) Other service. Where service is made pursuant to subdivision four of section three hundred eight of this chapter, proof of service shall also specify the dates, addresses and the times of attempted service pursuant to subdivisions1 one, two or three of such section.

(d) Form. Proof of service shall be in the form of a certificate if the service is made by a sheriff or other authorized public officer, in the form of an affidavit if made by any other person, or in the form of a signed acknowledgement of receipt of a summons and complaint, or summons and notice or notice of petition as provided for in section 312-a of this article.

(e) Admission of service. A writing admitting service by the person to be served is adequate proof of service.

N.Y. CPLR § 306-B. Service of the Summons and Complaint, Summons with Notice, Third-Party Summons and Complaint, or Petition with a Notice of Petition or Order to Show Cause

Service of the summons and complaint, summons with notice, third-party summons and complaint, or petition with a notice of petition or order to show cause shall be made within one hundred twenty days after the commencement of the action or proceeding, provided that in an action or proceeding, except a proceeding commenced under the election law, where the applicable statute of limitations is four months or less, service shall be made not later than fifteen days after the date on which the applicable statute of limitations expires. If service is not made upon a defendant within the time provided in this section, the court, upon motion, shall dismiss the action without prejudice as to that defendant, or upon good cause shown or in the interest of justice, extend the time for service.

N.Y. CPLR § 306-C. Notice of Commencement of Action For Personal Injuries by Recipient of Medical Assistance

In the case of an individual who has suffered personal injuries and has received medical assistance pursuant to titles eleven and eleven-D of article five of the social services law on or after the date of such injury, notice of the commencement of an action by or on behalf of such individual for such personal injuries shall be sent to the social services district in the county in which such recipient resides, or to the department of health, by certified mail, return receipt requested, or electronically in accord with regulations promulgated by the commissioner of the department of health, within sixty days of the completion of service upon all parties to such action. Proof of sending such notice shall be filed with the court in accordance with rule three hundred six of this article. Sending such notice shall not be a jurisdictional requirement to commencing an action.

N.Y. CPLR § 306-D. Additional Mailing of Notice in an Action Arising Out of a Consumer Credit Transaction

(a) At the time of filing with the clerk of the proof of service of the summons and complaint in an action arising out of a consumer credit transaction, the plaintiff shall submit to the clerk a stamped, unsealed envelope addressed to the defendant together with a written notice in clear type of no less than twelve-point in size, in both English and Spanish, and containing the following language:

ADDITIONAL NOTICE OF LAWSUIT
(NAME OF COURT)
(COUNTY)
(STREET ADDRESS, ROOM NUMBER)
(CITY, STATE, ZIP CODE)

(NAME OF DEFENDANT)

(ADDRESS OF DEFENDANT)

Plaintiff:
Defendant:
Name of original creditor, unless same:
Index number:

Attention: a lawsuit has been filed against you claiming that you owe money for an unpaid consumer debt.

You may wish to contact an attorney.

You should respond to the lawsuit as soon as possible by filing an "answer" which may be done at the court clerk's office listed above.

If you do not respond to the lawsuit, the court may enter a money judgment against you. Once entered, a judgment is good and can be used against you for twenty years, and your personal property and money, including a portion of your paycheck and/or bank account, may be taken from you. Also, a judgment may affect your credit score and can affect your ability to rent a home, find a job, or take out a loan.

You CANNOT be arrested or sent to jail for owing a debt.

Additional information can be found at the New York state court system website.

Sources of information and assistance:

The court encourages you to inform yourself about your options as a defendant in this lawsuit. In addition to seeking assistance from a private attorney or legal aid office, there are free legal assistance computer programs that you can use online to help you represent yourself in this lawsuit.

For further information, or to locate a legal aid program near you, you may visit the LawHelpNY website or the New York state court system website, which has information for representing yourself and links to other resources at: ______________.

(b) The face of the envelope shall be addressed to the defendant at the address at which process was served, and shall contain the defendant's name, address (including apartment number) and zip code. The face of the envelope also shall state the appropriate clerk's office as its return address.

(c) The clerk promptly shall mail to the defendant the envelope containing the additional notice set forth in subdivision (a) of this section. No default judgment based on the defendant's failure to answer shall be entered unless there has been compliance with this section, and at least twenty days have elapsed from the date of mailing by the clerk. No default judgment based on the defendant's failure to answer shall be entered if the additional notice is returned to the court as undeliverable. Receipt of the additional notice by the defendant does not confer jurisdiction on the court in the absence of proper service of process.

(d) The chief administrative judge shall issue a Spanish translation of the notice in subdivision (a) of this section and shall maintain and publish the URL address for the web page containing consumer resources for unrepresented litigants.

N.Y. CPLR § 308. Personal Service Upon a Natural Person

Personal service upon a natural person shall be made by any of the following methods:

1. by delivering the summons within the state to the person to be served; or

2. by delivering the summons within the state to a person of suitable age and discretion at the actual place of business, dwelling place or usual place of abode of the person to be served and by either mailing the summons to the person to be served at his or her last known residence or by mailing the summons by first class mail to the person to be served at his or her actual place of business in an envelope bearing the legend "personal and confidential" and not indicating on the outside thereof, by return address or otherwise, that the communication is from an attorney or concerns an action against the person to be served, such delivery

and mailing to be effected within twenty days of each other; proof of such service shall be filed with the clerk of the court designated in the summons within twenty days of either such delivery or mailing, whichever is effected later; service shall be complete ten days after such filing; proof of service shall identify such person of suitable age and discretion and state the date, time and place of service, except in matrimonial actions where service hereunder may be made pursuant to an order made in accordance with the provisions of subdivision a of section two hundred thirty-two of the domestic relations law; or

3. by delivering the summons within the state to the agent for service of the person to be served as designated under rule 318, except in matrimonial actions where service hereunder may be made pursuant to an order made in accordance with the provisions of subdivision a of section two hundred thirty-two of the domestic relations law;

4. where service under paragraphs one and two cannot be made with due diligence, by affixing the summons to the door of either the actual place of business, dwelling place or usual place of abode within the state of the person to be served and by either mailing the summons to such person at his or her last known residence or by mailing the summons by first class mail to the person to be served at his or her actual place of business in an envelope bearing the legend "personal and confidential" and not indicating on the outside thereof, by return address or otherwise, that the communication is from an attorney or concerns an action against the person to be served, such affixing and mailing to be effected within twenty days of each other; proof of such service shall be filed with the clerk of the court designated in the summons within twenty days of either such affixing or mailing, whichever is effected later; service shall be complete ten days after such filing, except in matrimonial actions where service hereunder may be made pursuant to an order made in accordance with the provisions of subdivision a of section two hundred thirty-two of the domestic relations law;

5. in such manner as the court, upon motion without notice, directs, if service is impracticable under paragraphs one, two and four of this section.

6. For purposes of this section, "actual place of business" shall include any location that the defendant, through regular solicitation or advertisement, has held out as its place of business.

N.Y. CPLR § 310. Personal Service Upon a Partnership

(a) Personal service upon persons conducting a business as a partnership may be made by personally serving the summons upon any one of them.

(b) Personal service upon said partnership may also be made within the state by delivering the summons to the managing or general agent of the partnership or the person in charge of the office of the partnership within the state at such office and by either mailing the summons to the partner thereof intended to be served by first class mail to his last known residence or to the place of business of the partnership. Proof of such service shall be filed within twenty days with the clerk of the court designated in the summons; service shall be complete ten days after such filing; proof of service shall identify the person to whom the summons was so delivered and state the date, time of day and place of service.

(c) Where service under subdivisions (a) and (b) of this section cannot be made with due diligence, it may be made by affixing a copy of the summons to the door of the actual place of business of the partnership within the state and by either mailing the summons by first class mail to the partner intended to be so served to such person to his last known residence or to said person at the office of said partnership within the state. Proof of such service shall be filed within twenty days thereafter with the clerk of the court designated in the summons; service shall be complete ten days after filing.

(d) Personal service on such partnership may also be made by delivering the summons to any other agent or employee of the partnership authorized by appointment to receive service; or to any other person designated by the partnership to receive process in writing, filed in the office of the clerk of the county wherein such partnership is located.

(e) If service is impracticable under subdivisions (a), (b) and (c) of this section, it may be made in such manner as the court, upon motion without notice directs.

N.Y. CPLR § 311. Personal Service Upon a Corporation or Governmental Subdivision

(a) Personal service upon a corporation or governmental subdivision shall be made by delivering the summons as follows:

1. upon any domestic or foreign corporation, to an officer, director, managing or general agent, or cashier or assistant cashier or to any other agent authorized by appointment or by law to receive service. A business corporation may also be served pursuant to section three hundred six or three hundred seven of the business corporation law. A not-for-profit corporation may also be served pursuant to section three hundred six or three hundred seven of the not-for-profit corporation law;

2. upon the city of New York, to the corporation counsel or to any person designated to receive process in a writing filed in the office of the clerk of New York county;

3. upon any other city, to the mayor, comptroller, treasurer, counsel or clerk; or, if the city lacks such officers, to an officer performing a corresponding function under another name;

4. upon a county, to the chair or clerk of the board of supervisors, clerk, attorney or treasurer;

5. upon a town, to the supervisor or the clerk;

6. upon a village, to the mayor, clerk, or any trustee;

7. upon a school district, to a school officer, as defined in the education law; and

8. upon a park, sewage or other district, to the clerk, any trustee or any member of the board.

(b) If service upon a domestic or foreign corporation within the one hundred twenty days allowed by section three hundred six-b of this article is impracticable under paragraph one of subdivision (a) of this section or any other law, service upon the corporation may be made in such manner, and proof of service may take such form, as the court, upon motion without notice, directs.

TEXAS

Tex. R. Civ. P. 106. Method of Service

(a) Unless the citation or court order otherwise directs, the citation must be served by:

(1) delivering to the defendant, in person, a copy of the citation, showing the delivery date, and of the petition; or

(2) mailing to the defendant by registered or certified mail, return receipt requested, a copy of the citation and of the petition.

(b) Upon motion supported by a statement — sworn to before a notary or made under penalty of perjury — listing any location where the defendant can probably be found and stating specifically the facts showing that service has been attempted under (a)(1) or (a)(2) at the location named in the statement but has not been successful, the court may authorize service:

(1) by leaving a copy of the citation and of the petition with anyone older than sixteen at the location specified in the statement; or

(2) in any other manner, including electronically by social media, email, or other technology, that the statement or other evidence shows will be reasonably effective to give the defendant notice of the suit.

VIRGINIA

Va. Code § 8.01-296. Manner of Serving Process Upon Natural Persons

In addition to any other manner of service upon natural persons prescribed elsewhere in the Code, and subject to the provisions of § 8.01-286.1, in any action at law or in equity or any other civil proceeding in any court, process, for which no particular mode of service is prescribed, may be served upon natural persons as follows:

1. By delivering a copy thereof in writing to the party in person; or
2. By substituted service in the following manner:

a. If the party to be served is not found at his usual place of abode, by delivering a copy of such process and giving information of its purport to any person found there, who is a member of his family, other than a temporary sojourner or guest, and who is of the age of 16 years or older; or

b. If such service cannot be effected under subdivision 2 a, then by posting a copy of such process at the front door or at such other door as appears to be the main entrance of such place of abode, provided that not less than 10 days before judgment by default may be entered, the party causing service or his attorney or agent mails to the party served a copy of such process and thereafter files in the office of the clerk of the court a certificate of such mailing. In any civil action brought in a general district court, the mailing of the application for a warrant in debt or affidavit for summons in unlawful detainer or other civil pleading or a copy of such pleading, whether yet issued by the court or not, which contains the date, time and place of the return, prior to or after filing such pleading in the general district court, shall satisfy the mailing requirements of this section. In any civil action brought in a circuit court, the mailing of a copy of the pleadings with a notice that the proceedings are pending in the court indicated and that upon the expiration of 10 days after the giving of the notice and the expiration of the statutory period within which to respond, without further notice, the entry of a judgment by default as prayed for in the pleadings may be requested, shall satisfy the mailing requirements of this section and any notice requirement of the Rules of Court. Any judgment by default entered after July 1, 1989, upon posted service in which proceedings a copy of the pleadings was mailed as provided for in this section prior to July 1, 1989, is validated.

c. The person executing such service shall note the manner and the date of such service on the original and the copy of the process so delivered or posted under this subdivision and shall effect the return of process as provided in §§ 8.01-294 and 8.01-325.

3. If service cannot be effected under subdivisions 1 and 2, then by order of publication in appropriate cases under the provisions of §§ 8.01-316 through 8.01-320.

4. The landlord or his duly authorized agent or representative may serve notices required by the rental agreement or by law upon the tenant or occupant under a rental agreement that is within the purview of Chapter 14 (§ 55.1-1400 et seq.) of Title 55.1.

Va. Code § 8.01-299. How Process Served on Domestic Stock Corporations, Nonstock Corporations, and Limited Liability Companies Generally

Except as prescribed in § 8.01-300 as to municipal and quasi-governmental corporations, and subject to § 8.01-286.1, process may be served on a domestic stock corporation, nonstock corporation, or limited liability company created by the laws of the Commonwealth as follows:

1. By personal service on any officer, director, or registered agent of any such corporation or on the registered agent of such limited liability company;

2. By substituted service on stock corporations in accordance with § 13.1-637, on nonstock corporations in accordance with § 13.1-836, and on limited liability companies in accordance with § 13.1-1018; or

3. If the address of the registered office of the corporation or limited liability company is a single-family residential dwelling, by substituted service on the registered agent of the corporation or limited liability company in the manner provided by subdivision 2 of § 8.01-296.

This section does not prescribe the only means, or necessarily the required means, of serving a domestic stock or nonstock corporation or limited liability company.

FRCP ESSENTIALS

Your Exam Checklist

FRCP 11: Motion for Sanctions

1. Make sure you are in federal court. (State courts have their own rules.) Remember also that Rule 11 is only one avenue for regulating misconduct. There are also professional responsibility rules and statutes; the contempt power; and inherent authority to discipline.
2. Is the offense contained in a "pleading, written motion, or other paper"/ Rule 11(a)?
   This Rule does not apply to discovery/11(d).
3. Violations/11(b) — 4 types of conduct prohibited
   a. Improper purpose/11(b)(1)
      - Violation of Rule 11 if improper purpose such as to harass, cause unnecessary delay, or needlessly increase the cost of litigation.

   b. Failure to do legal homework/11(b)(2)
      - Violation of Rule 11 if claims, defenses, or other legal contentions are not warranted by existing law (or by nonfrivolous arguments for new law).

   c. Failure to do factual homework (Claimant)/11(b)(3)
      - Violation of Rule 11 if factual contentions) do not have evidentiary support.
      - Exception: Need only be likely to have evidentiary support if specifically identified this way in the complaint.

   d. Failure to do factual homework (Responding party)/11(b)(4)
      - Violation of Rule 11 if denials of factual contentions do not have evidentiary support.
      - Exception: Denial can be based on a reasonable belief or a lack of information if specifically identified this way in the answer.
4. How Raised/11(c)
   a. Raised on Court's Initiative/11(c)(3)
      - Judge must issue show-cause order and allow party to respond.

   b. Raised by Party/Safe Harbor/11(c)(2)
      - Three-step process

    i. Serve (but do not file) the Rule 11 motion describing sanctionable conduct.
    ii. Give opposing party 21 days to cure (amend, withdraw, correct).
    iii. File the motion only if challenged conduct is not cured.

5. Determine the appropriateness of the sanction/11(c).
    a. Attorney, law firm, or party that violated rule may be sanctioned/ 11(c)(1).
    b. Sanction should be limited to what is sufficient to deter/11(c)(4).
    c. Sanction can be monetary or nonmonetary/11(c)(4) & (c)(5).
        i. Monetary sanctions are generally payable to the court. Exception: Attorney's fees payable to the movant if imposed on their motion and where warranted for effective deterrence.
        ii. Represented parties should not suffer a monetary sanction for their lawyers' failure to do their legal homework.
        iii. Judges should not impose monetary sanctions on their own initiative unless their show-cause order was issued prior to voluntary dismissal or settlement.
    d. Law firms jointly responsible for violation committed by partner, associate or employee/11(c)(1).
    e. Sanctions are not mandatory even when Rule is violated/11(c)(1).

FRCP 12(b)(6): Motion to Dismiss for Failure to State a Claim

1. Make sure you are in federal court. (State courts have their own pleading rules. And even when they adopt the text of FRCP 8(a) and 12(b)(6) they may interpret those rules differently.)
2. Tackle each cause of action separately — one at a time.
3. Analyze the legal sufficiency/cognizability of the claim.
    - What is the plaintiff's cause of action?
    - Does the jurisdiction recognize that alleged harm as actionable?
4. Analyze the factual sufficiency of the claim.
    a. For each element of the cause of action, aggregate all of the corresponding allegations in the Complaint.
        - Is the allegation conclusory (e.g., mere recitation of element, bare assertion, bald allegation)?
        - Conclusory allegations will be ignored in the next step.
        - Non-conclusory allegations will be accepted as true in the next step.

b. Analyze the plausibility of the claim.
   - Is the plausible inference that the defendant is liable?
   - Compare/contrast with scenarios where all of the non-conclusory allegations in the complaint are true yet defendant is not liable.

FRCP 14: Third Party Practice / Impleaders

1. Make sure you are in federal court. (State courts have their own rules.) Remember that impleaders are never compulsory.
2. Identify the third-party plaintiff (i.e., the party that is asserting this claim).
   - The plaintiff on the impleader (the third-party plaintiff) is always a defendant on some other claim.
3. Identify the third-party defendant (i.e., the party that is the target of this claim).
4. Confirm that the target of this claim is not already a party in the lawsuit.
   - Proper third party claim only if the third-party defendant is not already a party to the action.
   - If that party is already named in this suit, consider, instead, a cross-claim, or a counterclaim.
5. Identify the third-party plaintiff's cause(s) of action.
   - There must be some cognizable claim.
6. Analyze the claim to make sure that there is derivative liability.
   - At least one of the third-party plaintiff's causes of action must be "for all or part of the [third-party-plaintiff's liability on the] claim against it"/14(a)(1).
   - Contract or law can create such a right of reimbursement from the third-party defendant (e.g., indemnification, subrogation, warranty, contribution).
   - On a proper impleader, the third-party claim should evaporate if the third-party plaintiff prevails on the claims against it (because the third-party claim is derivative).
7. Procedure after a third-party defendant is added
   a. The third-party defendant may assert affirmative defenses that the third-party plaintiff had on the claims asserted against it (the third-party plaintiff)/14(a)(2)(C).
      - This prevents third party defendant from being derivatively liable for claim where third-party plaintiff could have avoided liability on the claims against it (the third-party plaintiff).
   b. The third-party defendant may assert claims against the original plaintiff that arise out of the same transaction or occurrence as the plaintiff's claim against the third-party plaintiff/14(a)(2)(D).

c. The original plaintiff may assert claims against the third-party defendant that arise out of the same transaction or occurrence as the plaintiff's claim against the third-party plaintiff/14(a)(3).
d. Like any other defendant, the third-party defendant may assert other defenses, counterclaims, crossclaims and third-party claims, per FRCP 8, 13, and 14/14(a)(2) & (a)(5).

FRCP 15: Motion to Amend / Amendments Before Trial

1. Make sure you are in federal court. (State courts have their own rules.)
2. FRCP 15(a): All amendments must satisfy FRCP 15(a) — Three alternative possibilities.
   a. Freebie/15(a)(1). If amending complaint, apply 15(a)(1)(B).
      - Open for 21 days after the earlier of defendant's answer or motion.
      - Can only do this "once."

      or
   b. Consent/15(a)(2)
      - Opposing party may consent.

      or
   c. "When justice so requires"/15(a)(2)
      - Analyze delay of moving party.
        - How long since they filed the pleading they seek to amend?
        - Why has it taken them this long? (Diligent?)
        - The longer and less excusable the delay, the less likely the amendment will be allowed.
      - Analyze prejudice to non-moving party.
        - How/why has the delay made it harder for non-moving party to defend?
        - The more prejudicial the delay, the less likely the amendment will be allowed.
      - Court should "freely give leave."
3. Statute of Limitations problem?
   - Are you adding/amending a claim (including a party and a claim) that would be barred by the statute of limitations if it were filed as a new separate action today?

   If no, then stop here. Otherwise, continue (because you need the doctrine of relation-back).
4. Will relation-back solve your statute of limitations problem?

- If claim would be time-barred even if it had been in the pleading that you're amending, then relation-back will not solve your statute of limitations problem. Futile to continue.
  - Watch for different dates triggering the statutory period.
  - Watch for different statutory periods for different types of claims.
- If claim would have been timely if it had been in that pleading, then continue.

5. Relation-back — Three alternative possibilities to earn relation-back.
   a. State law and State relation-back/15(c)(1)(A)
      - If the claim (including a party and a claim) you're seeking to add arises under state (as opposed to federal) law, then go to that state's rule of civil procedure on relation-back and apply it if it is more generous than this Federal Rule.

      or
   b. Adding a related claim (not adding a party — just adding/amending a cause of action)/15(c)(1)(B)
      - Claim will relate-back if this new claim arises out of the same transaction or occurrence as the claims in the original pleading.

      or
   c. Adding/Amending a party/15(c)(1)(C)'s conjunctive three-part test
      i. Same Transaction or Occurrence
         - Claim will relate back if the claim against this new party arises out of the same transaction or occurrence as the claims in the original pleading.

         and
      ii. Notice
         - Notice of what? The filing of the claim.
         - Notice when? New party must have received this notice within 90 days of filing of complaint.

         and
      iii. Mistake
         - The new party knew or should have known that the moving party was mistaken about the proper party's identity.
         - Lack of knowledge is not a mistake. The classic mistake is a typographical error.

FRCP 19: Required Joinder of Parties / Necessary and Indispensable Parties / 12(b)(7)

1. Make sure you are in federal court. (State courts have their own rules.)

2. Defendant's motion: The triggering event is that the defendant is moving to dismiss because the complaint fails to include a party (a plaintiff or a defendant) that defendant claims is required (or necessary).
3. FRCP 19(a)
   - There are two alternative possibilities where the unnamed party is required (or necessary).
     a. Inability of the court to award complete relief to plaintiff/19(a)(1)(A)
        Ask: can named defendant perform the relief that plaintiff requests in the complaint?
        If not (e.g., relief requests conveyance of property that is jointly owned with unnamed party), then the unnamed party is a required party.
        or
     b. Unnamed party has an interest in the present action, and litigating this action without them could be prejudicial.
        - The prospect of prejudice usually stems from a request for equitable relief (or a request for damages that can be analogized to equitable relief — e.g., a limited fund). Consider, for example, a classmate brings a disability discrimination lawsuit seeking to change the way that the law school determines class rank. The law school could move to dismiss under 12(b)(7) claiming that you are a required (necessary) party.
        - A request for equitable relief can create prejudice because, in a *subsequent* suit involving the *unnamed* party (e.g., you versus the law school), the court could either: (i) allow the outcome of the earlier litigation to affect the subsequent litigation (arguably prejudicing you, since you and your interests weren't represented in that earlier suit); or (ii) ignore the outcome of the earlier litigation in the subsequent litigation (arguably prejudicing the law school, since they now might face inconsistent obligations from the judges in the two suits).
4. Feasibility of Joinder
   - An unnamed party that is required (or necessary) per FRCP 19(a) (Step 3 above) must be joined if it is feasible.
   - Joinder is not feasible if the court would no longer have subject-matter jurisdiction (because the joinder would destroy complete diversity). Joinder is not feasible if the unnamed party enjoys sovereign immunity, or if it cannot be served, or if it is not subject to personal jurisdiction, or if venue would be improper.
5. If joinder is not feasible, the court must choose between two unattractive options: proceed without a required (necessary) party or dismiss the case (because the unnamed party is indispensable). The following three

factors should be considered by the court in making that choice. FRCP 14(b).

a. Revisit the prejudice/impairment inquiry that made the party "required" and consider whether that harm actually will occur and, if so, how severe it is. The more theoretical, speculative, and unlikely that prejudice/impairment, the easier to proceed without them.
b. Consider whether the inadequacy of the relief can be improved or the prejudice/impairment be lessened or avoided/19(b)(2) and (b)(3).
   - This usually means awarding money damages instead of equitable relief.
   - Other procedural devices may also be available. (Could the defendant bring a third-party claim? Could the nonparty avoid injustice by intervening?)
c. Practical effect of dismissal: If the plaintiff could find adequate relief elsewhere (e.g., in a state court), then the existence of an alternative forum militates in favor of dismissal.

FRCP 20: Joinder of Parties

1. Make sure you are in federal court. (State courts have their own rules.)
2. This rule applies to joinder of plaintiffs and joinder of defendants. This is not a motion; the claim merely joins parties by adding the names of more than one plaintiff and/or more than one defendant.
3. Joinder of parties is proper when two-part test is satisfied.
   a. The claims by/against the parties must arise out of the same transaction or occurrence (or series of transactions of occurrences).
      - Consider proximity of time.
      - Consider proximity of space.
      - Consider any logical relationship or connection.
   b. There must be a common question of fact or law.
      - E.g., A common question of fact for a plaintiff suing multiple defendants in a personal injury suit could be the plaintiff's damages. ("What are plaintiff's medical expenses?")
      - E.g., a common question of fact for multiple plaintiffs suing their employer in a discrimination action could be the defendant's policies? ("What does the personnel manual say about *x*?")

  - E.g., a common question of law in a case involving a plaintiff suing multiple defendants in a breach of contract action could be whether a novel theory of comparative fault is available."
  - E.g, a common question of law in a case involving multiple plaintiffs suing a defendant is whether a charitable immunity defense applies.

  Common mistake by students: Thinking that any case involving the same cause of action involves common questions of law or fact.
4. Remember that even when joinder is proper, judges have to discretion to sever. FRCP 42(b)
   - Look for prejudice, complexity/inefficiency.

FRCP 26: Scope of Discovery

1. Make sure you are in federal court. (State courts have their own rules.)
2. Request must be *relevant* to the claim or defense of any party.
   - Ask: Could this document (or could the answer to this interrogatory or deposition question) have any tendency to make any fact of consequence in determining this action more or less probable? If so, it is relevant.
   - Tip: If relevance is contested, posit a hypothetical response to the question that would show relevance.

   If the request information is not relevant, then stop here because the request is beyond the scope of discovery. Otherwise, continue.
3. Request must not be *privileged* information.
   - This tends to be tested only superficially, if at all, in a Civil Procedure course. You will learn about privileges in Evidence.
   - Commonly recognized privileges include: attorney-client privilege, work product doctrine, doctrine-patient privilege, psychotherapist-patient privilege, clergy-penitent privilege, martial (spousal) privileges.

   If the request information is privileged, then stop here (or, if responding to a document request, log the privilege FRCP 26(b)(5)(A)), because the request is beyond the scope of discovery. Otherwise, continue.
4. Request must be proportionate — Six factor balancing test.
   (a) Importance of the issues at stake in the litigation
      - Ask: Does this case have impact beyond the parties to this suit?
      - Ask: Is there a social problem here demanding accountability?

   (b) Amount in controversy
      - Ask: What amount is demanded in the complaint?

- Ask: Is there a better way of determining the magnitude of the litigation?

(c) Parties' relative access to information
- Ask: are there other sources for the information sought?

(d) The parties' resources
- Ask: Does the request pose an undue burden on the responding party?

(e) Importance of the discovery in resolving the issues
- Ask: Is the requested information about the crux of the case?
- Ask: Is there other evidence or other ways to obtain information like this?

(f) Whether burden/expense outweighs likely benefit.
- Burden is not always monetary. Think: privacy, dignity.

www.ingramcontent.com/pod-product-compliance
Lightning Source LLC
LaVergne TN
LVHW080025210926
848481LV00011B/3107